Colorado Restaurants and Recipes

from small towns

Written by: Benjamin James Bennis

Edited by: Linda P. Viray

Small Town Publications
Littleton, Colorado

Front Cover Sketch: The Ranch House Restaurant and Saloon at Devil's Thumb Ranch
in Tabernash (see page 276)

Back Cover Sketch: The Back Narrows Inn and Restaurant in Norwood (see page 225)

Photos and sketches of restaurants provided by the restaurants themselves.

First Printing: November 1995
Second Printing: April 1996

Published by Small Town Publications
PO Box 621275
Littleton, CO 80162

Printed in Canada.

To obtain additional copies, write directly to the publisher, above, or call (303)978-0316.
Please see order form right before the Table of Contents.

ISBN 0-9629799-2-9

Dedicated to my mother, a kind, sweet, generous, loving person and the gentlest human I've yet to know. She was also a very neat lady in more ways than one.

Rose Middione Gruber
1914-1994

ACKNOWLEDGEMENTS

I would like to thank the Colorado Center For The Book for nominating <u>Colorado Restaurants and Recipes</u> as one of four finalists in 1996 for the Colorado Book Award in the category of Non-fiction, Reference. I want to express my gratitude to the many newspapers and magazines that mentioned <u>Colorado Restaurants and Recipes</u>, including Bill St. John of the Rocky Mountain News, John Kessler of The Denver Post and Westword; and to those who reviewed this guide: Mildred Brodbeck of the Douglas County News Press in Castle Rock, Susan Sherwood at the Colorado Beverage Analyst, Anne M. Thompson of the Rocky Ford Daily Gazette, Arlene Shovald at The Mountain Mail in Salida, Dusty Smith of the Jackson Country Star in Walden, Wanda Lowe at the La Junta Tribune-Democrate, Linda Funk of the Dove Creek Press and a special thank you to Mona Neeley at Colorado Country Life Magazine who's article generated an enormous response. I also want to thank Mike Boyle, KHOW Restaurant Show Host, and Warren Byrne, Host of The Restaurant Show on KEZW, for their helpful suggestions and references when I began this project one year ago. A special note of gratitude goes to Jim Hoysick, for his patience and understanding over these past several months. I would also like to express my appreciation to the many individuals who stopped by my booth at one of the many shows that I do during the year (like the People's Fair, Taste of Colorado, the Rocky Mountain Book Festival and the Holiday Food and Gift Festival) and offered their restaurant recommendations around the state. While I did not have the opportunity to dine at all of them, many of the restaurants in this guide, and the last, were the direct result of these proposals. Finally, and by far most importantly, I would like to express my deepest gratitude to my editor, Linda P. Viray, for her constant dedication and vigilance over the past year. Without her diligent support, this book wouldn't have half the quality nor would it have likely been released this year, let alone this millennium. I could not have done it without her.

INTRODUCTION

Colorado Restaurants and Recipes (CR&R) is the third restaurant guide on Colorado small towns that I've come out with in the last 4 years. The original, The Colorado Small Town Restaurant Guide, featured 200 restaurants from 50 Colorado small towns. It was a beginning — an appetizer for things to come. A year later, I published Restaurants from 101 Colorado Small Towns — the main course, all meat and potatoes, a fat red book over 500 pages (200 pages more than its predecessor) that presented 365 restaurants. It was intended to be a comprehensive guide that would offer the Colorado traveler an ample selection of restaurants to choose from no matter what section of the state he or she were traveling in. Now with this third installment, I've changed directions and trimmed down to just 101 restaurants (if I could only lose the 20 pounds that I put on while researching the book!). This is the "dessert" book — the Grand Marnier souffle following the appetizer and main course.

Whereas quantity of restaurants was my primary goal with the second book, quality restaurants was my main motivation with this latest guide. I've managed to take 34 of the best restaurants from the first two guides (less than 10% of the second guide) and add 67 new discoveries. I dined at all of the restaurants in all 3 books and with a few exceptions, I dined at all of the restaurants in this book in the 11 months prior to printing. Colorado Restaurants and Recipes has many new highlights not found in either of the first 2 editions. Beginning with the restaurant reviews themselves, I've completely revamped my style, replacing those space-consuming town maps with easy-to-follow, precise (down to the 10th of a mile) directions to each restaurant. Then I placed all the essential information about each restaurant — address, phone number and restaurant policies on hours of operation, reservations and the like — in a separate section. Following this, I included a special section just to talk about the history of the restaurant and the personalities (people) who operate it, from owner(s) to manager(s) and chef(s). Finally, there is, of course, a discussion of food, service and ambiance based on my personal dining experiences.

There are 2 new sections to this guide. One is the recipe. There is 1 recipe from each restaurant (101 in all) ranging from appetizers and sauces, soups and salads to entrées and desserts. So, not only do you get a guide to some of the state's best restaurants, but you get a cookbook as well. I felt compelled to go all out with this book (after all, following dessert there may be nothing but a quiet ride home), so in addition to being the only restaurant guide to Colorado's small towns and a cookbook, I decided to include SPECIAL ONE-TIME OFFERS that could save you, the traveler/cook, literally hundreds of dollars.

Who is This Guide For

My first two restaurant guides were for anyone who liked to travel and eat (and who doesn't?). Now, with recipes included, this third edition is for anyone who likes to travel and eat or anyone who likes to stay home and cook which means, it's for anyone who likes to eat. It's also for people who like to save money when they dine out. Two people traveling together could save over $1,200 using this guide (and how much did you pay for it?). Big spenders and those of you traveling in groups could save even more by taking advantage of the special one-time offers that are based on a percentage of the bill or have no limit on the number of people who can use the offer (just remember, it is a ONE-TIME ONLY SPECIAL OFFER).

So whether you're a Coloradan planning to travel through our beautiful state on business or pleasure, an out-of-stater visiting for the first time, a frequent guest or planning to move here, Colorado Restaurants and Recipes will be an invaluable guide to your dining enjoyment and will save you money as well (up to 75 times the price you paid and maybe more!). You'll also be able to use this guide to keep a record of the restaurants that you've been to (your host at each restaurant will initial and date your Special One-Time Offer) and, when you return home from your Colorado adventure, you can try some of the same recipes that you tried at the restaurants you visited. From Alamosa in the San Luis Valley to Winter Park in the Fraser Valley, you'll discover restaurants to dine at with the help of this guide. If you're interested in travel guides, cookbooks or saving money, then Colorado Restaurants and Recipes is for you.

How to Use This Guide

You can use this book either as a travel guide on your sojourns around Colorado or as a cookbook in your own kitchen at home. If you use Colorado Restaurants and Recipes as a travel guide, the first thing you should note is that the book is laid out alphabetical by town. So once you've decided where you're going, or if you're already there, just flip through the book, or look in the Table of Contents, to see if your town is included. If it is, you're in business. If not, try another town that might be suitable for dining. By the way, don't forget to read the brief town histories. There are some interesting highlights about each town including the town's population (1990 U. S. Census figures are used unless stated otherwise) and elevation as well as its zip and area codes.

Once you have selected a town, take a look at the restaurants that I reviewed. The review is divided into 3 sections. The first section provides you with essential information that you will need to make a (hopefully wonderful) dining experience happen. This includes the address and telephone numbers to the restaurant, directions on how to get there and restaurant policy information (the type of cuisine, when they are open, what meals they serve and the price range of entrées, whether they have a nonsmoking section, whether they provide take-out service, whether they serve alcohol, what credit cards they take, their policy regarding accepting personal checks, their policy on reservations, whether they are wheelchair accessible, how most of the restaurant's diners dress (if there is no mention of dress, it means dress is casual) and other pertinent facts you should know about). All of this is in the ESSENTIALS section. Abbreviations are used to indicate months and days of the week. The months are all 3-letter abbreviations, all in capital letters, like JAN for January and SEP for September. The <u>days</u> are all in 3-letter abbreviations, in upper and lower case, like Sun for Sunday and Thu for Thursday. Many of the restaurants who have seasonal hours informed me that the dates that they change their hours is not exact, so check with those restaurants to make sure they're open before you waste a trip. The <u>dollar signs</u> under **Meals and Prices** refers to the price range of the vast majority of entrées on the restaurant's menu (80% or better). Each dollar sign represents $5. For example, $$ means you can expect entrées to run between $5 and $10; $$$-$$$$ means entrées are between $10 and $20. The abbreviations for **Credit Cards** are as follows: MasterCard (MC), Visa (just Visa), American Express (Amx), Discover (Disc) and Diner's Club (DC). If a restaurant accepts all five of the major credit cards, "All 5" is indicated.

Once you get past the nitty-gritty details under <u>ESSENTIALS</u>, the real fun begins. This time I've spent considerably more time researching the history of each restaurant and the backgrounds of the people who operate them. This is the area I like to call <u>HISTORY, PERSONALITY AND CHARACTER</u>. In it you will learn about the building that you're dining in, when it was built, what it was originally built for, what it has been used for in the past, whether other restaurants occupied the same space or something totally unrelated used to be there like a blacksmith shop or auto garage. You will also know who your hosts are and who will be cooking your food (or at least who heads up the kitchen staff). This way you'll know who to thank (or blame) personally for your dining experience. (I have a feeling that with the restaurants that I have selected, you will be doing a lot of praising and little, if any, criticizing of the restaurants that you visit). The information provided in this section is courtesy of the owners and managers of each restaurant.

The third and final section of the review is <u>FOOD, SERVICE AND AMBIANCE</u>. That is, after all, why you probably bought the book. Here I start talking about my own dining experiences at each restaurant. What I savored or relished and what I particularly liked about each dish. In situations where there were fellow diners along, I also made comments about their meals, as well. Following this empirical discussion is a brief description of the restaurant's menu for each meal. Then there are a few comments about the service and an exposé of the ambiance — the decor and atmosphere and how it enhanced the restaurant's overall exposure.

Positioned between the review of the restaurant and the restaurant's recipe is the <u>SPECIAL ONE-TIME OFFER</u>. This is just what it says it is: a special offer that can be used just one time. In order to use the SPECIAL ONE-TIME OFFER, you MUST bring this book into the restaurant. None of the 101 restaurants in this guide will accept copies of these offers. Second, you must present this offer at the time you order your meal (unless it states otherwise). Also, unless stated otherwise, the special offer is limited to 2, that is 2 desserts, 2 drinks, 2 appetizers or whatever with appropriate purchase. When you receive the special offer, the owner or manager will initial and date your book. Once he or she has done this, the special one-time offer becomes invalid and cannot be used again. Please be sure that you have your book opened to the right page so as NOT to have some other restaurant's offer signed-off in its place. In the event that a restaurant has changed owners since the printing of this book (you can confirm this by checking the section on HISTORY, PERSONALITY AND CHARACTER), it is entirely up to the discretion of the new owners whether or not to accept the special one-time offer. New owners which Small Town Publications has not contracted with are under no obligation to honor these special offers. (I don't think you will run into this situation very often, but it could happen). Also, please remember that the gratuity is not included in the special offers and that your tip should be based on the amount of the bill before the special offer is deducted. Please contact Small Town Publications (see back of title page) if you encounter difficulty when using the SPECIAL ONE-TIME OFFERS.

If you purchased this book primarily to try out the recipes, there is a recipe index in the back of the book which may help you decide which recipe to try. All of the recipes are provided compliments of the restaurants. They have been written by one of the chefs, manager or owners. All of the recipes are taken from items offered from the restaurant's menu or, in a few cases, items that the restaurant frequently offers as a special. In some instances, the quantities and proportions had to be cut considerably so that you could feed your family or a small dinner party and not the 4th Infantry. I, and I'm sure the restaurants, sincerely hope that this necessary procedure will not affect the quality of the final product. Questions concerning the recipes should be directed to the restaurant providing the recipe. Decisions on the spelling of certain ingredients used in the recipes were based on one of two criteria. Wherever possible, I strived to be consistent with the spellings. For example, you will see "spaetzle" rather than "spatzle" and "omelet" as opposed to "omelette". The second criteria, in the case of more unusual or exotic terms, was to use the spelling provided by the restaurant — words such as "Kirschwasser", "aromat" and "frikadeller". This, by the way, also applies to the spellings used in the reviews of the restaurants' food.

How I Wrote the Guide

Each of the 3 restaurant guides that I wrote took about 1 year to research and write. This last guide, however, was far more difficult than the first two. With the first 2 guides, when I completed my review of a restaurant, whether it was good, bad or indifferent, I was finished. Not so with Colorado Restaurants and Recipes. Since I included both a recipe and a special one-time offer, I had to have a written agreement with each restaurant. This meant 2 things. First, any restaurant that I did not review favorably would not be included in the book. Second, I had to make frequent telephone calls to the restaurants over a 5-month period from May to October. For most of the restaurants, this was their busy summer season and although they expressed interest in being in the book, they nonetheless failed to provide me with either a recipe or signed agreement or both. By far, the biggest delay was with the recipes. Many of the chefs do not have recipes written down and to get them to take the time to write one down on paper, well . . . let's just say it took a lot of time and patience (a lot of time and patience). Without exaggeration, I spent on the average $300 per month on telephone bills over this 5-month period calling these Colorado restaurants from the Denver area.

My research for the first printing of this book included visits to 190 restaurants and took me all around the state several times. On my last tour, I did a figure 8 through Colorado, leaving Denver and making stops in Winter Park, Grand Lake, Steamboat

Springs and Meeker, then over to Grand Junction and down through Delta and Montrose, across to Gunnison and Crested Butte, then south to Lake City and Creede, a swing over to Durango, a weekend in Silverton and Ouray, and it was back to Denver. The largest town in <u>Colorado Restaurants and Recipes</u> is Durango with a population of 13,200 and the smallest village is Heeney with a mere 40 inhabitants. Of the 190 restaurants that I mentioned, I rejected 22 as not being of the calibre that I wanted in the book. All of the restaurants in this guide come either recommended or highly recommended. The remaining 168 restaurants were given every opportunity to be included in this guide and the fact that 67 of them are not here is their decision, not mine. Of those 67, 2 went out of business (about 1% of the total number that I originally visited), 5 others had plans to sell in the near future, although only one appeared to have a serious buyer, 4 either refused to part with one of their secret recipes or failed to provide a recipe, 3 had changes in ownership and significant menu changes making my review obsolete and several just failed to respond (after saying they would) or were left out for a variety of reasons like "I don't need more business", the restaurant was undergoing changes or the owner simply was not interested. However, the largest number of restaurants decided not to participate because of the special one-time offer.

      With the exception of the Tivoli Deer in Kittredge, where I've dined at least a dozen times, and The Fort in Morrison, where I've eaten 10 times so far, the other 99 restaurants I reviewed were based on 3 or fewer visits and 65 of those were based on just a single stop. I offer this as food for thought for the inquiring mind, but make no mistake, I make no apologies for the lack of multiple visits to each restaurant. Traveling throughout the state is a time consuming venture. Realistically, to print a book of this nature requires a minimum number of visits to each restaurant. There are just too many restaurants and too little time. Also, these 3 guides remain the only small town restaurant guides on Colorado, making them unique. Nobody else has attempted to come out with an in-depth guide to the state's restaurants outside of the major metropolitan areas.

      Don't be surprised if one of your favorite small town restaurants is not included in this guide. There are far more restaurants in the state than one person could possibly get to in one year. In addition, my intention in writing this third edition was to come up with a smaller book than the 500+ page monster I wrote the second time. To do this, I set a self-imposed rule of visiting no more than 4 restaurants per town and you'll find no more than 3 restaurants from any town. I was, therefore, very selective as to who I would include in the guide. Also, don't forget that some restaurants did not choose to be in the guide because of objections to the recipe, special offer or other reasons. For myself, there were about 25 restaurants, mostly close to Denver, that I would have liked to have dined at and included in this guide, but time did not permit. Nonetheless, you should have a great time with the 101 restaurants, recipes and special offers. So let <u>Colorado Restaurants and Recipes</u> turn your Colorado vacation into an adventure. Bon appetite!

<u>Special Notes about Second Printing</u>

      All of the restaurants in Colorado Restaurants and Recipes were updated with the second printing of the book which took place in April 1996. (The first printing was released in November 1995). A notice was sent out to all restaurants who then had an opportunity to notify Small Town Publications of any changes since the first printing. In addition, my most competent editor, Linda Viray, went through the book looking for minor spelling and punctuation errors which were corrected. Two restaurants were deleted from the first printing: the Country Side Inn in Lyons which went out of business and Penelope's in Crested Butte which was scheduled to be under new management with a new menu and a new concept (a bistro) in May 1996. La Mariposa in Lyons was added to take the place of the Country Side Inn.

Disclaimers

Reviewing restaurants is a subjective endeavor and no matter how objective one may try to be, this business is still opinions and perspectives. I have dined at all of the restaurants at least once, some more than once, and some with fellow diners. Without exception, I have approached each restaurant without prejudice or preconceived notions and have attempted to be consistent and fair in all respects. I have no reason to rate any restaurant unfairly one way or the other. I am not a paid consultant or advisor for any restaurant. Many food critics differ on their opinions of the same restaurant and your opinion may differ as well. Please keep in mind that I am reporting what I encountered at the time(s) that I dined at each restaurant. Knowing that, it should also be remembered that restaurants, like everything else, do change over time. Occasionally I will quote the price of a certain item. I should point out that these prices were in effect when I visited the restaurant. They may have changed since. Hence, these prices should be used as a guide only, not an absolute, and under no circumstances should they be presented to restaurant management as a guaranteed price.

Comments and Additional Copies

Comments about The Guide or restaurants are most welcome. Comments and/or requests for additional copies of this book may be addressed to:

Small Town Publications
P.O. Box 621275
Littleton, CO 80162
(303)978-0316

Please see order form right before the Table of Contents.

Benjamin James Bennis

April 7, 1996

Other Books by Benjamin James Bennis:

The Colorado Small Town Restaurant Guide — 1991
Restaurants from 101 Colorado Small Towns — 1992

"Colorado Restaurants and Recipes can take you to great restaurants in Colorado's small towns. It is a great handbook to take along as you travel the state."

> Mona Neeley
> Colorado Country Life Magazine

"Written by Benjamin James Bennis, [Colorado Restaurants and Recipes] is one man's saga of eating his way across the state of Colorado visiting many interesting restaurants along the way."

> Dusty Smith
> Jackson Country Star
> Walden, CO

"Littleton author Benjamin James Bennis has eaten his way through every bitsy burg in the state. It makes a good travelogue for anyone planning a driving trip through the state."

> John Kessler
> The Denver Post

"Benjamin James Bennis has done it again. This book is a must for anybody traveling through Colorado with an appetite."

> Warren Byrne
> Host, The Restaurant Show
> AM 1430 KEZW

"This book is an absolute must. Whether you're traveling to the ski areas, Rocky Mountain National Park or any of Colorado's great out-of-the-way places, Benjamin's book will make the trip that much more enjoyable."

> Mike Boyle, Host
> Newstalk 63 KHOW
> Restaurant Show

"Bennis has done it again! Braving alimentary overload, he has munched away hours and dollars surveying Colorado's eateries. Now, with no punches pulled, you'll find an evaluation of Colorado Restaurants and Recipes, so you can have it here and at home. Tuck a copy in your glove compartment when you travel this state. It'll pay you!"

> Sam Arnold
> Food Critic, Historian and Owner of
> The Fort restaurant

ORDER FORM

SMALL TOWN PUBLICATIONS
P.O. BOX 621275
LITTLETON, CO 80162
(303)978-0316

NAME _____

ADDRESS_____
_____

Telephone _____

_____ Copies of **Colorado Restaurants and Recipes** @ $16 each $_____

_____ Copies of **Restaurants from 101 Colorado Small** Towns @ $10 each
(regular price $14.95 — **SAVE 33%!**) $_____

        Sub-Total $_____

Sales Tax (4.8% of sub-total) $_____
Packaging and Postage ($2.95 for
1st copy. $.50 for additional copies
up to $5.95 maximum) $_____

        TOTAL (Add last 3 lines) $_____

Please send check to address above. (Sorry, no credit cards). Please allow 10 days for delivery.

TABLE OF CONTENTS

TABLE OF CONTENTS

TABLE OF CONTENTS

TABLE OF CONTENTS

TABLE OF CONTENTS

TABLE OF CONTENTS

TABLE OF CONTENTS

TABLE OF CONTENTS

Writer and editor, 1 year and 30 pounds ago with friends Chauncey (the corgi), Ferdinand (the beagle) and Sam (the German shepherd mutt).

ALAMOSA

Alamosa, Spanish for "cottonwood grove", was originally a stage coach stop in 1876 called Wayside before being named by ex-Governor A. C. Hunt, President of the Denver and Rio Grande Construction Company. It is the crossroads of the Navajo Trail and Pan-American Highway (Highways 160 and 285, respectively) and a narrow gauge railroad terminal for minerals, agricultural products and passengers from the San Juan Mountains. The Alamosa National Wildlife Refuge, 3 miles southeast of town on the Rio Grande River, is an 11,158-acre waterfowl habitat for numerous bird species including Canadian geese and whooping crane. Bluff Overlook Road offers excellent wildlife viewing. Zip Code: 81101. Area Code: 719 Population: 7,579. Elevation: 7,544'.

Oscar's

710 Main Street, 589-9230

Directions: From Highways 17 and 160, go west on Highway 160, over the bridge, and turn right at the first signal which puts you on Main Street. Go 3½ blocks. The restaurant is on the left just past San Juan Avenue and before the movie theater. From Highways 160 and 285 heading east on Main Street, go to the east end of town. The restaurant is on the right just past Edison Avenue and the movie theater.

ESSENTIALS

Cuisine: Mexican
Hours: APR-OCT: Tue-Sun 11AM-9PM. Closed Mon. Nov-Mar: Sun and Tue-Thu 11AM-8PM. Fri/Sat 11AM-9PM. Closed Mon.
Meals and Prices: Lunch/Dinner $-$$
Nonsmoking: Yes. The right side of the restaurant.
Take-out: Yes
Alcohol: Beer, wine coolers, margaritas only.

Credit Cards: MC, Visa
Personal Check: From San Luis Valley only and with I.D.
Reservations: Accepted
Wheelchair Access: Yes
Other: Additional 15% service charge for parties of 6 or more. Can accommodate large groups with 1 hour notice; 120 person seating capacity for banquets, parties and receptions.

HISTORY, PERSONALITY AND CHARACTER

Owner Oscar Orozco opened Oscar's Restaurant in 1977 on State Street in Alamosa. Two years later, he moved to his current location on Main Street. Oscar's wife, Dolores, is the manager. Both Oscar and Dolores do the cooking. The building they occupy now dates back to the 1930s and used to be a hardware store where Dolores' family would buy Christmas presents when she was a little girl. The building was remodeled in January 1990.

FOOD, SERVICE AND AMBIANCE

Their homemade chips and salsa are deliciously different. The chips are made from white corn tortillas and they fluff up when they are fried (in cholesterol-free canola oil) so they actually have a double layer. They are crispy and lightly salted. The salsa has more tomato flavor and is all liquid with no tomato, onion or chili pieces. It has a spicy flavor that will make your tongue tingle! Oscar buys his dried red and green chilies from New Mexico and roasts them himself. Many of the ingredients come from New Mexico. Their entire menu is by the number (1-78). I ordered #27 - the chili rellenos plate. These are probably the best chili rellenos I have had since Maria's in Trinidad (see page 459 in Restaurants from 101 Colorado Small Towns. Unfortunately, Maria's is closed). They have a crispy inner shell and soft outer shell, come smothered with cheese, green chilies and onion, and are stuffed with cheese as well. It is just the way I like my chili rellenos! They come with beans in a thick sauce and white rice with a touch of tomato sauce. Their menu carries a full Mexican fare including red or green chili with pork, menudo, chalupas (a flour tortilla fried into a bowl, like a taco salad), chili burgers, huevos rancheros, chili caribe (pork), chicken flautas, tamales, carne adovada, fajitas, chimichangas and (cow) tongue burrito. The American dishes include fried chicken, pork chops, jumbo shrimp, and steaks. They also have burgers, sandwiches and pie and ice cream for dessert.

My server was young, friendly, relaxed and attentive. Country music played in the background. You seat yourself when you enter. The restaurant interior features white adobe walls with indented Spanish arches, pinewood vigas and posts, and red and green chili-shaped lights on a string. Inside the indented Spanish arches on the walls are colorful paintings of Indian pottery with flowers, cactus and a coyote.

SPECIAL ONE-TIME OFFER: Buy one entrée at the regular price and receive 50% off a second entrée of equal or lesser value. This offer NOT valid in combination with any other offers. _____ Manager/Owner. _____ Date.

Reading the introduction in the front of the book
will help you get more out of this guide.

RECIPE

Calabacitas
Sautéed Baby Pumpkins

3 small baby pumpkins, when in season   1 16-ounce can vacuum-packed
  (Zucchini will do)   sweet corn
1 medium onion   Salt to taste
1 teaspoon oil

1. Dice baby pumpkins and onion.
2. Place in frying pan along with 1 teaspoon oil.
3. Fry until tender. Put in corn.
4. Cover and simmer for about 10 minutes. Salt to your own taste.

Piñons Dining Room in Aspen

ASPEN

Originally named Ute City by H. B. Gillespie in 1879 for the local Ute Indians, Aspen's name was changed by B. Clark Wheeler for the abundant quantity of trees by that name. Another Wheeler, Jerome B. (no relation to the first), built the Wheeler Opera House, the Hotel Jerome and the Wheeler-Stallard House. In the late 1940s, Friedl Pfeifer, a ski enthusiast, and Walter Paepcke, who was interested in starting a musical and cultural festival, combined their efforts into a year-around program that offered a festival in the summer and skiing in the winter. Over the last 12 decades, Aspen has gone from a booming silver mining town to a sleepy cow town following the establishment of the gold standard in 1893, to a prosperous, world-renowned resort for skiing and festivals. Zip Code: 81611. Area Code: 970 Population: 5,049 (1990). Elevation: 7,907'.

Guido's

403 South Galena Street, 925-7222

Directions: From the northwest (Glenwood Springs), stay on Highway 82 as you enter town, make a right on 7th Street and a left on Main Street. Go 11 blocks. Turn right on Galena Street (one block past Mill Street). The restaurant is 3 blocks down on your right, on the northeast end of the Cooper Avenue Mall, above Stefan Kaelin's sporting goods store. It is on the west corner of Galena Street and East Cooper Avenue. From the southeast (Independence Pass), you will enter town on Cooper Avenue. The restaurant is one block past Hunter Street, on the northeast end of the Cooper Avenue Mall, on your left above Stefan Kaelin's sporting goods store.

ESSENTIALS

Cuisine: Swiss/French
Hours: Thanksgiving to Mid-APR: 7 nights 5:30PM-10PM. Mid-JUN to Mid-OCT: 7 days 9AM-3PM and 5:30PM-10PM. Closed Mid-APR to Mid-JUN and Mid-OCT to Thanksgiving.
Meals and Prices: Breakfast $, Lunch $$, Dinner $$$$-$$$$$
Nonsmoking: All

Take-out: Yes (on their own plates which they request to be returned).
Alcohol: Full Bar
Credit Cards: MC, Visa, Amx, Disc
Personal Check: Yes, with I.D.
Reservations: Recommended for dinner, accepted otherwise
Wheelchair Access: Yes, by elevator
Other: 17% service charge on parties of 6 or more

HISTORY, PERSONALITY AND CHARACTER

Guido and Trudi Meyer opened their first restaurant in 1951 where the Hickory House Restaurant stands now, at 730 West Main Street in Aspen. In 1953, they built and moved into a building at the corner of South Galena Street and East Cooper Avenue. The downstairs was the restaurant while the upstairs was used as living quarters for the Meyers and their employees. In 1971, the Meyers retired and left the business to

4

Hermann and Lulu Gasser, a couple from Switzerland. The Gassers returned to their native country in the summer of 1988 and Rosie Wettstein, Guido and Trudi's daughter, took over. Rosie grew up in Guido's (pronounced Gee-Does, like the baby deer, not the verb), putting in her time as "forced labor" doing things like bussing tables. She also spent 5 years in Switzerland working in her aunt's hotel and restaurant. In 1990-91, the original building was torn down and replaced. The restaurant was moved upstairs and the downstairs is now occupied by a sporting goods store. Rosie and I chatted in a corner of the bar where her bedroom used to be. Her motto for the restaurant is "Adapt, adjust and accommodate". She is assisted by her hostess, Anna Marie, who has been with the restaurant since 1971, and chef, Brent C. Holleman, who joined in 1991. Brent graduated from the Culinary Institute of America in Hyde Park, New York in 1984. He did his apprenticeship at the Green Briar in White Sulphur Springs, West Virginia. His experience dates back to 1973 and includes the Pier House and the Bonaventure Resort in Florida, the Fairmont Hotel in New Orleans, Louisiana and 14 months of training in Switzerland and France.

FOOD, SERVICE AND AMBIANCE

After much self-debate, I finally decided on the "petto di pollo alla Ticinese," a top quality, moist chicken breast stuffed with finely chopped wild (but delicate tasting and highly flavorful) mushrooms (portobello, shiitake and morel) and herbs on a bed of sautéed spinach topped with a natural sherry chicken glaze. Choosing the rice pilaf with sundried tomatoes and mushrooms over the späetzle or potatoes was easier. Thoroughly cooked purple cabbage, asparagus and red peppers came with the meal. For an appetizer, you can have a warm artichoke, poached jumbo shrimp, escargots or duck liver pâté. Soup and salad are extra, but you may want to order their French onion soup made with caramelized onions or a salad, like grilled chicken with spinach and wild mushrooms, or proscuitto and tomatoes with one of their homemade dressings.

The entrées feature several veal dishes including scallopinis with wild mushrooms and artichoke hearts, veal cordon bleu and Wienerschnitzel. Also on the menu are shell loin steak in either a three peppercorn sauce or grilled with Swiss herb butter, poached seafood with penne pasta, beef tenderloin with roasted garlic, and several dinners for two. I sampled their apple strudel with its light, chewy crust, raisins and a sprinkle of powdered sugar. It is one of several homemade desserts on their menu: chocolate mousse, créme brûlée, cheeses and fruits, and chocolate fondue for 2. A selection of American and French wines, by the glass or bottle, is available as well. A light breakfast menu offers espresso and cappuccino, New York bagels, lox and Belgian waffles. Soup, salads and sandwiches (roasted turkey, avocado and vegetables, and a couple of unusual selections that use Jarlsberg cheese, vegetables, homemade basil mayonnaise, peppers, eggplant or French goat cheese) are offered for lunch.

ASPEN

Service was provided by Rick and his British accent, an accommodating duo. Brazilian jazz and classical songs were played. This second-floor restaurant with a view of the ski lift and slopes was decorated in Ansel Adams photographs; large color blow-up photos of Aspen, a creek, and mountains; a frosted-glass winter mountain scene with log cabins and pine trees; a World Cup ski poster; pastel paintings and a panoramic view of Aspen taken in 1987.

SPECIAL ONE-TIME OFFER: Buy one entrée at the regular price and receive 50% off a second entrée of equal or lesser value. This offer NOT valid in combination with any other offers. _____ Manager/Owner. _____ Date.

RECIPE

Zurichoise

½ ounce clarified butter
6 ounces veal emincé (thin slices)
2 ounces mushrooms, sliced
1 medium shallot, chopped
½ white wine
2 ounces Bordeaux sauce
1 ounce cream

Salt and pepper to taste
1 each lemon, anchovy and caper, for garnish
1 each Roesti - Swiss-style shredded potato like a hashbrown (made by shredding a potato, adding bacon and onion and then frying)
½ ounce whole butter

1. Heat clarified butter. Season veal with salt and pepper. Sear on all sides, remove.
2. Sauté shallots and mushrooms in butter.
3. Deglaze with white wine and Bordeaux sauce. Reduce. Add cream.
4. Reduce to consistency. Salt and Pepper to taste. Finish with whole butter.
5. Serve with roesti.

A recipes index is located at the end of the book.

Mirabella

216 South Monarch Street, 920-2555

Directions: From the northwest (Glenwood Springs), stay on Highway 82 as you enter town, make a right on 7th Street and a left on Main Street. Go 9 blocks. Turn right on Monarch Street (one block past Aspen Street). Go 1 block. The restaurant is on the left just past Hopkins Avenue. From the southeast (Independence Pass), you will enter town on Cooper Avenue. Follow it to where you are forced to turn right on to Galena Street. Proceed 2 blocks to Hopkins Avenue. Turn left and go 2 blocks to Monarch Street. Turn left again, the restaurant is on the left.

ESSENTIALS

Cuisine: Mediterranean

Hours: MON-SAT 11:30AM-3PM.
7 days 5:30PM-10PM.

Meals and Prices: Lunch $$$,
Dinner $$$$-$$$$$

Nonsmoking: Smoking only permitted at bar.

Take-out: Yes

Alcohol: Full Bar

Credit Cards: All 5

Personal Check: Local only

Reservations: Not for lunch.
Recommended for dinner, especially for parties of 5 or more.

Wheelchair Access: Yes

Dress: Casual to fine.

Other: There is a private dining room for parties of up to 24.

HISTORY, PERSONALITY AND CHARACTER

Mirabella was built on National Historic Registry property by Gibraltar, Inc. in the early 1990s. The restaurant opened on July 8, 1994. Richard Sultani, who has been in the restaurant business since 1975 and operates restaurants in Washington, D.C., including Les Champs in the infamous Watergate Complex, is the owner and general manager. Janet Lightfoot, who served as construction manager and decorator before the restaurant opened, is the office manager. Michel Wahaltere and Benoit Marande are the executive chefs. Joseph Munoz is the pastry chef.

FOOD, SERVICE AND AMBIANCE

This is a very unpretentious restaurant with sundry seasonings and spices to incite your senses. Their red lentil soup with caramelized onion and fresh roasted cumin was very (temperature) hot and zesty. The maniish, a Mediterranean pastry, was more like a mini-pizza topped with tomatoes, Moroccan spices and kasseri cheese, then cut up in 8 pieces around the outside of the plate with a center of diced tomato, cucumber and scallions. Fresh parsley sprinkled on the edge of the plate completed this enticing dish. My meal came with an appetizing light and fluffy pita bread, dusted with flour and made with unbleached and duram flour from Morocco. For my final course, I had the cherry clafouti, a French country custard with Italian cherries, a sprinkling of powdered sugar, and 3 big blackberries with a sprig of fresh mint on top. I strongly recommend this ethereal, delectable dessert. It will freshen your palate and clean your breath in a most delightful way.

Mirabella is a must for ethnic food lovers. Their fares come from France, Morocco, Lebanon, Greece, Turkey, Spain and Italy. You can order a combination of soup, salad, hot or cold appetizers, like I did, or one of their featured entrées. If you follow my route, you may find yourself selecting chilled Spanish gazpacho; tabouleh (parsley salad); fettoush; feta cheese, yogurt or lentil salad; a hot appetizer of crisp fried chick pea patties with fava beans, a savory spinach pastry, or spicy homemade sausage; or a cold appetizer like hummos tahini (chick pea purée with sesame paste and lemon), dolma (stuffed grape leaves) or roasted eggplant. The main courses include marinated lamb or chicken, minced lamb and beef, langoustinos, linguini and vegetables, gyros, cous cous (an authentic Moroccan dish with chicken and lamb), paella and a mixed grill. They also offer three nightly specials, one being a fish dish. A few of their other delightful desserts are zuccoto, Italian raspberry and banana cream spongecake with roasted bananas; kunefé, Palestinian ricotta and mozzarella pastry with ice cream; and Turkish baklava with hazelnuts and pistachios.

My server was sociable and willing to help. Light rock music played quietly in the background. The dining room is designed in white adobe with turquoise shutters matched with a turquoise slanted roof and vegas. Huge bottles of pickled scallions, carrots, hot peppers and raspberries, along with dried flower arrangements, decorate the white adobe shelves. The kitchen in the rear is open for your viewing pleasure. Hiding downstairs in the hallway next to the restrooms is an exhibition displaying images from the Wheeler Opera House by Susan Slater displaying rocks, water and a nude in an underground grotto. The arched ceiling, columns and painted mural of a coastline of the Mediterranean give the feeling of dining on the patio of an old villa. If you haven't discovered Mirabella yet, you know about it now. I thought this was an outstanding find!

SPECIAL ONE-TIME OFFER: Buy one entrée at the regular price and receive a second entrée of equal or lesser value FREE. This offer NOT valid in combination with any other offers. Please present to server at time of ordering. _____ Manager/Owner. _____ Date.

This is the 3rd small town restaurant guide on Colorado by Benjamin James Bennis.

RECIPE

Clafouti
(Serves 6)

Seeds from ½ fresh vanilla bean or
  substitute 1 teaspoon vanilla extract
12 ounce milk
8 ounce heavy cream
8 egg yolks

1 tablespoon all-purpose flour
6 ounce granulated sugar
Pinch of nutmeg
½ pound Amarone cherries

1. Scald the milk and heavy cream with the vanilla bean seeds.
2. Combine egg yolk, sugar, flour and nutmeg.
3. Add a small amount of the scalded milk to the sugar/flour mixture until smooth and then add the remaining milk making a custard mixture.
4. Place seeded cherries in a shallow custard dish and pour custard mixture over the cherries.
5. Bake in water bath at 325 degrees for 25 minutes or until set.

Piñons

105 South Mill Street, 920-2021

Directions: From the northwest (Glenwood Springs), stay on Highway 82 as you enter town, make a right on 7th Street and a left on Main Street. Go 10 blocks. Turn right on Mill Street (one block past Monarch Street). The restaurant is in the first block on the right. From the southeast (Independence Pass), you will enter town on Cooper Avenue. Follow it to where you are forced to turn right on to Galena Street. Proceed 2 blocks to Hopkins Avenue. Turn left and go 1 block to Mill Street. Turn right. The restaurant is on the left.

ESSENTIALS

Cuisine: American with a Colorado Touch
Hours: 7 nights 6PM-10PM. Closed Mid-APR to Mid-JUN and OCT to Thanksgiving.
Meals and Prices: Dinner $$$$$$$
Nonsmoking: All
Take-out: No
Alcohol: Full Bar

Credit Cards: MC, Visa, Amx
Personal Check:
Reservations: Highly recommended.
Wheelchair Access: Yes. They have an elevator. Please call ahead.
Dress: Aspen casual with a western motif.
Other: $6 surcharge for entrées split in kitchen.

ASPEN

HISTORY, PERSONALITY AND CHARACTER

Piñons is a world-class restaurant recognized in the 1992 through 1996 Directory of Award Winning Restaurants in North America (DiRōNA) and listed #2 among the Top 40 Rocky Mountain Restaurants, #2 among the Top American Restaurants, and the #1 Top Celebrity Scene in the Zagat Survey. The restaurant was built in turn-of-the-century style and opened in February 1988 under original owner, Fred Mayerson. Paul Chanin became a partner right after the restaurant opened and shortly thereafter was and still is the sole owner. In 1993, Piñons was followed by Chanin's Grill, just one block south. Mr. Chanin was a philanthropic real estate developer from New York who moved to Aspen in 1980 where he has carried on his community and philanthropic activities. The Restaurant Manager/Maitre d' is Frank Chock, from Hawaii, who has been in the restaurant business in the Aspen area since the early 1970s, having previous experience at Shavano's (now Il Poggio) and Krabloonik's, both in Snowmass Village, and Gordon's (now Chanin's Grill). The Executive Chef is Robert Mobilian, from New York, who started at Piñons in 1988. Joe Flamer and Betty Shurin are the sous chefs and Damon Ornowski is the sommelier.

FOOD, SERVICE AND AMBIANCE

Dinner was a 4-course treat. I whet my appetite with a tantalizing lobster strudel with morel and chanterelle mushrooms with a tomato base sauce in a flaky, filo pastry. I must have been on a fungi funk this evening because I followed my appetizer with wild shiitake and portobello mushroom soup with celery, onions, parsley and tomato in a fabulous broth. The main course was a satisfying, medium-rare, grilled rack of lamb with roasted figs and pink peppercorn sauce. A medley of mixed vegetables and a fresh sage sprig were served on the side. The finale was a piece of scrumptious fallen chocolate soufflé cake with warm chantilly cream and Crème Anglaise.

The soups, deserts, ice creams and sorbets are all homemade. A few of the pre-entrée preferences are pheasant quesadillas, Thai- seared beef tenderloin with peanut sauce and pan-seared scallops with tomatilla sauce. Some of the favorite entrées include sautéed Colorado pheasant breast, elk tenderloin, roasted Colorado striped bass, blackened pork tenderloin, ahi and roasted dover sole. To accompany your meal, you have about 400 wines from France, Spain, Italy, California, Germany and elsewhere around the world to choose from. To conclude your dinner, you can enjoy a cappuccino, espresso, cognac or dessert wine with a piece of chocolate macadamia nut tart, fresh fruit gratin or old-fashioned fruit cobbler.

My server was a member of Piñons' knowledgeable, experienced staff who has been working in the Aspen Valley for a long time. New Age music, like George Winston, fits in perfectly with the mood and setting of the restaurant. There are great views of the Aspen ski slopes from this second-story location. The 1900 western motif includes mandellas and large paintings of Mount Sopris, the Grand Canyon and cowboys on the plains and plateaus; a green-color tin ceiling; Piñon pinewood logs, posts, and window frames; and tan stucco walls.

Special One-time Offer: Buy one entrée at the regular price and receive a second entrée of equal or lesser value FREE. Maximum Value $28.00. This offer NOT valid in combination with any other offers. Please present to server at time of ordering. _____ Manager/Owner. _____ Date.

RECIPE

Pan-Seared Thai Beef with Watercress Salad, Spicy Onions and Peanut Sauce

Thai Spice:
- 1 tablespoon garlic powder
- 1 tablespoon chili powder
- 1 tablespoon white pepper
- 1 tablespoon black pepper
- 1 tablespoon cayenne pepper

Peanut Sauce:
- ¼ cup olive oil
- 1 teaspoon curry
- 1½ cups ground peanuts
- 1 teaspoon minced garlic
- ½ cup chicken stock
- 1 teaspoon Thai spice
- 1 cup coconut milk
- ½ teaspoon salt
- 1 tablespoon sugar
- 1 lemon, juice only

Beef:
- 1 pound beef tenderloin
- Olive oil for sautéing

Watercress Salad:
- ¼ cup rice vinegar
- ¼ cup peanut oil
- 2 tablespoons sesame oil
- 1 teaspoon minced shallots
- 1 teaspoon minced garlic
- ¼ cup Tamari sauce
- 1 tablespoon chopped fresh cilantro
- 1 tablespoon lime juice
- Salt and pepper to taste
- 4 bunches watercress, cleaned

Spicy Onions:
- ½ cup all-purpose flour
- 1 tablespoon paprika
- 2 teaspoons Thai spice
- 1 large red onion, thinly sliced
- ½ cup buttermilk
- Peanut oil for frying

1. Thai Spice: Combine all ingredients in small bowl.
2. Peanut Sauce: Mix all ingredients in sauce pan and simmer for 15 minutes. Keep warm.
3. Spicy Onions: Mix together flour, paprika and 2 teaspoons Thai spice. Soak onions in buttermilk, then toss in flour mixture. Fry in peanut oil until golden brown and set aside.
4. Watercress Salad: Mix rice wine vinegar, peanut oil, sesame oil, shallots, garlic, Tamari, cilantro and lime juice. Salt and pepper to taste. Toss with cleaned watercress.
5. Beef: Cut beef into 8 2-ounce portions and dredge in remaining Thai spice. Heat olive oil over high heat, add beef, and sear on both sides until rare or medium-rate. Cut each piece into 4 slices.
6. Serving: Place salad in middle of plate, top with onions, drizzle peanut sauce on plate and fan beef slices around salad.

A Festive Place Setting at Ricardino's in Avon.

AVON

Avon, named by an Englishman for England's Avon River, was spelled Avin in 1889 when it was listed as a railroad station in 1889.
Zip Code: 81620. Area Code: 970. Population: 1,798. Elevation: 7,440'.

Ricardino's
82 East Beaver Creek Blvd in the Benchmark Shopping Center, 81620, 949-6000
Directions: Take Exit 167 from I-70. Proceed south .1 miles to the first signal. Turn left on East Beaver Creek Boulevard, then take your first right into the Benchmark Shopping Center and look for the blue doors.

ESSENTIALS
Cuisine: Mediterranean
Hours: 7 days 11:30AM-10PM. Lunch served until 5PM when dinner starts. Call for hours during off-seasons: Mid-APR to Mid-JUN and OCT.
Meals and Prices: Lunch $$, Dinner $$$-$$$$.
Nonsmoking: Yes. Smoking permitted at the bar before 6PM and after 10PM.

Take-out: Yes
Alcohol: Full Bar
Credit Cards: MC, Visa, Amx
Personal Check: Yes, with I.D. if out-of-town.
Reservations: Recommended
Wheelchair Access: Yes

HISTORY, PERSONALITY AND CHARACTER
Ricardino's is in a building built in the late 1970s, and at that, it is the second oldest building in town (Avon is fairly young, as Colorado towns go). This spot was originally a deli. In the late '80s, it became Pizza Express & Pasta Pub for a few years. Then it had a short run as Rockies (a bar with pool tables) before opening on December 31, 1993 as Ricardino's. This is owner Richard Gollub's first restaurant. He has been in the restaurant/hotel consulting business since 1974 and worked as a cook at restaurants in the Lodge at Vail (Wildflower and Cucina Rustica) as well as the Hotel Splendido in Porto Fino, Italy from 1990 to 1993. The Lodge at Vail and Hotel Splendido are both owned by Orient Express Hotels (the same people who own the train). It is while at the Lodge at Vail that his friends from Italy began calling him "Ricardino" (the diminutive form of Richard) and the name just caught on. Richard also attended Diana Folinari's Cooking School in Positano, Italy (south of Naples). Most of the recipes on the menu are his.

FOOD, SERVICE AND AMBIANCE
I was looking for something exotic on their lunch menu, and when I didn't find it, I asked to see the dinner menu. They were very accommodating in letting me order

the paella off the dinner menu for lunch. This was one "fiery" paella and not for the faint-hearted or weak-stomached. I thoroughly enjoyed it! This dish, with clams, mussels, squid, shrimp, and scallops, is spiced up with roasted red peppers, garlic and pepperincino (not to be confused with pepperoncini) - small red chilies from southern Italy. It is served with Spanish saffron rice with tomatoes. The table bread was special, too - homemade tomato parmesan and chibata (a mixture of three flours: whole wheat, all purpose and light rye). This was accompanied by dahl, prepared with basil, garbanzo beans, garlic and olive oil. If you like ethnic food, dine here. Their pastas are made fresh or purchased from Italy. Soups and sauces are all made from scratch with the stock used to enhance the sauces. The pastries, foccacia (Italian flat bread) and desserts (cookies, biscotti, tiramisu, chocolate truffle cake, Grand Marnier cheesecake and dauphinoise - a pecan pie bottom brushed with dark almond custard) are all homemade. Their coffee beans come from Lavazza, a company in Milan, Italy. Some highlights from the lunch menu are hummis (with tomatoes, red onions, calamata olives and pita bread), Greek salad, grilled polenta (peppers, vegetables and greens), grilled chicken (with pancetta -Italian bacon - provolone, and pesto mayonnaise) and pasta dishes including linguini with fresh clams. A few of the more exotic dinner items are toasted ravioli with marinara, seafood risotto in a saffron stock and Aunt Sadie's (Richard's aunt) rosemary roasted chicken. The summer menu tends to be lighter with dishes like fettuccine al limone and falafel - a Greek pita sandwich with chick-peas. There are daily specials: every Wednesday is vegetarian day, Thursday is for lasagna, and Friday features eggplant Parmesan. There is a junior citizen's (children's) menu. The wine list offers about 40 American, Italian, Greek and Spanish red, white and sparkling wines and champagnes. If you prefer, have one of their freshly made espressos or cappuccinos.

Richard and his staff will try to accommodate your special requests, as they did mine. Blue chairs and colonial-style shutters match the blue doors. There are several Van Gogh prints - sail boats in Aurel, France, sailing ships in the Mediterranean, and Starry Night, but the picture I liked best was the one of an outdoor cafe in Porto Fino. It reminded me of the time I was just 14 when my Italian cousin, 11 of his friends, and I piled into 3 Fiats and drove from Genoa to Porto Fino and stopped for espresso in an outdoor cafe, very similar to the one in the picture. In fact, it may have been the same one. The picture definitely brought back memories. The terra cotta faux walls are signed by the maker, Carlo D'Allissio. Soft jazz and mild rock play in the background. In the evening, wine bottles filled with test tubes of lamp oil are set on the tables. You can purchase an oil test tube for about $13 to use in your own wine bottle when you return home. Patio dining with covered umbrellas is available during nicer weather.

SPECIAL ONE-TIME OFFER: Buy one entrée at the regular price and receive your choice of a free dessert or a free glass of wine. Limit two desserts or two glasses of wine with the purchase of two entrées. Maximum value $4.25 per dessert or glass of wine. This offer NOT valid in combination with any other offers. _____ Manager/Owner. _____ Date.

RECIPE

Escoffier
(Serves 1)

1 tablespoon garlic, chopped
1 tablespoon pomace, celio olive oil
4 fluid ounces clam, ocean juice
4 fluid ounces white wine
12 each Manila clams

1 pinch crushed red chili pepper
Salt and pepper to taste
Pinch of fresh parsley
7 ounces cooked linguine

1. Heat oil in sauté pan. Add clams, deglace with wine. Add garlic, pepper flakes and clam juice.
2. Reduce and as clams open, pull from pan and set aside. Keep reducing until sauce has been reduced by ⅔.
3. Add butter and clams. Toss with pasta that has been reheated in water bath. Add parsley, season with salt and pepper.
4. Serve in a decorative bowl, pulling clams to the top outside edge of bowl.

Restaurants from 101 Colorado Small Towns, also by Bennis, is a thorough guide to 365 restaurants. See your local bookstore or call Small Town Pub. at (303)978-0316.

BERTHOUD

Berthoud, formerly known as "Little Thompson" in 1875, was named after Captain Edward L. Berthoud, chief civil engineer of the Colorado Central Railroad. Zip Code: 80513. Area Code: 970. Population: 2,990. Elevation: 5,030'.

The Savoy Restaurant Français
535 3rd Street, 532-4095

Directions: Take Exit 250 from I-25 and go west on Highway 56 for 5 miles into Berthoud. (There's a little jog in the road right before you get to town where the highway bends to the right and you have to turn left at a stop sign). Turn right at the first street past the railroad tracks onto 3rd Street. The restaurant is on the left.

ESSENTIALS

Cuisine: French
Hours: TUE-SAT 5:30PM-9:30PM. SUN 4PM-8:30PM. Closed MON.
Meals and Prices: Dinner $$$$-$$$$$
Nonsmoking: All
Take-out: No
Alcohol: Full Bar
Credit Cards: MC, Visa, Amx
Personal Check: Yes
Reservations: Recommended, especially on weekends and holidays

Wheelchair Access: Yes
Dress: From nice casual to coat/tie and gown
Other: Specialty dinners of your choosing (minimum 4) can be arranged with at least 1 week's notice. Appetizers and desserts may be ordered only with an entrée. The Savoy can be rented for a special lunch or dinner on weekends.

HISTORY, PERSONALITY AND CHARACTER

The Savoy is in a century-old building that used to serve as a mercantile and a coffee shop. In September 1992, Jean and Chantal Martini purchased the restaurant from the Barats who had operated The Savoy since 1988. Prior to 1988, the restaurant had been called Chez François. Jean and Chantal were both born in Paris where Jean started out as a butcher and Chantal owned and operated her own restaurant, La Grillade. Jean has been cooking since 1970 and is featured in the book Colorado's Greatest Chefs by Marilyn Booth. The Martinis had spent 9 years at the high-class Jonathan Club in Los Angeles when they saw The Savoy for sale in a French-American newspaper. The switch from big-city U.S.A. to small-town Colorado was executed much to the chagrin of Californians and the delight of Coloradans, myself included.

FOOD, SERVICE AND AMBIANCE

This elegant dining experience began with a Kir Royale aperitif, champagne and crème de Cassis — a black currant liquor. It was cool, refreshing and whetted my appetite. Escargots — sturdy, tasty, intact snails, poached in burgundy and served in

16

Roquefort butter with just a touch of garlic — aroused my taste buds further. The Roquefort butter was just fine for dunking their thin sliced French bread. The two soups du jour were heavenly creamy creations: cream of carrot with curry and vegetable purée with fresh basil. Chef Jean is an accomplished artist when it comes to plate presentations. The mixed green salad was laced with a red beet ribbon and served with Dijon vinaigrette. When it came time to order our entrées, my editor, Linda, and I went in separate directions. She chose vegetarian linguini, the pasta du jour in a colorful assortment of vegetables — French green beans, carrots, red peppers and mushrooms — spiced with tarragon in a very rich cream sauce topped with grated parmesan. I selected a special that I've only had this one opportunity in my life (so far) to order, although Chantal says that it is on the menu more and more. You don't see this dish offered on this continent too often, but you may see it quite often on another continent. I'm talking about kangaroo. (When Chantal told the folks at a table next to us what the special was, one woman asked "Is that legal?"). The kangaroo was excellent. It was the back portion, prepared in raspberry sauce, less beefy than meat, less of a gamey taste than venison, very tender, practically 100% lean and very flavorful without being overpowering. I savored every morsel of this dish and was wanting more when I finished. Those guys can hop onto my plate anytime! The vegetables for this dish (mashed broccoli, cauliflower and carrot) were very attractively arranged to resemble a flag and were placed along side Peru purple potatoes, braised purple cabbage with juniper berries, snow peas, fresh carrots and squash stuffed with ratatouille — a delightful mixture of flavors and textures.

As a prelude to the exquisite cuisine that follows, Jean and Chantal recommend an aperitif, such as Kir Imperial (champagne and raspberry liquor) or Ricard a Pernod (French anise). Chef Jean's creative touch is revealed in first-course appetizers of gravlax, freshly marinated apricot dill salmon served with toast points and capers; gratinee, French onion soup with Port wine; and grilled shrimp marinated in soy and ginger oil and served with sweet pepper salsa. Spotlighting the selection of entrées (the preparation and presentation of which, including the selection, Chef Jean changes regularly) are tournedos au poivre (a house favorite) — beef tenderloin medallions with cracked black, pink, white and green peppercorn sauce, flavored with cognac; breast of duckling with cassis, a dry blueberry sauce; and fruit de mer Savoy — shrimp and scallops sautéed with shallots, ginger, tomatoes and vermouth. The chef's deft hand is also applied to baby rack of lamb, filet mignon, veal scallopini and chicken. Accompanying the menu are nightly specials of appetizers and game and fish entrées. The chef's nightly dessert selections vary. You may be enticed by black currant and raspberry mousse, baked Alaska or crème brûlée.

Our gracious host and server, Chantal, was an expert on Jean's cooking and very attentive to our needs. She met us as we entered through a majestic carved wooden door. Inside, soft jazz played quietly in the background and there was a scent of incense in the air. This 19th century building is adorned with white linen tablecloths and napkins, stained-glass lamps, fine china plates, brass sconces covering tan and white wallpaper, chandeliers, hardwood chairs and red brick walls. This is regal dining in an atmosphere that couldn't be more comfortable.

SPECIAL ONE-TIME OFFER: Buy one entrée at the regular price and receive a complimentary kir (white wine and crème de Cassis). Good for every member of your party who purchases an entrée. This offer NOT valid in combination with any other offers. Please present to server at time of ordering. _____ Manager/Owner. _____ Date.

RECIPE

Pan Seared, Oven Finished Filet of Halibut
with Fresh Beet Sauce, Asparagus, Wild Rice with Three Color Pepper
(Serves 6)

Wild Rice:
 2 cups cold water
 4 ounces wild rice
 1 ounce each red, green and yellow
  bell peppers
 ½ tablespoon fresh crushed garlic
 1 ounce extra virgin olive oil
 1 pinch salt
 1 pinch white pepper

Beet Sauce:
 16 ounces of whole fresh beets
 ½ ounce shallots chopped very fine
 2 bay leaves
 5 whole black peppercorns
 2 ounces extra virgin olive oil
 ½ cup clam juice
 1 tablespoon cornstarch
 2 tablespoons cold water

Halibut:
 6 5-ounce pieces of filet of Halibut
 2 ounces of clarified butter
 Salt to taste
 White pepper to taste

Asparagus:
 12 medium asparagus tips, 3 inches
  in length
 1 quart of cold water
 Pinch of salt

1. Rice: Wash the rice and dry. Place rice in cold water and bring to a boil. Cover loosely with foil. Place over low heat for 20-25 minutes. While the rice is cooking, prepare a brunoise of yellow, red and green peppers. Sweat the peppers and garlic in olive oil until tender or until transparent. When rice is cooked, add brunoise, add salt and pepper to taste, mix together and put rice in 2-ounce soufflé cups and cover with clear film. Press firmly into the cup to make a mold.

2. Sauce: Peel the beets and place them in a vegetable juicer. Extract 10 ounces of beet juice. Sweat shallots, bay leaves, peppercorn and olive oil together until transparent. Add clam juice and reduce by half. Add beet juice and bring to a boil. Remove from burner. In a cup, mix cold water and cornstarch. Add cornstarch mixture to beet sauce and wave with a rubber spatula. Return to burner, bring to low boil and remove. Strain in fine chinois. Once strained, keep warm in water bath.

3. Halibut: Pan sear halibut for 1½ minutes face down in a non-stick pan in clarified butter. Place in over for 4 minutes at 375 degrees for medium rare. For medium, turn and add 3 more minutes. Salt and pepper to taste.

4. Asparagus: Peel asparagus. Place water in a pan with salt. Bring water to a boil, add asparagus and boil for 4 minutes. While asparagus is boiling, prepare a bowl with water and ice. When asparagus is cooked, place in bowl with ice and water.

5. Steam and place asparagus in a "V" from the center of the plate up. Put rice mold in center of asparagus "V". Using a 2-ounce ladle, pour sauce on lower half of plate. Using a spatula, take each filet and let drain. Press with a paper towel to remove excess moisture. Place over sauce on plate. Decorate with one edible pansy at point of "V" of asparagus.

The Black Forest Inn in Black Hawk

BLACK HAWK

Black Hawk derived its name when an early mining company brought a quartz mill into the area bearing the name of the famous Indian chief. Along with Central City, Black Hawk produced over a half million dollars in gold and other metals during the great mining days of the 19th century. Rich in history, as well as precious metals, Black Hawk has several distinctions including the establishment of the first smelter in Colorado in 1868, the first telephone in Colorado and the Gilpin House where President Grant slept. Black Hawk was 1 of 3 Colorado towns to legalize limited-stakes gambling in October of 1991.

Zip Code 80422. Area Code: 303. Population 227 (1990). Elevation: 8,056'.

Black Forest Inn

260 Gregory Street, PO Box 11, 279-2333 (local call in Denver), 582-9971 (Black Hawk)

Directions: Take Exit 244 from I-70 and head north on Highway 6. Where Highway 6 meets Highway 119, continue north on Highway 119. It's 8 miles from I-70 to Black Hawk. When you get into town, turn left at the second signal onto Gregory Street. Go .2 miles. The restaurant is on the left just after the road bends to the right.

ESSENTIALS

Cuisine: German/American
Hours: 7 days 11AM-9:30PM (8PM on Sun and Holidays).
Meals and Prices: Lunch $$, Dinner $$$-$$$$
Nonsmoking: Yes
Take-out: No
Alcohol: Full Bar

Credit Cards: No
Personal Check: Yes, with I.D.
Reservations: Always recommended
Wheelchair Access: Yes
Other: Gregory Hall, their banquet room seats 250 and is the largest banquet facility in Black Hawk. Ample valet parking across the street.

HISTORY, PERSONALITY AND CHARACTER

Part of the building now occupied by the Black Forest Inn was originally constructed in the late 1860s as housing for gold miners. John Doe (actual name), a tailor from England who was Baby Doe Tabor's husband before she married Horace Tabor, was one of the establishment's guests. Prior to 1958, 10 different businesses operated from these premises including an old-fashion homecooking diner called Chicken Bruster ran by Bell Tobin, the J. and M. Diner owned by Jesse and Margaret Clemens, a fountain laundry, a grocery store and a warehouse for the St. Charles Hotel. In March 1958, current owner Wilhelm "Bill" Lorenz opened the Black Forest Inn in what is today the front right dining room. In 1963, he added 4 dining rooms on 3 levels to the left of the entrance, including a Rathskeller. In June 1989, after 2½ years of construction, Gregory Hall (named after John Gregory, the famous discoverer of gold in Central City and

Georgetown) was opened as a banquet facility for up to 250 people. It is constructed of natural rock, midwestern oak and iron.

Bill, who is a former mayor of Black Hawk, grew up in the restaurant business in Mainz, Germany. His father owned a half-dozen restaurants and Bill himself served apprenticeship for Maitre D' in Germany. Bill's general manager since 1989, Randy Young, started out in the restaurant business in 1965 as a bus boy. He owned and operated a restaurant/casino in Las Vegas, Nevada, before taking over the management of the Wuthering Heights Restaurant in Lakewood, Colorado, from 1976 to 1989. Alfredo Aries, who has been with the Black Forest Inn since 1973, is the executive chef.

FOOD, SERVICE AND AMBIANCE

It's nice to know that the high quality of a restaurant doesn't change over the years. Such was the case with the Black Forest Inn when I dined here in 1991, before gambling, and again a few years later after gambling. But then, it shouldn't be much of a surprise to find that a restaurant that has been under the same tutelage for 38 years has remained constantly commendable over just a few years.

On my initial visit, I savored my well-done sauerbraten (beef roast) smothered in a rich, thick brown sauce and served with potato pancakes that were crisp and dark on the outside and moist on the inside. The red cabbage had a pleasingly tart taste. I actually preferred my dinner companion's filet of stroganoff to my own meal: very tender medium rare tenderloin tips on a bed of homemade noodles with mixed steamed vegetables. On my latest visit, my dinner companion mistakenly ordered the Russian egg appetizer thinking this would just be a tasty tid-bit. Wrong! This was a mountain of an appetizer that balanced brackish anchovies and caviar with the temperate tastes of salmon, German potato salad, tomatoes, pickles, hard-boiled egg and lemon wedges on a bed of lettuce that filled an entire dinner plate. My own entrée selection was soft, 12-day well-aged loin elk pan-fried and seared on the outside with button mushrooms and wide egg noodles sprinkled with parsley. Cranberry sauce was always one of my favorite dishes on Thanksgiving, but the Black Forest's creamy cranberry sauce with orange peel and wine was better than anything my mother or aunts ever came up with for the holidays. No matter how delectable these two preferences were, we still had enough left over for lunch the next day. The heartiest of appetites can be gratified at Bill's Black Forest. I also enjoyed both their house oil and sweet vinegar dressing and the honey-Dijon on their dinner salads. Dinners come with a hardy German sour-dough rye bread.

Other appetizers to start your dining are goose liver pâté with truffles, marinated herring, cold vichyssoise and German oxtail soup. Their specialties, wild game and fowl, accompany their regular menu highlighted by Hungarian goulash, ground sirloin Burgunion, kassler rippchen, schnitzel holstein, fresh calves liver and Australian rock lobster. The lunch menu features salads (fruit plate, avocado seafood, avocado chicken Waldorf and stuffed tomato), sandwiches (burgers, German cold cuts and ham and cheese) and entrées (pork chops, wiener schnitzel, New York cut sirloin, vegetarian plate and Glacier Bay halibut). German, French and domestic beer can enhance your meal. Complete your meal with homemade ice cream, German cheesecake, fresh strawberries in cream, German apple streudel or rainbow sherbet.

Service starts with Bill greeting you at the door and escorting you to your table; continues with the amiable, efficient, prompt and professional staff; and ends where it began with Bill confirming that you had a memorable experience and bidding farewell. German and Austrian orchestrated waltzes enrich each dining moment. The cherrywood, knotty walls are trimmed with gold-framed paintings of the German countryside, castles, hunters in suspenders and knights in armor; a boar's head; a cuckoo clock and pictures of a big surf á la Big Sur style, aspen trees, still-lifes, party scenes and a house overgrown with vines. You'll also find tapestries, a large, black "Denver Gold & Silver Exchanges Safe" and a piano. Patio dining and an outdoor German beer garden that seats 200 are available. Whether you're planning a romantic dinner for 2 or a banquet, you'll treasure Bill Lorenze's warm, robust hospitality and fine German and American cuisine provided in an old European atmosphere in the wild west.

SPECIAL ONE-TIME OFFER: Buy one entrée at the regular price and receive a Fun Book (valued at $15) good at the Black Forest Inn and Otto's Casino next door. This offer NOT valid in combination with any other offers. Please present to server at time of ordering. _____ Manager/Owner. _____ Date.

RECIPE

Sauerbraten
(Serves 6 to 8)

3 pounds beef round roast	1 carrot, sliced
2½ red wine	½ onion, diced
2½ cups white vinegar	3 garlic cloves
½ cup brown sugar	2 tablespoons pickling spice
2 celery stalks, sliced	1 tablespoon salt

1. Combine all ingredients. Marinate roast for at least 48 hours under refrigeration.
2. Pre-heat oven to 350 degrees. Place roast in baking pan with 1 inch water. Bake one hour, then add marinade. Cook one more hour. Remove roast, strain ingredients from stock (vegetables, picking spice).
3. Use a cornstarch roux to thicken the stock for sauerbraten gravy.
4. Slice roast against the meat grain, ¼-inch thick and add to gravy.

BLANCA

Blanca, Spanish for "white", was named for its location at the foot of Mount Blanca. The town was established in 1908 as the result of a land lottery. People from across the country were sold small tracts of land making them eligible for larger plots of ground later.
Zip Code: 81123. Area Code: 719. Population: 272. Elevation: 7,750'.

Mt. Blanca Gamebird & Trout, Inc.
PO Box 236, 379-3825

Directions: 3½ miles southwest of Blanca. From Highways 17 and 160 in Alamosa, go 19 miles east on Highway 160. There will be a big sign on your right announcing Mt. Blanca Gamebird & Trout. Turn right, go 2½ miles on a gravel road. There will be another sign on your right. Turn right, go 1 mile to the restaurant and lodge. Coming from the east on Highway 160, there will be a big sign on your right just past Blanca announcing the restaurant. Turn left onto the gravel road, go 2½ miles, turn right, go 1 mile to the restaurant.

ESSENTIALS

Cuisine: Steak, Seafood and Wildgame
Hours: FEB-MAY: Wed-Sun Breakfast 7:30AM-9:30AM, Lunch 12PM, Dinner 6PM. Closed Mon/Tue. JUN-DEC: 7 days, same hours as above. Closed JAN. NOTE: Lunch and Dinner are single seatings.
Meals and Prices: Breakfast $6, Lunch $7, Dinner $17.
Nonsmoking: No
Take-out: No

Alcohol: Full Bar
Credit Cards: MC, Visa
Personal Check: Yes, with I.D.
Reservations: REQUIRED. You will not be served without one.
Wheelchair Access: No
Other: 15% service charge for parties of 8 or more. Open for business and social groups: banquets, meetings, parties, wedding receptions, seminars. Conference room and lodging available.

HISTORY, PERSONALITY AND CHARACTER

The restaurant, lodge and wildgame bird and trout preserve were built in 1987 by current owners, Bill Binnian, Jerry Smith and Rodger Wakasugi. Jerry and Rodger farm in the local area, while Bill operates and manages the facility. Former football great Dick Butkis and race car driver Jack Baldwin filmed a segment for ESPN here in October 1993 and enjoyed the same pheasant dinner (with a different pheasant, of course) that I had. The on-premises preserve, for the propagation of gamebirds and fish, raises in excess of 7,000 gamebirds per year under a 5-acre net and 3,000 pounds of trout in 3 man-made ponds. Most of the gamebirds - pheasants, chukar partridge, quail, ducks and geese - are released to the wild for hunters. The rainbow and German brown trout can be caught and released, or they will cook your catch for breakfast, lunch or dinner. This is a very popular place for bird hunters, trout fisherman and sporting clay shooters (they have 10 shooting fields). The lodge has also been used as a base camp for assaults on Mt. Blanca and other "Fourteeners" nearby.

FOOD, SERVICE AND AMBIANCE

I had a very pleasant 3-hour dinner here on a balmy February evening with my gracious and gentlemanly host, Bill. The fare for the evening started off with a house salad that included sunflower seeds, mushrooms, green peppers and pepperoncini. The main course was pheasant, wrapped in bacon and ham, covered with a cream sauce and served on a bed of wild rice. The pheasant was cooked thoroughly and had a nice mild flavor, nothing too spicy. The side dishes were mixed vegetables and whole cranberry sauce. We finished off the meal with several cups of coffee and Chocolate mousse cakes. Dinner was served by the friendly Mt. Blanca staff with pleasant smiles.

Much of the meal comes from frozen, packaged or canned ingredients. However, that should not deter you from taking the short 3½-mile trip off the main highway to dine here. You will be treated to some wild gamebird or trout grown right on the premises. They also offer T-bone, ribeye, prime rib, locally grown tilapia, barbecue baby-back ribs, occasionally buffalo and lobster, and other specialties on request. When you call to make your reservation, tell them what you would like to have for dinner and they will do their best to accommodate your desires. Crackers, rolls and butter, non-alcoholic beverage and dessert are included with dinner. Breakfast is short-order. When you arrive you can choose from pancakes, eggs, bacon, sausage, ham, hash browns, biscuits and gravy, coffee, tea and juices. Lunch is family style and chef's choice. It will include casseroles, soups, sandwiches, a non-alcoholic beverage and dessert.

The location and ambiance are also good reasons for stopping here when you are in the area: a great view of Mt. Blanca and the Sangre de Cristo Mountains and the perfect setting for a gorgeous Colorado sunset. Inside the lounge and dining area, you will find stuffed Hungarian partridge, ring-neck pheasant, trout, marlin, Canadian geese, fox and coyote skins, and a head of antlers on their big rock fireplace, all under a vaulted knotty-pine ceiling with walnut-stained vegas.

SPECIAL ONE-TIME OFFER: Buy one entrée at the regular price and receive a second entrée of equal or lesser value FREE (up to $17.00 value) OR 50% off a single entrée (maximum discount $8.50). This offer NOT valid in combination with any other offers. _____ Manager/Owner. _____ Date.

RECIPE

Pheasants in Sour Cream

3 pheasants, cut up
½ teaspoon pepper, poultry
   seasoning
½ teaspoon thyme, basil
1 medium onion, chopped
1 cup chicken broth

1 cup sour cream
½ cup butter
¾ cup white wine
½ cup mushroom
2 teaspoon garlic

1. Marinate cut-up pheasant in wine early in the day and refrigerate. Turn occasionally.
2. In large frying pan, sauté onions, garlic and mushrooms in butter until brown. Put in casserole dish.
3. Coat pheasant in flour seasoned with pepper, poultry seasoning, thyme and basil.
3. Add more butter to pan and lay in the pheasant.
4. Brown all pieces and put in casserole dish.
5. Add broth to pan and work until clean.
6. Add wine and heat a few minutes. Pour over pheasant.
7. Bake one hour; 15 minutes before pheasant is ready, add sour cream.
8. Bake covered until you add sour cream and then uncovered for the last 15 minutes.
8. Serves 5 to 6 people.

The Dining Area at Mt. Blanca Game Bird and Trout, Inc. in Blanca

BRECKENRIDGE

Named after former U. S. Vice President, John Cabell Breckinridge, the spelling was changed because of Breckinridge's sympathy for the Confederacy during the Civil War. The town's citizen's were fervent Unionists who petitioned Congress to change the name of the town. Hence, the spelling change to disassociate the town of Breckenridge from the Vice President. On July 23, 1887, the largest single gold nugget ever found in Colorado was discovered by miner Tom Groves at nearby Farncomb Hill. It weighed in at 13 pounds, 7 ounces! Today, Breckenridge can boast that they have over 350 buildings on the National Register of Historic places.

Zip Code: 80424. Area Code: 970. Population: 1,285. Elevation: 9,602'.

Cafe Alpine

106 East Adams Avenue, PO Box 173, 453-8218. Fax 453-6936.

Directions: From the North on Highway 9, proceed two blocks past the signal at Lincoln. Turn left on Adams Avenue. The restaurant is ½ block down on the left. From the South, on Highway 9, proceed 2 blocks past the signal at South Park Avenue. Turn right on Adams Avenue. The restaurant is ½ block down on the left.

ESSENTIALS

Cuisine: International
Hours: Memorial Day through SEP: Mon-Fri 11AM-9PM (Lunch until 3PM, Appetizers and Tapas 3PM-5PM, Dinner 5PM-10PM). Sat/Sun 10AM-9PM (Brunch 10AM-2PM). Late NOV to Mid-APR: Tapas 3PM-10PM, Dinner 4PM-10PM (Note: closing may be earlier on slow evenings). Closed from Mid-APR to late MAY and from late OCT to late NOV.
Meals and Prices: Lunch/Brunch $$, Dinner $$$$, Tapas $
Nonsmoking: All
Take-out: Yes

Alcohol: Full Bar
Credit Cards: MC, Visa, Amx, Disc
Personal Check: In-state with I.D.
Reservations: Recommended
Wheelchair Access: Yes, for the 1st floor only.
Other: Available for large parties, local groups, business meetings, wedding receptions and catering. Additional 15% service charge for parties of 6 or more. No separate checks. $1 split plate charge for lunch. $3 split plate charge for dinner includes soup or salad.

HISTORY, PERSONALITY AND CHARACTER

Cafe Alpine is in a building that dates back to the 1880s and was a residence until 1967 when it underwent major remodeling to become an office building. In 1988, when the Japanese purchased the local ski area, the building transformed into the Kanda Sushi Bar. Tom and Theresa Franco took over in the summer of 1992, gutted the downstairs, added new paint and carpet, remodeled everything from the tapas bar to the

26

banisters, and opened Cafe Alpine on November 22, 1992. The Francos' philosophy is to set their own standards, raise the level of sophistication of the local diners, and provide quality and consistency in both food and service. Tom started as a waiter in Orlando, Florida, in 1982. He took a year of management training before moving to Woodland Park, Colorado, in 1985. A year later, he was a general manager and host at the Adams Street Grill in Breckenridge. When Tom opened Cafe Alpine, he brought with him 8 of the staff from the Adams Street Grill. Theresa's background is in public relations and photography. She has handled banquets at Beaver Run and Horseshoe II in Breckenridge and managed retail as well. She's a service-oriented perfectionist in charge of looks at Cafe Alpine. R. Hanes Hoffman Jr., restaurant general manager, has been in the restaurant business since 1990. He worked at the Four Seasons Resort in Maui, Hawaii, for 2½ years before coming to Denver to become general manager at Brendan's. In July 1994, he moved to Breckenridge to manage, host and tend bar at Cafe Alpine. Carol Kruer, their manager, who has been in the restaurant business since 1987, is one of the "Alpine Street Grill 8". She also worked at The Historic Mint in Silverthorne. A long-time local resident named George was born and married in the top level dining room. He always returns to the Cafe Alpine on his birthday and wedding anniversary to dine by the fireplace.

FOOD, SERVICE AND AMBIANCE

I relished dipping their fresh, soft, homemade sesame and poppy seed white bread into a spicy basil/pesto vinaigrette while I waited for lunch. The asparagus soup was creamy, but without asparagus, which they included, lightly steamed, slightly warm and crunchy, on my lunch plate. The spanikopita was a delectable flaky, phyllo pastry stuffed with spinach, feta cheese, black olives and olive oil served with a tangy marinara sauce and white rice. It brought back pleasant memories of my trip to Greece just a year earlier.

Their eclectic international lunch menu highlights dishes from around the world: baked peppercorn brie, grilled salmon in a honey Dijon rosemary glaze, and French toast are expressions of France; quesadillas and chicken burritos provide a taste of Mexico; chicken satay, blackened tuna sashimi and Viet-Thai peanut stir-fry are samples from the Orient; shrimp and scallop al fresco, piñon pasta and homemade thin-crust pizza symbolize Italy; grilled smoked turkey with sharp cheddar, dry-aged New York steak and J. J. Limousine filet mignon stand for America; curried pork tenderloin is a swatch of Indian cuisine; the hummus duet and Crete benedict demonstrate Mediterranean dishes; a Belgian chocolate bag filled with white mousse on raspberry syrup with créme en glaze exemplifies that country; and, closer to home, smoked Colorado trout canapes, fresh tilapia filet, and roast duck breast in a Sante Fe pepper sauce offer a regional representation.

BRECKENRIDGE

Tapas, a creation from the taverns of Andalucia in southern Spain dating back several centuries, are "little meals" or appetizers, such as roasted red pepper roulade, pork and garlic sauce, savory cheesecake, pepper shooters, and tomato and pesto, that you can enjoy at Cafe Alpine's tapas bar or at the dinner table with 20 different ½ glass wine selections. The original tapa, meaning "to cover" in Spanish, was simply a slice of cured ham or chorizo sausage placed over the mouth of a wine glass, possibly to keep the flies out. Cafe Alpine won the 1994 and 1995 Wine Spectator Award of Excellence for their tapas wines and 100 specially selected bottles and 40 wines by the glass. They were also honored with the Three Diamond Award from AAA for food, service and ambiance, and the 1993 and 1994 Taste of Breckenridge Award.

My server was a likeable young lady who made me feel welcome and very comfortable. In fact, I found Cafe Alpine to be entirely down-to-earth. This restaurant is adorned with a vaulted ceiling; oak wood vegas, posts, door and window frames, stair railing and banisters; and a rock fireplace. It is further beautified by a caricature map of Cafe Alpine; an old pair of wood skis, snowshoes and a snowboard; and exceptionally clear, bright, enlarged photos taken by Tom on a bicycle trip through Europe in 1982. Some of the more engaging pictures reveal Lake Annecy in the French Alps; Bruggs, Belgium, the only city Hitler would not bomb; the Loire River region in the French white wine district; Mt. Blanc Ski Resort in Chamonix, France; sheep in Bath and Cornwall, England; grapes in Beaune, France; some little kids on roller skates following Tom in Venice, Italy; Tom and Theresa camping on a pass in the French Alps; and Tom's favorite, Old Stockholm on South Brenner Pass in the Italian Alps.

SPECIAL ONE-TIME OFFER: Buy one entrée at the regular price and receive a second entrée of equal or lesser value FREE. Maximum Value $18.00. This offer NOT valid in combination with any other offers. Please present to server at time of ordering.
_____ Manager/Owner. _____ Date.

Comments or suggestions? Send them to
Small Town Publications, PO Box 621275, Littleton, CO 80162.

RECIPE
White Chocolate Bread Pudding

1 pound fresh French bread
6 ounces weight, white Belgium
  chocolate
18 fluid ounces, whole eggs
12 fluid ounces, egg yolks
38 ounces weight, granulated sugar
2 fluid ounces, vanilla extract
56 fluid ounce, extra heavy cream
  or 3 pints, 8 ounces
38 fluid ounces, half and half
  or 2 pints, 6 ounces

Cream Anglaise:
  1 whole egg
  2 fluid ounces, egg yolks
  12 fluid ounces, extra heavy cream
  12 fluid ounces, half and half
  6 ounces weight, granulated sugar

Raspberry Sauce:
  30 ounces weight, fresh or frozen
   raspberries
  20 ounces weight, granulated
   super fine sugar (for sweeter berries,
   use less sugar)
  6 fluid ounces, fresh lemon juice
  4 fluid ounces, water

1. Coat a glass baking dish. We used an 8"x11.5"x2" or 2-quart dish with pan release spray and then flour. Remove the excess flour.
2. Cut the bread into half-inch slices and using half of the bread, overlap the pieces, covering the bottom of the dish.
3. Cut the white chocolate into small pieces and spread over the bread in the dish. Cover with remaining bread slices.
4. Mix the remaining ingredients in a large bowl and slowly pour over the bread.
5. Pat the contents of the dish to ensure that bread is completely saturated with custard.
6. Cover the pan tightly with plastic wrap and then aluminum foil. Bake in a 400-degree preheated oven for 1-1½ hours or until center temperature reads 150 degrees.
7. Prepare the cream anglaise and the raspberry sauce while pudding is cooking or one or two days in advance.
8. Allow bread pudding to cool.
9. In our restaurant, we place the warm bread pudding on the raspberry sauce and drizzle the cream anglaise over it.

10. Cream anglaise: In a large bowl, mix ingredients until well blended. Heat mixture in a double boiler over medium-high heat, stirring frequently until the sauce coats the back of a spoon or till it reaches 150 degrees. Strain through a fine mesh strainer. Lay plastic wrap on top of the sauce to prevent a crust from forming and serve chilled. Makes 24 ounces of sauce.

11. Raspberry sauce: Purée the raspberries and force through a fine mesh strainer. Discard seeds in strainer. In a stainless steel, ceramic or plastic bowl, mix the strained puree with the water and lemon juice. Add the sugar, slowly in 5-ounce increments, stirring well. Taste frequently until desired sweetness is achieved.

The St. Bernard Inn in Breckenridge

St. Bernard Inn

103 South Main Street, PO Box 960, 453-2572

Directions: From the north (Frisco) on Highway 9, go to the signal at Lincoln Street in the center of town. The restaurant is just past the signal on the right. From the south (Fairplay) on Highway 9, the restaurant is on the left, ½ block past Washington Street, just before the signal at Lincoln Street.

ESSENTIALS

Cuisine: Northern Italian

Hours: Mid-MAY through NOV: 7 Days 5:30PM-9:30PM. DEC to Mid-APR: 7 days 5PM-10PM. Closed Mid-APR to Mid-MAY.

Meals and Prices: Dinner $$$-$$$$

Nonsmoking: All. Smoking permitted in the bar and lounge in the rear.

Take-out: Yes

Alcohol: Full Bar

Credit Cards: All 5

Personal Check: Yes, with I.D.

Reservations: Recommended

Wheelchair Access: Yes

Other: Additional 15% service charge added to parties of 8 or more. No separate checks.

HISTORY, PERSONALITY AND CHARACTER

Named after the famous alpine pass between Italy and France, the St. Bernard Inn specializes in the cuisine of northern Italy: the egg pastas of Bologna, the beef dishes of Piemonte and Tuscany, the seafood of Venice, the veal dishes of Florence, Milan and Parma, the game dishes of Milan, and the lamb of Emilia Romagna. Built in 1890, the St. Bernard was originally a two-story mercantile for miners. In 1899, the building became a grocery store. In 1908, it turned into a pharmacy and continued as such through the 1930s. In the 1940s, the building turned back into a grocery store again and it was not until 1971 that Tom Bauder, the current owner, established the premises as a restaurant. Tom is assisted by his floor manager, Shirley Rainey. The head chef, Sylvia Smith, has been with the restaurant since 1993. She has been cooking since 1987, having worked previously at the Vista House at the top of Peak 8 and the Briar Rose, both in Breckenridge. She also helped to set up the kitchen and menu at the Gold Dredge on the Blue River in town. The St. Bernard Inn has been the recipient of the Wine Spectator Award of Excellence for several years in the 1980s and in 1990.

FOOD, SERVICE AND AMBIANCE

I have dined here twice, trying both their homemade pastas (lasagna and fettucine) and veal chop, both with very favorable results. The lasagna is baked to a an overflowing "gooey" perfection of mozzarella, ricotta, tomatoes, meats and Italian spices. The veal chop with port wine, shallot and veal stock demi-glaze was juicy, but I would have liked more of the demi-glaze. The bed of homemade al dente egg and spinach noodles that the veal chop was served on was fresh and flavorful. The side dishes to these two wonderful meals were spinach squash topped with marinara sauce and fresh steamed broccoli. Olive oil with basil and garlic is on the table for the warm dinner rolls. I liked their fresh tomato and basil soup with pieces of fresh garlic. Their salad comes with a good house honey-vinaigrette, homemade toasted sesame or creamy garlic dressings. Grated parmesan is served on the side.

Their menu offers a variety of freshly-made pastas and sauces with fresh seafood, beef tenderloin, veal, chicken or fresh vegetables. The homemade desserts include tiramisu; cannoli filled with ricotta cheese, chocolate cinnamon, a raspberry cream sauce and topped with pistachios; hazelnut liquor-flavored pudding with toasted coconut topping; cheesecakes (chocolate or berry); and ice cream. There is a children's menu and a wine list that offers 101 (a number that I am partial to!) Italian red, white and sparkling bottled wines from Trentino Alto Adige to Sicily. Wines by the glass are also available nightly.

Service was attentive, helpful and pleasant. The atmosphere in the restaurant is filled with sounds of violin music and classical piano. The decor features photos by Alan Klug of Monet's garden in Giverny, France and Shakespeare's House in Stratford, England. Original street signs of the Naval Reserve, Hobbs Fishery and a consulting physician are symbols of the restaurant's past along with the original gold-painted tin ceiling from the turn of the century. Red table cloths and cloth napkins along with oil table lamps and brass wall lamps add some pleasing touches. The bar and lounge in the rear has a picture history of the St. Bernard, darts, and two couches to relax in before or after dinner.

SPECIAL ONE-TIME OFFER: Buy one entrée at the regular price and receive a complimentary "wine by the glass" selection. Limit two glasses of wine with the purchase of two entrées. This offer NOT valid in combination with any other offers. _____ Manager/Owner. _____ Date.

Looking for more great small town restaurants to visit in Colorado?
Pick up Restaurants from 101 Colorado Small Towns by Benjamin James Bennis
at your local bookstore or order by calling (303)978-0316.

<u>RECIPE</u>

Pollo ai tre Formaggi
(Serves 6)

Cheese Mix: 1 cup flour
  1½ cups ricotta cheese
  ¼ cup Parmesan, grated   Apricot Glaze:
  ½ cup asiago cheese, grated   ½ cup sliced, dried apricots
  1½ cups grated mozzarella cheese   ½ stick of butter
  ⅛ cups dried or fresh basil   ½ cup orange juice concentrate
                                      1 shallot, chopped fine
Egg Wash: ¼ cup chopped fresh basil
  3 eggs   ½ cup white wine
  ¼ cup cold water   ¼ cup water

Breading:
  2 cups dried bread crumbs
  ¼ cup parmesan
  ¼ cup pine nuts

1. Cheese Mix: Mix all ingredients in a mixing bowl.
2. Egg Wash: Whip both ingredients together.
3. Lightly pound 6 chicken breasts. Divide cheese mix and flip chicken, smooth side down and stuff with equal parts of cheese mix. Flip over other side, gently mash with palm of hand.
4. Breading: Add all to food processor and chop. Blend well.
5. Fry chicken in oil on medium heat.
6. With 1 cup flour in bowl, dip each chicken in flour, egg and bread crumbs. Fry in medium high heat until good and brown on one side. Flip.
6. Place whole pan in 500-degree oven for 10 to 15 minutes or until cheese is oozing out.
7. Sauce: Put all ingredients in a pan and reduce until thick and bubbly.
8. Serve chicken on fresh fettuccine. Top with apricot glaze.

See the introduction for an explanation of abbreviations used in the Essentials Section.

BUENA VISTA

Buena Vista, Spanish for "beautiful view", is located near the geographic center of Colorado in the Upper Arkansas River Valley and lives up to its name. Twelve "Fourteeners" (14,000' peaks), including the Collegiate Peaks, are located in the Buena Vista region. The town lies in Chaffee County where the residents changed the county seat in 1880 by stealing the courthouse records from Granite and transferring them to Buena Vista. From the adage "what goes around, comes around," the records were stolen from Buena Vista in 1928 and moved to Salida, the present-day county seat.
Zip Code: 81211. Area Code: 719. Population: 1,752 (1990). Elevation: 7,955'.

Casa del Sol

303 Highway 24, PO Box 1395, 395-8810, 395-6340
Directions: From the intersection of Highways 285 and 24, 2 miles south of Buena Vista, go north 2.4 miles to the signal at Main Street. Continue north for ¼ mile. The restaurant is on the right at the southeast corner of Highway 24 and Arkansas Street.

ESSENTIALS

Cuisine: Mexican/New Mexican
Hours: Memorial Day Weekend to Mid-OCT: 7 days 11:30AM-3PM and 4:30PM-9:30PM. End of DEC through MAR: Thu-Sun 11:30AM-3PM and 4:30PM-8:30PM. MAY: 11:30AM-3PM and 4:30PM-8:30PM. Closed Mid-OCT to end of DEC and APR.
Meals and Prices: Lunch $$, Dinner $$-$$$
Nonsmoking: Yes

Take-out: No
Alcohol: No
Credit Cards: MC, Visa
Personal Check: Yes, with 2 forms of I.D.
Reservations: Highly recommend JUN-SEP.
Wheelchair Access: Yes
Dress: Casual to sportswear for skiing, hiking, cayaking etc.

HISTORY, PERSONALITY AND CHARACTER

The building occupied by Casa del Sol is a "tale of two centuries". The front dining room was originally constructed of logs in 1880 as a blacksmith shop, while the back dining room was added 100 years later in 1980. Paul and Marjorie Knox purchased the structure in 1974. Their son, Jeffrey, started out in the early years waiting tables then moved on to cooking. Today, he has taken over the restaurant while Paul and Marjorie operate The Adobe Inn next door.

FOOD, SERVICE AND AMBIANCE

I thoroughly relished my two dining experiences here and part of the reason is Casa del Sol's recipes. For the past 30 years, the Knoxes have been traveling throughout Mexico sampling the cuisine and bringing back authentic recipes from Sonora, Jalisco,

Guerrero and Chihuahua. On my first visit, I delighted in their most popular dish, the Pechuga Suiza — a lightly toasted flour tortilla stuffed with chicken, Monterey jack cheese, mild green chilies, onion and sour cream: a delectable combination. My second time at the restaurant was equally gratifying when I ordered the enchilada Casa del Sol in an appealing plate presentation with lettuce along the edge; a black olive in the center; ground beef, cheese and red chili powder sauce on top (a real "nose runner" but short of a "barn burner") and sprinkled with chives. All meals made to order with fresh ingredients is another reason why this is one of my favorite Mexican restaurants in Colorado. Chips with homemade salsa — thick with tomato, onion and green chilies and hot with jalapeño — are served with each meal. For dessert, I'd recommend their fresh rum butter pecan cake served warm with a scoop of whipped ice cream on top. It was soft (easily pierced with a fork) with a sugary top — delicious!

Other Mexican delicacies found on the lunch and dinner menus include chicken, cheese, beef and crab/seafood enchiladas with frijoles; shrimp quesadillas; a green chili bowl; tacos and burritos. Highlighting the dinner menu are traditional Mexican dishes: chicken móle — a broiled breast topped with a mild exotic sauce of green chilies, tomatoes, onion, garlic, almonds, spices and chocolate; carne asada — a broiled New York strip smothered in green chili; a cheese enchilada with a special homemade, mild sauce made from the flavorful pulp of Rio Grande Valley chilies and a fluffy egg chili relleno. American dishes are also offered: broiled New York strip and shrimp scampi cooked in garlic butter. Homemade soups are served: French onion for lunch and beef consommé with sherry and meat balls for dinner. They have a children's plate. Homemade hot fudge sundae, ice cream and sherbet are available for your enjoyment.

Service was cheerful, efficient and smiling. All orders are individually baked after you order so, if the restaurant is full, you may wait a few extra minutes for your meal, but it will be well worth it. Mexican guitar and classical violin music provided pleasing entertainment. Aged and weathered stained plywood in the rear dining room gave it a much older than 15-year look. The shelves in this room were decorated with brass, iron, wood, porcelain and hand-painted carvings of animals, eggs hatching, clowns and a nativity scene — all made in Mexico and all for sale in the $5 to $80 price range. Kachina and paper mache dolls, Mayan masks, Mexican rugs, several gold-framed mirrors and small tapestries enhance the Mexican medium. Orange is the predominant color with matching wood tables and chairs, paper napkins and place mats and curtains. A narrow, circular stairway leads up to a pair of booths with two small windows overlooking the highway and a view of Mt. Princeton to the west. An enclosed, gravel-covered courtyard was added in 1987 with a fountain, aspen and fir trees, red-rock walkway and dining on wood benches under canvas canopies and cushioned iron-frame chairs under umbrellas. A separate enclosed dining room off the courtyard featured cowhide chairs, a black iron Cameron stove, a shelf with Mexican pottery and colored-pencil sketches of assorted wildflowers and plants (Indian paintbrush, yucca, fire weed, western red lily, lupin and golden bowl mariposa). Take pleasure in "a little bit of Mexico in the Rockies" with Casa del Sol's bona fide Mexican cuisine.

<u>SPECIAL ONE-TIME OFFER:</u> Buy one entrée at the regular price and receive a complimentary beverage or dessert (up to $2.50 value). Limit 2 beverages or desserts with the purchase of 2 entrées. This offer NOT valid in combination with any other offers. Please present to server at time of ordering. _____ Manager/Owner. _____ Date.

<u>RECIPE</u>

Chicken Mole Recipe
(Serves 6)

8 ounce chicken breast, skinless and boneless	½ tablespoon sesame seed
	½ tablespoon chile powder
	½ teaspoon cinnamon
8 ounces canned tomatoes, diced	½ teaspoon coriander
7 ounces green chilies, diced	½ teaspoon salt
¼ medium onion	¼ teaspoon ground cumin
1 teaspoon diced garlic	¼ teaspoon ground cloves
⅓ cup almonds	1 cup chicken broth
¼ cup raisins	1 square unsweetened chocolate

1. Fry onions and garlic in a little oil. Set aside.
2. Blend the rest of ingredients, except chicken broth and chocolate in a blender. Add blended mixture to the onions and garlic, then add the chicken broth and chocolate. Simmer until chocolate is melted.
3. Grill chicken breast. Put on a plate and cover with about ½ cup of the mole sauce and bake at 400 degrees for a few minutes. Top with toasted almonds.

Evergreen Cafe

418 Highway 24 North, 395-8984

Directions: From the intersection of Highways 285 and 24, 2 miles south of Buena Vista, go north 2.4 miles to the signal at Main Street. Continue north for .3 miles. The restaurant is on the left just past Arkansas Street.

ESSENTIALS

Cuisine: American

Hours: 7 days 6:30AM-2PM (Breakfast until 11:30AM, lunch from 11:30AM)

Meals and Prices: Breakfast $, Lunch $-$$

Nonsmoking: All

Take-out: Yes

Alcohol: Wine and beer

Credit Cards: No

Personal Check: Yes with I.D.

Reservations: Not accepted

Wheelchair Access: Yes

Dress: Outdoor wear: hiking and cayaking gear

Other: Available for special parties and business meetings from NOV-MAR. Information on hiking, mountain climbing and kayaking available.

HISTORY, PERSONALITY AND CHARACTER

The Evergreen Cafe started out as a rail car diner in the early 1950s with 10 stools occupying the right half of the present-day cafe. At the time, it was one of only 3 such diners in Colorado, the other two located in Fairplay and on West Colfax in Denver. Over the past 40 years, the diner was expanded by 6 different owners into its contemporary state with a counter, 2 dining areas and a sun room (or green house) which was added in 1983. Current owner John Nale took over in 1985. He's assisted in the kitchen by Vicky James, who started with the Evergreen Cafe in 1987 and has been in the restaurant business since 1970, and Patsy Elifritz who moved to the Evergreen Cafe after 13 years at Casa del Sol.

FOOD, SERVICE AND AMBIANCE

I had two exceptional breakfasts at the Evergreen Cafe. They used fresh blueberries in making their very tasty and fluffy pancakes, a meal that I normally steer clear of because it's "heavy" and "weighs me down". I made an exception for these, however, and recommend them. They also serve appetizing, locally-produced sausage patties. For my second breakfast, I ordered the scrumptious eggs Vicksburg (named after the nearby ghost town, not the Civil War battle) — home fries topped with two eggs, melted cheese, green peppers, onion and picante sauce, a delicious combination of ingredients sure to please vegetarian and non-vegetarian alike. Everything is made to order at the Evergreen Cafe. Pies, coffee cakes, cinnamon rolls, biscuits, sausage gravy, green and red chili, soups and salsas are all made in-house.

BUENA VISTA

Spotlighting the breakfast specialties are eggs benedict and variations with mushrooms, asparagus or sausage. Other morning delights include huevos rancheros, breakfast tacos with chorizo and green chilies, breakfast crêpes with asparagus and hollandaise or mushroom and onion, egg sandwiches, omelets, Belgian waffles, French toast, biscuits and gravy and for lighter appetites, breakfast shakes and yogurt topped with granola. The lunch menu features burgers, with toppings like guacamole and jalapeño peppers, sandwiches (turkey breast, veggie, cod fillet, grilled chicken breast barbecued or with guacamole, sirloin steak and melts — turkey, tuna or ground beef), chicken fried steak, burritos, nachos, soup, salads and homemade chili. For dessert, try one of their delectable homemade pies, fruit-filled crêpes, cheesecake or carrot cake.

Service was provided by a very friendly and hospitable host. This quaint, quiet cafe has a shingled roof, an evergreen-colored front, evergreen trees and a small patio. Inside, you can revel in the sunlight in their all glass-enclosed green house with hanging ferns and crocuses. The front dining area has a green acoustical tile ceiling complementing a green carpet and is decked with a photo of the St. George (Utah) Marathon from 1987 and a poster of a runner in autumn titled "There is no finish line." John, by the way, is a marathon and long-distance runner and has ran in the Boston Marathon and several 100-mile runs, including one from Silverton to Telluride to Ouray to Lake City and back to Silverton. A caricature map of Buena Vista and a print of the Mountain Top Mine above Ouray supplement the decor. Relax and enjoy some good home cooking in the sun at the Evergreen Cafe.

SPECIAL ONE-TIME OFFER: Buy one entrée at the regular price and receive a second entrée of equal or lesser value FREE (up to $5.00 value) OR 50% off a single entrée (maximum discount $2.50). This offer NOT valid in combination with any other offers. Please present to server at time of ordering. _____ Manager/Owner. _____ Date.

RECIPE

Breakfast Taco

2 eggs	1 large flour tortilla
1 ounce chorizo sausage	2 ounces grated cheddar cheese
1 tablespoon diced green chilies	3 ounces salsa, picante or green chili

1. In a sauce pan, brown chorizo, add diced green chilies, then blend in the 2 scrambled eggs. Once this mixture is uniform, place it into the tortilla, roll it and cover with your choice of Picante, salsa or green chili.
2. Place grated cheese on top and microwave until cheese is melted. Serve with hashbrowns or refried beans on the side.

Casa del Sol in Buena Vista in summer

The Evergreen Cafe in Buena Vista in winter

CARBONDALE

Carbondale was named by one of the town founders, John Mankin, for his home town in Pennsylvania. Good fishing is available nearby on the Roaring Fork and Crystal Rivers. Zip Code: 81623. Area Code: 970 Population: 3,004. Elevation: 5,170'.

The Village Smithy Restaurant, Inc.
26 South Third Street, 963-9990

Directions: From the signal at the intersection of Highways 82 and 133, 12 miles south of Glenwood Springs, go west on Highway 133 for 1 mile to the first signal. Turn left onto Main Street. Go .6 miles. The restaurant is on the right at the corner of 3rd Street.

ESSENTIALS

Cuisine: Country

Hours: 7 days. 7AM-2PM. Lunch starts at 11:15AM.

Meals and Prices: Breakfast/Lunch $$

Nonsmoking: All, including the patio.

Take-out: Yes, except on weekends.

Alcohol: No

Credit Cards: MC, Visa

Personal Check: Local only

Reservations: No, but call ahead for groups of more than 6. They will try to accommodate.

Wheelchair Access: Yes

Dress: Very casual, but wear shirt and shoes.

Other: Additional 15% service charge added to parties of 6 or more if separate checks are requested or if children are running in aisles! Senior citizen discount for those 65 years young or older.

HISTORY, PERSONALITY AND CHARACTER

The Village Smithy began as an old blacksmith shop (hence, the name Village Smithy) around the turn of the century. Some of the locals still talk about the days when horses were brought in here. In 1914, Roy D. Pattison came to Carbondale and took over the blacksmith shop from his uncle, H. C. Pattison. Two additional blacksmiths followed before a few unrelated businesses occupied the premises: a shop that made looms; a woodworking shop, then a kitchen, for the local school; and the western slope's largest tropical fish store. Chris and Terry Chacos, a couple of former registered physical therapists, introduced the Village Smithy in May 1975. Pat Daily has been their manager since 1981 and Chris Rayne, formerly of the Daily Bread in Glenwood Springs, Colorado, has been their kitchen manager since 1994.

FOOD, SERVICE AND AMBIANCE

This is a great little mountain sojourn for breakfast or lunch. Friendly people; good, nutritious and innovative food; and, in the summer, a most appealing lawn and patio for dining and viewing Mt. Sopris: a must stop if you're between, or near, Glenwood

Springs and Aspen. I had lunch here on two occasions and have enjoyed an appetizer, homemade soup, salad with homemade dressing, and sandwich. For a scrumptious treat that will tantalize the taste buds without interfering with your appetite, try their lightly-breaded, non-greasy jalapeños stuffed with black beans and sour cream. Their beef-vegetable soup is chock-full of vegetables and meat. You can order salad with a novel Tamari dressing prepared with soy sauce, lemon, garlic, honey and yogurt (the blue cheese dressing is also homemade). The savory, southwestern chicken sandwich was top quality, moist, not overcooked, chicken marinated in Mexican seasonings and orange juice, grilled and served with a whole green chili and Monterey Jack cheese. Very tasty!

In 1994, Chris and Terry brought in a nutritionist who ran their recipes through a computer and suggested ways to reduce fat, calories, cholesterol and sodium. The result was the "Lite Fare" items you will see identified on their menu. Canola oil is used for all their deep frying and polyunsaturated oil is used in their recipes. Their baked goods (which can be purchased at the entrance for take-out), salsa and hollandaise sauce are all made from scratch. Eggs and meats, omelets, huevos rancheros and egg burrito are served all day. Espresso drinks, fruit smoothies, hot cakes, Belgian waffles, French toast, bagels, yogurt, fruit and granola, hot cereals, huevos rancheros and various other specialties are served for breakfast. Chicken, turkey and fish plates; burgers; and daily Mexican and pasta specials are on the lunch menu. Weekend specials highlight eggs benedict; eggs vegetarian; and for those of you, like me, who find hollandaise sauce something less than palatable, sample the salmon benedict with cream cheese and pesto sauce or the Don Quixote benedict with melted cheese and pork or veggie green chile.

The folks that work here seem more like a family than a staff of workers. There is a lot of camaraderie among the employees. On my last visit, I arrived when they were switching over to lunch (about 11:15AM) and had to wait a few minutes before they could take my order. Once they got started, though, the host with an infectious smile, was very helpful and brought a to-go menu without my asking.

The artwork changes every 6 weeks. They look for local artists from the Glenwood Springs to Aspen area to display, and sell, their creations. In the past, they have exhibited various works of art by local high school students, color photography, oils, watercolors, even rugs. The front of their menu has a quote by Thoreau: "To affect the quality of the day is the highest of arts". Drop in on the Village Smithy and enrich the quality of your day!

SPECIAL ONE-TIME OFFER: Buy one entrée at the regular price and receive 50% off a second entrée of equal or lesser value. This offer NOT valid in combination with any other offers. Please present to server at time of ordering. _____ Manager/Owner. _____ Date.

RECIPE

McGurk's Crispy Cheese and Potato Breakfast

12-inch skillet with a lid

¼ cup diced tomatoes
¼ cup diced green onions

¼ cup sliced mushrooms
¼ cup grated cheddar cheese
1 teaspoon oil
1 teaspoon margarine

1. Preheat your skillet with about 1 teaspoon of oil and 1 teaspoon of margarine.
2. Spread enough grated potatoes to cover the bottom of the skillet. Spread potatoes evenly.
3. When brown on the bottom, turn them over and break them up a bit.
4. Add your tomatoes, onions and mushrooms. Top with cheese. Cover.
5. Toast to desired crispiness.

Variations: On Southwestern McGurk's, replace green onions with red and add broccoli. Place the broccoli stems down in the potatoes and leave covered until they change to bright green! Include whole green chilies, marinated chicken and guacamole.

Pat McGurk was an employee with the restaurant in 1978 to 1980. Pat enjoyed ordering different creations of his own for his employee meals. One of Pat's particular breakfast creations became popular with Pat's associates with the Village Smithy. They would say, "I'll have Pat's special potato dish today." We all contributed to modifying it a little over time and we'd offer Pat's Potato dish as a breakfast special. Then people started coming back and asking for Pat McGurk's special potato breakfast. We just had to add the dish on our menu as a regular item after that and it was appropriately named McGurk's! Pat McGurk went on to finish college, became a teacher, has married and started a family and they are now living in Kansas last we heard from them. Pat McGurk, lots of folks would like to say, "Thank you".

Chris Chacos

CASTLE ROCK

Castle Rock, named for the large rock formation at the top of the hill, is a community nestled among thousands of acres of rolling hills, scrub oak and ponderosa pine that used to be the hunting grounds for the Ute, Arapahoe and Cheyenne Indians. In the last quarter of the 19th century, Silas W. Madge quarried lava stone in the area which was used as building material. In March of 1978, the county courthouse was destroyed by fire by a distraught lover who tried to free her imprisoned boyfriend. The new courthouse now stands in its place. Each year for the Holiday Season, a yule star is lit on top of the large rock marking the town. In the summer, Castle Rock is home to a PGA golf tournament — the International at Castlepines. Another major attraction is the factory outlet stores just north of town.

Zip Code: 80104. Area Code 303. Population: 8,708. Elevation: 6,200'.

Pegasus

207 Wilcox Street, 688-6746

Directions: From the north on I-25, take Exit 182 and head east. The street will bend to the right (south) and become Wilcox Street. Go straight at the signal at 5th Street. The restaurant is on the right just past 3rd Street. From the south on I-25, take Exit 181 and head north on Wilcox Street. The restaurant is on the left just before 3rd Street.

ESSENTIALS

Cuisine: Mexican/Greek/American
Hours: Mon-Fri 6:30AM-9PM, Sat/Sun 7:30AM-9PM. JUN-AUG: Closing time is 10PM.
Meals and Prices: Breakfast $, Lunch $$, Dinner $$-$$$.
Nonsmoking: Yes
Take-out: Yes
Alcohol: Full bar

Credit Cards: MC, Visa, Amx, Disc
Personal Check: Yes, with I.D.
Reservations: Recommended for groups of 6 or more; not accepted otherwise.
Wheelchair Access: Yes
Other: Outside catering available through Colorado Cookhouses Catering

HISTORY, PERSONALITY AND CHARACTER

The building occupied by Pegasus was constructed in 1971. It was originally used as a tire store, followed by the Broiler Restaurant and Bar in 1974 and finally Pegasus in 1988. Owner John T. DeLay has been in the restaurant business since 1975 and helped to open the original Pegasus in the Capitol Hill area of Denver in 1985. It took 6 months of renovation before he was ready to open Pegasus in Castle Rock, but it seems to have been all worth it. The Renaissance Festival in Larkspur, the Castle Pines International Golf Tournament and the Castle Rock Factory Outlet Stores have all assisted in Castle Rock's tremendous growth in the 1990s. As John says, "I've been living happily ever after in Castle Rock!" John employs the Torres Brothers from Chihuahua,

Mexico to do the cooking: David, who has been with John since the Capitol Hill Pegasus opened in 1985 and Roberto who has been with John since 1986.

FOOD, SERVICE AND AMBIANCE

I've dined here for dinner on two occasions and found the Grecian platter to be mouth-watering and delicious, the smothered sirloin to be a good cut prepared just the way I like it and even sampled one of their Mexican combinations. The Grecian platter was a flavorsome combination of Greek salad, a generous portion of marinated and grilled pork, a blend of lamb and beef ground together, two pita breads to make your own souvlaki and gyros and tzatziki sauce. My savory, medium-rare sirloin was covered with cream cheese and smothered with mushrooms and oodles of sautéed onions. The Mexican combination offered a tasty deep-fried chili relleno topped with cheddar, onion, tomato and lettuce; a peppery beef burrito with onion; a mildly spicy cheese enchilada and a great tasting green chili sauce (one of the Torres Brothers' creations, along with their own picante salsa).

Headlining the other dinner entrées are top sirloin, chicken fried steak with homemade mashed potatoes, chicken smothered or marinated with teriyaki and charbroiled, a fresh fish of the day and on Fridays and Saturdays, prime rib. Lunch menu items that are served through the dinner hours include appetizers (Buffalo wings, fresh guacamole dip, stuffed jalapeños, nachos and dolmades), salads (a create your own, Greek, chef or dinner), Mexican fare such as chicken or steak smothered in green chili and melted cheddar, sandwiches (cheese steak, barbecued chicken, souvlaki, gyros and a club) and burgers with favorite toppings like guacamole, sautéed mushrooms and whole green chilies. You can finish your meal with one of their homemade dessert: a piece of Dutch apple, cherry or peach pie; a brownie; a cookie or a piece of chocolate cake.

Breakfast is a popular meal at Pegasus and for good reasons. They serve a few items that you don't see on many breakfast menus like souvlaki and eggs, huevos Monteleños (with vegetarian salsa, corn tortillas, frijoles and cheddar) and a Grecian omelet (with lamb, beef, feta cheese and onions). Accompanying these delights are piping hot cinnamon rolls, chicken fried steak, huevos rancheros, breakfast burritos, create your own omelets, French toast and buttermilk pancakes. Eggbeaters are available on request.

The servers at Pegasus were accommodating (they don't have frosted mugs but that didn't stop my server from chilling my beer glass on ice) and helpful in answering my questions. The restaurant was garnished with Mexican and American Indian adornments and divided into three dining areas with a small bar at the front. A white stucco divider with crystal-glass bricks on top separated two dining areas. Decorating the walls were Mexican rugs, a colored etching by Frank Howell in turquoise and peach portraying American Indians called "April's Song", an Indian feather headdress ornament, paintings by Julie Krammer Cole called "He Who Watches" showing a wolf in a tepee village and one that I called "Indian Spirits in the Wind", and artworks of Indians that blend in with the scenery — the rocks, trees and water. Stop by Pegasus and take pleasure in their Mexican cuisine prepared by fellows from the heart of Mexico who also know how to serve delectable Greek and American food as well.

SPECIAL ONE-TIME OFFER: Buy one entrée at the regular price and receive a complimentary appetizer. Maximum Value $6.00 per appetizer. Limit 2 appetizers with the purchase of 2 entrées. This offer NOT valid in combination with any other offers. Please present to server at time of ordering. _____ Manager/Owner. _____ Date.

RECIPE

Guacamole

5 avocados

¼ cup chopped onions

1 tomato, diced fine, drain juice

¼ teaspoon garlic powder

¼ teaspoon garlic salt

2 tablespoons mayonnaise

Dash cilantro

2 tablespoons Picante salsa

Jalapeño, optional

1. In a bowl, mash the avocados until smooth, add mayonnaise then add spices. Stir in other ingredients.

If you have a restaurant recommendation, please contact Benjamin James Bennis at Small Town Publications (see back of title page for telephone number and address).

CIMARRON

Cimarron, named after the river on which it is located, is Spanish for "wild" or "unruly" and also the Mexican name for Big Horn sheep.
Zip Code: 81220. Area Code: 970. Population: 80. Elevation: 6,906'.

Inn at Arrowhead
21401 Alpine Plateau Road, 249-5634

Directions: From Gunnison on Highway 50, travel west for 35 miles. Look for the blue Inn sign and turn left onto Alpine Plateau Road, a forest access. From Montrose on Highway 50, travel east for 30 miles. Go .8 miles past the black-iron gate for the Arrowhead Sales Office, ½ mile past mile marker 123, and turn right onto Alpine Plateau Road. From here, it is 5½ miles over gravel road along the east fork of Little Blue Creek, which comes right up to the roadside in some places, to the restaurant which is on the right.

ESSENTIALS

Cuisine: Creole, Continental and Down-home Country
Hours: 7 days 7AM-11AM, 11:30AM-2PM and 6PM-10PM. Closed Mid-NOV to Mid-DEC and APR.
Meals and Prices: Breakfast/Lunch $$, Dinner $$$-$$$
Nonsmoking: Yes
Take-out: Yes

Alcohol: Full Bar
Credit Cards: MC, Visa, Amx
Personal Check: In-state with I.D.
Reservations: Recommended JUL to Mid-SEP, OCT to Mid-NOV and over the Holidays. Accepted otherwise.
Wheelchair Access: Yes
Other: Available for small conferences, weddings and receptions.

HISTORY, PERSONALITY AND CHARACTER

The Inn at Arrowhead was originally built in 1974 as a cafe and grocery store. In 1990, it was converted into a restaurant with 12 rooms upstairs. The ranch itself has been in the Squirrel family since 1937, beginning as an old cattle and sheep ranch before Jim Squirrel, son of original owner, Don, developed Arrowhead Ranch, a series of homesteads scattered among the trees. Today, he and his wife, Linda, run the ranch and inn. The executive chef and Culinary Institute of America (CIA) graduate, Michael Thompson, grew up in New Orleans and has been cooking since 1980. His culinary experience and travels have taken him from Bermuda and the Dominican Republic to Oklahoma City and Colorado Springs before coming to Arrowhead in April 1994. He has worked as a private chef for "the rich and famous" and nourished dignitaries and members of Congress.

FOOD, SERVICE AND AMBIANCE

Bean soup has never been one of my favorites, but it definitely moved up a couple of notches after I finished a bowl of Chef Michael's very thick, 100% black bean soup topped with scallions. It was delicious with a mini-loaf of fresh, crispy crust white bread. The grilled quail was tasty, cut-up morsels with a flavorful, spicy Cajun-mix coating: cayenne, red and black peppers; granulated garlic; paprika; onion and salt. It came with a hearty portion of wild rice mixed with mushrooms, green peppers and onions and a serving of herbal carrots — positively down-home country cooking with a Cajun flair! If you prefer a dinner or avocado salad, you have your choice of homemade blue cheese or ranch as well as vinaigrette dressings. The other dinner entrées were 10-ounce, bacon-wrapped filet mignon, sautéed Cajun catfish and fried shrimp. Other evenings you may see prime rib, different steaks, red deer, pheasant sausage, elk or duck. Michael emphasizes freshness so the menu changes nightly. Finish your meal with one of their homemade desserts like blueberry pie, chocolate brownie sundae, cheesecake, bread pudding or Kay's famous apple dumpling. If you arrive for breakfast, expect to choose from a long list of omelets; steak, quail or Rocky Mountain trout with eggs; buttermilk pancakes; Belgian waffles with fresh strawberries; or French toast. Catch and clean your own fish on the premises and they'll grill it with two eggs and home fries. Lunches feature sandwiches, burgers, made-from-scratch soups, salads, fruit plates, box lunches to go and specials: meatloaf, pork chops and roast beef.

My server was courteous, prompt and helpful. Vocal country music played through the restaurant. The windows over the boardwalk face a serene setting of aspen and pine across the road. Photos next to the rock fireplace present a common blue grouse, a rare pine martin, an ermine and a couple of comical poses showing a bear taking a drink from a hummingbird feeder and a pica thoroughly enjoying himself in a cup of sunflower seeds. I found the Inn at Arrowhead to be a peaceful place to experience world-class dining.

SPECIAL ONE-TIME OFFER: Buy one entrée at the regular price and receive a second entrée of equal or lesser value FREE (up to $15.00 value) OR 50% off a single entrée at the regular price (maximum discount $7.50). This offer NOT valid in combination with any other offers. Please present to server at time of ordering. _____ Manager/Owner. _____ Date.

BBQ Shrimp
(Yields 2 appetizers or 1 entrée)

8 jumbo shrimps, peeled and deveined   2 ounces Worcestershire sauce
2 teaspoons coarse black pepper   1 cup heavy cream
Juice of ½ lemon   2 tablespoons butter
1 jalapeño, cut in half

1. In a dry sauté pan over high heat, add black pepper to extract pepper oil.
2. Add shrimp, lemon and jalapeno. Cook for 1 minute. Add Worcestershire sauce and reduce to syrup stage.
3. Add heavy cream and reduce by half. Swirl in butter to thicken.
4. Serve in bowl with French bread for dipping.

Having worked in two of the best and most famous restaurants in New Orleans, Pascal's Manale and Emerils, I have combined two of their dishes (Manale's famous BBQ Shrimp and Emerils Crawfish and Angle Hair Pasta) to come up with my version of BBQ Shrimp.

Michael Thompson

The Inn at Arrowhead in Cimarron

COAL CREEK CANYON

Coal Creek Canyon is an unincorporated community in Boulder County. It is located 5 miles east of the town of Pinecliffe. Originally called Gato, the Spanish word for "wildcat", Pinecliffe was named around the turn of the century by Dr. Craig, a minister, for the beautiful pines on a nearby cliff.

Zip Code: 80471. Area Code: 303. Population: 4,500 (1995 estimate by the Coal Creek Fire Department). Elevation: 8,200'.

Copperdale Inn

32138 Highway 72, Golden, CO 80403, 642-9994 or 642-3180

Directions: From Highway 93 between Golden and Boulder, proceed west on Highway 72 through Coal Creek Canyon for 9½ miles. The restaurant will be on your left.

ESSENTIALS

Cuisine: German/Austrian

Hours: Wed-Sat 5PM-9PM. Sun 12PM-8PM. Closed Mon and Tue.

Meals and Prices: Dinner $$$-$$$$. Sandwiches and salads $$. Early dinners, Wed-Fri before 6:30PM, $9.95.

Nonsmoking: Yes

Take-out: Yes, except on weekends.

Alcohol: Full Bar

Credit Cards: All 5

Personal Check: In-state only with guaranteed check card.

Reservations: Highly recommended.

Wheelchair Access: Yes. There is a ramp by the kitchen door.

Other: $5.00 charge on split dinners. No separate checks. Additional 15% service charge for parties of 5 or more.

HISTORY PERSONALITY AND CHARACTER

Three different owners have occupied the Copperdale Inn building. The first was Black's Cottage, a coffee shop, in the 1960s. This was followed by the Western Lamp Inn, a German café, in the early 1970s. In September 1975, Marie and John Wallinger bought the establishment and named it the Copperdale Inn. They enlarged the restaurant in 1979. John is a musician who studied in Salzburg and plays the accordion, piano and organ. He has performed in the USA, Canada, Africa and New Zealand. Marie and John worked at the five-star Lodge at Smuggler's Notch and the Von Trapp Family Lodge of "The Sound of Music" fame in Stowe, Vermont. Marie does the cooking while John entertains the dinner quests playing Viennese waltzes, Austrian folk songs, polkas and show tunes on the organ and piano.

FOOD, SERVICE AND AMBIANCE

I have enjoyed several items on their menu: the homemade soups (a vegetable with slivered almonds and a mildly seasoned cream of potato with nutmeg, bay leaf and black peppercorns), salad with a sweet poppyseed dressing, very lean bratwurst and

49

smoked pork loin, sauerbraten (beef top round) that is marinated in burgundy wine and spices for 5 days and zigeuner schnitzel (veal cutlet) with sautéed peppers, onions and paprika. I preferred the quality and taste of the veal and I recommend the noodles that are fried in butter and are crisp on the edges. They buy pre-baked bread and finish the baking here. The result is close to homemade quality. An outside baker makes their apple streudel according to Marie's specifications.

If you arrive before 6:30PM on Wednesday, Thursday or Friday, you can order one of their special early dinners (wiener schnitzel, beef stroganoff, bratwurst, rib eye steak or trout). The German specialties on the regular menu include vegetarian cabbage rolls, Vienna rostbraten (braised sirloin), chicken Kiev, beef stroganoff, schnitzel holstein (milk-fed veal), veal cordon bleu and New Zealand farm-raised venison. They also offer seafood (Rocky Mountain rainbow trout, fantail shrimp, shrimp scampi, Norwegian salmon filet and lobster), steaks and sandwiches (corned beef and Swiss, reuben, knackwurst and burgers). The sandwich and salad menu is not offered on Saturdays and holidays. For dessert, you can order chocolate raspberry black forest cake, Viennese walnut and German chocolate torte, mint parfait, chocolate sundae or frozen raspberry yogurt to go with fresh espresso or cappucino. Domestic, German and non-alcoholic beers and wines will whet your appetite.

I found the service here to be friendly and courteous. German tunes were played by John in this restaurant that is decked with posters of Innsbruck and Tirol, Austria, a sketch of the Trapp Family Lodge in Stowe, Vermont, and paintings of castles, snow-capped peaks and pine forests. The Inn has a "woodsy" feel that will make you feel like you are in the Old Country. The scenic view overlooks the valley to the south with several hills beyond.

SPECIAL ONE-TIME OFFER: Receive 20% off one to four entrées. This offer NOT valid in combination with any other offers. _____ Manager/Owner. _____ Date.

Benjamin James Bennis would like to hear about your restaurant experiences. Contact him at Small Town Publications. See back of title page for telephone number and address.

RECIPE

Spiced Sauerkraut
(Serves 4 to 6)

2 pounds canned sauerkraut (do not drain or wash)
½ pound bacon, cubed
1 cup onion, chopped
2 cups cold water

6 whole juniper berries
6 whole black peppercorns
1 tablespoon whole caraway seeds
6 whole cloves
2 whole bay leaves

1. Place sauerkraut in large pot. Add water and 1 tablespoon of caraway seeds and bring to a boil. Reduce to low heat.
2. Meanwhile, cook bacon in frying pan until crisp (do not drain fat). Add 1 cup onion, cook on medium. Heat for 5 to 10 minutes until slightly cooked. Add bacon and onion to sauerkraut.
3. Place remaining ingredients in cheese cloth. Tie cheese cloth. Crush with mallet. Add cheese cloth into sauerkraut mixture. Cook 1½ to 2 hours until liquid is almost gone.

Copperdale Inn in Coal Creek Canyon

COPPER MOUNTAIN

Copper Mountain is often referred to a "the skier's mountain" and has been voted No. 1 trail and slope design by "Snow Country Magazine". The resort underwent a $40 million dollar expansion, including a second high-speed quadruple chairlift and offers ski lessons, snowboarding and cross-country skiing. In the summer, there is Copper Creek Golf Club, one of the highest golf courses in the U.S.

Zip Code: 80443. Area Code: 970. Population: 150. Elevation: 9,700'.

Rackets

0509 Copper Road, 968-2882 X6386

Directions: Take Exit 195 from I-70. You will be heading south on Highway 91. Take the first right onto Copper Road. Go .6 miles. The restaurant, located in the Copper Mountain Racket and Athletic Club, will be on your right.

ESSENTIALS

Cuisine: Southwestern
Hours: JUN-SEP: Tue-Sat 11:30AM-2PM, 5PM-9:30PM. Sun 10AM-2PM, 5PM-9:30PM. Closed Mon. DEC to Mid-APR: 7 days 5:30PM-9:30PM. Closed Mid-APR through MAY and OCT-NOV.
Meals and Prices: Lunch $$, Dinner $$$$, Sunday Brunch $$-$$$

Nonsmoking: All
Take-out: Yes
Alcohol: Full Bar
Credit Cards: All 5
Personal Check: Yes, with I.D.
Reservations: Recommended
Wheelchair Access: Yes, by elevator

HISTORY, PERSONALITY AND CHARACTER

Rackets, part of the Athletic Club, was built in 1982 and is operated by Chris Martell, Director of Food and Beverage; Trish Dixon, Director of Restaurants; and Dan Kibbie, Restaurant Manager. Dan has been with the restaurant since 1990. The executive chef is Ron Sampson, who has been in the restaurant business since 1984 and at Rackets since 1991. Prior to that, he worked at The Steak Out, Pesce Fresco and Mogul Fields (now Double Diamond) in Copper Mountain and the Garden Room and Edgewater in Keystone. He has kitchen experience for restaurants as well as banquets.

FOOD, SERVICE AND AMBIANCE

Chef Sampson serves 9 or 10 special salad selections at the soup and salad bar, such as Szechwan noodle with peanut butter and red peppers, pasta with pesto and sun-dried tomatoes, mushrooms and fennel in anisette dressing and southwestern corn salad with jicama (a rutabaga, similar to a turnip, sometimes referred to as a Mexican potato). The dressings for the greens are equally creative: sun-dried cranberry and mandarin orange vinaigrette (a sweet combination), green peppercorn ranch, creamy avocado, and creamy Caesar. The soup for the evening was seafood bisque - an oceanic offering of clams, halibut, crab, shallots, paprika, white wine, fresh lemon juice and cream prepared in a fish stock of boiled salmon. It was fantastic! I could have easily made a whole meal out of the soup and skipped the rest. Two kinds of homemade rolls are served at your table — Anna/Damma (cornmeal and molasses) and jalapeño cheddar. A specially prepared butter with the texture of whipped cream and made with lime, cilantro, honey and a dash of crushed New Mexico red chilies accompanies the rolls. The entrée was a game combination of rack of fallow deer and stuffed pheasant breast. The platter presentation was very attractive. The deer rack was char-grilled with a brown prickly pear, juniper, cabernet sauce on top. Next to it was the char-grilled pheasant breast with a red, dried cherry veloute on top of a hazelnut stuffing mix. On the side were wild, long-grain rice, yellow spaghetti squash with a touch of burgundy-colored cranberry on top, a green-colored pepperoncini, and a fresh rosemary sprig. It tasted as good as it looked!

Bring a good appetite when you come here. Despite the plentiful supreme soup and salad bar that comes with your entrée, you will probably want to order one of their scrumptious appetizers, like the black bean chipotle (peppers) quesadilla with tomatilla scallion salsa and goat cream cheese, calamari breaded with blue corn meal, or the chili rellenos stuffed with smoked duck and goat cheese. There is a lot of southwest flavor to this menu. For lunch: wild game stew, slow-smoked roast chicken, smoked chorizo with green chili and a char-grilled ground elk burger. A few of the desert dinner delights are char-grilled trout with Alaskan crab meat, baked cilantro lime scallops, wild mushrooms enchiladas and New Zealand lamb with roasted garlic and shiitake mushrooms. For dessert, if you still have room, add a créme brûlée, chocolate mousse with raspberry chambord sauce or a piece of New York cheesecake with fresh strawberries. The wine list is predominantly from California. Sunday summer brunch includes the supreme soup and salad bar with your choice of entrée: crab benedict, Belgian waffle, salmon with raspberry basil vinaigrette and chicken piccata.

Service was very helpful, pleasant and eager to provide answers to my questions. Very quiet slow jazz played somewhere in the background mixed with sounds of the aerobics class next door. The main feature of the dining room is the high picture windows providing a scenic view of the ski area. A rock fireplace with a long, wide ledge provides a home for several tall cactus and yucca plants. There are several rectangular light fixtures hanging from the high ceiling and a bookshelf with books, handwoven baskets with plastic flowers and dried corn. Take a break and enjoy some great southwestern dishes served-up at Rackets.

COPPER MOUNTAIN

SPECIAL ONE-TIME OFFER: Buy one entrée at the regular price and receive a second entrée of equal or lesser value FREE (up to $24.95 value) OR 50% off a single entrée at the regular price (maximum discount $12.45). This offer NOT valid in combination with any other offers. Please present to server at time of ordering. _____ Manager/Owner. _____ Date.

RECIPE
Sundried Cranberry Mandarin Orange Vinaigrette

1 cup dried cranberries	2 cups salad oil
1 cup white wine	1 cup mandarin oranges, chopped
1 pinch saffron	2 ounces honey
1 cup orange juice, fresh is best	1 teaspoon salt
1 cup rice wine vinegar	

1. In a pan, combine wine, cranberries and saffron. Bring to a boil and simmer until cranberries are soft and alcohol has evaporated.
2. Mix the cranberry mixture with all other ingredients.
3. Chill and mix well before serving.

The Patio at the Countryside Coffeehouse in Crawford

CORTEZ

The town, originally called the Mitchell Springs Settlement, was named after Hernando Cortez (1485-1547, 16th century Spanish explorer and conqueror of Mexico) despite the fact that the man never stepped foot in this area. The Navajos call Cortez "Tzaya-toh" meaning "rock water" — the water from Mitchell Springs that watered Navajo sheep and attracted ranchers. The town was planned by M. J. Mack of the Montezuma Valley Water Supply Co. A homesteader, who sold the site to the same company, proposed the name Cortez. Located in the heart of the Montelores Valley where the San Juan Mountains meet the Arizona desert, the town is centrally situated for excursions to Mesa Verde National Park, Hovenweep National Monument, the Four Corners and Monument Valley. During the 1950s, the town boomed as a result of the area's oil, gas and uranium activity. Zip Code: 81321. Area Code: 970. Population: 7,284. Elevation: 6,201'.

Earth Song Haven
34 West Main Street, 565-9125

Directions: From the East, Highway 160 becomes Main Street in Cortez. Go to the west end of town. The restaurant is on the right just past Market Street. From the West, Highways 666 and 160 turn into Main Street. The restaurant is on the left just past Chestnut Street.

ESSENTIALS

Cuisine: Vegetarian/Light Gourmet
Hours: APR-SEP: 7 days
7AM-9PM. OCT-MAR: 7 days 7AM-6PM.
Meals and Prices: Breakfast/Lunch $
Nonsmoking: No, but you have to ask for an ashtray.

Take-out: Yes
Alcohol: No
Credit Cards: MC, Visa, Amx, Disc
Personal Check: Yes
Reservations: Accepted, not required.
Wheelchair Access: Yes, including restrooms.

HISTORY, PERSONALITY AND CHARACTER

The place now occupied by Earth Song Haven was originally a pharmacy built in 1886 by Dr. G. H. Harrington. When the pharmacy burned to the ground, Dr. Harrington was determined to prevent such a mishap from ever happening again. In 1910, he rebuilt his pharmacy to last with stones from McElmo Canyon just west of Cortez. The building was leased to the post office until the 1950s when it was converted into Kosmolski's Drug Store. During the 1960s, Bill Runck ran an appliance store, then it became a pet store, and eventually sat vacant for a couple of years until Goldie Fowler purchased the place and opened up a book store in March 1972. In 1990, she began a light menu of teas, coffees and desserts. In 1991, she added lunch to the menu and in 1992, she went to a breakfast and lunch menu. Goldie broke through a section of the stone wall into the adjacent building and now has a 10-table dining area with wall-to-wall books combined with a complete room for books (the Quality Bookstore). The bricks from the two fireplaces that frame the connecting pathway between bookstore and restaurant were quarried from Aztec, New Mexico, and used for the front of the building.

FOOD, SERVICE AND AMBIANCE

If you enjoy a good book with good food, come to this bookstore/restaurant where you can read your favorite piece of literature over breakfast or lunch. Breakfast is served all day, so I had a mid-day order of cottage and cheddar cheese crêpes (they usually use ricotta cheese, but ran out preparing the lasagna special) with fresh strawberries and topped with whipped cream. The crêpes were light and fluffy and served with a fresh, warm, homemade blueberry muffin. I also sampled their vegetable egg rolls made with fresh celery and carrots. I could eat it without getting any grease on my fingers.

They also have homemade cinnamon rolls, pies (key lime is their specialty), carrot cake, bread pudding (their own recipe of marinated pastry in brandy custard with extra fruits and nuts and a homemade wine sauce) and calas tous chauds (little rice dumplings sprinkled with powdered sugar). They buy fresh vegetables and fruits in season from local growers, as well as fresh chicken from local farmers when it is available. Wheat flour is purchased from a company that grinds its own wheat and white flour is home-grown from Cortez. The menu is for vegetarian and carnivore alike. Meat dishes are made as fat free as possible and greens are home-grown when possible and organic when available. Breakfast offers eggs, omelets, meats, vegetables, pancakes, waffles, crêpes and yogurt sundaes with fresh fruit and granola. For lunch, served from 11am, you can order a crêpe or pita pocket with vegetables, chicken, shrimp or salmon served with a salad, fruit and cookie; an open-faced sandwich like roasted turkey with pineapple and almonds, or honey-baked chicken and pecans; quiche; salad; or homemade soup. They also have specials like broccoli beef with lo mein noodles and a veggie or beef burrito. For beverages, you can choose from special coffees, herbal teas, espressos, flavored or iced cappuccinos, café lattés, frappés and Perrier.

Servers are quick to take your order and they keep returning to your table (you will not be ignored here). I found this to be a quiet place (as a bookstore should be). They do have a tape player so you might hear some light, easy-listening music. Don Quixote is their logo ("the impossible dream" — which is how Goldie describes putting together her venture in bits and pieces). When you enter the restaurant, take a quick look behind you. Over the door you will see a stained-glass picture of Don Quixote riding his donkey. The big table in the front and the hutch in the rear are antiques. The walls above the bookshelves are decorated with prints from Portraits West by Thomas Fitzwater - western scenes with buffalo, Indians, mountains and deserts - for sale at about $40; watercolors by Carolyn Fosdick - the mountains of the southwest and adobes - for sale at around $350; and pastels by Lois Fox between $40 and $70. The hardwood floors are original but the fireplace in the rear is electric and gives off no heat. (It does look like a gas burning stove, however.) The high tin ceiling dates back to the turn of the century when they were very popular. Other nice touches include glass-plated chandeliers, a single-piece coach and coffee table, a turquoise carpet and cloth napkins.

SPECIAL ONE-TIME OFFER: Buy one entrée at the regular price and receive a second entrée of equal or lesser value FREE. Maximum Value $5.00. This offer NOT valid in combination with any other offers. _____ Manager/Owner. _____ Date.

RECIPE
San Carlos

1 slice of fresh baked sourdough bread, deli size	Alfalfa sprouts
Slices of ham and cheese	Sliced avocado
Green chilies	Sour cream
	Black olives

1. Slice fresh baked sourdough bread. Top with generous slices of ham and cheese.
2. Smother with green chilies. Top with sprouts and avocado.
3. Garnish with sour cream and black olives.
4. Serve with a fresh tossed salad, fresh fruit and a homemade cookie.

Table setting at the Bristol Inn Restaurant in Creede
with Bristol Head Mountain in the Background

CRAWFORD

Crawford was named after frontier capitalist, speculator and former governor of Kansas, George A. Crawford, who started many towns on Colorado's western slope in the 1880s. Zip Code: 81415. Area Code: 970. Population: 221. Elevation: 6,520'.

Countryside Coffeehouse
356 Highway 92, 921-3560
Directions: From the intersection of Highways 92 and 133 in Hotchkiss, go 11 miles south on Highway 92. The restaurant is on the right side before the Country Store at the corner of E Street.

ESSENTIALS
Cuisine: Country	**Credit Cards:** No
Hours: Tue-Sat 11AM-3PM. Closed Sun/Mon.	**Personal Check:** Local only
Meals and Prices: Lunch $	**Reservations:** Recommended for lunch.
Nonsmoking: All	**Wheelchair Access:** Yes
Take-out: Yes	**Other:** Conference space available upstairs.
Alcohol: Beer and Wine	

HISTORY, PERSONALITY AND CHARACTER
The Countryside Coffeehouse is in a home that dates back to 1906. In the early 1990s, it was used by a seamstress, Mary Rister, who ran a daycare center. In May 1994, Michelle and Dylan Bethge purchased the house and opened the restaurant. It is the first restaurant for this young couple. Dylan bakes the breads while Michelle prepares the desserts and waits the tables.

FOOD, SERVICE AND AMBIANCE
I tried their ham and Swiss croissant, beef on whole wheat sandwich, salad with parmesan peppercorn dressing (which I recommend), and cream of broccoli soup. The breads are baked here and the meats (ham, roast beef, turkey) and vegetables are fresh from Kraft and Red Hat Produce in Austin, just down the road. The meat portions are generous, too. The soups are homemade. Other lunch items include a classic BLT, French dip, turkey and cheese and an occasional hot dish special like stew or burritos. If you are coming down this way to see the Black Canyon of the Gunnison from the north ridge or just driving through Hotchkiss at lunch time, it would be worth your while to stop here for a fresh, homemade, tasty lunch. They also serve several gourmet coffees and teas, rolls, strudels, pastries and cakes. All the baked goods are prepared from scratch, starting with the kneading of the dough. Their desserts are also made in-house: chocolate mousse cake, a no-bake strawberry cheesecake, Napoleons (a puff pastry with homemade chocolate pudding in the middle) and apple pie. Steve Duffy, my lunch companion, and

I split a piece of Jamoca almond fudge ice cream pie on homemade vanilla cake topped with whipped cream and chocolate syrup. The single serving cut in half probably was a quarter piece of the pie and would have easily been two servings in any other restaurant. By the way, it was as good as it sounds!

Michelle was our server and Dylan prepared our lunches in the kitchen. This is a cozy little place with vaulted ceilings and an upstairs dining area for small parties. There are a couple of pieces of artwork by Jim Tanaka depicting jazz musicians, one called "Running Wild", a photo from Ducks Unlimited, and a stained-glass window and lamp shade made locally. In the summertime, they have patio dining which is visible from the highway.

SPECIAL ONE-TIME OFFER: Buy one entrée at the regular price and receive a second entrée of equal or lesser value FREE (up to $5.20 value) OR 50% off a single entrée at the regular price (maximum discount $2.50). This offer NOT valid in combination with any other offers. Please present to server at time of ordering. _____ Manager/Owner. _____ Date.

RECIPE

Basil Chicken with Parmesan

2 tablespoons water
1 tablespoon butter
2 tablespoons of basil

1 8-ounce boneless, skinless
    chicken breast
1 cup heavy cream
½ to 1 cup grated Parmesan cheese

1. In a sauté pan, mix 2 tablespoons water, 1 tablespoon butter and 2 tablespoons of basil.
2. Add 1 8-oz boneless, skinless chicken breast and heat over medium flame. Sauté chicken until browned.
3. Add 1 cup heavy cream. Mix in ½ to 1 cup grated parmesan cheese. Sauté until cream sauce is thick and chicken is thoroughly soaked.
4. Serve over your favorite pasta with fresh vegetables.

An order form is located right before the Table of Contents to order additional copies of Colorado Restaurants and Recipes or Restaurants from 101 Colorado Small Towns.

CREEDE

Creede was named after Nicholas C. Creede whose mineral discoveries resulted in several mining camps and led the way to Creede's growth to 10,000 people. Bob Ford, Jesse James' killer, died here while poet Cy Warman immortalized the town with the lines, "It's day all day in the daytime and there is no night in Creede."
Zip Code: 81130. Area Code: 719. Population: 362. Elevation: 8,838'.

Bristol Inn Restaurant

39542 Highway 149, 658-2455
Directions: Located on Highway 149, 18½ miles from Creede and 32 miles from Lake City between mile markers 39 and 40. From Creede, the restaurant is on the right, ¼ mile past Freeman's Guest Ranch.

ESSENTIALS

Cuisine: Continental
Hours: Mother's Day 2PM-7PM. Memorial Day Weekend to Father's Day and Labor Day through SEP: Fri-Sat 5PM-8:30PM, Sun 10:30AM-2PM. Father's Day to Labor Day: Wed-Sat 5PM-8:30PM, Sun 10:30AM-2PM. Closed Mon/Tue. Closed OCT to Mother's Day.
Meals and Prices: Dinner $$$$, Brunch $$
Nonsmoking: All. Smoking area on the deck.

Take-out: Yes
Alcohol: Full Bar
Credit Cards: MC, Visa
Personal Check: Yes
Reservations: Required
Wheelchair Access: Yes. They will carry you upstairs or serve you in the studio downstairs.
Other: Available for special events. Free seasonal calendar of events available listing dinner specialties and arts and crafts workshops. Write or call.

HISTORY, PERSONALITY AND CHARACTER

Rick and Teri Inman built the Bristol Inn Restaurant which opened in 1977. In 1981, they added a gallery with Teri's handweavings; sister Kathy Killip's dried-flower wreaths and ornamental angels and Clem Robertson's photography. Teri's weaving studio was added in 1983 and the kitchen was expanded to include a steamer and charbroiler in 1990. Rick has been a chef since 1973 starting at Tony's in Houston. From there he "chefed" at Rudy's and the Host International Hotel at Houston Continental Airport, before moving to Creede to start the Bristol Inn. Teri is your hostess who does the baking, prepares the desserts and manages the front.

FOOD, SERVICE AND AMBIANCE

The dinner menu changes nightly but always includes 4 entrées featuring charbroiled steak, meat, seafood and poultry (a land, sea and sky selection). I went to the

60

sky and elected charbroiled game hen. It had been marinated in a vinaigrette and was very moist, tender, non-spicy and slightly crisp. As an appetizer, I enjoyed a serving of sautéed and deep-fried artichoke hearts with a light breading and a touch of lemon. The food here is high on quality and low on spice. Fresh, very tender, steamed asparagus, baked parmesan potato and a mini-loaf of homemade stoneground whole wheat bread, made with local wheat and honey, accompanied the meal. Everything is cooked to order. All of the soups, like Bavarian lentil (with sausage), shrimp and chicken gumbo and Parisian duck, are all homemade by Rick, as are the salad dressings: chive-vinaigrette, honey-Dijon ranch and, their house specialty, a lemon-pepper with Parmesan cheese.

Some appetizers that might be available when you dine here include crab meat turnover, Cajun popcorn shrimp with sweet and sour sauce, Piroshki (a cream cheese pastry with spinach, Swiss cheese and mushroom stuffing) and smoked salmon with capers. You can also choose from a spinach salad, tossed salad or pink grapefruit and avocado salad. Chef Rick has a delectable assortment of entrée recipes to tantalize your appetite including steak au poivre, salmon Wellington, prime rib of beef or buffalo, sautéed quail with shiitake port sauce, several veal dishes, rack of lamb, creole pasta, Rouladen, paella, lobster, fresh bass, rainbow trout and tilapia from the San Luis Valley. Occasionally, they will serve home-grown ostrich. Rick says the ostrich is a firm red meat similar to beef; however, low in fat and cholesterol, much like wild game but with less marbling. For a delicious dessert, you can decide on one of Teri's homemade creations: pecan or fresh French apple pie, flourless mocha fudge cake or cheesecake topped with a strawberry/raspberry sauce, blueberry cinnamon sauce or strawberries and cream. The Sunday brunch selection includes eggs Nona (artichoke hearts, prosciutto ham and mushrooms); a shrimp, mushroom and artichoke heart omelet; a frittata made with egg beaters; Philly cheese steak sandwich; Southwestern rib eye and fruit plates.

My server was cheerful, pleasant and smiling. Indian flute and new age music by David Lanz played quietly. This second floor restaurant has windows on three sides with picturesque views of Clear Creek flowing by and Bristol Head Mountain. The fourth side leads up to the gallery. Flowering pots and hummingbird feeders are set on the deck, but I only saw one lonely hummingbird (and a lazy one at that. He stopped fluttering and sat down to eat). In middle to late summer, you'll see some wildflowers. Once in a while they have elk, deer or bighorn sheep visit. A wreath hangs on a two-story white brick fireplace next to a banner for "Rick's Bar and Grill". The banner was made by Rick's brother-in-law for a Fourth of July parade.

The gallery upstairs, which you should visit before, during and/or after dinner, displays placemats, rugs and distinctive clothing by Teri; angel figures on a Christmas tree and woven swags and wreaths by her sister, Kathy Killip; pottery from Arlington, Texas; photographs of the Commodore Mine, Lake San Cristobal, the Great Sand Dunes and Monument Valley by Clem Robertson; paintings of Navajo Indians by Irvine Manuelito, a Navajo himself, and a melange of related artworks from jewelry and silversmith pieces to hand woven baskets and handmade baby quilts. I have been to restaurants with bookstores and greenhouses, restaurants in former banks and churches and now I've been to a restaurant with a gallery. Delight in some of the best arts and crafts this side of Taos, New Mexico while you regale Rick's superb cuisine.

SPECIAL ONE-TIME OFFER: Buy one entrée at the regular price and receive 20% off the purchase of one Renaissance Angel in the Gallery. Good for every member in your party. This offer NOT valid in combination with any other offers. Please present to server at time of ordering. _____ Manager/Owner. _____ Date.

RECIPE

Salmon Wellington
(Serves 6)

6 8-ounce salmon fillets
6 10"x15" sheets of puff pastry
3 tomatoes
2 onions
2 green bell peppers
6 mushrooms
Melted butter to taste

Salt, paprika and aromat (Knorr seasoning, if available) to taste
White wine Worcestershire sauce to taste (Lea and Perrin, if available)

Egg Wash:
1 egg
A little bit of water

1. Place salmon fillet on puff pasty sheet.
2. Slice tomatoes, onions and bell pepper into rings. Slice mushrooms.
3. On each fillet, alternately place a tomato slice, an onion slice and a pepper slice, until there are 2 of each item.
4. Top with 1 sliced mushroom and season with salt, paprika, aromat and white wine Worcestershire sauce.
5. Fold puff pastry sheet over and trim off excess dough. Make a rolled edge then prick top with a fork to allow steam to escape. Brush with egg wash (one egg beaten with a little water).
6. With remaining dough, cut out designs to place on top of pastry and brush with egg wash.
7. Bake at 400 degrees for 15 to 20 minutes or until pastry has browned evenly.
8. Serve with a lemon wedge and garnish with parsley.

Creede Hotel Restaurant
120 North Main Street, 658-2608
Directions: From South Fork, go north on Highway 149 for 22 miles to Creede. Turn left onto 7th Street. Go over the bridge and at the next intersection, turn right onto Main Street. Go .4 miles. The restaurant is on the right ½ block past 1st Street. From Lake City, go south 50 miles to Creede. When you get to the yield sign, continue straight on Main Street for .4 miles. The restaurant is on the right ½ block past 1st Street.

ESSENTIALS
Cuisine: Charbroiled meats/Seafood/Pasta/Vegetarian
Hours: MAY and OCT: Tue-Sun 11AM-2:30PM. Closed Mon. JUN to Mid-SEP: 7 days 7AM-10:30AM, 10:30AM-2:30PM and 4:30PM-8:30PM. Mid-SEP to end of SEP: Tue-Sun: 11AM-2:30PM, Fri/Sat 5PM-8PM. Closed Mon. Closed NOV-APR.
Meals and Prices: Breakfast/Lunch $, Dinner $$$

Nonsmoking: All, including the deck and patio.
Take-out: Yes
Alcohol: Full Bar
Credit Cards: MC, Visa, Disc
Personal Check: Yes, with I. D.
Reservations: Strongly recommended for dinner during theater season (JUN-SEP) or for groups of 8 or more. Not necessary otherwise.
Wheelchair Access: Yes

HISTORY, PERSONALITY AND CHARACTER
The Creede Hotel, built in 1892, was originally called Zang's Hotel, after its first owner. At the time, there were nearly 100 places offering accommodations in the Creede area and Zang's was "the place to stay". The hotel housed miners and businessmen as well as some famous boarders like town boss and con-artist Soapy Smith, poker-playing/cigar-smoking Alice Tubbs, Calamity Jane and Bob Ford (the baby-faced killer of Jessie James). Some of these boarders may still be around in spirit as many guests have reported hearing or seeing strange things in the night. The current owners can tell you a few ghost stories of their own. The restaurant, back then, was a cafe serving three meals a day. Zang's annex, in what is now called the Green Room, used to be a bath house before it became a lobby area and then a saloon. Lillian Hargraves ran a boarding house out of Zang's and served fried chicken dinners. In the years that followed, the apartments were converted into "cribs" for prostitutes and Zang's went from being considered one of the town's best hotels to being "extremely rustic". Wallpaper began resembling window shades and you could literally put your hand through the walls. Nonetheless, the rowdy bar downstairs still provided plenty of entertainment. In the 1950s and 1960s, Chester Brubaker, a piano player who liked to drink and turned to the lingerie section of the Sear's Roebuck Catalog for rhythmic inspiration, led the fun-filled nights of singing and dancing. The saloon became more of a rough, tough, brawling

drinking place in the 1970s during Creede's last major mining boom. That image was rectified by current owners, Rich and Cathy Ormsby.

When the Ormsbys leased the hotel in 1984 and 1985, they removed half the seating area at the bar, took out the pool table and juke box and converted the space to dining. They returned in 1988 as owners and brightened up the restaurant with paint and new carpet. The menu was enlivened with fresh fruits and vegetables, the deep-fat fryer was "canned" and more interesting, healthful foods were being served. In 1995, Rich and Cathy began serving lunch and dinner on the patio. Cathy is from the mid-West, has been in the restaurant business since 1975 and is the head chef. Rich worked in restaurants in Connecticut, is in charge of "maintenance and quality control" and is a member of the board of the nationally recognized Creede Repertory Theater next door to the hotel.

FOOD, SERVICE AND AMBIANCE

I had a delightful lunch on the patio on a warm, windy, afternoon in early summer, combining a cup of black bean soup, the house specialty, with a Mandarin orange sausage sandwich, a lunch special. The soup, made from scratch starting with vegetables, was in a medium-thick broth and the sandwich had a hint of orange with a sharp red pepper taste — a good light, but tangy, summertime meal. For dessert, I had a piece of Cathy's fresh, delicious carrot cake made with pineapple, raisins and white frosting. Cathy also prepares the mustard-tarragon, creamy-garlic and Italian vinaigrette dressings, all the soups, breads (like canola potato bread and French rolls), pasta sauces and desserts (pecan-brandy apple pie, brownie sundae, triple-berry shortcake and cheesecakes).

Enjoy a breakfast burrito, whole grain cereal, pancakes or a fruit bowl for breakfast. For lunch, you can choose from Mandarin chicken salad, soup, grilled eggplant sandwich, barbecue beef brisket or a burger made with beef, lamb or vegetarian-style. A children's lunch menu is available. Start off dinner with spanakopita or artichoke-green chili casserole. The appetizing entrées feature tilapia, bass and trout from the San Luis Valley; tamari-honey chicken, a hotel favorite; orange-glazed pork chops; lemon-dill lamb chops; a variety of steaks; prime rib on most Fridays and Saturdays; and several pasta selections in marinara, Alfredo and red meat sauces. Enhance your meal with one of their wine selections from California, Colorado, Italy or Yugoslavia; or try a bottle of Xingu Black Bear from Brazil or their own Creede Hotel Brown and Golden Ale brewed in Vail.

Outside dining is very pleasant on either the deck under a slanted fiberglass roof or down below on gravel amongst aspen trees. Inside there are two dining rooms decorated with artwork representing the region. The original dining room is adorned with sketches and paintings of the Creede Hotel, the Commodore Mine and the town of Creede in Winter (with piles of snow) by local artist, Steve Quiller. The lounge/dining room, to the left, has a small bar; an upright piano; a Woodland wood-burning, black-iron stove; photographs of Adolph J. Zang's tombstone and San Luis Peak from the Continental

Divide by John Gary Brown; a photograph of the Wheeler Geological Site in the San Luis Valley, Colorado, by J. D. Marston; a print of a painting of Indian blankets (with marvelous detail to the threads) and pottery by Turid Pederson; and posters from Gentleman's Magazine in 1851 and the Creede Repertory Theater. Rich and Cathy Ormsby have brought the Creede Hotel back to life with good-tasting, quality food; friendly, special service and a warm, comfortable atmosphere.

SPECIAL ONE-TIME OFFER: Buy one entrée at the regular price and receive a second entrée of equal or lesser value FREE (up to $12.00 value) OR 50% off a single entrée at the regular price (maximum discount $6.00). This offer NOT valid for dinner on theater nights (when the Creede Repertory Theater has a production) until 7:30PM. This offer NOT valid in combination with any other offers. Please present to server at time of ordering. _____ Manager/Owner. _____ Date.

RECIPE

Tamari-Honey Chicken

2 whole chickens   1⅓ cup water
6 cloves garlic   ¼ cup honey
⅔ cup tamari (or soy sauce)

1. Quarter chickens and place in a baking dish, skin side down.
2. Press garlic into a small bowl.
3. Add tamari, honey and water.
4. Whisk together and pour marinade over chicken. Cover and refrigerate 4 to 8 hours.
5. Turn chicken quarters so skin side is now up.
6. Cover and bake in tamari mixture for about one hour at 325 degrees.
7. Finish by charbroiling (or oven broiling) until skin is nicely browned.
8. Chicken may be baked in advanced, refrigerated and finished just before serving.

Belong to a group or organization? Quantity discounts of this book and Restaurants from 101 Colorado Small Towns are available. Call (303) 978-0316 for more information.

CRESTED BUTTE

The town derived its name from a nearby mountain whose top resembles the crest of a rooster's head. Since the 1860s, Crested Butte has been blessed with gold, silver and coal mining and now benefits from the ski industry with Mt. Crested Butte Ski Resort next door. The world record elk — the largest rack ever measured — was killed in 1899 in the Dark Canyon of Anthracite Creek, 12 miles west of Crested Butte by John Plute. The head is displayed at the Conoco Station on the northwest corner of Elk Avenue and 4th Street.

Zip Code: 81224. Area Code: 970 Population: 878. Elevation: 8,908'.

Gourmet Noodle

411 Third Street, PO Box 1238, 349-7401

Directions: From the intersection of Highways 50 and 135 in Gunnison, go 28 miles north on Highway 135 to Crested Butte. At the 4-way stop, turn left onto Elk Avenue. Go 3 blocks to Third Street and turn left. The restaurant will be 100 feet down on your right.

ESSENTIALS

Cuisine: Italian

Hours: 7 nights 6PM-10PM. Closed Mid-APR to Mid-JUN and Mid-SEP to Mid-NOV.

Meals and Prices: Dinner $$$-$$$$

Nonsmoking: All, except the bar area.

Take-out: No

Alcohol: Full Bar

Credit Cards: MC, Visa, Amx ($15 minimum on any credit card)

Personal Check: Local only

Reservations: Highly Recommended

Wheelchair Access: No

Other: Additional 15% service charge added to parties of 6 or more. No separate checks. Plate charge included in all split meals. No ordering off the child's menu if you're over 12 years of age.

HISTORY, PERSONALITY AND CHARACTER

The building occupied by the Gourmet Noodle was constructed in 1978. It was originally built as condominiums by a town councilman who managed to side-step the residential zoning laws. Current owners Scott and Kiffani Sylvester leased the property in 1982 when it was a steak house. This is their first restaurant as proprietors. Kiffani has been in the restaurant business since 1966 and worked at Penelope's in Crested Butte for three years while catering. Kiffani also manages and cooks at "the Noodle".

FOOD, SERVICE AND AMBIANCE

Despite the wide selection of sauces and pastas, I decided to order the elk and spinach cannelloni. I was not disappointed. The spinach cannelloni noodle was stuffed with ground elk and ricotta cheese, topped with tomato basil sauce and bechamel sauce. I liked both the sweet tasting bechamel and the more traditional Italian tomato basil. The noodles are from Pasta Fresca in Boulder, but they make all their own sauces and soups. Sweet tasting homemade sourdough bread (that's not a contradiction in terms), with garlic butter was brought to the table. Salad with feta cheese and a bitter, basil vinaigrette was served with the meal. They have a list of nightly specials in every category, like an antipasto of vegetables and cheese stuffed with basil, lemon, cream sauce; Mexican black bean soup; tequila lime crab cream sauce with broiled shrimp; three linguini pasta flavors: saffron, red chili, or lemon basil; rainbow cheese tortelini; a couple of veal dishes; salmon filet with leek and scallop cream sauce; and elk medallions with apple raisin glaze. As for the regular menu items, they include antipasto dishes; roast game hen, chicken piccata, Italian steak, veal, meat or vegetarian lasagna, and eggplant Parmesan; and a variety of sauces (Italian sausage, pasta insalata, sauce Alfredo, red or white clam sauce, cilantro and goat cheese pesto and fresh pesto Genovese); and pastas (egg, black pepper, spinach, whole wheat, and garlic parsley). There is also a children's menu.

The homemade desserts feature peanut butter ice cream with hot fudge sauce, tiramasu, bread pudding filled with different fruits and served warm with Jack Daniels bourbon sauce, cheesecakes and nightly specials like Grand Marnier chocolate mousse cake, créme brûlée and apple pie. Meals are made to order and if you have a special request, like if you're allergic to garlic, they will prepare a special sauce for you. (If you're allergic to garlic, though, what would you be doing in an Italian restaurant?)

Service is with a smile, most appealing and accommodating. Music from the 1930s and 40s - Sarah Vaughn vocals with brass accompaniment - along with some low-keyed jazz and Elvis Presley are the main mood setters for this dimly-lit restaurant with candles. The rest of the ambiance is provided by lace curtains, green tablecloths, white cloth napkins, frosted glass, a poster of the Crested Butte Wild Flower Festival, and a painting of a cactus and crescent moon.

SPECIAL ONE-TIME OFFER: Buy one entrée at the regular price and receive a complimentary dessert. Limit 2 desserts with the purchase of 2 entrées. This offer NOT valid in combination with any other offers. _____ Manager/Owner. _____ Date.

RECIPE

Stuffed Mushrooms

Large mushrooms
Green onions
¼ cup butter
2 cloves garlic or 1 tablespoon
  ground garlic

3 teaspoons Italian seasoning
¼ teaspoon salt and pepper
4 teaspoons chervil (or pinch of herbs)
1½ cups sour cream
Fresh ground Parmesan cheese

1. Take stems out of large mushroom caps. Chop, or cuisinart on pulse, stems along with green onions. (Approximately 2 dozen caps to 1 bunch onions).
2. Sauté mixture in butter with garlic. Add Italian seasoning, salt, pepper and chervil.
3. Drain in coriander and cool. When cool, add sour cream and mix well. Stuffing can be made ahead and refrigerated for up to four days.
4. When ready to serve, sauté caps in garlic and butter. Brown both sides.
5. Remove from pan, place caps in oven-proof dish. Place spoonful of stuffing mixture in each cap forming a mound.
6. Sprinkle generously with Parmesan cheese. Place under broiler until cheese is slightly browned. Serve at once.
7. If stuffing was refrigerated, heat up slightly in microwave before using. If you desire to dress up caps, you can add chopped crabmeat or shrimp to filling. You can also exchange Monterey Jack cheese for parmesan cheese. Caps can be slightly sautéed in advance but remember that mushrooms have a lot of water and will start to shrivel up and look old and loose shape if done too far in advance.

Victorian Enchantment in the Parlor of Slogar's in Crested Butte

Le Bosquet

201 Elk Avenue, PO Box 1350, 349-5808

Directions: From the intersection of Highways 50 and 135 in Gunnison, go 28 miles north on Highway 135 to Crested Butte. At the 4-way stop, turn left onto Elk Avenue. Go 4 blocks. The restaurant is on the right at the corner of 2nd Street.

ESSENTIALS

Cuisine: French

Hours: Mother's Day through OCT: MON-SAT 11:30AM-2PM, 7 days 6PM-10PM. Thanksgiving to Mid-APR: MON-FRI 11:30AM-2PM, 7 days 5:30PM-10PM. Closed Mid-APR to Mother's Day and NOV 1st to Thanksgiving.

Meals and Prices: Lunch $$, Dinner $$$$

Nonsmoking: All. Smoking only permitted on patio.

Take-out: Yes

Alcohol: Full Bar

Credit Cards: MC, Visa, Amx, Disc

Personal Check: Yes, with 2 IDs

Reservations: Recommended for Dinner, not accepted for Lunch.

Wheelchair Access: Yes

Dress: Casual for lunch, relaxed dressy for dinner

Other: Banquet room upstairs available for rehearsal dinners and graduation and birthday parties.

HISTORY, PERSONALITY AND CHARACTER

Le Bosquet, Crested Butte's longest continuously owned and operated restaurant, was built in 1976. A year later, Victor and Candace Shepard purchased half of the restaurant and a year later, they purchased the other half. Victor, the Executive Chef, has been in the restaurant business since 1964, starting out as a waiter in Washington, D.C.; Los Angeles, California and Columbus, Ohio. Candace, a retired school teacher, manages the dining room and handles the books. Le Bosquet has been awarded the Wine Spectator Award of Excellence in 1992, 1993 and 1994. A few notable celebrities who have dined here in the past include Jill St. John, Jimmy Carter, Tom Skeritt, Michael Keaton and Richard Dreyfus.

FOOD, SERVICE AND AMBIANCE

I've dined at Le Bosquet for lunch, dinner and even brunch when they were serving it a few years back. I've always been impressed with the quality of their food, the friendliness of the staff and the comfortable atmosphere of the dining room and patio. But then, one would expect that from a restaurant that has been around for two decades. I found the lamb sandwich to be similar to roast beef in appearance and texture, but with an unmistakable lamb flavor. It was served with cole slaw that was easy on the mayo and sweetened with raisins — a good-tasting lunch to enjoy while I sat on the patio and beheld Gothic Peak. Their salads are fresh and light. I'd recommend the toasted sesame seed vinaigrette for a different sweet and sour tang. The roast leg of lamb was two healthy slices with chives in a rich brown sauce accompanied by French-style scalloped potatoes and yams. The salmon and asparagus, both fresh, in a flaky and fluffy pastry shell was topped with "old fashion" hollandaise sauce, made without a blender. Their strawberry sorbet was cool, refreshing, slightly frosted and got better as it melted. I don't think you'll be disappointed with anything on their menu.

Their lunch menu is highlighted with soups, salads, sandwiches, pastas and pizzas. French onion soup, of course, is a main stay. There are a myriad of salads: Caesar, chevre with warm goat cheese in a balsamic vinaigrette, grain salad trio (tabbouleh, gingered millet and barley corn) with French green beans, smoked trout and spinach with Roquefort cheese. Sandwich selections include Cajun chicken, classic Reuben and mesquite smoked turkey. The diversified menu also offers pita crust pizza, fresh salmon with linguini and meat and veggie burgers. Dinner appetizers include pheasant and porcini mushroom raviolis and carpaccio of beef. Headlining the dinner entrées are warm lobster and scallop salad with mango basil vinaigrette, seafood risotto with shell fish and salmon, Colorado roast rack of lamb and hazelnut chicken. You have the opportunity to enrich your dining experience with a collection of predominantly French wines, rare for a Colorado restaurant, from lesser known châteaus at reasonable prices, several in the teens and twenties. Homemade desserts, like crème brûlée, French apple tart, double chocolate moussecake, lemon or chocolate napoleans, ice cream and sorbet, bring a sweet ending to your meal.

My last visit was for lunch and my server was courteous, attentive and smiling. They play a variety of jazz, big band and classical tunes in the background. Victor and Candace brought back several colorful posters from the Galerie La Palette D'Or in Paris and displayed them in the dining room for your viewing pleasure. The cumulation comprises a park in Paris and St. Emilion vineyard by Jacques Huet, wild flowers by E. Begarat and pastoral scenes by Anselme and Harold Altman. A large mural on the right wall brings to light a forest of aspen trees. White-laced curtains, hanging ferns and spider plants and a wine bottle hanger further embellish this unpretentious French restaurant. Relax and delight in Chef Victor's cuisine.

SPECIAL ONE-TIME OFFER: Buy one entrée at the regular price and receive a second entrée of equal or lesser value FREE (up to $30.00 value) OR 50% off a single entrée at the regular price (maximum discount $15.00). This offer NOT valid in combination with any other offers. Please present to server at time of ordering. _____ Manager/Owner. _____ Date.

RECIPE

Seafood Risotto
(Serves 8, yields 2 quarts)

Risotto:
  2¼ cups arborio rice
  1 ounce garlic, minced
  1 medium yellow onion, diced
  ¼ pound butter
  10 cups clam juice (2½ quarts)
  ¾ cup red bell pepper brunoise,
    finely chopped
  Saffron

Seafood (per serving):
  3 mussels, preferably New Zealand
    green-lipped mussels, available
    fresh or frozen at most fish
    markets
  3 large shrimps, peeled and
    deveined
  3 ounces fresh salmon filet, cut
    into 6 cubes
  1 ounce cleaned calamari (squid)
    including tentacles, with body
    tubes cut into rings

1. Set aside 4 cups of the clam juice for later use. Add saffron to remaining 6 cups of the clam juice and heat to simmer.
2. Heat butter in large, heavy casserole over medium heat. Add the garlic and onion and sauté until translucent and soft, about 5 minutes, being careful not to brown them.
3. Add the rice and stir for one minute, making sure all the grains are well coated. Add the wine and stir until it is totally absorbed. Then add ½ cup of clam juice stirring constantly. When the clam juice is almost completely absorbed, add the next ½ cup, again stirring until almost totally absorbed.
4. Continue this process until all but ½ cup of clam juice has been used, about 20 minutes. Remove from heat and stir in remaining ½ cup of clam juice. The rice should be tender but firm.
5. Stir in the red bell pepper, then cool, cover and refrigerate. This step can be done one day ahead.
6. Seafood: To cook per serving - in a medium sauté pan, place one cup of the risotto. Stir in ½ cup of remaining clam juice. Add the above seafood ingredients. Cover and heat on low heat, stirring often, until seafood is cooked and risotto is creamy, about 4 minutes.
7. For additional creaminess, add more clam juice. Serve immediately in large bowls.

The Slogar

Second and Whiterock, PO Box 386, 349-5765

Directions: From the intersection of Highways 50 and 135 in Gunnison, go 28 miles north on Highway 135 to Crested Butte. At the 4-way stop, turn left onto Elk Avenue. Go 4 blocks to Second Street and turn left. Go two blocks. The restaurant is on the right.

ESSENTIALS

Cuisine: Fried Chicken/Steak

Hours: 7 days 5PM-9PM. Closed Mid-APR to Mid-JUN and late SEP to Mid-NOV.

Meals and Prices: Dinner $$$-$$$$

Nonsmoking: All. Smoking only permitted in the bar.

Take-out: Yes

Alcohol: Full Bar

Credit Cards: MC, Visa

Personal Check: Yes with I. D.

Reservations: Recommended

Wheelchair Access: Yes

Other: Available for private party dinners. Special menus for special occasions.

HISTORY, PERSONALITY AND CHARACTER

The Slogar was originally built in 1882 by Thomas W. Lipcomb as a tavern and brothel. The Slogar was one of 18 taverns in town and the first one miners came to as they returned from work. Almost a century later in 1976, the Slogar was restored, a Victorian motif was selected and a dining room was added to the right of the entrance. The ornate bar was built by local carpenters, Joe Grabowski and Dave Bennett. Robin Grabowski designed the stained-glass artwork behind the bar unveiling a lady in white with a blue hat.

Mac and Maura Bailey have owned the Slogar since June 1985. They have been in the restaurant business since 1982 and own Penelope's (see previous restaurant review) and Soupçon, both in Crested Butte. Guest Service Manager Katrina Angier handles the front of the restaurant while Kitchen Manager Don "Peel" Richardson takes care of the back. Katrina has been in the restaurant business since 1986 having worked previously in Massachusetts and several establishments in Crested Butte: Penelope's, Angelo's and Brick Oven Pizza. She came over to The Slogar in the fall of 1993. Peel, from Kansas, got his start cooking at Angelo's and has been at The Slogar since 1987.

FOOD, SERVICE AND AMBIANCE

The Slogar presents family-style dinners of skillet-fried chicken or steak. This is a 3-course meal beginning with a cold relish tray of carrot and celery sticks, sugar and spiced cinnamon pears and sweet pickles; homemade tomato chutney prepared with ginger, garlic, onion and a touch of vinegar; cottage cheese; and cole slaw sweetened with sugar and cream and soured with salt and vinegar. I liked the sweet, seasoned pears as well as the tangy chutney. The cole slaw was "deliciously different", which is the motto they use at The Slogar to describe their dining. The second hot course features one-half, non-greasy, crisp on the outside, moist on the inside, skillet-fried chicken; homemade mashed potatoes; savory chicken gravy with black pepper and paprika; homemade sweet honey-butter and strawberry preserves to put on fresh baking powder biscuits that break apart easily; and sweet, whole kernel, creamed corn. You finish this feast with a refreshing scoop of ice cream. Decaffeinated coffee, tea or milk is also included. A wine list, Genesee Cream Ale and Sioux City soft drinks, including birch beer and sarsaparilla, are available. This is a very different restaurant, indeed. They keep it plain and good.

My server was cheerful, smiling and accommodating. Light trumpet jazz music played quietly in the bar. You'll appreciate the antique charm of this place from the Victorian-style furniture in the parlor, to the many artistic stained-glass pieces and the cloth wall-covering. Adorning the walls are posters of Monaco-Monte Carlo and the Crested Butte Wildflower Festival and an aerial photograph of the towns of Crested Butte and Mount Crested Butte with Axtel Mountain and Wet Stone Mountain in the background. For small parties, there are a couple of cozy dining areas in the back. The Slogar was a fun, popular spot the evening that I visited. Dining here is like taking a step back in time to a simpler era. Join the friendly staff here for down-home cooking and a nostalgic look and feel back to the past.

SPECIAL ONE-TIME OFFER: Buy one entrée at the regular price and receive 50% off a second entrée (maximum discount $10.00). This offer NOT valid in combination with any other offers. Please present to server at time of ordering. Special Offer EXPIRES: March 31, 1997. _____ Manager/Owner. _____ Date.

RECIPE

Tomato Chutney

7 pounds of tomatoes,
  peeled and coarsely chopped
3 cups apple cider vinegar
1 cup sugar
2 medium onions, coarsely chopped

1 tablespoon salt
2 ounces garlic, finely chopped
2 ounces ginger, finely chopped
1½ teaspoon Tabasco

1. Throw them all in a pot and cook until desired consistency.

DELTA

George A. Crawford established the townsite of Uncompahgre, named after the nearby river, mountain range and plateau. However, because the name Uncompahgre proved so difficult to pronounce, the town was later renamed for its location on the delta at the mouth of the Uncompahgre River. The Ute Indians named the river "Anacopogri" or Uncompahgre meaning Red Lake because there is a spring of reddish color water near the source of the river. The first white man to visit the delta area was Don Juan Rivera in 1761.

Zip Code: 81416. Area Code: 970. Population: 3,789. Elevation: 4,953'.

The Eatery
305 Main Street, 874-9634

Directions: From the north on Highways 50 or 92, go south on Main Street (Highway 50). The restaurant is on your right just past 3rd Street. From the south on Highway 50, go through town. The restaurant is on your left past 4th Street.

ESSENTIALS

Cuisine: Soup and Sandwich Shoppe
Hours: Mon-Fri 11AM-3PM. Closed Sat/Sun.
Meals and Prices: Lunch $
Nonsmoking: Yes, in the front of the restaurant
Take-out: Yes
Alcohol: No
Credit Cards: MC, Visa
Personal Check: Yes
Reservations: No
Wheelchair Access: Yes

Other: Catering and lunch delivery available in the Delta area (minimum 4 lunches). They have a list of 78 different kinds of pies, strusels, cobblers and stratas (cream cheese with fruit on top). Give them a day's notice and you can pick up your pie fresh. Breads, buns and cinnamon rolls can also be purchased with the same advanced notice. Extra plate $1, except for children. Free refills on most beverages.

HISTORY, PERSONALITY AND CHARACTER

The Eatery is in a building that began as a grocery store back in 1893 and is currently on the National Registry of Historic Places. It was a Hallmark card store in the 1970s before lying vacant from 1983 to 1985. In August 1985, Jim Kearas and Pat Dickensheets purchased the building and opened The Eatery. Pat worked for four years in a sandwich shop called "The Kitchen Koop" in Washington State. She bakes the breads and pies. Pat's daughter, Julie, prepares the soups, salads and specials.

FOOD, SERVICE AND AMBIANCE

This is a marvelous little place to stop for lunch. Just be prepared for a crowd, and possibly a short wait to be seated, if you come between 11:30AM and 1PM. A few days before I arrived, they got so busy that Jim had to run to the hardware store down the street to buy two chairs (which, I might add, he paid for later as he was in a hurry. This is a small town so you can get away with taking merchandise without paying for it - if they know you!). I wound up sharing a table with a couple of charming locals. I ordered a cup of their chili - spicy hot with beans, beef, melted cheddar and scallions - and the Monterey chicken breast on a homemade bun with green chilies. This was a great combination. Their meats and vegetables are fresh, coming from distributors in the local area. In addition to baking bread and making desserts, soups and pastries from scratch, their Thousand Island and sweet-tasting poppyseed dressings are also made in-house. The special for the day, which I had a hard time passing up, but my two table companions will vouch for, was a pesto burger on a light rye bun.

The regular menu features burgers, salads, and sandwiches (beef or white turkey with Swiss, ham and cheddar, vegetarian with cream cheese, tuna, Philly steak, French dip). Their extensive homemade dessert list changes daily and includes fruit and cream pies like caramel apple and chunky monkey (chocolate cream with banana, walnuts and marshmallows); half-baked chocolate mousse; toffee torte; and fruit strusels, cobblers and stratas. Come here for lunch and I guarantee you will agree this is the "feel good food place"!

Service is fast and courteous! My meal was served within two minutes. This is a long, single-room restaurant with an attractive beige-pattern wallpaper on the left decorated with wicker baskets, a washboard, tin angelfood cake molds, and a pitcher. The red brick wall on the right has several still-life paintings, one of a woman and child carrying firewood from a barn in the dead of winter, all by Pat's mother, Marion McCombs, a local artist. They are for sale in the $125 to $175 range. An outdoor patio in the back was just added in the summer of 1995.

SPECIAL ONE-TIME OFFER: Buy one entrée at the regular price and receive a free dessert. Limit two desserts with the purchase of two entrées. This offer NOT valid in combination with any other offers. _____ Manager/Owner. _____ Date.

RECIPE

Tampico Torte

2 bananas

8 ounces cream cheese

1 orange peel, grated

1 cup whipping cream

1 cup powdered sugar

Caramelize:

¾ cup butter, melted

⅔ cup brown sugar

2 tablespoon corn syrup

1. Cool pie shell. Mix and boil the caramel for 2 minutes in the microwave or on top of the stove.
2. Pour in the bottom of the pie shell.
3. Slice 2 bananas into the caramel.
4. Whip cream cheese with 1 cup powdered sugar.
5. Add grated orange peel. Fold in one cup whipped cream.
6. Pour over caramel. Chill.
7. Dollop remaining cream on top.
8. Garnish with orange slices.

Old Germany Restaurant in Dolores

DILLON

Dillon was named after gold digger Tom Dillon who, after becoming lost and ending up in Golden, described it as a wide valley where three rivers met. Later, explorers upon finding this area named it in his honor. (Sometimes getting lost has its advantages!) This town has moved three times since its original townsite in 1881: in 1882 when the railroads came to town, in 1883 when the town was moved between the three rivers and in 1961 to make room for Dillon Lake. The original townsite lies under water on the south end of the lake and many of the original buildings are still visible.

Zip Code: 80435. Area Code: 970. Population: 553. Elevation: 9,156'.

Arapahoe Cafe

626 Lake Dillon Drive, 468-0873

Directions: Take Exit 205 from I-70. Go south on Highway 6 for 1.2 miles. Turn right at the signal for Lake Dillon Drive. Go .3 miles. The restaurant will be on your right at the corner of West La Bonte.

ESSENTIALS

Cuisine: American Cafe and Country
Hours: 7 days 7AM-2:30PM and 5PM-9:30PM.
Meals and Prices: Breakfast/Lunch $$, Dinner $$$-$$$$
Nonsmoking: All. Smoking only permitted in the bar/lounge downstairs.
Take-out: Yes
Alcohol: Full Bar

Credit Cards: All 5
Personal Check: Yes, with I.D.
Reservations: Accepted for dinner only.
Wheelchair Access: No
Other: Additional 15% service charge for parties of 6 or more. No separate checks.

HISTORY, PERSONALITY AND CHARACTER

The Arapahoe Cafe, one of the historic landmarks in Dillon, was built back in the early 1950s by Faye and Lenore Bryant in the old town of Dillon before the reservoir was built. The original restaurant was to the left of the entrance and the current dining area to the right used to be the Bryants' living quarters. In 1960, with the building of Dillon Reservoir, the Bryants moved their restaurant up the hill to avoid destruction. The move left the restaurant intact, but the floors are a bit uneven and the original pine panel walls meet at a place somewhere more or less than 90 degrees. In 1972, the restaurant changed owners and became the Tappan House. In 1988, George Blincoe, current manager, took over operations under new ownership and returned the restaurant to a classic mountain-style cafe with its original name and historic charm. George has been in the restaurant business since 1966, previously managing The Navigators (now Nonnino's) for 7 years at the Keystone Resort. In 1991, he was joined by Bruce Ganoung who worked as chef and manager in Keystone and at The Maggie Hut in Breckenridge.

In 1994, Mountain Valley Properties, which also owns the adjacent Best Western Ptarmigan Lodge, became the new owners. Dave Vopalecky, a self-trained chef who's been cooking since 1980 and who worked previously at Spencer's in the Beaver Run Resort in Breckenridge, has been the head chef since May 1995. Dan Pierce from Wisconsin, who started cooking in the late 1980s, has been the night chef since 1992.

FOOD, SERVICE AND AMBIANCE

I can recommend the Arapahoe Cafe for its lunch specials. Both times that I dined here, I decided to go with the special rather than order off the menu. The first time, I was introduced to their huge portions and "down-home" cooking that they are known for: a big plate of beef stroganoff with about a half-pound of pasta noodles with more than two dozen chunks of beef in a brown gravy with peas on fresh hot biscuits. On my second visit, I was ready to order "Mom's liver and onion" (I'm one of those rare few who happens to like this dish), but changed my mind when I heard the special was Greek pasta. It is a combination of spinach, artichoke hearts, black olives, feta cheese, tomatoes, cheddar and mozzarella, and sautéed mushrooms, placed over linguini - like a pasta primavera, only better. Good home cooking that's high in quality and wide in quantity (and so will you be after you've eaten here). Make sure you bring your appetite.

Their soups, muffins, biscuits and salad dressings (burgundy vinaigrette, peppercorn Parmesan) are all made in-house. Breakfast is served all day, except for pancakes and French toast which is only served until 11AM. A few of their special breakfast entrées are Belgian malted waffles with fresh strawberries, sautéed fresh vegetables with low-fat mozzarella and non-yolk egg mixture and ruby red trout. (The trout is fed a diet high in keratin, including fresh water shrimp, that give the fish the red, salmon-looking color). Lunch offers chicken fried steak with real mashed potatoes, an open-faced quesadilla, burgers (like the guacabacacheezahburgah), sandwiches (including an open-faced blackened steak sandwich), veggie sandwiches, and salads (spinach and bacon, and oriental chicken). A few of the dinner entrées that deserve closer attention are the chicken Mediterranean, roast duck lingonberry and the Greek-style shrimp. Each evening, they present a different fresh seafood and wild game special. Afterwards, you can relax with an espresso, cappuccino or flavored latté with one of their desserts (Rocky Mountain or key lime pie, cheesecake, a fruit pie or tin roof sundae). Micro brewery beers from Colorado, Oregon and Montana are also available.

Service is friendly and attentive with a homey attitude, but you may wait a few extra minutes for your meal. Not too worry, it's worth the wait. If you are here in the summertime, you may want to make a point of having breakfast here on a sunny day under one of the umbrellas on their patio. At 9,156 feet above sea level, the air is crisp and the view of Dillon Reservoir and the mountains is exceptional. Inside this log cabin, you will find several old photos of the original Arapahoe Cafe when it was down where the reservoir is now. The Pub Down Under, located under the restaurant, features a pool table, photos of W. C. Fields and Jackie Gleason shooting pool and live entertainment from 9:30PM to 12:30AM on Friday and Saturday nights.

SPECIAL ONE-TIME OFFER: Buy one adult dinner entrée at the regular price and receive a complimentary glass of wine. Good for every member of your party. This offer NOT valid in combination with any other offers.

_____ Manager/Owner. _____ Date.

RECIPE

Grilled Salmon with Squash Noodles

6- to 7-ounce salmon fillets
Salt and pepper, as needed
Clarified butter, as needed
Lemon juice, as needed
1 teaspoon fresh parsley
1 summer squash
1 zucchini squash

6 ounces red wine
6 ounces cranberry juice
3 ounces fresh cranberries
2 ounces mixed berries and
  peppercorns
Honey, as needed

1. Combine red wine, cranberry juice, cranberries and peppercorns.
2. Let reduce by half. Then thicken with honey.
3. Grill salmon to medium-rare. Place on cooked squash noodles.
4. Nape with sauce when thick.
5. Cut summer squash and zucchini into very long julienne and sauté in butter until tender.
6. Garnish with fresh parsley.

Ristorante Al Lago

240 Lake Dillon Drive, 468-6111

Directions: Take Exit 205 from I-70. Go south on Highway 6 for 1.2 miles. Turn right at the signal for Lake Dillon Drive. Go .2 miles. The restaurant will be on your right at the corner of West Buffalo Street.

ESSENTIALS

Cuisine: Northern Italian
Hours: Mid-JUN to OCT and Mid-DEC to APR: Tue-Sun 5PM-10PM.

Closed MAY to Mid-JUN and NOV to Mid-DEC.
Meals and Prices: Dinner $$$$

Nonsmoking: All. Smoking only permitted in the lounge.
Take-out: No
Alcohol: Full Bar
Credit Cards: MC, Visa, Amx, Disc
Personal Check: Local only with I.D.
Reservations: Recommended

Wheelchair Access: Yes, through the kitchen.
Other: Additional 15% service charge for parties of 6 or more. Surcharge of $5 for splitting an entrée or any person not eating. No separate checks. Available for special parties.

HISTORY, PERSONALITY AND CHARACTER

The building occupied by Ristorante Al Lago was built in the mid-1960s, originally as the Hearth Steakhouse. It was replaced in 1973 by a French restaurant, La France. On July 1, 1988, the third and current owners, the Ottoborgo Family, opened Ristorante Al Lago, less than one year after their first restaurant, the Berthoud Falls Inn on Berthoud Pass, burned down. The Ottoborgos, Alessandro (Alex), Mary Lou, their three daughters, Diana, Elisabetta (Lisa) and Loredana, and son, Ivano, are a charming, traditional family who manage the restaurant together. Mary Lou used to be in the real estate field. Diana and Loredana wait tables. Lisa has married and moved to Denver. Ivano, who started cooking at the age of 12, is the chef.

FOOD, SERVICE AND AMBIANCE

I have tried something from each part of their menu in my two visits here: pasta, veal, chicken, seafood and eggplant. All dinners include a warm, fresh loaf of homemade Italian bread, homemade soup, salad and pasta. Dipping the bread in olive oil with multi-colored peppers is an appetizing endeavor while you work your way to the main course. That effort could include some delicious chicken tarragon with rice soup or veal broth with whipped eggs. You will also have to exert your palate on their salad with house dressing made from herbs, balsamic vinegar, virgin olive oil and garlic. On my last visit, I put some additional muscle into an appetizer of fresh mussels and clams in Diavolo, a spicy tomato sauce with basil, red pepper, oregano, parsley, white wine and garlic — great for dipping the homemade bread into. I found their veal dishes, both the sautéed medallions with seasoned spinach and fontina cheese, and the veal and shrimp topped with prosciutto and melted mozzarella to be savory and mouth-watering. The chicken breast with onions, mushrooms and fresh tomatoes was flavorful and the eggplant with marinara sauce was very tangy. The pasta is imported and everything on the menu is prepared to order. Children can receive half portions at half price on any menu item excluding seafood and special entrées. Save room for dessert and delight in one of their homemade creations like tiramisu, strawberry shortcake made with yellow cake, chocolate cappuccino mousse, walnut torte with Ghiradelli chocolate, French apple pie, cognac cake or créme caramel custard.

The warm-heartedness of the Ottoborgos complements the warmth from their double-sided rock fireplace. The Ottoborgos are genuinely friendly, affectionate people who are happy to share their compassion for good food and each other with their guests. Italian songs, classical violin and instrumental pieces augment the at-ease Ristorante Al Lago atmosphere. The dining room walls are adorned with frosted-glass chandeliers, pictures of the Venice canals, needlework of a rabbit hunt with a celebrative picnic afterwards, a photo of a gondola in Venice at sunset, brass utensils, and small china pieces on the wall shelves above the windows. There is an intriguing stained-glass piece in the lounge along with a classy china cabinet. Windows along the back wall of both dining rooms look down on their small farm with its circular pond, reindeers, pigeons, deer, ducks and Hungarian sheep dog.

SPECIAL ONE-TIME OFFER: Receive 10% off the entire bill for your table. This offer NOT valid in combination with any other offers. Please present to server at time of ordering. _____ Manager/Owner. _____ Date.

RECIPE

Petti di Pollo alla Diana
(Serves 2)

2 tablespoon butter
4 chicken breasts, skinned and boned
1 tablespoon brown sugar
¼ cup champagne

2 shots Grand Marnier
1 can 8-ounce frozen strawberries in juice, or make your own strawberry reduction

1. Sauté chicken breasts in brown sugar and butter.
2. Add champagne. Let reduce.
3. Add Grand Marnier and strawberries.
4. Cook until it thickens.
5. Garnish with an orange swirl.

Benjamin James Bennis does several Denver shows during the year. Stop by his booth at the People's Fair or Taste of Colorado in Civic Center Park.

DOLORES

Dolores was named after the river on which it is located. The Dolores River was given the name "Rio de Nuestra Señora de las Dolores," or "river of our lady of sorrow," by Father Escalente in 1776. More than 1,380 Anasazi ruins and archaeological sites have been identified in the Dolores area and an extensive collection from the excavations are on display in the Anasazi Heritage Center, which opened in August 1988 just two miles west of Dolores. Dolores was one of the last sections of the state to be settled by the white man. In 1877, William, Richard, and George May settled on the Dolores River. From that beginning, Dolores developed over the years as a shipping point for cattle and sheep. Ranching, farming and lumber have been the town's major sources of survival and prosperity. Today, Dolores is a small recreational town, a gateway to the Dolores River Canyon and the Mount Wilson Primitive Area. McPhee Reservoir, which extends downstream 11 miles from Dolores, is open for fishing, camping and boating.
Zip Code: 81323. Area Code: 970. Population: 866. Elevation: 6,936'.

Old Germany Restaurant
200 South 8th Street (Highway 145)
Directions: From the north or south on Highway 145, go to the southwest corner of Railroad Avenue (Highway 145) and 8th Street. (Note: Highway 145 is an east/west route through Dolores).

ESSENTIALS

Cuisine: German
Hours: Tue-Sat 4PM-9PM (10PM from MAY-OCT). Closed Sun/Mon.
Meals and Prices: Dinner $$$
Nonsmoking: Yes
Take-out: Yes
Alcohol: Full Bar

Credit Cards: MC, Visa
Personal Check: Yes
Reservations: Recommended in summer. Accepted otherwise.
Wheelchair Access: Yes
Other: Dining room and bar downstairs available for special parties.

HISTORY, PERSONALITY AND CHARACTER

Old Germany is in a house built in 1908. It was converted into a restaurant in May 1986 by current owners James and Rita Blount. James is a certified German chef having completed his apprenticeship in Schweinfurt, Germany. He operated the Old Germany Restaurant in Mesa, Arizona, from 1981 to 1984 before moving to Colorado for health reasons. He has been cooking since 1980. Rita works the front of the restaurant.

FOOD, SERVICE AND AMBIANCE

I have tried both their jaegerbraten (pork roast in mushroom sauce) and sauerbraten (sweet and sour marinated roast beef with purple cabbage). The soup and 14-item salad bar - with pasta salad, pickled okra and homemade dill dressing - is included with dinner. Their beef noodle soup is homemade with ground beef and pork dumplings, a nice German touch. The sauerbraten is thick and tender (can be eaten with just a fork) with a rich, thick gravy from the beef stock. They use top-quality cuts of meat that they marinate for 7 to 10 days. You have your choice of potatoes - like their chewy potato dumplings or spätzle noodles that I recommend - or French fries, mashed or baked potatoes, German potato salad or fried potatoes.

The other dinner entrées include New York strip with mushroom sauce or fried onions, breaded porkloin steak filled with ham and cheese, grilled porkloin steak or chicken breast with bell peppers and onions in paprika sauce, wiener schnitzel, breaded cod, fried trout, and German-style meatloaf. Wednesday and Friday are all-you-can-eat cod and/or shrimp days. If you have a small appetite, order some homemade bratwurst, knackwurst, kasseler (smoked porkchop), soup and salad, one of their toast entrées or a sandwich. Accompany your meal with a German beer or wine and finish it off with some homemade apple strudel, a chocolate cream torte, a piece of the cake of the day like black forest, or one of their Bavarian creams (chocolate, pineapple, butterscotch, raspberry, blueberry, hazelnut or strawberry). They grow their own herbs, sour cherries, raspberries and strawberries.

Service is friendly and accommodating. Rita will make you feel right at home. Vocal German folk songs and polkas play quietly in the background. Since my first visit, they have paved the parking lot, added new sidewalks and a garden at the entrance. This is a nicely refurbished old house with two dining rooms in the front and one in the rear. It is decorated with a wood china cabinet holding beer steins and mugs, deer antlers, philodendrons, a chandelier, a framed page out of the February 3, 1918, edition of the Denver Post with the headlines: "Hun Strikers, Kiev Victory", "America must recognize Reds", and "Americans must smash Detachment/Huns attack". Hanging on the wall in the rear dining room in a hermetically sealed frame is the emblem of the village of Wipfeld in northern Bavaria. This priceless 800-year-old flag was once carried into battle. The flag was discovered in 1974 by the Blounts who were remodeling a Bavarian house built in the 1200s. When a portion of the roof was ripped out, the flag of Wipfelt fell to the ground. It had been hidden in the roof, covered with boards.

SPECIAL ONE-TIME OFFER: Buy one entrée at the regular price and receive a complimentary glass of wine or beer of your choice. This offer NOT valid in combination with any other offers. _____ Manager/Owner. _____ Date.

<u>RECIPE</u>

Cordon Bleu

Veal steak or butterflied pork loin steak	Flour
Salt	Milk/egg mixture
Pepper	Bread crumbs
Ham	Vegetable oil
Cheese (Swiss or Monterey Jack)	Lemon Slice

1. Use either veal steak or butterflied pork loin steak. Tenderize it.
2. Lightly add salt and pepper.
3. Lay ham and cheese on one half, fold over and push together.
4. Flour both sides, then dip in milk/egg mixture.
5. Dip in bread crumbs.
6. Fry in half-full pan of hot vegetable oil until golden brown on both sides.
7. Serve with lemon slice.

Rio Grande Southern

101 South 5th Avenue, PO Box 516, 882-7527, 1-800-258-0434

Directions: Dolores is on Highway 145, 11 miles north of Cortez. From the south on Highway 145, turn left at 5th Street, go to the end of the block. The restaurant is on the corner of Center Street on your right. From the north on Highway 145, turn right at 5th street, go to the end of the block. The restaurant is on the corner of Center Street on your right.

<u>ESSENTIALS</u>

Cuisine: Country
Hours: APR-NOV: Mon-Sat 8AM-2PM, 5PM-9PM. Sun 8AM-2PM. DEC-MAR: Mon-Fri 8AM-2PM. Breakfast ends and lunch begins at 11:30AM.
Meals and Prices: Breakfast $, Lunch $$, Dinner $$-$$$
Nonsmoking: No
Take-out: Yes
Alcohol: Full Bar

Credit Cards: MC, Visa, Disc
Personal Check: Local only
Reservations: Recommended for evening, accepted otherwise.
Wheelchair Access: Yes
Other: Picnic baskets available. To-go orders 50¢ charge. Additional 15% service charge for parties of 5 or more. No separate checks for large parties.

HISTORY, PERSONALITY AND CHARACTER

The Southern Hotel and Restaurant, also known as the Old Railroad Hotel, was built in 1893 by E. L. Wilbur who served as proprietor. The hotel provided lodging for travelers, including railroad and mining millionaires, and a congregation point for locals to obtain news from the incoming trains. The restaurant was the only eating establishment between Telluride and Durango. Around the turn of the century, the name was changed to the Rio Grande Southern and over the years, the hotel served as a brothel and flop house. For a while after World War II, the establishment was called Benny's Hogan. The current restaurant was opened in June, 1989. The kitchen is where part of the old dining room used to be. The current owners and managers, Fred and Cathy Green, purchased the restaurant in February, 1993. This is their first restaurant venture. Cathy bakes the muffins and makes the desserts, the cakes and pies. Fred prepares the breads, soups, sauces, breakfasts, lunches and does a little bit of everything in the kitchen. Scotty McEwen has been the night cook preparing dinners since May, 1995. He has been cooking since 1980, graduated from the Emily Griffith Institute, was certified by Hans Nobler and Wayne Krebs in Denver and worked previously at the Brown Palace and Regis College Marriott in Denver and C.C.'s Finest in Cañon City.

FOOD, SERVICE AND AMBIANCE

I stopped here for lunch on two occasions so I have had the opportunity to sample their homemade soup; salad with honey-raspberry, walnut vinaigrette dressing and homemade croutons; grilled chicken sandwiches; fries and pasta platter. The ingredients are fresh. The breads, croutons, pies, cakes, soups, sauces, biscuits and gravies are all homemade. The salad dressings, served on the side, are not homemade but they offer both poppyseed and honey-mustard. The spicy Italian sauce has green peppers, mushrooms and charbroiled ground steak. The al dente noodles are wider than a spaghetti, but narrower than a fettuccini. On the breakfast menu are interesting little histories about the local notables, but the items are fairly standard. The quality, though, would be well above standard, if lunch is any indication. Lunch burgers come with bacon, ham, turkey, American and Swiss cheeses (all on the same burger!); grilled onions, mushrooms, Monterey Jack and blue cheeses; or green chilies and cheese. The list of sandwiches includes steak with grilled onions and mushrooms, French dip, grilled ham and cheese, chicken or tuna salad, and lo-cal grilled beef. Prime rib is their dinner time specialty, but they also offer New York strip, top sirloin, T-bone, filet mignon, barbecue spare ribs, charbroiled chicken breast, butterfly shrimp, chicken fried steak and shrimp scampi. You can finish your meal with a homemade fruit or cream pie, cake and/or ice cream. There is also a children's menu. Wednesday is Mexican specialty night, Friday is "all you can eat fish fry" and Sunday brunch offers breakfast and the best of lunch menu.

DOLORES

Service is fast and friendly. It had to be my last time here. They were short of people because of spring break, so Cathy was "a husslin' and busslin' tables" while a jovial Rhonda (their accountant) provided me with information on the restaurant. This is a small place that can hold 35 people in pinewood booths, so calling ahead for reservations would not be a bad idea. The walls are decorated with several old town photos, including one of a group of men standing in front of the "Dolores Akin Mercantile Co. General Merchandise Store", and sketches of Rio Grande Southern Railroad cars.

SPECIAL ONE-TIME OFFER: Buy one entrée at the regular price and receive a second entrée of equal or lesser value FREE (up to $17.95 value). This offer NOT valid in combination with any other offers. _____ Manager/Owner. _____ Date.

RECIPE
Cathy's Coconut Cream Pie

9-inch pie crust, baked and cooled	2 tablespoons butter or margarine, softened
⅔ cup sugar	1 tablespoon vanilla
¼ cup cornstarch	1 teaspoon coconut flavoring
½ teaspoon salt	2 cups coconut
3 cups milk	
4 egg yolks, slightly beaten	¼ cup coconut to garnish

1. Stir together sugar, cornstarch and salt in a saucepan. Blend together milk and egg yolks.
2. Gradually add egg mixture to sugar mixture.
3. Cook over medium heat, stirring constantly (whip with whipper if it begins to lump).
4. Boil one minute. Remove from heat and stir.
5. Add butter, vanilla and coconut flavoring.
6. Add 2 cups coconut.
7. Immediately pour into baked and cooled pie crust. Chill 2 hours.
8. Toast remaining ¼ cup coconut under broiler. Cool.
9. Top cooled pie with Rich's Whipped Top Base using pastry bag. Sprinkle with toasted coconut.
10. Keep chilled until ready to serve.

DURANGO

The town was named by former Territorial Governor A. C. Hunt upon his return from Durango, Mexico. The name Durango itself is derived from the town Urango (meaning "water town") in the Basque Province of northern Spain. The "D" was added by the Spanish. Durango reflects three cultures — Native American, Anglo and Hispanic — and is a center for ranching, farming and recreational activities. Once a predominant coal mining community and commercial center, Durango is known today for its Victorian architecture and the Durango to Silverton narrow gauge railroad. The railroad offers daily round trips, from May to October, through the scenic San Juan Mountains. The train depot, the Palace Grill Restaurant located in what used to be the Palace Hotel and the Strater Hotel are three of the best examples of early architecture that still remains today. Zip Code: 81301. Area Code: 970. Population: 13,200 (1/1/94 est.). Elevation: 6,523'.

Cafe Cascade
50827 Highway 550 North, 259-3500
Directions: Located 30 miles north of Durango and 18 miles south of Silverton.
From the entrance to Purgatory Ski Resort on Highway 550, go 1.9 miles north. Cascade Village is on the west (left). As you pull up the drive, the restaurant is in the first building to your right.

ESSENTIALS
Cuisine: California Eclectic (Fresh Seafood/Wild Game/Steak)
Hours: Thanksgiving to MAR: 7 days 5:30PM-9PM. Memorial Day to Mid-OCT: 6PM-9.30PM. Closed APR to Memorial Day and Mid-OCT to Thanksgiving.
Meals and Prices: Din $$$$-$$$$$
Nonsmoking: All
Take-out: Yes
Alcohol: Full Bar
Credit Cards: All Five

Personal Check: Yes
Reservations: Definitely Recommended
Wheelchair Access: Yes, through elevator.
Dress: Casual (or as owner, Tom Hamilton says, "the only thing we take seriously is food and drink!")
Other: One check per table. Additional 17½% service charge added for parties of 8 or more.

HISTORY, PERSONALITY AND CHARACTER
Cascade Village and The Meadows Restaurant were created in 1980. In 1985, current owner Tom Hamilton, who has been in the restaurant business since 1976, replaced The Meadows with Cafe Cascade. Tom also owns the Trough Restaurants in Gunnison (see page 148) and Farmington, New Mexico, and has a share of Señor Peppers and the Rocky Mountain Rib Company in Farmington and the Chelsea's Restaurants in Durango, Grand Junction, Longmont and Farmington. His newest restaurant venture is

the New Sheridan Restaurant and Bar in Telluride. John Shaddock, who has been with Tom since 1980 at the Trough Restaurant in Gunnison, assists Tom in managing Cafe Cascade. They have three talented chefs, each with 9 to 10 years' experience, rotating duties between the broiler, vegetables and sautées: Steve Maddalena who started in 1991, Roy Perkins in 1992, and Paul Atkinson in 1994. Steve and Roy hail from back East. Paul used to work at the Santa Café in Sante Fe, New Mexico. Cafe Cascade has enjoyed rave reviews from the Rocky Mountain News to the Los Angeles Times.

FOOD, SERVICE AND AMBIANCE

I enjoyed a feast when I dined here, starting off with Cajun barbecue rock shrimp. It was easily 4 dozen shrimps (I estimate 3/4 pounds) in a hot seasoning sauce with red pepper, rosemary, thyme, Worcestershire and lots of garlic. (Garlic lovers take note - you won't want to miss this!) The shrimps somehow managed to maintain their texture in this rather potent mixture. This was followed by a well-organized salad - celery, carrots, cucumbers, bell peppers, black olives, tomato, lettuce and red cabbage neatly separated on the plate - with the house creamy Caesar dressing. Fresh vegetables are one of their mainstays and this was continued on the entrée platter with fried (in vegetable oil) spinach, carrots, ratatouille, acorn squash, tomato (topped with parmesan cheese, garlic, basil and oregano), broccoli, black-eyed peas, roasted potatoes with tarragon, and spaghetti squash. Nine vegetables in all. You're guaranteed a minimum of 7, but it is usually 9 or 10 vegetables with each entrée. Tom tells me the record is 17! The fried spinach is a favorite, and now mine too. It's crunchy and has a different texture. The other vegetables are baked, sautéed or steamed, but the flavor remains intact. Oh, and yes, there was room left on the platter for my entrée - a combination of elk and rack of lamb prepared medium rare with three different sauces: minted rosemary demiglace, four peppercorn (white, pink, black and green) demiglace and orange hoisin sauce. The meats were pink to red, but with warm centers. Overall I preferred the lighter, milder demiglaces to the sweet, thick Hoisin sauce made with soy sauce, but it was a nice alternative every few bites. You won't be disappointed with the quality nor will you go away hungry here. You can count on receiving value for your money.

Bread is home baked and some desserts, like chocolate chip and coconut cheesecakes, are homemade. The salad dressings, stocks and sauces are all made from scratch. Soup is not part of the menu. Wild game, one of their changing specialties, includes caribou, kangaroo, boar, quail and duck. The regular menu and the list of nightly specials feature a number of steak entrées, like ribeye with 7 mushroom madeira sauce, and seafood entrées including prawns, scallops, ahi, salmon, grouper, Florida swordfish, Alaska halibut and king crab, Chilean sea bass, escolar, and lobster in a variety of tempting sauces. A different chicken and veal entrée is also offered each evening. Three minds are better than one or two so the selections from the kitchen are imaginative and unique. Some items are available in reduced portions at a 20% savings if you have a lighter appetite. Wines are primarily from the Napa and Sonoma Counties, California, but they also have a few from Idaho, France, Germany and Portugal. I recommend the Pine Ridge Merlot, smooth and elegant, to accompany a wild game or steak selection.

Service is very attentive. Top notch. The restaurant is in two tiers. The lower level overlooks the lounge and fireplace and has a view of the forest and hills beyond the parking lot. Wreaths of garlic and Indian blue corn hang on the green walls along side pictures of mallard ducks. The upstairs dining area has large green-cushioned booths and a painting of "hounds" on a successful fox hunt. This is a spacious dining area with a high-vaulted ceiling. Sophisticated violin instrumental and classical Bach music enhanced the mood for the evening. Cafe Cascade is remote but not undiscovered. You'll revel in their refined, yet friendly, atmosphere as you delve into their exquisite cuisine. This find was one of my favorites on the western slope.

SPECIAL ONE-TIME OFFER: Buy two entrées at the regular price and receive a complimentary appetizer (up to $10 value). Limit 1 appetizer with the purchase of 2 entrées. This offer NOT valid in combination with any other offers. Please present special offer to server at time of ordering. _____ Manager/Owner. _____ Date.

RECIPE

Spaghetti Squash with Blueberry Maple Cream
(Serves 8 to 12)

1 small spaghetti squash	1 tablespoon brown sugar
1 tablespoon fresh parsley	1 teaspoon white sugar
½ pint of blueberries	¼ cup port wine
1 teaspoon roasted shallots	¼ cup of pure maple syrup
1 teaspoon honey	1 cup heavy cream
1 teaspoon of roasted and ground coriander and fennel	

1. Cut squash in half and scrape out seeds. Place on baking sheet face down, cover the bottom of the sheet with water and bake for 18 minutes at 400 degrees.
2. Place blueberries in sauce pan with brown sugar, white sugar, pure maple syrup, honey, coriander, fennel and roasted shallots. Cook until liquid consistency.
3. Once sauce is liquid, pour in port wine, then reduce by half. Add heavy cream and once again reduce by half.

> 4. Take fully baked spaghetti squash and scoop out the meat of the squash. Place the scooped squash directly in sauce which you have just made and toss around.
> 5. Reheat to near boil, sprinkle on fresh parsley, salt and pepper to taste.

Red Snapper

144 East 9th Street, 259-3417

Directions: From the intersection of Highways 160 and 550, go north on Highway 550 for 4 blocks, turn right on 9th Street and go 2½ blocks. The restaurant is on your right ½ block past Main Street. From the north on Highway 550, continue on Main Avenue to 9th Street. Turn left and go ½ block. The restaurant is on your right.

ESSENTIALS

Cuisine: Seafood

Hours: 7 days 5PM-10PM

Meals and Prices: Dinner $$$-$$$$

Nonsmoking: All. Smoking is only permitted in the adjacent lounge area by the restrooms.

Take-out: Yes

Alcohol: Full Bar

Credit Cards: MC, Visa, Amx

Personal Check: Local area only

Reservations: Only accepted for parties of 7 or more

Wheelchair Access: Yes

Other: Special room available for parties up to 20 people; 15 % gratuity added to parties of 7 or more. One check per table.

HISTORY, PERSONALITY AND CHARACTER

The building now occupied by the Red Snapper was completed in 1907. In the 1910s, it was a Masonic Lodge called Redman Hall. By 1920, it became the Durango Business College and in the 1930s it was a post office. In November 1985, current owners Rick and Karen Langhart opened the Red Snapper. Rick has been in the restaurant business since 1975 working previously at the Chart House in Aspen. Karen, who has a degree in architecture, designed the interior of the restaurant. Both Rick and Karen manage the restaurant along with Sven Brunso. The head chefs are Joel "Buzz" Campbell and Mike Weist. Buzz has been with the Red Snapper since 1989 and prepares the specials and sauces. Mike started in 1993 and has been to culinary school in Denver. Karen makes the pies and other desserts.

FOOD, SERVICE AND AMBIANCE

I deemed it appropriate to have red snapper on my first visit here. On my second visit, I ordered a dozen fresh oysters on the half shell and baked orange roughy mozzarella. The oysters, appalachicolas from Florida (they also get blue points from Connecticut and oysters from Texas and Virginia depending on the season), slid right over the palate. The only problem with these delectable little guys is they are gone so quickly. They go down too easily. White and caraway seed bread baked fresh that day from Jean Pierre's bakery in town and a 36-item salad (and vegetable) bar comes with the meal. It is one of the freshest I have found. In particular, I found the spinach and beets had a profusion of flavor. The bar also features homemade salad dressings, including poppyseed made with rice wine vinegar which gives it a purple color, honey-mustard and raspberry vinaigrette. The fish was flaky and easy to break apart with a fork. I found the roughy to be a particularly taste-pleasing treat with mozzarella cheese, fresh tomatoes, basil and oregano baked on top.

Their fish entrées are either baked, like the red snapper with Monterey jack cheese and tarragon or the orange roughy in orange and Grand Marnier; or grilled, like the rainbow trout with lemon, caper, white wine and butter. Catches of the day could also include blackened marlin, Cajun mahi-mahi, Hawaiian ahi, swordfish and halibut. If you prefer shellfish, there is shrimp (teriyaki, cajun style or scampi), baked scallops, lobster, and king crab. For the carnivore, they have prime rib, filet mignon, top sirloin and Hawaiian chicken. The only soup you can get here is New England clam chowder but it is homemade. Wines are primarily from the Sonoma and Napa Valleys in California with a few from France. In the summer months, May through August, they serve sushi. The dessert menu includes death by chocolate, mint Alaskan pie, and New York cheesecake, along with a homemade dessert of the day like praline pecan cheesecake, Bailey's cream pie, or key lime pie (a house favorite specialty).

The restaurant is well staffed with knowledgeable, experienced people and they have very little turnover. The servers are friendly and show genuine interest in their customers. The decor is most appropriate for a seafood place. They have several fish tanks with colorful fish and coral, posters of ocean whales from California and Hawaii by Robert Lyn Nelson, frosted glass dividers with pictures of ocean fish or clouds and seagulls, a couple of brass dolphins hanging on the rear wall, and, in the foyer, a model of the Aliser Smith clipper ship from 1872 made entirely out of wood, sails included. The tables are from the original Chart House in Aspen. Each table has a different wood design. Take a short walk to the back hallway where the restrooms are located, whether you need to or not, and take a look at some of the old enlarged photographs of the hotel and town dating back to the turn of the century. Also, stand in front of the bar and gaze up the four-story atrium (just don't waddle into the way of one of the waiters).

SPECIAL ONE-TIME OFFER: Buy one entrée at the regular price and receive a complimentary dessert. Limit 2 complimentary desserts with the purchase of two entrees. This offer NOT valid in combination with any other offers. _____ Manager/Owner. _____ Date.

<u>RECIPE</u>

Salmon Dijon

1 cup mayonnaise	Juice of 1 lemon
2 cups sour cream	¼ of 8-ounce jar of Dijon mustard
1 cucumber, peeled, seeded and diced	1 teaspoon white pepper
1 tablespoon dill weed	1 tablespoon chopped fresh parsley

1. Mix all ingredients together in mixing bowl. Spoon over broiled or grilled salmon filets.

The Covered Awning Entrance at the Red Snapper in Durango

EDWARDS

Originally named Berry's Ranch after Harrison Berry, the townsite owner, there are two versions of the town's name derivation. One version names the town after Melvin Edwards, Colorado Secretary of State in 1883. The other gives credit to a post office inspector of 1887 with the railroad changing the name of the station to Edwards in 1912. Zip Code: 81632. Area Code: 970. Population: 500. Elevation: 7,226'.

Fiesta's

57 Edwards Access Road in Edwards Plaza, 926-2121, fax 926-3048
Directions: Take Exit 263 from I-70. Proceed south ½ mile. The restaurant is on the right in the Edwards Plaza, just past the Eagle River and just before Highway 6.

ESSENTIALS

Cuisine: New Mexican
Hours: Mon-Fri 10:30AM-10PM.
Sat/Sun 7:30AM-10PM (Breakfast served until noon).
Meals and Prices: Breakfast $, Lunch/Dinner $$
Nonsmoking: Yes
Take-out: Yes
Alcohol: Full Bar
Credit Cards: MC, Visa, Amx, Disc

Personal Check: Eagle County only with I.D.
Reservations: Accepted only for parties of 8 or more.
Wheelchair Access: Yes
Dress: Mountain comfortable (casual).
Other: Catering available. Additional 15% service charge added for parties of 6 or more.

HISTORY, PERSONALITY AND CHARACTER

Fiesta's is in a building that was built in 1975, originally as an auto garage. It was later converted into the Golddust Cafe operated by the liquor store next door, before the Marquez sisters (Susan, Cheryl, Debbie and Anna) opened Fiesta's in December, 1989. The entrance dining area and bar were added in 1993. Debbie has been in the restaurant business since 1974, working for Aircoa Hotels and Restaurants. She was an assistant manager at the Stouffer's Hotel (now called the Red Lion) at the old Stapleton Airport in Denver. Cheryl and Susan have both worked in restaurants waiting tables. Anna now lives in Denver. The Marquez sisters come from a restaurant family. Uncle Ed used to operate the Hungry Dutchman (now called Hans Brinkers) in Englewood, Colorado. Their aunt in Albuquerque, New Mexico, owns the Tia Florencias Cafe. Their family members encouraged them to open this restaurant and even helped out with the design, equipment and set-up. Kitchen manager, Mariano Ledezma, has been with Fiesta's since 1992. Debbie says that "the sauces are the key to our success". The locals seem to agree. Fiesta's was voted "Best of Vail/Most Authentic Mexican Food" for 1993 (the first year the award was given) and 1994 in a People's Choice Award run by the Vail

Daily Newspaper. In 1995, Fiesta's was listed number 55 in "The 100 Fastest Growing Companies" by Hispanic Business Magazine.

FOOD, SERVICE AND AMBIANCE

Whenever possible, I try to get a sampling of different foods when I visit a restaurant. So I ordered a small (but plentiful) combination: the chili relleno and shredded-beef, blue corn tortilla enchilada smothered with rich, red chili and cheese and served with refried beans, Mexican rice, shredded lettuce, diced tomatoes and black olives. The green chile on the chili relleno is fresh roasted. It is also used in their chili verde, white jalapeño sauce and green chili salsa. Pulp from New Mexico red chilies are used in the enchilada sauce, as well as in the menudo (made from tripe and hominy), carne adovadá, and spicy chicken wings. The Marquez sisters use recipes brought to Colorado from New Mexico by their great-grandparents and taught to them by their mother and grandmother. It is easy to see why Fiesta's was voted "Most Authentic Mexican Food".

The smothered burrito with chorizo, egg and potato is the favorite dish on the breakfast menu. Other items include Santa Fe enchiladas; menudo; omelets with green chili strips, chorizo or avocado; pancakes and French toast. The lunch and dinner menus are identical with two differences: chips and salsa are extra at lunch and the dinner entrées cost a little more. The meat in their carnitas (fajitas) is cut up first, marinated in a recipe that includes tequila, then grilled with chilies, onions and tomatoes. Whether you order the taco salad, stuffed sopapilla, chimichangas, chicken fried steak, or one of their grand burritos, you'll enjoy their special and unique sauces. A children's menu and 20 different tequilas are available and, for dessert, try their fried ice cream (I did): vanilla ice cream with a crunchy coating of corn flakes soaked in honey then fried, (frozen) strawberries, and, if they have them, nuts (they were out of nuts the day I was here). They also serve a flan, fruit chimichangas, and homemade cinnamon sopapillas.

Service was busy, but quick at lunch time. They were dumped on because the pizza place next door was closed for an employee party. There wasn't any follow-up after my meal was served, which I could understand because they were packed, but when my server rushed my check without checking to see if I wanted dessert, I said "Wait a minute, aren't you going to ask if I want dessert?" She said they don't get many dessert orders for lunch.

There are several piñatas (made from paper mache) hanging from the ceiling - figures of bulls, fish, chickens, red chili peppers, mermaids, donkeys, a hot air balloon and, my favorite, a blue triceratops. They are for sale for $15 ($19 if you want it stuffed with goodies). An entire row of red chilies hangs in front of the middle dining room window. There are Indian rugs and posters of Great Chilies and Indian Corn of the Americas, but the prize piece of artwork is the mural on the far left wall by local artist Natalie DeStefano who occasionally tends bar here. The mural at Fiesta's depicts the Marquez family members, either eating or playing cards, with a church modeled after one in Vallecitos, New Mexico (near Chama) and a portrait of the grandparents' wedding in the background. There is a second mural at the end of the bar with a different scene. This one shows several señoritas standing in front of vine-draped Spanish arches. Natalie's works can also be seen in the Uptown Grill (see page 293).

SPECIAL ONE-TIME OFFER: Buy one entrée at the regular price and receive a second entrée of equal or lesser value FREE (up to $10.00 value). This offer NOT valid in combination with any other offers. _____ Manager/Owner. _____ Date.

RECIPE

Spanish Rice
(Serves 4 to 6)

1 cup long grain white rice	Dash of cumin
1 small can tomato sauce	Chopped fresh jalapeño pepper,
¼ cup diced white onions	optional
¼ cup diced tomatoes	Chopped green bell pepper, optional
Salt and pepper to taste	

1. Over medium-high heat, heat 1 tablespoon vegetable oil in a 12-inch skillet. Brown rice until uniform golden color.
2. Remove skillet from heat. Add tomato sauce, water, onion, diced tomatoes and spices. Stir gently.
3. Return to burner over medium heat. Cover.
4. Allow to simmer until all water is absorbed. Remember, don't stir. Serve piping hot.

Feasting at Fiesta's in Edwards

EMPIRE

Empire, located beside the west fork of Clear Creek, was named after New York, the "Empire" state, and the original home of the men who founded the town. It is an old gold and silver mining area comprising several old mines including the Hartford, the Gold Dust, Gold Fissure, Atlantic, Empire City Mine, the Mint and McKinley. Zip Code: 80438. Area Code: 303. Population: 401. Elevation: 8,614'.

The Peck House

Sunny Street at Freeman Street, PO Box 428, 569-9870, Fax 569-2743
Directions: Take Exit 232 from I-70 and head north on Highway 40 for 2 miles into Empire. Turn right on Main Street. Go one block and turn left. The restaurant is on the right.

ESSENTIALS
Cuisine: Continental/Colorado
Hours: Year around: Sun-Thu 4PM-9PM, Fri/Sat 4PM-10PM. Sun 10AM-2PM.
Meals and Prices: Brunch $$$, Dinner $$$$-$$$$$
Nonsmoking: No. If someone complains, they will request the smoker move to the bar.
Take-out: Yes
Alcohol: Full Bar
Credit Cards: All 5
Personal Check: Yes, with I.D.
Reservations: Strongly recommended on holidays, suggested otherwise

Wheelchair Access: Only in dry weather from the side of the building, passing over the porch
Dress: Casual to dressy
Other: Smaller public rooms and dining room available for specially catered luncheon groups. Rated ★★★ by AAA, finalist for Uncle Ben's 1992 10 Best Country Inns of the Year Award. Winner of the Governor's Award for Colorado Cuisine. Listed on National Register of Historic Places.

HISTORY, PERSONALITY AND CHARACTER
The Peck House, built in 1862 by wealthy, adventurous Chicago merchant James Peck as a 4-room home for his family, is Colorado's oldest hotel still in operation. The current kitchen, bar and reception area were the original dwelling. In 1872, he converted the home to The Peck House to accommodate eastern travelers, investors, prospectors and visiting mining executives. P. T. Barnum, Ulysses S. Grant and General Sherman are three names that appear in the old Peck House registry. The Peck House became a stage coach stop for stages running over Berthoud Pass. Generated by power from their own water wheel, The Peck House was the first building in Empire with electric lights. The

property remained in the Peck Family until 1945 when it was sold to Joseph Emerson Smith, who in turn sold it to the two granddaughters of Adolph Coors, founder of Coors Brewery in Golden, and Henry Colbran, one of the founders of the Colorado Midland Railroad. The two granddaughters renamed the Peck House, the Hotel Splendide, but it became The Peck House again in 1972. In March 1981, Gary and Sally St. Clair took over operation of the inn and restaurant. Gary has been in the restaurant business since 1958, formerly owned Carlson's in Greeley and used to be associated with the Marriott Corporation.

FOOD, SERVICE AND AMBIANCE

I've had two exquisite meals here, one for Sunday brunch, the other for New Year's Day dinner. They were both outstanding in their own way. For brunch, I delved into a prosciutto, cream cheese and asparagus omelet that was incredible (a word that doesn't come to mind too often when I think of omelets). This one was superior! It was served with fried potatoes, champagne, fresh strawberries and raspberries and a plate of homemade breakfast breads and coffee cakes. For the holiday dinner, the finale for my New Year's Eve Tour to Grand Lake, I relished a plate of tender veal medallions sautéed in butter, wine and garlic then covered with lightly sautéed vegetables (which I prefer because the vegetables were still crisp and maintained their flavor) — fresh mushrooms, bell peppers, onion, celery and tomato (actually, the toppings would go well on a pizza). This was a dish for those who don't like a rich, thick sauce. The others in my "Restaurant Adventure Plus (RAP) Tour" enjoyed a tender New York strip with little fat, a superb duck in raspberry sauce or the dish that got the highest praise, a flaky and moist baked salmon filet in butter, brown sugar and lime juice. Delicious homemade soft dinner rolls with a light, crisp crust and salad greens with cream of Dijon dressing (mayonnaise texture, mustard taste) accompanied the dinners. All of the meals featured top quality ingredients expertly brought together.

Chef Gary's menu combines several specialties from the northwest with Colorado cuisine. His Washington State salmon is smoked in alderwood (a wood indigenous to the northwest) to make the fish dryer and sweeter. The items from Colorado include Colorado mountain bass macadamia, pheasant in the fall season, lamb Dijon, Rocky Mountain oysters, smoked Colorado clam chowder and Colorado peach sundae.

Headlining the brunch entrées were eggs or crab benedict; quail, smoked trout or steak with eggs; shrimp jambalaya crêpe, seafood potpourri consisting of jumbo shrimp, smoked trout and salmon; and a pâté platter. You can start off dinner with fresh sautéed mushrooms, baked French onion soup or a combination seafood appetizer. Follow this with an entrée of beef (sautéed tenderloin cuts with bernaise sauce or pressed New York Strip in cracked peppercorns and flamed with brandy), seafood (rainbow trout stuffed with wild rice, artichoke and baby shrimp; and broiled jumbo shrimp covered with chutney-curry sauce), chicken in a sour cream and vegetables sauce, wild game (roast duck with raspberry Grand Marnier, roasted quail and venison medallions with fresh mushrooms and scallions) and a dish that I've got to try next time, Mrs. Peck's beef and oyster pie containing a secret sauce. A cognac, liquor or after dinner drink will go well with one of their tortes, concocted of pound cake, fruit fillings, liquors, dark chocolate and nuts; hot fudge cake; turtle sundae; a daily baked cheesecake or apple streudel.

The service at The Peck House is splendid — always there to warm the coffee, fill the water and see to your every need. They take great care of their customers. Softly playing classical music serenades your elegant dining while you peer through a window at a majestic view of the Empire mountain valley that carries over to Georgetown. Although, the best view is from the front porch which is used for dining in the summertime. Much of the furniture dates back to the days of the original owners. A pair of deer racks form bookends over the white-brick fireplace mantel. Farm implements — a pick, hay saw and branding iron — create a homestead feeling to the dining room. Colored lithographs by J. Bien showing mining era scenes and mining machinery from Big Chief Mill and Empire hang from the white walls next to a changing display of contemporary watercolors and historic artwork. Victorian grandeur and gold-mining ruggedness combined with shining service and a luscious cuisine characterize The Peck House.

SPECIAL ONE-TIME OFFER: Buy two entrées at the regular price and receive 20% off the price of a guest room. Advanced room reservations required. Holiday periods excluded. This offer NOT valid in combination with any other offers. Please mention this offer when making room reservation and present to server at time of ordering two entrées. _____ Restaurant Manager/Owner. _____ Date. _____ Innkeeper. _____ Date.

RECIPE

Shrimp Sarah
(Serves 4)

¼ cup sliced mushrooms
3 tablespoons golden raisins
2 heaping teaspoons Major Grey's
  Chutney
¼ tablespoon curry powder
Dash each of cayenne pepper and
  Worcestershire sauce

½ heavy cream
20 large shrimps, shelled and deveined
3 cups cooked long grain and wild rice
  (1 cup uncooked)
A little melted butter, oil or margarine

1. Cook the mushrooms, raisins, chutney, spices, Worcestershire sauce and cream in a small skillet over medium heat for 5 minutes or until thickened.
2. Arrange the shrimp on 4 skewers. Brush the shrimp with a little melted butter, oil or margarine.
3. Broil 4 to 5 inches from the heat for 4 to 5 minutes, turning once or until cooked.
4. Serve on rice with sauce.

The Pecks on the Front Porch of the Peck House in 1880

ESTES PARK

Formerly known as Estes Park Village, the town was named after the first white people to settle the area — Joel and Patsy Estes. Joel discovered this valley on a gold-hunting expedition in 1858, brought his family to a homestead claim in 1859, built a cabin on Fish Creek and stayed until the severe winters convinced him to leave in 1866. In the 1870s, an Irish Nobleman, Lord Dunraven, would pay itinerants — drunks and derelicts from Denver's lower downtown district — to purchase homesteads in the valley (then purchase the 5-acre lots from them) in an attempt to gain control and maintain it as a private hunting preserve. He built a 6,000-acre empire before his neighbors challenged his deeds and forced him to return to England. After the turn of the century, F. O. Stanley used his invention, the Stanley Steamer, to bring guests up the canyon into Estes. He later built his own hotel in 1909. Enos Mills was instrumental in creating Rocky Mountain National Park in 1915, which today, is entered through Estes Park.
Zip Code: 80517. Area Code: 303. Population: 3,184. Elevation: 7,522'.

The Dunraven Inn
2470 Highway 66, 586-6409
Directions: From the intersection of Highways 34 and 36 in Estes Park, go west on Highway 36 for .4 miles. Turn left at the 2nd signal. Stay on Highway 36 for 3.3 miles (bearing right after ¼ mile). Turn left onto Highway 66. Go 1.4 miles. The restaurant is on the right.

ESSENTIALS
Cuisine: Italian
Hours: 7 days 5PM-10PM (11PM Fri/Sat)
Meals and Prices: Dinner $$-$$$
Nonsmoking: No, but smoke-eater on premises
Take-out: Yes

Alcohol: Full Bar
Credit Cards: MC, Visa, Amx, Disc
Personal Check: In-state with I.D.
Reservations: Highly recommended JUN-SEP, recommended otherwise
Wheelchair Access: Yes

HISTORY, PERSONALITY AND CHARACTER
The Dunraven Inn was built circa 1920 and is located at the original entrance to Rocky Mountain National Park. The building has a storied past having existed as a house, lodge, boarding house and Mexican restaurant before The Dunraven Inn opened in 1976. Dale Hatcher, who's been in the restaurant business off and on since 1974 and previously managed Crawdaddy's Restaurant in Tampa Bay, Florida, took over in September 1994. He manages a staff of long-term employees and is the head chef as well.

FOOD, SERVICE AND AMBIANCE

I savored a cup of their homemade Caribbean black bean soup prepared with carrots, celery and tomato and topped with a dollop of sour cream to sweeten and cool the palate. This was followed by one of their more popular entrées, shrimp Da Vinci — tender, tasty shrimp with capers and vegetables, sautéed and simmered to bring out the flavors, on top of al dente spaghetti. It was scrumptious! A delicious mini-loaf of garlic bread with oregano was served hot and stayed hot in aluminum foil. You can substitute plain Italian bread. For dessert, I found the amaretto ice cream to be an irresistibly rare treat.

You can start your meal with an appetizer of cold or hot antipasto, sausage and peppers, liver pâté or shrimp scampi. If you elect to go with salad instead of soup, you can have one of their homemade dressings: Italian vinaigrette or creamy garlic. All of their sauces are New York City recipes and are made in-house as well. Highlighting the pasta dishes are spaghetti with homemade meatballs or sausage, three-cheese ziti, manicotti filled with seasoned cheese, ravioli stuffed with ricotta cheese, cannelloni filled with meat and spinach, lasagna and linguini with white clam sauce. The house specialties include shrimp in a basil-marinara sauce; chicken cacciatora; veal, eggplant or shrimp parmigiana, lobster, charbroiled sirloin, lemon sole almondine and sole Newburg. Select a bottle of wine from their very reasonably priced wine list, mostly in the teens and mostly from Italy or California, to sparkle your dining experience. There is a children's menu. You can complete your evening with a delectable dessert like spumoni, canoli filled with sweet ricotta cheese and chocolate chips, tiramisu, chocolate suicide cake, cheesecake, raspberry sorbet or a chocolate sundae.

I was served by a very personable, courteous and helpful gentleman. Orchestrated classical and operatic music played in the restaurant. There are two distinguishing elements of decor at The Dunraven Inn. The first is the literally thousands of one-dollar bills, signed by the people who have dined here and pinned to the walls of the entrance and lounge — sort of the same fashion style that Beau Jo's Restaurants have with autographed napkins, only this has monetary value. The second notable feature is the pictures of Mona Lisa — over 20, from enlarged to snap shot size, some in gold frames, some in black frames, with or without borders — that adorn the second-hand barn wood walls of the dining room. Additional rustic charm is created by old world maps, exposed sections of the red brick inner wall, a wine shelf, fireplace with black-iron hood, red curtains and a stucco ceiling with wood beams. The Dunraven Inn offers authentic Italian cuisine in a romantic, dimly-lit atmosphere that lets you capture a piece of "The Rome of the Rockies".

ESTES PARK

SPECIAL ONE-TIME OFFER: Buy one entrée at the regular price and receive a complimentary dessert. Limit 2 complimentary desserts with the purchase of 2 entrées. This offer NOT valid in combination with any other offers. Please present to server at time of ordering. _____ Manager/Owner. _____ Date.

RECIPE

Eggplant Soup

4 tablespoons extra virgin olive oil
1 clove garlic, peeled and diced
2 medium red onions, peeled and diced
3 tablespoons flour
1 large eggplant, peeled and chopped
⅓ cup parsley, chopped

¼ cup oregano, chopped
4 to 5 ounces sundried tomatoes
Salt and pepper to taste
Dash chopped cilantro
4 to 5 cups of stock
Grated Parmesan cheese

1. In a large sauce pan, heat the oil. Cook the garlic and onion until translucent.
2. Stir in the flour and over gentle heat, cook the mixture for a few minutes. To the contents of the sauce pan, add the eggplant, stock, tomatoes and seasoning.
3. Bring the liquid to a boil; reduce the heat and simmer the eggplant, covered, for 30 minutes.
4. Season the soup to your taste. Serve it hot and offer the Parmesan cheese to top the soup.

This soup can be made with either a chicken, beef or veal stock. My customers prefer chicken and this is the stock I use most of the time. This recipe has been modified and updated from an old, untitled cookbook I bought at a garage sale in Key West, Florida.

Dale Hatcher

Restaurants from 101 Colorado Small Towns is an ideal companion to Colorado Restaurants and Recipes and will expand your selection of restaurants to visit in the state.

EVERGREEN

Formerly called The Post, after Amos F. Post, the son-in-law of Thomas Bergen who first settled nearby Bergen Park, the name was changed to Evergreen by D. P. Wilmot in honor of the huge evergreen trees in the area. Ute Indians used to camp along nearby Soda Creek. Evergreen has had a varied history of trappers, traders, gold miners, ranchers and lumberjacks.

Zip Code: 80439. Area Code: 303. Population: 4,500. Elevation: 7,040'.

The River Sage Restaurant
4651 South Highway 73, #103, 674-2914

Directions: Take Exit 252, for El Rancho, from I-70 and follow Highway 74 south for 8 miles into Evergreen. The restaurant will be on your right where Highway 74 intersects with Highway 73. Parking for the restaurant is on both Highways 74 and 73.

ESSENTIALS

Cuisine: Rocky Mountain/Caribbean

Hours: 7 days 7AM-9PM (9:30PM on Fri/Sat). Breakfast 7AM-11AM, Lunch 11AM-5PM, Dinner 5PM-9PM (9:30PM on Fri/Sat), Breakfast with Brunch on Sat/Sun 7:30AM-2PM.

Meals and Prices: Breakfast $-$$, Lunch/Brunch $$, Dinner $$-$$$

Nonsmoking: Smoking only permitted on streamside deck

Take-out: Yes

Alcohol: Beer and wine

Credit Cards: MC, Visa, Amx

Personal Check: Yes

Reservations: Suggested for Fri/Sat night or groups over 6. Accepted otherwise.

Wheelchair Access: Yes

Other: Outside catering available. No separate banquet room, but they will try to accommodate special events.

HISTORY, PERSONALITY AND CHARACTER

The River Sage occupies what used to be two separate buildings constructed in 1890 as the Liston Lodge and a lumberyard. The buildings were joined together in 1982, remodeled and used for a hobby shop. In June 1985, Alan and Vanessa Werthan leased the property and opened The River Sage. The initial restaurant only comprised the current large dining room and a small kitchen. The River Sage has expanded 4 times since its beginning, expanding the kitchen, adding a prep kitchen, a walk-in refrigerator, a second dining room, an entrance room and a streamside patio which was later expanded. Alan grew up in the restaurant business and started catering at the age of 14. He managed a Harvest Restaurant in Denver for 4 years before coming to Evergreen. The kitchen crew consists of Jim Carlson, their baker since 1988 who prepares all the rolls, breads and desserts; Ricky Seepaul from the Island of Trinidad who brought all the island grill recipes and Glenda Buchannan who develops original recipes for soups, salads, marinades, dressings, seasonings and spiced blends.

The River Sage not only has a history, it also has a dream. There is a legend of an old wise man who lived long ago on the banks of Bear Creek. He lived a reverent, harmonious life, respected the wisdom and balance of nature and appreciated the gift of life. His life reflected the tranquility and gentle energy of the water by which he lived and he became known as the River Sage. The dream behind this restaurant is to pass on some of the wisdom and inspiration of the Old River Sage by providing nourishment for both body and spirit.

FOOD, SERVICE AND AMBIANCE

I've dined here twice for dinner, once alone and once with a group of 8 including 2 children. On the two visits combined, with some sharing, I managed to try 3 seafood selections (mesquite yellow fin tuna, mesquite marlin with sage and shrimp and salmon Alfredo), 2 beef entrées (beef sirloin and chopped buffalo) and 2 chicken choices (marinated and grilled jerk chicken breast and chicken parmesan). The tuna, in a dill butter sauce, was mild, tender and cooked medium rare. It was a delicious meal served with baked potato and fresh vegetables. The marlin was firm and savory with melted dill butter. The Alfredo, with fettuccine and onions in a parmesan garlic cream sauce, was thin and light as opposed to rich and heavy. The buffalo, grilled in a mixture of Caribbean spices with green peppers and onions, and accompanied by green chilies on the side was a tasty dish next to real mashed potatoes with black pepper in a brown sauce. The grilled sirloin was plain, tender and flavorful. The jerk chicken was zesty with chilies and spices from Trinidad. The chicken parmesan, covered with marinara and mozzarella, was mouth-watering. I especially liked the curry vegetables — spicy green peppers, carrots, squash and onion — that come with the island grill recipes (the beef, buffalo and jerk chicken). For dessert, we tried four of their scrumptious homemade concoctions: chocolate buttermilk cake with ¼-inch deep, rich chocolate frosting; a thick peanut butter mousse topped with chocolate and whipped cream; strawberry cheesecake in a graham cracker crust with fresh strawberries; and blueberry tofu cheesecake made without wheat, milk or eggs and rice syrup substituted for sugar. Their out-of-house desserts, pecan and apple caramel Granny Smith pies, were delectable as well. Other homemade desserts that evening were chocolate tofu mousse, walnut baklava and blueberry pie.

For appetizers, we whet our appetites with appetizing stuffed mushrooms sautéed in soy sauce and sherry and gado gado — steamed vegetables with spicy hot Indonesian peanut dip. All their soups, breads, sauces, house dressing and desserts are homemade. The corn chowder bisque came in a crock bowl, was thick, creamy, lightly seasoned, and served with corn bread. The tomato and rice with garbanzo and kidney beans was not spicy while the Indian split pea with curry was toothsome and mildly spicy. Lemon tahini is the house dressing. They also have balsamic vinaigrette, creamy cucumber and honey-mustard.

The weekend brunch specials feature eggs Benedict or Florentine, seafood crêpes and a fresh trout and eggs platter. Their regular breakfast menu is most innovative offering turkey sausage; Cajun sausage and vegetarian Cajun skillets; an assortment of whole grain buttermilk pancakes (with nuts and fruits), omelets (that include seafood or bison) and scrambles; and healthy, low cholesterol, lower fat, low salt and no sugar choices. Their lunch menu is no less innovative or extensive. Their sandwiches, served closed or "bubbly" style (open faced with broiled cheeses) include cream spinach and mushrooms, turkey with roasted cashews and raisins, and roast chicken chunks with toasted almonds. They have lunch specialties like spinach or seafood lasagna, spanikopita Indian vegetable curry and Indonesian vegetable wok; a variety of soups and salads; Chef Ricky's Trinidad recipes prepared streamside and an assortment of southwestern specialties from buffalo burrito to tempeh sauté. The dinner highlights include fresh seafood (seafood lasagna or fettuccine, blackened red snapper or Cajun blackened trout), vegetable creations like vegetarian Alfredo and oriental 9 vegetable wok, Ricky's Trinidad recipes using seafood, beef chicken or vegetables, and chicken specialties (Tahitian, blackened Cajun, Indonesian, tandoor, Alfredo or Baja style). If you have room for dessert, you can choose from a flan, mocha custard pie, white raspberry chocolate swirl cheesecake or carrot cake. They serve espresso, cappuccino and latte. There is a children's menu.

Service was very friendly, helpful, courteous and relaxed. If you make reservations for a large group on a Saturday night, like us, you should expect a bit of a wait for your meals, which is understandable. They played new age music inside while on the streamside patio, they were setting up for live ragae music. The patio is connected to Highway 74 by a foot bridge and features lit torches that lean over Bear Creek, green-striped awnings to go with green-checkered table cloths and a grill. Inside, impressive wood carvings by Matthew Mazarin portray faces in logs like an Indian woman wearing feathers. A color crayon picture of the "Land of Puff, the Magic Dragon", amethyst in a hollowed out lava log, and a lithograph of a bald eagle are a few of the unusual adornments that embellish this unique restaurant. Idyllically situated on Bear Creek, The River Sage Restaurant carries a romantic spirit to your table.

SPECIAL ONE-TIME OFFER: Buy one entrée at the regular price and receive 50% off a second entrée of equal or lesser value (maximum discount $7.50). This offer NOT valid in combination with any other offers. Please present to server at time of ordering. _____ Manager/Owner. _____ Date.

RECIPE

White Chocolate Raspberry Cheesecake

Basic Filling:
- 1½ pounds cream cheese
- 1 cup ricotta cheese
- 1 cup yogurt or sour cream
- ⅔ cup turbinato sugar
- 4 eggs
- 1 teaspoon vanilla
- ¼ teaspoon salt

Crust:
- 1½ cups crushed graham crackers
- ¼ cup butter softened
- 1 tablespoon whole wheat pastry flour
- 1 tablespoon honey

Additions:
- ½ cup raspberry melba
- 6 ounces white chocolate, melted

1. Crust: Combine all ingredients until fine and crumbly. Press into a 10-inch springform pan.
2. Filling: Whip cream cheese until light and fluffy and add ricotta and sour cream. Add sugar mix until smooth. Add eggs, vanilla and salt. Remove ½ cup filling and mix with raspberry melba sauce. Melt 6 ounces white chocolate and add to the rest of filling and pour in pan. Swirl in raspberry filling. Bake for 40 minutes at 350 degrees.

The Old River Sage

FORT GARLAND

Fort Garland, Colorado's first military post, was named after John Garland, commander of the military district when the post was founded in 1858. Kit Carson was commander here from 1866 to 1867. The post was abandoned in 1883, but the settlement that had grown around it retained the name.

Zip Code: 81133. Area Code: 719. Population: 350. Elevation: 7,932'.

Mt. Blanca Supper Club
Highway 160, 379-2555

Directions: On the southside of Highway 160 at the west end of town. From Highway 17 and Highway 160 in Alamosa, go 24.0 miles east on Highway 160. The restaurant is on the south (right).

ESSENTIALS

Cuisine: Steak, Seafood and New Mexican

Hours: Sun 11AM-10PM, Tue-Sat 4PM-10PM, closed Mon

Meals and Prices: Lunch $, Dinner $$

Nonsmoking: No

Take-out: Yes

Alcohol: Full Bar

Credit Cards: MC, Visa, Disc

Personal Check: Yes, with I.D.

Reservations: Accepted. Recommended for Friday or Saturday dinner in the summer.

Wheelchair Access: Yes

Other: Catering. Meeting room behind main dining room for banquets, wedding receptions.

HISTORY, PERSONALITY AND CHARACTER

Robert and Freda Vasquez opened the Mt. Blanca Supper Club in December 1993, the first New Mexican restaurant to occupy the premises. The building itself dates back to the late 1940s and was originally just a bar owned by a man named Cannon. The second owner was a gentleman named Klockenbrink who turned the bar into a steak place for a few years in the mid-50s. He was followed by Jim and Shirley Washington, owners from about 1957 to 1990. They operated a steak and seafood restaurant. Fred Maes took over in 1990 (another steak joint) followed by a man named Johnson and a few other owners before the Vasquezes purchased the restaurant from German owners. Robert operates the restaurant and prepares all the New Mexican cuisine while Freda lives and works in Albuquerque, New Mexico. This is their first restaurant. Robert is retired from the Sandia National Laboratories. When he wasn't busy with nuclear tests at the laboratories, he developed a few of his own award-winning chili recipes. He has worked the chili cookout circuit since 1983 and earned several awards: 9 blue ribbons and one 2nd place at the 1987 Hatch (New Mexico) Chili Festival over Labor Day Weekend and best of show and grand prize for red and green chilies at the 1987 New Mexico State

Fair. Robert was born and raised in Fort Garland, lived most of his adult life in Albuquerque, then retired back in his home town.

FOOD, SERVICE AND AMBIANCE

I went with a winner for dinner — the Carne Adovada Burrito: blue ribbon and best of show at the New Mexico State Fair and blue ribbon at the Hatch Chili Festival (chili capital of the world). The recipe has also appeared in the book, "America's Best Recipes". The flour tortilla and red or green chili are homemade. The beef or pork (I was served pork without being asked which I preferred) is marinated in red chili before being topped with your choice of chili , lettuce, tomatoes, onions and cheese. The dish comes with authentic tasting refried beans with melted cheese, Spanish rice made with homemade tomato sauce and sopapilla or flour tortilla (my waitress guessed right again and brought me the tortilla). The folks down in New Mexico considered this to be the best and I, for one, would not argue. All their chilies come from Hatch, New Mexico. The green chili will help to open up that stuffy nose. They also make their own salsa and chips which are served at your table after you order your meal. If you opt for the surf or turf, you have prime rib, filet mignon, T-bone, Cajun catfish, deep-fried shrimp, crab legs and lobster to choose from. They also offer chicken fried steak, fried chicken, roast beef, pork chops and a tortilla burger. If you arrive for lunch in the summertime, you can order one of the homemade pizzas, burgers or sandwiches.

This is another one of those restaurants on the main highway that if you judge the quality of the food by the appearance of the building, you are going to miss out! The interior has all been remodeled since Robert took over to give the place a New Mexican look. He has put in stucco walls and ceilings, Spanish archways, colorful (red, pink, blue, green, tan and beige) tablecloths and a few paintings of desert scenes, pheasants and a mountain mine. The floors are hardwood. The bar and lounge (including a juke box) are in the front of the building. The entrance to the main dining room is to the rear. The meeting room is behind the dining room. They do not play any music, but occasionally have live music (Mexican or country western) on Friday or Saturday evening or on holidays.

SPECIAL ONE-TIME OFFER: Buy one entrée at the regular price and receive 50% off a second entrée of equal or lesser value (up to $5.00 value). This offer NOT valid in combination with any other offers. _____ Manager/Owner. _____ Date.

<u>RECIPE</u>

Carne Adovada Burrito Casserole
(Serves 8 to 10)

Carne:
  10 pods red chile
  1 cup water
  Onion, garlic, salt to taste
  5 pounds lean pork

Tortillas:
  1½ cups white flour
  ½ teaspoon baking powder
  ⅛ teaspoon salt
  1 tablespoon (heaping) unmelted lard
  ½ cup water

Green Chile Salsa:
  Lean pork (remaining third of
    5 pounds)
  2 tablespoons white flour
  3 tablespoons meat drippings
  14 pods green chile, cooked,
    peeled and chopped
  1½ cups water
  ¼ teaspoon monosodium glutamate
    (MSG)
  Garlic salt to taste
  Salt to taste
  1 pound cheddar cheese,
    grated lettuce, tomato and onions

1. Carne: In a blender or by hand, mix the red chile pods, water, MSG and garlic salt to make a medium paste. Prepare ⅔ of the meat by slicing very thinly (easier if meat is partially frozen). Save the remainder of the meat for green chile salsa. Marinate the sliced pork in red chile sauce at least 2 hours. In a frying pan, cook the marinated meat slowly, being careful not to scorch. Do not simmer, but cook until liquid has evaporated and meat is well done. Allow to cool before burritos are prepared.

2. Tortillas: Mix the flour, baking powder, salt, lard and water into dough. If the dough is sticky, add extra flour, 1 teaspoon at a time, until smooth. Let stand for 5 minutes. Separate and form into a dozen small balls. Roll out into round tortillas and fry on an unoiled iron skillet or griddle on high heat until lightly browned. Turn and brown on other side. Cool.

3. Salsa: Cube the meat and fry in a medium-size pan without oil. When the meat is brown, push to one side of the pan and brown the flour in the drippings, being careful not to burn the flour. When browned, mix in the meat, chile and water (do not make too thin). Bring to a boil and add garlic salt and salt to taste. Lower heat and simmer for 15-20 minutes.

4. Casserole: Spread the cool carne adovada over the cool tortilla. Fold the ends of the tortilla in on four opposite sides and then fold in the middle (to keep the meat from spilling out). Place side by side in a large pan. Sprinkle 1 pound grated cheese over burritos and place in oven preheated to 350 degrees, long enough for the cheese to start melting. Pour green chile sauce over the top and serve immediately, before the tortillas get soggy. Garnish with chopped tomatoes, shredded lettuce and chopped onions, if desired.

FRISCO

A Swedish emigrant, Henry A. Recen, built the town's first log cabin in 1871 and four years later the townsite was named "Frisco City" by an old Indian scout named Henry Learned. Learned also discovered the Kitty Innes Mines in 1878. In its early days, Frisco was known for its dance halls and saloons. Today, it is the center of Summit County with easy access to several surrounding ski areas.
Zip Code: 80443. Area Code: 970 Population: 1,601. Elevation: 9,050'.

Blue Spruce Inn
20 Main St, PO Box 269, 668-5900
Directions: Take Exit 201 from I-70. Proceed east on Main Street for ½ mile to the first 4-way stop. Turn right on Madison, then an immediate left into the restaurant parking lot. From Highway 9, go west on Main Street for ½ mile to the second 4-way stop. Turn left on Madison, then an immediate left into the restaurant parking lot.

ESSENTIALS:

Cuisine: Continental
Hours: Year-around: 7 nights 5PM-10PM. Memorial Day Weekend to Mid-OCT: Sun 9AM-1:30PM.
Meals and Prices: Brunch $$-$$$ Dinner $$$$-$$$$$
Nonsmoking: All. Smoking only permitted in lounge upstairs.
Take-out: Yes

Alcohol: Full Bar
Credit Cards: All 5
Personal Check: Yes, with I.D.
Reservations: Recommended
Wheelchair Access: Yes
Dress: Casual
Other: Catering available for parties up to 1,000: special parties, wedding receptions, business open houses.

HISTORY, PERSONALITY AND CHARACTER

The Blue Spruce Inn has always been called the Blue Spruce Inn since it was built in 1947, but it has occupied three different locations in its lifetime. It originated as an inn and restaurant in the Old Town of Dillon (now occupied by Dillon Reservoir). In 1961, when the Dillon Dam was built, it was moved to Highway 9 and Main Street where it existed as a roadside cafe. In 1966, it was moved to its current location where it stands as the finest dining establishment in Frisco. The restaurant has been owned and operated by Annie and Travis Holton since 1986. They also own Pug Ryan's and the Corona St. Grill in Dillon. Travis has been in the restaurant business since 1970 and used to manage The Historic Mint in Silverthorne and restaurants in Vail. Meade Parks has been the manager at the Blue Spruce Inn since 1991. Prior to moving to Colorado, Meade was a head waiter at the Maison et Jardin Restaurant in Orlando, Florida, from 1984 to 1988. Pat Sullivan, who has been cooking since 1980 and graduated from the Culinary Institute of America in Hyde Park, New York, has been the chef at the Blue Spruce Inn since 1990. He trained at Martha's Vineyard, an island off the Massachusetts coast.

FOOD, SERVICE AND AMBIANCE

I dined here on two occasions and tried both their seafood and steak. On my first visit, I selected the seafood special: salmon with shrimp, spinach and Parmesan, topped with lemon beurre blanc, a dish that was simply wonderful. I decided to give their meats a try on my second visit and ordered the stuffed New York: aged beef stuffed with roasted garlic, black peppers and bleu cheese with a green peppercorn cognac demi-glace. I'm a big pepper steak fan and the roasted garlic and bleu cheese just made it that much better. You can't go wrong with either of these two selections, or with any other entrée on their menu, for that matter. Dinners include homemade bread, like a warm, freshly baked demi-loaf (double thickness) of whole wheat sesame seed bread, and soup or salad. I've had their cream of broccoli with smoked jalapeño cheese and vegetable beef with pasta (beef chunks, square dumplings, fresh stewed tomatoes, mushrooms and onions. The chef calls it Hungarian beef stew). They were both delicious. Entrées also include long-grain wild rice, baked or new potatoes and seasonal vegetables. They also have Nilgai antelope (a native to the foothills of the Himalayan Mountains) and wild lamb from Corsican Mouflon sheep and Iranian Red Sheep. These are raised and harvested on the Broken Arrow Ranch in South Texas.

If you are in the area in the summer or early fall, you may want to stop in for Sunday brunch. They have several entrées that sure look appealing to me: a southwestern frittata — green chilies, sundried tomatoes and scallions baked with eggs and cheese; scrambled eggs with cilantro, sour cream and green chili salsa; and leg of lamb with pesto served with green peppercorn demi-glaze. For you eggs Benedict fans, they have an orange hollandaise and serve a couple of special Benedicts: one with crabmeat, almonds and spinach, the other with filet mignon topped with sundried tomato hollandaise.

Moving on to dinner, they have some appetizers that sound terrific: red trout (raised on a Rocky Mountain farm) that is smoked at Pug Ryan's, quail marinated in a Thai chili sauce, and crab-stuffed artichokes. Chef Sullivan's dinner entrées offer variety and taste: vegetarian pasta; roast duckling; roasted chicken breast rolled with spinach, bacon, and provolone cheese; pork tenderloin amaretto; lamb chops baked with pesto and bread crumbs; prime rib; veal scallopine and seafood. Their homemade desserts vary, but may include sundried cherry bread pudding with chantilly sauce, a no-flour chocolate torte (similar to fudge) with caramel sauce, blueberry cobbler and marble cheesecake. They have about 100 wines on their wine list mostly from California.

Service was top notch on both occasions, offering plenty of advice and information. Their whole staff is very efficient and relaxed, which made me feel comfortable and welcome. Soft, light, easy jazz seems to be what they like to play the most. Walls made of full-length pinewood logs, a rock fireplace with a deer head mounted over the mantel, and brass, hexagonal wall and ceiling lamps with yellow-tinted glass provide the mood, and look, of an old log cabin home. A painting by Peggy Ramsey next to the host's station is a good representation of the Blue Spruce. The

FRISCO

downstairs dining area is decorated with framed posters of Cakebread (wine) Cellars in California, Panoramic Arch in Arches National Park, Utah, a pair of skiers in Megeve, France in 1938, a blue wing teal duck and Chateau St. Jean. The upstairs has been remodeled to provide more space and more of an open-look and feel. Overhead, there are three skylights and wood beams that support an old toboggan, snowshoes, ice skates and original skis used by the 10th Mountain Division out of Leadville (they were trained mountain fighters in World War II). Next to the lounge is an interesting computer-generated map of the Rockies, high plains and intermountain west. A romantic, enchanting evening awaits you when you dine at the Blue Spruce Inn.

SPECIAL ONE-TIME OFFER: Buy one entrée at the regular price and receive a second entrée of equal or lesser value FREE (up to $19.95 value) OR 50% off a single entrée (maximum discount $10.00). This offer ONLY VALID from MAY through OCT. NOT valid from NOV through APR or in combination with any other offers. From NOV through APR, receive 20% off your total food bill (not including beverages).
_____ Manager/Owner. _____ Date.

RECIPE

Lamb Chops Blue Spruce
(Serves 6 to 8)

16 to 20 lamb chops, 2-3 ounces each
Salt and pepper
¼ cup olive oil
Seasoned bread crumbs
2 cups demi-glace (brown sauce)

Pesto:
½ cup pine nuts
½ cup fresh basil
½ cup chopped garlic
¼ cup olive oil
½ cup Parmesan cheese

1. Season lamb chops with salt and pepper.
2. Heat a large sauté pan with ¼ cup olive oil.
3. Sear lamb chops on both sides for 1 minute. Cool.
4. For the pesto, grind basil and garlic in a food processor. Add pine nuts and Parmesan cheese. Finish with olive oil.
5. Smear 1 teaspoon of pesto on each side of lamb chops, then cover each side with seasoned bread crumbs.
6. Bake in a 375-degree oven for 20 to 25 minutes (35 for well-done chops).
7. Heat demi-glace sauce. Serve chops on top of pool of sauce.
8. A fine bottle of Pinot Noir or Merlot complements this item nicely.

Charity's

307 Main Street, 668-3644

Directions: From the East on I-70, take Exit 203 and head south on Highway 9. Go 1.0 mile and turn right onto Main Street. Go three blocks to the stop sign at 4th Street. The restaurant will be in the next block on the right. From the West on I-70, take Exit 201 heading east on Main Street. Go .7 miles. The restaurant will be on your left just past 3rd Street. From the South on Highway 9, turn left onto Main Street. Go three blocks to the stop sign at 4th Street. The restaurant will be in the next block on the right.

ESSENTIALS

Cuisine: American with an Italian flair.

Hours: 7 days 11:30AM-10PM: lunch 11:30AM-3PM, dinner 5PM-10PM, Mid-day appetizer menu FROM 3PM-5PM.

Meals and Prices: Lunch $$, Dinner $$-$$$

Nonsmoking: Yes. Smoking limited to bar and lounge upstairs.

Take-out: Yes

Alcohol: Full Bar

Credit Cards: MC, Visa, Amx

Personal Check: Local with I.D.

Reservations: Not accepted unless a party of 10 or more.

Wheelchair Access: Yes, but for the bar/lounge area only.

Other: Additional 15% service charge for parties of 5 or more. No separate checks.

HISTORY PERSONALITY AND CHARACTER

The site that Charity's Restaurant occupies has a long, active and colorful history. Back in the 1880s, this was the site for Morrow's Saloon, located in the heart of Frisco's red light district. It was here, on October 20, 1881, that Frisco's "most vile crime" occurred. English saloon keeper James McWalters was murdered by Irish railroad workers. The Irish jury declared the action justifiable homicide after they observed the knifed and bludgeoned body laid before them on the courtroom floor for three days. About a half century later, Kenneth and Betty Chamberlain built the Frisco Cafe and Garage on this same site. It was the town's social gathering place in the 1920s and 1930s. A fire consumed the wooden frame building in 1942, but a year later a Texaco gas station was built in its place and it served the community for 40 years. The Chamberlain Family sold the building in 1981 and in 1982, current owners John Tuso and Susie Magrino, opened Charity's. Today, Charity's is listed on the National Register of Historic Places. John and Susie have been in the restaurant business since 1972. They also own Golden Annie's in Frisco and are former owners of Tuso's (from 1976 to 1982) at the B lift in Copper Mountain. Jason Hardwick, the General Manager, hails from Lynchburg, Virginia. He worked with Chilis on the East Coast and then decided to head west and relocate in Colorado. Jason Brown, who started cooking in 1985, is the head chef and has been with Charity's since 1988.

FRISCO

FOOD, SERVICE AND AMBIANCE

I had a tasty, light lunch here that included tomato Florentine soup and grilled shrimp with fresh corn cakes. The soup was thick with noodles, spinach, tomatoes, onions, fresh sage and topped with shredded Parmesan. The shrimp and cakes were topped with a cayenne/cilantro aioli made with mayonnaise. It was very mild, unless you had some on the side for dipping. Then, it had some "zip". The thin cakes were made from flour, eggs, chopped spinach, parsley and corn. They also make their own soup, sauces and dressings, like olive oil and gorgonzola. You will find a "little Italian touch" (I know what you're thinking. There's no such thing as a little Italian touch) in most of their menu items, like the artichokes hearts Romano and focaccia appetizers, the fresh mozzarella and tomatoes salad, the burgers with gorgonzola cheese or the sandwiches made with focaccia bread. A beef stew and tuscan bean and chicken stew are also popular entrées. The dinner menu adds on where the lunch menu leaves off with seafood pasta, peppered and seared tuna, grilled New York strip or pork chop, a mustard glazed salmon, pan-fried trout, and pine nut crusted chicken with a pesto cream sauce. There is a children's menu and desserts include flourless amaretto truffle torte, brownie sundae and New York cheesecake. The wine list is strictly American, mostly from California.

Service was attentive and friendly. Heads of deer, buffalo, elk and big horn sheep adorn the walls of this historic building with its vaulted ceiling, sun-roof dining area and rock, wood-burning fireplace. The back bar features some stenciled mirrors in arched-shaped fixtures. The airways were filled with medium-loud blues and rock music. Charity's is a fun and lively place to dine.

SPECIAL ONE-TIME OFFER: Buy 2 entrées at the regular price and receive a complimentary appetizer. This offer NOT valid in combination with any other offers. _____ Manager/Owner. _____ Date.

Reading the introduction to this book will enhance your understanding
of this guide and may answer questions that you have.

RECIPE

Charity's Hot Crab Dip

3 8-ounce packages cream cheese   1½ tablespoon lemon juice
1½ teaspoon Worcestershire   ½ cup chopped onion
¼ cup sherry   ½ cup chopped walnuts
½ cup chopped fresh spinach   ¼ teaspoon cayenne
8 ounce lump crabmeat   Dash tabasco

1. Sauté onion in 2 tablespoon butter.
2. Combine with all other ingredients. Mix well.
3. Place in baking dish. Top with ½ cup grated asiago cheese (or Parmesan).
4. Bake at 350 degrees for 20 minutes.

The Happy Cooker in Georgetown

GEORGETOWN

Georgetown was named after George Griffith, who, with his brother David, discovered gold here in 1859. Despite the discovery of gold, silver mining became the true source of wealth in the 1870s and 1880s. Georgetown, which become known as the "Silver Queen of the Rockies", and nearby Silver Plume, 2.1 miles away and 638 feet higher, became centers of Colorado's mining boom. To overcome the 6 percent grade between the two towns, Union Pacific engineer Robert Blickensderfer designed a circuitous route covering 4.47 miles, but with only a 3.5 percent grade. Today this stretch of railroad track is known as the Georgetown Loop and is open to the public. With the establishment of the gold standard in 1893, the value of silver plummeted and Georgetown dwindled. In 1966, the Georgetown/Silver Plume Mining Area was declared a National Historic Landmark District.
Zip Code: 80444. Area 303. Population: 891. Elevation: 8,512'.

The Happy Cooker
412 Sixth Street, 569-3166
Directions: From I-70, take exit 228. Go east (to the left if you are coming from Denver, to the right if you are coming from the mountains) to the stop sign. Turn right onto Argentine Street, go .6 miles, turn left onto Sixth Street, go three blocks. The restaurant is on your left at the corner of Taos.

ESSENTIALS
Cuisine: American/Continental
Hours: Mon-Fri 8AM-4PM. Sat/Sun 8AM-6PM (7PM from Memorial Day to Mid-OCT.
Meals and Prices: Breakfast/ Lunch $-$$
Nonsmoking: All
Take-out: Yes

Alcohol: Beer, wine and limited bar.
Credit Cards: MC, Visa
Personal Check: No
Reservations: Not required except for large parties over 20.
Wheelchair Access: Yes
Dress: Casual, T-shirts and shorts in the summer.

HISTORY, PERSONALITY AND CHARACTER
The Happy Cooker opened in 1974 in Taos Square, one block south of its present location. In 1976, it was purchased by Marilyn Pagano whose son, Shawn, waited on my table. In 1980, Ginny Fountain purchased the restaurant from Marilyn and in June 1987, she moved to her current location, a house built in the early 1900s. It was used as an antique shop during the 1970s before becoming The Happy Cooker. Dexter, Ginny's husband, does some of the cooking at the Happy Cooker and has created recipes for their new 1995 menu. He also caters and bakes at the bakery that he and Ginny own in Georgetown, The Rose St. Bakery.

FOOD, SERVICE AND AMBIANCE

I like coming to The Happy Cooker for its good homemade food, fresh ingredients and reasonable portions and prices. It is also an exceptionally clean restaurant. They came out with a new menu in the summer of 1995, after my visits but before this book went to press, so while the menu items may have changed, you should still expect the same high-quality food. I tried their light and different chipped beef and artichoke crêpe for breakfast, which you can still order as a European waffle; the shrimp and seafood crêpe in sherry wine sauce was also a savory delight; the vegetarian lasagna with spinach, broccoli and carrots layered in lasagna pasta noodles with ricotta and mozzarella cheeses and onion was lightly browned on top, without sauce and tasted homemade. Their homemade vegetable beef soup had plenty of ground beef, onion, broccoli, carrots, celery, red peppers, lima beans and cabbage in a beefy broth. It was very tasty and hearty.

The Happy Cooker is a great place to stop for breakfast or brunch on your way up to the mountains. Pick up energy for the day from a Belgian waffle, breakfast burrito, French toast made with French bread (a genuine idea!), quiche, chicken à la king with crunchy almonds or a fresh pastry from their Rose Street Bakery. If you arrive for lunch, plan on delving into some homemade soup, chili or vegetarian chili to go with homemade cheese caraway or fat-free yogurt dill bread; a host of salad selections from chicken Caesar to tuna and mostaccioli; a vegetarian burrito; a chicken or tuna croissant; a deli sandwich or a hot vegetarian pita. For dessert, partake a piece of fresh, homemade pie like apple or pecan. Whatever you decide, it will be wholesome and delicious.

Shawn was a very helpful and courteous waiter. The "Blue Danube Waltz" and other very relaxing instrumental pieces provided the background music. There are four dining rooms with mauve wallpaper and ceilings separated by arched doorways, fresh flowers at every table, and French impressionist paintings which are for sale. They also have a patio for summer dining. The Happy Cooker offers a "touch of class", fine cuisine and friendly service that should not be missed.

SPECIAL ONE-TIME OFFER: Buy one entrée at the regular price and receive a second entrée of equal or lesser value FREE (up to $7.25 value) OR 50% off a single entrée (maximum discount $3.60). This offer NOT valid in combination with any other offers.
_____ Manager/Owner. _____ Date.

<hr>

RECIPE

Tuna and Mostaccioli Salad
(Serves 10)

8 ounces mostaccioli pasta, uncooked
¾ cup water
3 tablespoons olive oil
2 tablespoons balsamic vinegar
1 teaspoon dried whole oregano
¼ teaspoon ground white pepper
⅛ teaspoon salt
1 14-ounce can artichoke hearts,
   drained and quartered

1 9¼-ounce can water-packed tuna,
   drained
2 cups coarsely shredded
   romaine lettuce
12 cherry tomatoes, halved
Red leaf lettuce, optional

1. Cook pasta according to package directions, omitting salt and fat; drain pasta well. Combine water and next 5 ingredients in a small bowl; stir well with a wire whisk.
2. Place pasta in a large bowl. Pour ½ cup vinegar mixture over pasta; toss gently. Add remaining vinegar mixture, artichoke hearts, tuna, lettuce, and tomato; toss gently to coat. Cover and chill.
3. To serve, spoon pasta mixture on individual lettuce-lined salad plates, if desired.

<hr>

Mostaccioli or little mustaches are large, 2-inch long macaroni tubes cut on the diagonal. They have either a ridged or smooth surface. There are several varieties of canned tuna: tuna packed in oil or spring water; chunk or solid pack; light tuna or albacore tuna. Tuna packed in water rather than oil nets a 60 percent savings in calories; that is, it contains 60 calories versus 150 calories per ¼ cup serving.

GLENWOOD SPRINGS

Previously called Defiance, Glenwood Springs was first called Glenwood Hot Springs for the mineral springs in the vicinity, and for Glenwood, Iowa. The Ute Indians were the first people to use the mineral hot springs. Later visitors included Doc Holiday, Kit Carson, Buffalo Bill Cody, President Theodore Roosevelt and Tom Mix. Today, Glenwood Springs is home of the world's largest hot springs pool.
Zip Code: 81601. Area Code: 970. Population: 6,561. Elevation: 5,763'.

Grand Lobby (Hotel Colorado)
526 Pine Street, 81601, 945-6511
Directions: Take Exit 116 from I-70. Go to the signal north of I-70 and turn right onto 6th Street (also Highway 6). Go straight at the next signal. The Hotel Colorado is on your left.

ESSENTIALS
Cuisine: American
Hours: 7 days 7AM-11AM,
11:30AM-2PM and 5:30PM-10PM
Meals and Prices: Breakfast $-$$,
Lunch $$, Dinner $$$$,
Sun Brunch $$$.
Nonsmoking: No
Take-out: Yes
Alcohol: Full Bar

Credit Cards: All Five
Personal Check: In-state with I.D.
Reservations: Recommended during summer and winter
Wheelchair Access: Yes
Dress: Casual to Dressy
Other: Items good for the heart identified on the menu by a ♥.

HISTORY, PERSONALITY AND CHARACTER
The Hotel Colorado was opened on June 10, 1893, by Aspen "Silver King", founder of Glenwood Springs and developer of the world's largest naturally-heated pool, Walter Devereux. Sandstone from the Frying Pan River south of Glenwood and Roman brick were used in its construction. The hotel was modeled after the Villa de Medici in Italy at a cost of $850,000. Over the past century, the Hotel Colorado has housed everyone from presidents and movie stars to gangsters. In 1905, President Theodore Roosevelt stayed here while bear hunting. When the President returned to the hotel empty-handed, the sympathetic maids stitched together a small bear out of scraps of cloth. A reporter coined the phrase "Teddy Bear" and a toy company snatched the idea and began making Teddy Bears. In 1909, the Hotel Colorado hosted President William Howard Taft and treated him to raspberries and mountain trout. Not too surprisingly, the 300+ pound President declined an invitation to dip in the pool. The Unsinkable Molly Brown was another notable guest of the era. During the "Roaring 1920s", the hotel took in many Chicago gangsters such as Bert and Jack Verain, alias Diamond Jack Alterie, and Al Capone. Anxious to please its lodgers (regardless of origin), the hotel provided an

awning from the curb to the hotel's west (or side) entrance so that the infamous characters could enter unseen. In 1926, Tom Mix stayed in the hotel with his cast while filming the movie, "The K&A Train Robbery." In 1977, the Hotel Colorado was officially entered into the National Register of Historic Places. The former Red Garter Room has been recreated into the Palm Court of years past, complete with reopened skylight. The Devereux Room is the formal dining area resplendent of the past.

With such a long and colorful history, it's not too amazing to find numerous "ghost" stories attached to the hotel: reports of cigar smoke in the lobby when no one is smoking, keys or files disappearing then reappearing in the same place that they vanished, a mysterious figure in charcoal gray slacks and a red and white vest, the elevator moving between floors late at night with no one aboard, doors opening and closing for no reason, lights turning on by themselves and lit candles appearing suddenly and burning beyond their life expectancy. Several stories relate to a former chambermaid named Florence who was murdered when she became part of a lovers' triangle, a little girl who is believed to have fallen from one of the balconies while chasing a ball, wallpaper that was inexplicably removed and replaced with another, and a telephone ringing occurrence in 1992 that started throughout the hotel when the concrete floor in the kitchen had to be drilled to install computers. If you dine or stay at the Hotel Colorado, you may experience more than you expect.

FOOD, SERVICE AND AMBIANCE

Linda, my editor, and I took pleasure in sharing the seasonings found in the vegetarian fettuccini and the tastes and textures present in the fish and chips when we dined in the Grand Lobby. The pasta special was highlighted by steamed broccoli and cauliflower, chicken, roasted red pepper, red onion, cilantro, reduced cream and red wine, cayenne pepper and garlic. The haddock was crisp but not heavy on the outside while light and fluffy on the inside. They were served with French fries. Other lunch selections included tortilla soup (Al Capone's favorite), thick and spicy chili, sandwiches (vegetarian, corned beef and pastrami), burgers, chicken, roast beef, turkey and salads. The prominent items on the breakfast menu are fresh fruits, hot oatmeal, granola, baked goods (Danish, croissants, muffins and bagels), Belgian waffles, omelets and specialties like smoked trout, eggs benedict or Teddy's huevos rancheros. Sunday brunch changes weekly, but the following should give you a good feel for what to expect (at least it's more definite than what you can anticipate from those pesky ghosts): raisin bread French toast, cheese blintzes with cherry sauce, a pasta station, hot entrées like hoisin basted roast beef with soy sauce or ginger-baked red snapper and salads such as Mandarin orange cole slaw or smoked capers and onion. Dinner emphasizes seafood, steaks, pasta, fowl and veal: smoked Colorado trout, Teddy's crab cakes and Scandinavian gravlax as appetizers; warm duck or spinach salads; and salmon florentine, veal medallions, Cornish game hen or filet mignon wrapped in pepper bacon for entrées.

Service was suitable and accommodating. New age music played softly in the background. There are actually four dining areas in the Hotel Colorado. The dining room in the lobby serves lunch and dinner from Labor Day to Memorial Day and is adorned with original turn-of-the-century furniture, oak and cherrywood wine cabinets and hutches, glass-topped circular tables with mauve linen, high ceilings with the pipes showing (characteristic throughout the hotel), white brass chandeliers and a wood-burning fireplace with a mural over the mantle. The courtyard cafe outside serves lunch and dinner in the summer on white brass tables and chairs overlooking the Florentine fountain and stone wall across the courtyard. The Devereux Room serves breakfast and banquets while the Palm Court is the bar and game room. You may not have a supernatural experience while you dine in the Hotel Colorado, but it will be enchanting.

SPECIAL ONE-TIME OFFER: Buy one entrée at the regular price and receive 50% off a second entrée of equal or lesser value (up to $12.00 value). This offer NOT valid in combination with any other offers. Offer NOT valid between and including Memorial Day Weekend and Labor Day Weekend. _____ Manager/Owner. _____ Date.

RECIPE

Oriental Pasta Sauce

2½ cups oyster sauce*   ¼ teaspoon cayenne
1¼ cups hoisin sauce*   ½ cup rice wine vinegar*
1¾ cups water   3 tablespoons pickled ginger*
¼ cup sesame oil*   2 tablespoons chopped garlic

1. Combine vinegar, ginger and garlic in blender or food processor. Mix well.
2. Whisk remaining ingredients together with blended mixture.
3. Store covered in refrigerator.

*Available in most oriental markets.

Rivers

2525 South Grand Avenue, 928-8813

Directions: Take Exit 116 from I-70. Go to the signal north of I-70 and turn right onto 6th Street (also Highway 6). Go to the next signal and turn right again onto Highway 82 or Grand Avenue. Go 1.4 miles (you will go over a bridge immediately after turning). Grand Avenue and Highway 82 split just past the Total gas station on your right. Stay to the right (on Grand Avenue) and go ¼ mile from the fork. The restaurant is on the right.

121

GLENWOOD SPRINGS

ESSENTIALS

Cuisine: American
Hours: Memorial Day to Labor Day:
Sun-Thu 11AM-9PM. Fri-Sat 11AM-
10PM. Lunch served until 2PM, Dinner
from 4PM, Bar Menu served all day.
Labor Day to Memorial Day: Sun-Thu
4PM-9PM. Fri-Sat 4PM-10PM. Sun
9AM-2PM.
Meals and Prices: Lunch $$,
Dinner $$$-$$$$
Nonsmoking: All, except the bar area.

Take-out: Yes
Alcohol: Full Bar
Credit Cards: MC, Visa, Amx, Disc
Personal Check: Yes
Reservations: Recommended for
Fri/Sat and the deck in summer.
Accepted otherwise.
Wheelchair Access: Yes
Dress: Casual to Dressy
Other: Additional 15% service charge
for parties of 6 or more.

HISTORY, PERSONALITY AND CHARACTER

Rivers is in a new building that only dates back to the early 1980s. It used to house Penelope's, owned by the same people who own Penelope's in Crested Butte (see page 73). In June 1994, Ben and Desirée Herr, along with Jack Pavell of Aspen, purchased the building and opened Rivers. The Herrs are from San Antonio, Texas, and also own the Cliff House on top of Tiehack (formerly Buttermilk) Mountain in Aspen. They have a most reliable and pleasant young lady named Katie O'Connell as their general manager. Head chef Michael Schlichel started working in restaurants at the age of 12 along the Jersey coast near his home. After attending Johnson and Wales Culinary Institute in Providence, Rhode Island, he set out for Aspen. Michael has been cooking and managing kitchens in the Roaring Fork Valley for the past 12 years.

FOOD, SERVICE AND AMBIANCE

It is fun to try something different sometimes that requires a little bit of work. It had been a few years since I "tackled" a whole lobster at the dinner table, and at a market price of $21.95, I could not resist the temptation. The live Maine lobster is prepared with new red potatoes, little neck clams and corn on the cob. They are all placed together in a net and boiled (I watched Chef Michael remove one of these steamer bags later in the kitchen). While it could not compare with the intoxicating experiences I remember on a trip through New England (quite a few more years ago), it was fun to put the "nutcracker and tiny fork" back to work! The dinner comes with a house salad with their own lemon tarragon vinaigrette dressing created by Richard and Rosemary Berkholder, Rivers' original chef, and a warm loaf of homemade white bread. The lobster, a special only offered on Tuesday and Wednesday, also comes grilled with angel hair pasta and a different sauce each week.

If you cannot make it here on lobster nights, don't worry. There are several creative dishes to choose from including oven roasted duckling with apples in brandy sauce; sautéed loin of pork with prosciutto, sage and fresh mozzarella; and pan-seared elk medallions with black currant sauce. There are equally interesting and enticing entrées featuring chicken, New York steak, prime rib, lamb loin chops, poached trout, grilled salmon filet, steamed vegetables, blue corn fettucini and salads (wilted spinach with applewood smoked bacon and an oriental, grilled chicken breast). A few of the desserts, like their four-layer chocolate cake and honey-rice pudding créme brûlée, are prepared in-house by baker, Charles Fortner. They plan to add more homemade desserts to the menu, which, as of this writing, featured fried ice cream with fresh strawberry sauce (there are strawberry fields in the local area), and a New York cheesecake. The wine list is mostly from California, with a few from Colorado and Europe.

My server was very attentive, returning to my table several times while I demolished by lobster. The restaurant has a first-rate vantage point, overlooking the Roaring Fork River with the massive south Glenwood Canyon wall that you can almost reach out and touch. As you follow your hostess to your seat, notice the wine cabinet on your right, the stenciled window dividers and hanging plants and ferns to your left, and the sun (or moon, depending on the time of day) roof overhead. Several watercolors of mountains, trees and flowers by local artist, Nancy Martin, decorate the restaurant and lounge. They are on sale for $200 and up. Rivers offers high-quality cuisine at reasonable prices, served by caring people in a refreshing environment

SPECIAL ONE-TIME OFFER: Buy one entrée at the regular price and receive a second entrée of equal or lesser value FREE (up to $24.00 value). Some entrées do not apply. This offer NOT valid in combination with any other offers. _____ Manager/Owner. _____ Date.

RECIPE

Red Curry Sauce
(Yields 2½ cups)

1 tablespoon crushed garlic
½ tablespoon Thai red curry paste
2 tablespoons white wine
½ cup fish or chicken stock

2 tablespoons sugar
6 ounces coconut milk
1½ cups heavy cream

1. Sauté garlic and curry paste in clarified butter, stirring regularly.
2. Add remaining ingredients and bring to a boil. Be sure to break up chunks of curry paste.

Sopris

Highway 82, PO Box 1985 (81602), 945-7771

Directions: Take Exit 116 from I-70. Go to the signal north of I-70 and turn right onto 6th Street (also Highway 6). Go to the next signal and turn right again onto Highway 82 or Grand Avenue. Go 7 miles towards Aspen. The restaurant is on the right.

ESSENTIALS

Cuisine: Elegant European
Hours: 7 days 5PM-10PM.
Meals and Prices: Dinner $$$-$$$$
Nonsmoking: No
Take-out: No
Alcohol: Full Bar
Credit Cards: MC, Visa, Amx,
Personal Check: Yes

Reservations: Recommended
Wheelchair Access: Yes, on folding ramps
Dress: Everything from casual to well-dressed to fine western wear to jeans
Other: Half orders for children at half price plus $1.50 are available for some entrées.

HISTORY, PERSONALITY AND CHARACTER

Current Owner and Executive Chef Kurt J. Wigger is a Swiss immigrant who has been in the restaurant business since he was 3. His father was a pastry chef, his mother was also a chef and his three sisters were waitresses. Kurt was brought to the U. S. in 1959 by Arnold Senn, owner of the Red Onion in Aspen, and appointed Executive Chef. In 1971, Kurt became a member of the Confrerie de la Chaine de Rotisseurs, International Chef's Organization, and proudly wears their medal. He is also a graduate of the Swiss National Chef School in pastry and cooking. While Kurt worked at the Red Onion, he met and married Elsbeth, from Switzerland, who was waitressing at Guido's. In 1974, Kurt, along with Werner Kuster and Jim Perry, purchased "Joe's Other Place" and renamed it the Red Onion. In 1978, Kurt became the sole owner and changed the name to Sopris after 12,953-foot Mount Sopris that lies in the Roaring Fork Valley between Glenwood Springs and Aspen. He became part owner of The Loft in Glenwood Springs from 1986 to 1989, Pepe's Hideout in Aspen from 1989 to 1991 and used to teach cooking at the Colorado Mountain School in Carbondale. Kurt, somewhat of a legend in these parts, estimates that he has served over 1,000,000 meals in his lifetime. His aim is to please young and old alike. He wants everyone who visits his restaurant "to leave feeling good about themselves and the time they've spent here." A few of the famous who have dined at Sopris include Jill St. John, John Wayne, Vic Damone, Robert Conrad, Clint Eastwood, the Kennedys, Rock Hudson, Henry Fonda, Lee Marvin, Wally Shirra, George C. Scott, and Buddy Hackett. Kurt has been Restaurateur of the Month in the Restaurant News and Sopris has been featured in Gourmet Magazine, Bon Appetit and Ford Times.

FOOD, SERVICE AND AMBIANCE

The veal forestiere with black morel mushrooms in a white wine sauce was tender enough to separate with a fork. I loved the sauce on this delicious dish, prepared with beef stock, cream, brandy, seasonings and onion. For the salad, I would recommend the garlic vinaigrette, but they also make a raspberry vinaigrette, creamy Italian, roquefort, and Thousand Island. Baked potato with sour cream and chives on the side and zucchini and carrots sprinkled with sage accompanied this delectable entrée. I savored every morsel!

For starters, you can order oysters, artichoke, escargots, jumbo shrimp cocktail, herring, show crab, French onion soup or vichyssoise. Highlighting the list of entrées are seafood like Colorado mountain trout and Australian lobster tail, several cuts of steak and pork chops charbroiled, popular entrées such as chicken livers stroganoff-style and veal parmesan with spaghetti and Sopris specialties: veal cordon bleu, rack of lamb, pepper steak flambe, "Wigger" shrimp wrapped in bacon, lobster Newburg, duck a l'orange and frog legs provençal. A selection of 45 wines, all chosen from vintage years, is available for your culinary pleasure. Conclude your delightful dining experience with peach Melba, pear Helen, chocolate mousse, custard, cheesecake, ice cream or cherries jubilee.

Service was top-notch, always present, but never intrusive. If you're looking for a dark, secluded, romantic place to dine where passers-by won't interfere, come to Sopris. It is decked in white linen, white candles, red velvet walls, fresh flowers and touches of cowboy elegance, like a wagon-wheel chandelier. The booths are trimmed with frosted and stenciled glass-works in imitation wood-frame doors with candle-shaped lights on either side. The pictures portray a steamship, hunting dogs, a flower basket and an elk.

Kurt Wigger is a renowned chef with the respect and experience that few restaurateurs in Colorado have. Combined with the intimate ambiance, this is one dining establishment that you won't want to pass by.

SPECIAL ONE-TIME OFFER: Buy one entrée at the regular price and receive $5 off a second entrée of equal or lesser value. This offer NOT valid in combination with any other offers. Please present to server at time of ordering. _____ Manager/Owner. _____ Date.

<u>RECIPE</u>

Bananas Flambé
(Serves 2)

2 bananas
Peel of 1 orange
1 tablespoon granulated sugar
1 tablespoon butter

¼ cup kirschwasser
½ cup heavy cream
Grand Marnier liqueur

1. Peel and slice bananas lengthwise. Cut the orange peel into thin slice.
2. Heat a pan and brown the sugar. Add butter and orange peel.
3. Put bananas in pan and turn them over very quickly several times. Flame bananas quickly with kirschwasser; add cream and cook until it thickens (about 2 minutes).
4. Place bananas on a plate. Add a dash of Grand Marnier to sauce and pour it over bananas.
5. Serve with vanilla ice cream.

Rivers Restaurant in Glenwood Springs

GOLD HILL

Gold Hill is an old gold mining community nestled beneath the Continental Divide, 10 miles west and 3,200' above the city of Boulder.
Zip Code: 80302. Area Code: 303. Population: 180. Elevation: 8,296'.

The Gold Hill Inn Restaurant

401 Main Street, 443-6461

Directions: From Broadway (Highway 7) and Mapleton Avenue (County Road 52) on the west side of Boulder, go west on Mapleton Avenue for 10 miles (bearing left at the fork after 5 miles). Stay on County Road 52 until you get to the town of Gold Hill. The restaurant and inn will be on the left just past the Bluebird Lodge.

ESSENTIALS

Cuisine: Mountain Gourmet
Hours: Mid-APR through OCT:
Wed-Mon 6PM-10PM. Closed Tue.
Closed NOV to Mid-APR.
Meals and Prices: Dinner $$$$
Nonsmoking: Yes
Take-out: No
Alcohol: Full Bar

Credit Cards: No
Personal Check: Yes
Reservations: Recommended. Made on the half hour.
Wheelchair Access: Yes
Dress: From casual to suits and ties.
Other: Available for weddings, conferences and private parties.

HISTORY, PERSONALITY AND CHARACTER

The Gold Hill Inn and Restaurant were built in the 1920s by the Bluebird Society, an all-female, bird-watching organization from Chicago, for their own personal use. In the 1930s, the "Bluebirds" abandoned the inn and restaurant which then remained vacant until 1962 when Barbara and Frank Finn acquired the property, remodeled and established the Gold Hill Inn Restaurant. In 1889, Eugene Field wrote about Gold Hill's hotel and the food service ran by a man named Casey, referring to it as "Casey's Table d'Hote" (table of the house). The Finns, who like Eugene Field, fell in love with the area, established "Casey's Table d'Hote" as their trademark. The Finns retired in the early 1980s and turned over the restaurant to their sons, Brian, who is the maitre 'd and manages the front of the restaurant, and Chris, who is the head chef.

FOOD, SERVICE AND AMBIANCE

Dinner at the Gold Hill Inn Restaurant is a 6-course affair with appetizer, soup, salad, entrée, dessert and an after-dinner tray of cheeses, crackers and fruits. Chef Christopher changes the selections nightly. When I dined here, the appetizer was zesty chili con carne with ground beef, tomato and cheese topping. This was followed by your choice of hot French onion soup that was high on onion flavor or cold Russian spinach à la Danish prepared with buttermilk, sour cream, cucumber, boiled egg and herbs. Even if you don't care for your soup cold, I think you'll like this. The salad was a medley of spinach, cucumber, radishes, red onion, mushroom, mildly sweet jicama and croutons with your choice of 3 in-house dressings: blue cheese, raspberry vinaigrette or Casey's, similar to Caesar's dressing with oil, vinegar, egg whites and herbs. The chef's entrée choices were roast leg of lamb with rosemary sauce, tournedos with green chili sauce, fresh striped marlin with hazelnut butter, smoked and stuffed broiled trout and stuffed broiled quail. The roast lamb, sliced thin, was tender and savory while the marlin had a delicate, sweet flavor and a firm texture. The tournedos and trout are regular stand-bys on the menu which may be joined by chicken country captain — a half chicken with curry and lentil sauces, escolar tuna or smoked brisket. The side vegetables included long grain and wild rice, a tasty zucchini pancake, scrumptious squash mixed with almonds and orange juice, and a delectable stuffed tomato. For dessert, choose from ginger pear or sour cream apple pie, chocolate torte, bundt cake — a delicious spice cake with real whip cream, or persimmon pudding. Following dessert, they serve a tray of cheeses (mild cheddar and Swiss) with assorted crackers, grapes and apples — a fitting ending to a wonderful meal.

A myriad of servers attended our table. I found them all very likeable and attentive. The Finns have taken every opportunity to add rustic touches to this building that is on the National Register of Historic Places. Table candles were in quaint tin candle holders filled with sand. The windows were draped with attractive white curtains with a fruit and leaf pattern. Dated photographs and old-fashioned snow shoes and wooden skis adorned the log and concrete walls. Candle-shaped light bulbs hang from the wood-beamed arched ceiling. A pumpkin, old kerosene lamp and a vase with dried flowers sat on the fireplace mantle at the end of the dining room. There were also a pot belly stove and antique furniture everywhere. The lounge in front of the dining room hosts a fireplace to either side, a bar in the back, an outmoded Fisher upright piano, a passé ice box converted into a wine cooler and an antiquated cabinet filled with crystal vases, canisters and books. One that caught my eye was titled "Ethics in the Dust: Ten Lectures to Little Housewives on the Elements of Crystallization" — they were lectures given at a girl's school on mineralogy. Photographs of Mason Williams, Dennis Weaver and Rod McQuen were hanging on the wall opposite the men's restroom. Inside the men's restroom (ladies, take note) there were outdated articles from the Denver Post and Saturday Evening Post and advertisements, like one inviting young men and boys to write in any question, but instructing them to avoid "silly questions" and to enclose a SASE. Charming! About twice a month on Friday nights, they have live music in the lounge — blue grass, folk or zydeco (similar to Cajun blue grass). Big outdoor barbecues that include live music are held outside on the lawn for holidays and special benefits. The Gold Hill Inn Restaurant offers world-class cuisine with an unpretentious style in an arcadian domain.

SPECIAL ONE-TIME OFFER: Buy one 6-course meal at the regular price and receive one complimentary glass of wine or one bottle of beer. Limit 2 glasses of wine or 2 bottles of beer with the purchase of two 6-course meals. This offer NOT valid in combination with any other offers. Please present to server at time of ordering. _____ Manager/Owner. _____ Date.

RECIPE

Leg of Lamb Venison

6 pounds leg of lamb
Tarragon vinegar
Buttermilk
3 cloves garlic, mashed
1 large onion, thinly sliced
1 small carrot, thinly sliced
10 whole cracked peppercorns
6 whole cloves
3 large bay leaves
10 sprigs of fresh parsley
6 sprigs of green celery leaves
3 crushed juniper berries
½ teaspoon each of ground mace,
  marjoram and allspice

For Roasting:
  2 dozens whole cloves
  ½ cup melted bacon fat
  ¾ cup dry white wine
  ½ cup red currant jelly
  1 tablespoon grated lemon rind
  Flour for thickening
  A little cold water

1. Rub lamb with vinegar and place in a crock. Cover with the rest of the ingredients (except those for roasting).
2. Cover and keep in a cool place, turning two times each day, making sure the meat is always covered with buttermilk.
3. After the fourth day, remove lamb (save the buttermilk mixture). Wipe dry and rub completely with a salt and pepper mixture.
4. Place in a roasting pan and insert 2 dozen whole cloves. Pour melted bacon fat and dry white wine over the lamb. Roast in a hot oven at 450 for 20 minutes, turning frequently. Lower the heat to 350 and allow 18 minutes for each pound. Baste frequently with the strained buttermilk.
5. When lamb is done, place on serving platter. Strain the liquor into a sauce pan. Skim off all fat and bring to a boil. Add ½ cup red currant jelly and a tablespoon of grated lemon rind, thickening with flour and a little cold water.
6. Pour part of sauce over sliced lamb and serve hot.

The Bluebird Lodge and Gold Hill Inn in Gold Hill

Silverheels Southwest Grill in Golden

GOLDEN

Originally called Golden City, the town was named after Thomas L. Golden. He and fellow settlers James Saunders and George W. Jackson established a temporary camp near the mouth of Clear Creek Canyon in 1858. The following year, the Boston Trading Company sent a wagon train led by General George West to partake in the gold discovery. From 1862 to 1867, before Colorado acquired statehood, Golden City was the capital of the Colorado Territory. The building used for the Colorado Territorial Capital is still located on the corner of Washington and 12th. Once a railroad center associated with the metal production industries, Golden today is a tourist center; the county seat of Jefferson County; and home to the Coors Brewery, established in 1872 by Adolph Coors Sr., the Colorado School of Mines founded in 1874 and Hakushika Sake U.S.A. brewery which opened in 1992.
Zip Code: 80401. Area Code: 303. Population: 13,116. Elevation: 5,674'.

Silverheels Southwest Grill
1122 Washington Avenue, 279-6390
Directions: From Denver, take 6th Avenue (Highway 6) west past C-470 and Colfax Avenue (Highway 40). Turn right at the signal at 19th Street. Drive 6 blocks and turn left onto Washington Avenue. The restaurant is 7 blocks down on the left at the corner of 12th Street. From north Denver, exit I-70 at Highway 58 and go west to the Washington Avenue Exit. Go south (left) on Washington Avenue for 5 blocks. The restaurant is on your right at the corner of 12th Street. From Boulder, go south on Highway 93 into Golden and turn left at the signal onto Highway 58. Exit Washington Avenue and go south (right) for 5 blocks to 12th Street. The restaurant is on your right.

ESSENTIALS
Cuisine: Southwestern
Hours: Open daily: 11:30AM-9PM (10PM on Fri/Sat). (Lunch until 2PM, cantina menu 2PM-5PM, Dinner from 5PM).
Meals and Prices: Lunch $$, Dinner $$$-$$$$
Nonsmoking: Yes
Take-out: Yes
Alcohol: Full Bar
Credit Cards: MC, Visa, Amx
Personal Check: Yes, with I.D.
Reservations: Suggested for Friday or Saturday evenings or for parties of 6 or more.

Wheelchair Access: Yes
Other: Service charge of 15% added to parties of 6 or more. No separate checks. Customized dinner banquets available. Outdoor parties serviced from a Conestoga wagon trailer. Dollar dining club for frequent customers. Early bird specials before 6PM. Heart smart items identified on menu by a ♥.

GOLDEN

HISTORY, PERSONALITY AND CHARACTER

Silverheels is in two historically significant structures in Golden. The main building, known as the Mercantile Building or Loveland Building, was originally constructed of wood in 1860 by W. A. H. Loveland. It was rebuilt in 1863 with brick and served as Loveland's Pioneer Store, Golden's first merchandise store. The second story of the building was constructed as a meeting hall that was used by the territorial legislature in 1866 and 1867 (when Golden was the capital of the Colorado Territory) and the Colorado School of Mines. The retail portion of the building continued as a grocery and dry goods store until 1884 when Nicholas Koenig bought out all other partners and ran his commercial enterprise, including a wholesale business with mountain towns and ranches. It stayed in the family for 57 years. From 1941 until 1971, the building remained in use as the Golden Mercantile, making a total of 108 continuous years in the same commercial use. After 1971, the building was used as a restaurant appropriately named, The Mercantile.

The second structure, the north side of Silverheels to the right of the bar, was built by Adolf Coors in 1906 as a distribution center and saloon featuring Coors products. Both structures were remodeled by Silverheels in 1992-93. The exterior and facade were restored to circa 1920 and the interior was designed to represent our American west heritage.

The story of Lady Silverheels is a bitter-sweet tale of a lovely dancehall girl who lived in the mining town of Buckskin Joe, Colorado. The click of her silver-plated high-heel shoes brought many a smile to the hard working miners. When a small pox epidemic hit the community in 1959, Lady Silverheels gave comfort and aid to the desperately ill miners until she too fell to the dreaded disease. When the epidemic passed, Lady Silverheels vanished into the mountains. No trace of her was ever found. The townspeople named Mt. Silverheels near Fairplay, Colorado, in her honor, a monument to a mysterious woman whose beauty and dancing gave pleasure to many and whose courage saved so many lives

Robert B. "Bobby" Starekow opened Silverheels in 1993. He has been in the restaurant business since 1975 and opened Silverheels in Silverthorne, Colorado, in 1988. Bobby started cooking at the age of 8, entering an igloo cake, with little bears and seals all around, in a Betty Crocker Bake-Off. He lost the competition. Undaunted by that early setback, between 1975 and the 1980s, he worked his way up from dishwasher to bartender to cook and finally owner of the Snake River Saloon in Keystone. Between 1979 and 1981, he was owner and executive chef of the Gore Range Inn, now Antonio's, in Dillon, and helped to build the inside including the bar. Between 1985 and 1988, he ran the Vintage House, a place with gracious southern dining, in Springfield, Missouri. Jim Welsch is co-general manager of both the Silverthorne and Golden restaurants.

FOOD, SERVICE AND AMBIANCE

I found the food simply scrumptious at Silverheels in Golden as well as in Silverthorne. You should visit both. See page 425 in <u>Restaurants from 101 Colorado Small Towns</u> for information on Silverheels in Silverthorne. Preceding dinner was a raw vegetable tray and green chili ranch dip with just a little "zing". The sirloin gordita was incredible — a puff of pastry dough stuffed with sirloin tips, sautéed onions, tomato and mild green chili, oozing with mild Monterey Jack cheese and topped with black bean salsa. This one has to be tried to be believed. For an appetizer, I found the quesadillas con legumes (crisp and golden grilled flour tortillas stuffed with cheese, green chilies, onion and julienne vegetables, then topped with green and red peppers) to be quite tasty. The pueblo barbecue ribs, smoked and charbroiled pork ribs in Spanish barbecue sauce with tomato chunks and coriander, were a flavorful alternative to traditional ribs. For seafood lovers, there's a savory, shrimp-fed, baked Rocky Mountain trout topped with cornbread, crab, sausage and chili and served with cilantro hollandaise that doesn't taste like hollandaise (for those of us that love cilantro, but don't care for hollandaise). Gnocchi sardi, a pasta vegetable dish with yellow squash and zucchini, livens up the trout. Dinners are served with very appetizing baked jalapeño-cheese onion rolls, corn bread and Monterey Jack cheese muffins with red-chili and raspberry-honey butter.

Highlighting the southwest American specialties are stone age cookery — steak, chicken or shrimp that you grill on a fiery hot granite slab; thinly cut steaks, fresh caught seafood and tender pork loins broiled over an open flame; Colorado wild sage smokehouse — Mojave hen, buffalo sausage and salmon with a light touch of smoke and a sweet hot sauce; and southwest tapas — little dishes of the Spanish southwest. A few of their signature dishes are pork loin medallions marinated, charbroiled and served with a fresh, cherry tamarind sauce; chicken Anasazi baked with cream cheese and crab and enchilada con hongos, a vegetarian meal. For lunch, there's a wide selection of sandwiches, platters, salads and stuffed pocket breads. The preparations, ingredients and combinations make this one of the best restaurants of southwest cuisine in Colorado. Desserts almost seems like just an afterthought after you've indulged on their exquisite main courses, but for the truly self-gratifying individual, there's a Mexican flan, carrot cake, chocolate mint mousse, apple and caramelized pecan pie with bourbon soaked raisins and a bittersweet chocolate brownie marbled with cream cheese.

My server was courteous, jovial and amiable. My editor, Linda, and I delighted in dinner in the rear dining room, its red brick walls brought to life by the old west imagery of Bobby Starekow's paintings portraying cow pokes and horse rustlers, color pencil of the original Cisco Kid series, old maps, chaps and rugs. Elsewhere in the restaurant, you'll find original Tom Goodan prints and watercolors representing the Grand Canyon and cowboys with their horses on the mesa. These were found in the attic of an old church in Sante Fe. A wood mosaic stagecoach created by Dan Richards from ebony, pine, oak cedar and red wood adds a nice touch to the environment. Other embellishments include peeled aspen log lattice over the bar, the 1862 photo of the first brick building, the 1906 photo of the Coors Distributorship, the original blueprints of the Coors building, and the safe of the Koenig Mercantile Company set in the wall with the stock certificate framed overhead. Silverheels offers some of the best regional foods in a distinctively southwest setting, both in Golden and Silverthorne.

SPECIAL ONE-TIME OFFER: Buy one entrée at the regular price and receive one complimentary appetizer OR one complimentary dessert (up to $5.95 value per item). Limit 2 appetizers or desserts with the purchase of 2 entrées. This offer NOT valid in combination with any other offers. Please present to server at time of ordering.
_____ Manager/Owner. _____ Date.

RECIPE
Silverheels Chile, Cheese and Onion Rolls

Rolls:
  2 tablespoons active dry yeast
  2 cups warm water (115 degrees)
  1 egg
  ½ cup sugar
  1 teaspoon salt
  3 tablespoons vegetable oil
  6½ cups flour

Filling:
  ½ cup melted butter
  1 cup dried cheese sauce mix
  ½ cup dehydrated onions
  ½ cup canned or frozen
    chopped chilies
  Egg wash - 1 egg beaten with water

1. Dissolve yeast in water in large mixing bowl. Stir in egg, sugar, salt and oil. Mix well. Add flour in small batches until dough is easy to handle. Put dough in large greased bowl and coat all sides with oil.
2. Cover, set in a warm place to rise until twice the original size. Punch down, cover and allow to rise once more to double size, this time in a cool spot.
3. Roll out dough to 3 sheets, ¼-inch thick.
4. Brush with melted butter, sprinkle liberally with cheese mix, onions and chilies. Roll into a tube with your hands, then cut in 1¼-inch rolls.
5. Place in oiled muffin tins and allow to rise to twice or three times its volume. Brush with egg wash and bake in 350-degree oven for 15 minutes till golden brown.

GRAND LAKE

Grand Lake is situated on the north shore of the largest natural body of water in Colorado, after which the town got its name, and on the headwaters of the mighty Colorado River. It was founded as a mining settlement at first, but today it is a popular summer resort, serving as the west entrance to Rocky Mountain National Park. In the winter, Grand Lake is a mecca for snowmobile enthusiasts.

Zip Code: 80447. Area Code: 970. Population: 259. Elevation: 8,380'.

Caroline's Cuisine

9921 Highway 34 (No. 27), 627-9404

Directions: From I-70, take Exit 232. Proceed north on Highway 40 for 46 miles to Granby. At the west end of town, turn right onto Highway 34. Go 10 miles to Soda Springs Ranch. Turn left, then take an immediate left and go .1 miles up to the hexagonal-shaped restaurant.

ESSENTIALS

Cuisine: French/American
Hours: Thanksgiving to Easter: Wed-Sun 5PM-9PM (9:30PM on Fri/Sat). Closed Mon/Tue. Mothers Day to Mid-OCT: Tue-Sun 5PM-9PM (9:30PM on Fri/Sat). Sat/Sun 11AM-2PM. Closed Mon. Closed Easter to Mother's Day and Mid-OCT to Thanksgiving.
Meals and Prices: Lunch $, Dinner $$$$
Nonsmoking: Yes. Smoking only permitted in the atrium and bar.

Take-out: Yes
Alcohol: Full Bar
Credit Cards: All 5
Personal Check: In-state with I.D.
Reservations: Suggested
Wheelchair Access: Yes
Other: No separate checks; 15% gratuity added to parties over 6 persons; $3 per plate charge for split entrées.

HISTORY, PERSONALITY AND CHARACTER

Caroline's Cuisine is located on the Soda Springs Ranch Resort built in 1982. The original restaurant was called the Soda Springs Ranch Restaurant until October 1991 when Caroline and Jean-Claude Cavalera opened Caroline's Cuisine. Caroline, who has been a chef since 1981, is a graduate of Culinary Institute of America in Hyde Park. She cooked at Callaway Gardens in Georgia from 1984 to 1986 and was sous chef at the Ritz-Carlton in Laguna Beach, California, from 1986 to 1989. Jean-Claude, who has a culinary degree from France, began cooking in 1973 in Nice and went to the Savoy Restaurant in London in 1975. He cooked at La Chaumiere in Washington, D.C., from 1979 to 1983, opened the Intercontinental in San Diego in 1983-84, was executive sous chef at the Ritz-Carlton in Laguna Beach from 1984 to 1989 and executive chef at the

135

Ritz Carlton in Boston from 1989 until 1991. Caroline and Jean Claude are currently chairpersons of the Grand County Food and Wine Festival. Caroline manages the kitchen and will prepare your fabulous dinner. Jean-Claude manages the front and will be your most gracious host.

FOOD, SERVICE AND AMBIANCE

Caroline changes the menu each season (summer and winter). Jean-Claude says their regular customers like the new menus because it's almost like coming to a new restaurant. At the same time, they will return popular, requested items to the menu. So while you may not see on the menu exactly what is presented here, you can expect similar creative continental cuisine. For example, in Restaurants from 101 Colorado Small Towns, I wrote about Caroline's roasted half chicken with sautéed mushrooms, bacon and pearl onions. The roasted half chicken is still on the menu, but with an onion soubise sauce. On my most recent visit, I ordered a roasted red pepper tapas appetizer and the duck confit entrée. The tapas — 3 half slices of red pepper served next to 2 slices of French bread with a tomato spread toasted on top, chopped tomatoes and a tapenade of crushed Nicoise olives, garlic and olive oil — were light and scrumptious. Definitely give this one a try as it will stimulate your appetite without filling it. The duck, served with a not-too-sweet dried cherry sauce, was tender to the degree of being soft. According to Jean-Claude, it's the confit style of cooking that gives the duck this texture. The duck is rubbed with rock salt and herbs (thyme, rosemary and garlic) and allowed to set overnight. The salt and herbs are washed off the next day. The duck is then cooked in some of its own fat at 200 degrees for 4 hours. The result was the most mouth-watering, succulent duck I've ever eaten!

You can start your dining experience at Caroline's Cuisine with escargot, shrimp and feta cheese quesadilla, herbed polenta or broccoli and onion tempura. Entrées include homemade soup or salad with homemade Caesar or bell pepper and Parmesan vinaigrette dressings. I chose the later and found the sweet bell pepper, sharp Parmesan and sour vinaigrette combination to my liking. Dinner rolls are served with an alouette (they call it Boursin in France) of cream cheese with fresh garlic, thyme and chives. This was very tasty but very filling as well. The other entrées were filet mignon in two sizes or with three jumbo shrimps, sautéed salmon, grilled ribeye steak or shrimp brochette, fettuccine with red pepper sauce (all of their pasta is made from scratch starting with a semolina machine to make the noodles) and an 8 oz. cheeseburger. They have a children's menu and a bar menu with appetizers, soup, salad and sandwiches. You can complete your meal with port, brandy, or on the lighter side, a cup of iced cappuccino or espresso to complement one of their homemade pies, cheesecakes or death by chocolate.

Service has always been pleasant and very attentive. The music has been a combination of French, Italian, classical and jazz. The decor has a distinctive food theme throughout the restaurant. You will find paintings of a food and wine festival and a classic dinner table and posters from Musee De L'art Culinaire, including two of Auguste Escofier and Nellie Melba. Escofier, known as the "chef of the king and the king of chefs" brought women out to restaurants in the 19th century by making dishes especially for women. His creations included peach Melba and Melba toast, named after the woman he fell in love with. The circular gallery upstairs has an art exhibit by Australian-born Ronda Eden, a collection of Native American and southwestern original watercolors, mixed media and prints that are for sale. The odd, hexagonal-shaped building has picturesque views of the rolling hillside. Plan to spend a little extra time here to view the art, chat with your hospitable host, Jean-Claude, and revel in an enchanting dining experience.

SPECIAL ONE-TIME OFFER: Buy one entrée at the regular price and receive a second entrée of equal or lesser value FREE (up to $15.75 value). This offer NOT valid in combination with any other offers. Please present to server at time of ordering. _____ Manager/Owner. _____ Date.

RECIPE

Shrimp and Feta Cheese Quesadilla with Fresh Salsa

1 flour tortilla
Clarified butter for sautéing
2 jumbo shrimps, diced
½ shallot diced
3 tablespoons feta cheese crumbled
Chopped chives

Salsa:
  2 medium tomatoes, small diced
  ¼ onion, small diced
  ½ bunch cilantro, chopped
  Salt and pepper to taste
  ½ lemon, juiced
  ¼ jalapeño, finely diced (optional)

1. In a small sauté pan, sauté shrimp in clarified butter until they just turn pink.
2. Add shallots and cook for one additional minute. Remove from heat.
3. In a large sauté pan, place tortilla flat on top of a bit of clarified butter.
4. Place shrimp and shallot mixture on one half of the tortilla and then put feta and chives over shrimp.
5. Fold empty half of tortilla over filled side and continue to sauté until golden on both sides.
6. Remove from pan and place on serving dish. Garnish with fresh salsa.
7. Salsa: Remove innards from tomatoes and purée. Dice remaining outer shell. In a bowl, combine all ingredients and let sit in refrigerator until ready to serve. Salsa can be made a day ahead of time.

GRAND LAKE

The Grand Lake Lodge Restaurant

15500 U. S. Highway 34, PO Box 569, Summer: 627-3185, Fax 627-9495. Off-season: (303)759-5848, Fax (303)759-3179.

Directions: From Highways 40 and 34 in Granby, drive 14 miles to Grand Lake. At the turn-off for Grand Lake (to the right), continue straight for 1 mile and turn right at the sign for the Grand Lake Lodge. Go another ½ mile to the lodge and restaurant. From Rocky Mountain National Park, the entrance to the lodge and restaurant is ½ mile south of the park entrance.

ESSENTIALS

Cuisine: American
Hours: JUN to Mid-SEP: 7 days 7:30AM-10AM, 11:30AM-2:30PM and 5:30PM-10PM. Closed Mid-SEP through MAY.
Meals and Prices: Breakfast $-$$, Brunch $$$, Lunch $$, Dinner $$$-$$$$
Nonsmoking: Yes. Smoking only permitted in the bar (no food service) and on the porch, deer deck or barbecue pit.
Take-out: No
Alcohol: Full Bar

Credit Cards: MC, Visa, Amx, Disc
Personal Check: Local only with I. D.
Reservations: Strongly recommended, especially in July or August.
Wheelchair Access: Yes. There is a ramp at the end of the building.
Other: One check per table. Additional 15% service charge added to parties of 6 or more. Available for business meetings, family reunions, anniversaries, weddings, receptions and other special events: two meeting rooms, barbecue pit and off-premise catering.

HISTORY, PERSONALITY AND CHARACTER

Roe Emery, the "Father of Colorado Tourism", began construction on the Grand Lake Lodge in April 1919, using native lodgepole pine. A year later, the Lodge opened with a grand ball on July 3, 1920. Emery successfully operated the Lodge for three decades before selling in 1953. I. B. and Ted L. James took control of the Lodge in the same year under the Colorado Transportation Company. On July 17, 1973, a kitchen grease fire burned the inside of the restaurant and main lodge. It took 7 years of repairs before the Lodge was ready to officially reopen in 1981. Three generations of the Ted L. James family have owned and operated the Lodge for over four decades. In 1993, the Grand Lake Lodge became a registered National Historic Landmark.

Mrs. Ted L. James, Jr. is the president of the company as well as the buyer and operator of the on-site specialty gift shop. Her son, Reed, is the general manager and her daughter, Kathy, is the controller. Her son-in-law, John Rinker, is the daytime dining room manager and has been at the Lodge since 1993. Food and Beverage Director Jay O'Neall and evening dining room manager Guthrie Schaffer have been with the Lodge since 1990 and 1991, respectively. Maitre d' Bob Scott has been at the Lodge since 1968 and can provide exact details on the 1973 fire, the rebuilding of the Lodge and other historical information. Executive Chef Paul Streiter has been at the Lodge since 1988. He is a graduate of the Culinary Institute of America (CIA) in Hyde Park, New York, and classically French trained. He completed his apprenticeship at the Waldorf-Astoria in New York and operated his own food delivery business in Ithaca, New York, where he attended Cornell University. In 1995, he was joined by another CIA graduate, Susan Kantor, who fulfilled her apprenticeship at Amy's Bakery in Manhattan. She is the Pastry Chef in charge of breads, pastries, desserts and wedding cakes.

FOOD, SERVICE AND AMBIANCE

I went vegetarian the evening that I dined at the Lodge, consuming an ample portabello mushroom with basil pesto and roasted peppers, topped with sharp, fresh romano cheese. If all vegetarian dishes were this good, I could turn into a vegetarian myself . . . for about a week. Chef Paul's plate presentation was attractive with parsley sprinkled on the plate edges and servings of new potatoes, sautéed mixed vegetables and a tomato with fresh basil roasted on top. Preceding the entrée was a salad and cilantro balsamic vinaigrette with fresh cilantro that you could really taste. Chef Susan prepared sesame and poppyseed twists and poppyseed rolls. Sometimes she'll make olive and garlic or chive and onion twists. The talents of two CIA chefs is unveiled in their mountain grill and pasta specialties, like rib-eye steak brushed with Thai sweet chili glaze, lamb chops and shrimp mix grilled with sundried tomato garlic glaze and lemon pepper pasta Alfredo with smoked salmon and scallops. Chef Paul says he likes to offer wild game specials; surf, turf and air specials; lighter fruit sauces and roasted vegetable sauces. For dessert, delve into a tempting piece of key lime pie with a homemade ginger snap crust, Grand Marnier and homemade Italian meringue; chocolate mousse; fresh apple Napoleon or chocolate cheesecake.

Their breakfast buffet is highlighted by 2-inch thick, homemade Belgian waffles made with malt and a fresh fruit bowl. On Sunday, they add champagne, a pasta bar, made-from-scratch pastries, ham, turkey, baron of roast beef, salads, peel-and-eat shrimp, marinated vegetables, and occasionally, Bob Scott's fried bananas. Lunch features soups, salads, burgers with a host of toppings, a spicy barbecue prime sandwich, grilled rainbow trout and focaccia pizza.

Service was very attentive, informative and helpful. Bob, Jay, Guthrie and my waiter all ministered to my inquiries and took me for a tour. Tom Scott, no relation to Bob, played the electric piano in the corner of the dining room. They provide live music Tuesday through Sunday. Weekly entertainment is also offered in the bar. I was here on a rainy day, yet I was still inspired by the view of Shadow Mountain, Grand Lake and Shadow Lake. Fresh flowers are a regular mainstay on every table. The dining room and adjacent bar are embellished with several stuffed animals and animal heads: mule and white tail deer, Canadian geese, pronghorn antelope, two trophy-sized elk, big horn sheep and a great horn owl. One of the most amazing facts about the lodge is that it has no foundation. The lodge pole pines used in construction were just set on rocks when the lodge was built. The stumps left behind from these pines are still in the basement of the lodge. Inside, you can watch the chefs prepare the meals from the open grill. Outside, you can sit on the porch facing the mountain and lakes or take a short walk down to the deer deck with its tables and umbrellas and park benches. Further below is the barbecue pit with picnic benches. Wherever you dine, you'll appreciate expertly prepared food, high-quality service and the best view in Grand County.

SPECIAL ONE-TIME OFFER: Buy one entrée at the regular price and receive a complimentary fresh, homemade dessert from on-site baker, Susan Kantor. Limit 6 desserts with the purchase of 6 entrées. This offer NOT valid in combination with any other offers. Please present to server at time of ordering. _____ Manager/Owner. _____ Date.

RECIPE

Sautéed Pork Loin with Crab Meat and Wild Mushrooms
(Serves 4 to 6)

2-3 ounces sherry or cooking sherry
1½-2 pounds pork loin, trimmed cut
   into 1½- to 2-ounce medallions,
   pounded
6-9 ounces lump crab meat
1-1½ cups shiitake mushrooms,
   julliened
4-6 tablespoons shallots, diced
2-3 cups heavy cream

5-7 ounces clarified butter or extra
   virgin olive oil
1 cup all purpose flour
Salt and pepper to taste
2-3 tablespoons parsley, chopped

Use one large sauté pan for 2 portions;
either repeat following process or use 2-
3 pans simultaneously

1. In large sauté pan, pour butter or oil. Turn heat up to high and let oil become hot.
2. As pan is heating, lightly flour pork medallions (3 medallions per person). When pan is hot, gently put pork medallions in pan, evenly spaced. Add a pinch of salt and pepper to the meat for seasoning.
3. After approximately 1-1½ minutes, turn pork over and allow the other side to cook for the same amount of time. Remove pork from pan and place on plate.
4. In the same pan, add 2 tablespoons of shallots and ½ cup of mushrooms. If pan is dry, add ½ ounce more oil or butter.

5. Sauté the shallots and mushrooms for 1 minute. Deglace pan with 1 ounce of sherry. Allow sherry to reduce by about 90 percent. When sherry has reduced, add 1 cup of heavy cream. Let cream reduce by about 50 percent (approximately 3 to 4 minutes).

6. At this point, add 3 ounces of crab meat, 1 tablespoon chopped parsley and salt and pepper to taste. Lightly mix ingredients into cream sauce and pour evenly over pork medallions.

7. It is important to let the sauté pan get hot before placing pork medallions in oiled pan. This way a light brown color will be noticed along the edges and center of each side of the medallion. When reducing the sherry, you do not need to add the cream until there is virtually no liquid in the pan. The final sauce should be an off-white color, not brown in color. If the color is brown, there is either too much sherry or not enough cream.

Toasting at Caroline's Cuisine in Grand Lake

The Rapids Restaurant

209 Rapids Lane, PO Box 1400, 627-3707

Directions: From I-70, take Exit 232. Proceed north on Highway 40 for 46 miles to
Granby. At the west end of town, turn right onto Highway 34. Go 14 miles to Grand
Lake. You will enter town on Grand Avenue. Go to the end of Grand Avenue and turn
left onto Rapids Lane. Go 1½ blocks. The restaurant and lodge are on your right.

ESSENTIALS

Cuisine: Italian
Hours: Memorial Day Weekend to
OCT: 7 days 5PM-9:30PM. DEC to
Memorial Day Weekend: Wed-Sun
5PM-9:30PM. Closed Mon/Tue.
Closed NOV.
Meals and Prices: Dinner $$$-$$$$
Nonsmoking: Yes
Take-out: Yes
Alcohol: Full Bar

Credit Cards: MC, Visa, Amx, DC
Personal Check: In-state only with
driver's license.
Reservations: Recommended for New
Year's Eve or parties of 8 or more.
Wheelchair Access: No
Other: $1 per ticket charge for
separate checks. Additional 15%
service charge for tables of 6 or more;
$9 minimum plate charge for adults.

HISTORY, PERSONALITY AND CHARACTER

In the early 1900s, John Lapsley Ish built the Rapids against the banks of the
Tonahutu River (the head waters for the Colorado River) so that he could divert water to
a private generator for electricity. The Rapids was the first building in Grand Lake to
have electricity or running water. The tree stumps, left behind from the logs used by Ish
to build The Rapids, are still in the basement of the lodge. In 1984, Toni Nigro
purchased the lodge and restaurant. Daughter Kathy manages the restaurant. Kathy has
also been the chef since 1984 with a sabbatical from 1986 to 1989 when she worked at
the Nigro's other restaurant, The Carousel (now the Divide Grill) in Winter Park. Ann
Newton, who has been with The Rapids since 1990, is their line chef. Her daughter,
Dana, started working here in 1987 as a busgirl and is now their sous chef. The Rapids
has been featured in Bon Appetit in January 1995, Better Homes and Gardens in March
1993 and Holiday Travel Magazine.

FOOD, SERVICE AND AMBIANCE

The Rapids has been a popular New Year's Eve destination for my tour
operation, Restaurant Adventure Plus (RAP) Tours. This has allowed me the opportunity
to dine here on three occasions and personally taste their prime rib, veal, shrimp and
pasta, not to mention the dozens of comments and opinions I received from the members
of my tour groups. I found the prime rib to be succulent, the veal was thick and
deliciously seasoned with pesto and sundried tomato sauce and the scampi Palermo, over

angel hair pasta, was spicy and flavorful in a red sauce with calamati olives, artichokes and feta cheese. Dinner at The Rapids is a four-course extravaganza starting with an hors d'oeuvre tray of boiled shrimp; prime rib, beef, chicken liver and/or blue cheese pâtés; assorted cheeses and vegetables and crisp crackers (I call them crackling bread because you can hear everyone in the dining room making crackling sounds when they bite into them). This is followed by a Caesar salad with a fresh baked roll, a fruit sorbet and the entrée, that includes fresh vegetables and potato, rice or pasta. The reaction from my group ranged anywhere from "fabulous" to "loved it"! Expect a fine dining experience when you come here.

Their pastas, which feature fettuccine and linguini, are imported from Italy and the sauce is made with their own special herbs. The Italian specialties include lasagna, manicotti and Nana's eggplant. Other entrée highlights to choose from are porterhouse steak, New York pepper steak, trout with almonds or capers, lamb chops, and Sicilian chicken. They have a children's menu, wine and champagne list that includes Dom Perignon and to finish your meal, cappuccino or espresso to go with one of their special desserts like cheesecakes, tortes, cakes, biscotti and ice cream drinks.

Service has always been friendly, professional and generally attentive. Although on a busy night, such as New Year's Eve, give your server a little consideration and offer a reminder if they need one. Eighty percent of their staff have been here 3 or more years, attesting to the experienced quality of the service you will receive. Exterior flood lights create a haunting image of the rock-filled waters below. Cocktails and hors d'oeuvres are served on the patio overlooking the Tonahutu River. In 1995, they added a gazebo. The decor inside includes stained-glass dividers, a log-beam ceiling slanting towards the river and art work from local artists. Many consider The Rapids to be the most romantic restaurant in Grand County.

SPECIAL ONE-TIME OFFER: Buy one entrée at the regular price and receive a complimentary glass of house wine. Limit 2 glasses of house wine with the purchase of 2 entrées. This offer NOT valid in combination with any other offers. Please present to server at time of ordering. _____ Manager/Owner. _____ Date.

If you traveled the state with both Colorado Restaurants and Recipes and Restaurants from 101 Colorado Small Towns, you'd have 433 different restaurants to chose from in 132 different towns.

RECIPE

19 Shrimp Palermo

Tiger shrimp size 6-8, cleaned and
shelled (4 per person)
1 cup of crumbled feta cheese

Sauce:
¼ cup olive oil
Chopped garlic to taste (1 teaspoon)
1 large chopped onion
1 cup of chopped celery
1½ cups of chopped plum
(roman) tomatoes
1 tablespoon tomato paste
1 cup of tomato sauce
2 cups of water
1 cup of white wine

½ cup of chopped pitted calamata
Greek black olives
½ cup of chopped sun-dried
tomatoes (marinade recipe
follows)
1 cup of marinated artichoke
hearts (Cara Mia)

1 tablespoon of sugar
Salt and pepper to taste
1 teaspoon of oregano
1 teaspoon of sweet basil
1 to 3 bay leaves

1. In a heavy sauce pan, heat olive oil; sauté garlic, onion, celery, and fresh tomatoes for 2 to 3 minutes or until the onions become transparent.
2. Add white wine, tomato sauce, tomato paste, spices and remaining ingredients (except feta cheese) and let sauce simmer for at least 1 to 2 hours. If sauce becomes too thick, add a small amount of water at a time to thin it down.
3. About 15 minutes before serving, bring sauce to a boil. Add raw, cleaned shrimp to cook. Shrimp are finished after they change colors.
4. Serving: Serve over fresh angle hair or linguini pasta. Place pasta on large plate. Dish sauce making sure to give vegetables generously over the center of the pasta. Arrange shrimps on top of sauce. To garnish, sprinkle dish with crumbled feta cheese. Serve with hot fresh Italian bread and a nice dry red wine.
5. Sun-dried tomatoes marinade: Buy sun-dried tomatoes in the package. In a tight lid jar, place tomatoes and equal parts of olive oil (salad oil, if you prefer) and red wine vinegar to cover tomatoes. Add a few tablespoons of sugar. Let tomatoes sit at least a week or until they start to soften. Use them in your favorite recipes or just eat them with bread in your antipasto.

The Rapids Restaurant in Grand Lake

The Staff at Garlic Mike's in Gunnison

GUNNISON

Gunnison was named after Captain John W. Gunnison who led a surveying team through the area in search of a railroad route to the west. He and most of his company were killed by Ute Indians in Utah in the fall of 1853. Today, the Pioneer Museum on Highway 50 displays many of the artifacts and buildings representing Gunnison's heritage, including a narrow gauge railroad engine, boxcar and caboose.

Zip Code: 81230. Area Code: 970. Population: 4,635. Elevation: 7,703'.

Garlic Mike's

2674 North Highway 135, 641-2493

Directions: From the intersection of Highways 50 and 135, go north on Highway 135 for 2.7 miles. The restaurant is on the right just past a bridge crossing the Gunnison River.

ESSENTIALS

Cuisine: Italian

Hours: 7 days 5PM-9PM. Closed for 1 week in APR and OCT.

Meals and Prices: Dinner $$$-$$$$

Nonsmoking: All. Smoking only permitted in bar area.

Take-out: Yes

Alcohol: Full Bar

Credit Cards: MC, Visa, Amx, Disc

Personal Check: Local only

Reservations: Recommended

Wheelchair Access: Yes, including bathrooms.

Other: Additional 15% service charge for parties of 6 or more. Major credit cards accepted with a $15 minimum.

HISTORY, PERSONALITY AND CHARACTER

Garlic Mike's was originally built about 1957 as a home. In the late 1960s, it was converted to the Ramble Inn, a 3.2 bar and restaurant. After going through several restaurant changes, it returned to the Ramble II in the early 1990s. On December 14, 1994, partners Larry Parachini and Mike Busse opened Garlic Mike's, named after both Larry's son and Mike Busse. Larry grew up in family-owned restaurants in New York and New Jersey. This is his first venture in Colorado. Executive chef Mike, a graduate of the Academy of Culinary Arts in Mayslanding, New Jersey, has been in the restaurant business since 1980 and worked at Larry's restaurant, L. C.'s Woodhouse in Allendale, New Jersey, from 1986 to 1994.

FOOD, SERVICE AND AMBIANCE

I had some good old-fashion pasta e fagoli alla Nonna (Grandma's macaroni and bean soup), a dry tasting, tomato base soup made with Northern cannelini beans, chick peas, smoked ham hocks, vegetables, pasta and white wine. I followed the soup with one of my favorite dishes, costolette — veal scallopine Marsala: thin, lean, tender, delicious medallions in Marsala wine with mushrooms. It was served with crunchy, thin, imported Italian breadsticks; soft and chewy bread rolls; sweet and creamy roasted garlic spread made with ricotta and mascarpone cheeses and fresh herbs; garlic mashed potatoes with a few lumps and skins left on (just the way I like them) and steamed broccoli. To finish things off, I made my way through homemade cannoli, a crisp, firm, fried pastry shell stuffed with smooth, saccharine, scrumptious pistachios, ricotta cheese and dried fruit, topped with whipped cream and fresh strawberries — an Italian delight!

This is one totally Italian restaurant with menus in both Italian and English. An extensive dinner menu offers hot and cold antipasto like calamari, mussels, ricotta-stuffed eggplant rolls and prosciutto with melon; soups; salads with homemade balsamic vinaigrette dressing; imported dry pastas and homemade raviolis; eggplant, chicken, veal or shrimp parmigiana; chicken; milk-fed, natural veal prepared in Madeira, white or sherry wines; a variety of seafood creations with halibut, salmon, scallops, shrimp or seafood stew and steaks. Their house specialty is sirloin carbonara. Enhance your dining experience with one of their red or white Italian wines and sweeten the end of your meal with homemade New York-style cheesecake, homemade Marsala egg custard with berries and ice cream, chocolate truffle cake, tiramisu, fresh berries, ice cream, rainbow sorbet or spumoni.

Service was most accommodating and Michael was a cheerful, energetic host. Dining is at tables with traditional red and white checkered table cloths. The first dining room has an arch-shaped, wood-burning fireplace while the second dining area, facing the patio, has storage shelves with a potpourri of pasta noodles, cans, fresh tomatoes, canisters and olive oils. Throughout the restaurant, you'll hear contemporary standard music and see modern, colorful artworks with a dining theme, dried-flower arrangements hanging over the entrances, and a series of old photographs, circa 1891 to 1922, from Italy, Portugal, California and New York. You can enjoy overseeing your meal being prepared through their open kitchen, with a wreath of garlic hanging overhead, or sit on the patio and watch the Gunnison River flow by amongst the river willows. Either way, you'll enjoy some authentic Italian cooking by a couple of east coast Italian guys who know how it should be done right.

SPECIAL ONE-TIME OFFER: Buy one entrée and receive a complimentary glass of house wine or a bottle of domestic beer. Limit two glasses of house wine or two domestic beers with the purchase of two entrées. This special one-time offer NOT valid in combination with any other offers. Please present to server at time of ordering. _____ Manager/Owner _____ Date.

RECIPE

Grilled Steak Giambotta
(Serves 6)

2 large potatoes, boiled in their skins, cooled and diced

3 bell peppers - red, green and yellow, if available, cut into ½-inch strips

2 medium yellow onions, peeled and cut into ½-inch strips

5 mild or hot cherry peppers, cut in half with seeds removed

1 cup diced zucchini, optional

¼ cup olive oil

1 teaspoon dried oregano leaf

1 tablespoon chopped garlic

⅛ cup balsamic vinegar or red wine vinegar

Salt and pepper to taste

1. While steaks are grilling, gather all ingredients. In large skillet, heat the olive oil until it just starts to smoke.
2. Toss in all ingredients, except the oregano, salt, pepper and vinegar.
3. Sauté all ingredients in a stir-fry fashion over high heat. The vegetables should be al dente (slightly undercooked).
4. Add the oregano, salt, pepper and vinegar. Cook for an additional minute. Put over steaks.

---

the Trough

West Highway 50, PO Box 1117, 641-3724

Directions: From the east, go 2½ miles past the intersection of Highways 50 and 135 on Highway 50. The restaurant is on the left. From the west on Highway 50, the restaurant is on the right immediately past the Water Wheel Motel at mile marker 155 before you get to Gunnison.

ESSENTIALS

Cuisine: Steak/Fresh Seafood/ Wild Game
Hours: Sun-Thu 5:30PM-10PM. Fri-Sat 5:30PM-10:30PM.

Meals and Prices: Dinner $$$-$$$$$
Nonsmoking: Yes
Take-out: Yes
Alcohol: Full Bar

Credit Cards: MC, Visa, Amx, Disc
Personal Check: Yes, with I.D.
Reservations: Recommended
Wheelchair Access: Yes, including restrooms.

Other: One check per table. Additional 15% service charge for parties of 6 or more. Banquet room available for special parties.

HISTORY, PERSONALITY AND CHARACTER

The Trough opened on October 28, 1980, and has retained its original name, decor and ambiance. The Trough is owned by Tom Hamilton who has been in the restaurant business since 1965 and also owns Cafe Cascade in Durango (see page 87) and the Trough Restaurant in Farmington, New Mexico. He also has a share of Señor Peppers and the Rocky Mountain Rib Company in Farmington and the Chelsea's Restaurants in Durango, Grand Junction, Longmont and Farmington. His newest restaurant venture is the New Sheridan Restaurant and Bar in Telluride. The Trough is managed by Stewart Barton and Cheri Meyer. Stewart has been working in restaurants since 1975 having worked previously in Denver before starting at the Trough on their opening night. Cheri has been in restaurants since 1980 and started at the Trough in 1984. Head Chef Stu Bob from Denver has been at the Trough since 1980.

FOOD, SERVICE AND AMBIANCE

I relished over the fresh southwestern marlin, a firm-textured fish, stuffed with a seasoned mixture of green chilies, pine nuts and fontina cheese, lightly breaded with a red chili pesto sauce baked on top for a crisp crust and sprinkled with grated Parmesan cheese. (Fish deliveries come twice a week. The fish is never frozen. It usually comes whole and is cut into filets at the restaurant). The combination of light, flavorful marlin with the chili spices made for an exquisite dish. It was served with a medley of 3 vegetables (a mini-representation of the Cascade Cafe tradition where you'll be served 9 or 10 vegetables) including crunchy fried spinach and tomato with melted cheeses on top. Also presented with dinner were fresh and slightly sweet, homemade poppyseed rolls and a salad with homemade sweet and sour French dressing prepared with red wine vinegar, caramelized sugar and pineapple juice. Salty sunflower seeds were served on the side. Their other homemade dressings are blue cheese, ranch and garlic Italian.

Their regular menu, one of the largest I've come across, measures about 3 square feet and they augment that with nightly fresh seafood and wild game specials. Your hearty selection includes slowly cooked prime rib (also available blackened), several cuts of steak, center cut pork chops or duck with an orange glaze, shrimp tempura, Alaskan king crab legs, lobster and chicken Mazatlan. The evening specials featured artichoke au gratin, Cajun barbecued rock shrimp and fresh soft shell crab for appetizers; opah, sesame seared ahi, salmon, trout, scallops and prawns for the fresh seafood choices offered that night and elk tenderloin, pheasant and quail in cranberry sage sauce and muscovy duck were the wild game entrées. To complement your meal, you have about 40 wines, mostly California with a few French, to choose from. To complete the dining experience, delve into a piece of amaretto cheesecake, key lime pie or chocolate ecstacy cake.

Service was very accommodating and attentive. They have a good flow from host to drink-taker to server. They also have very little turnover with staff. Some wait people have been there five years, which probably accounts for the excellent service. Country music played pleasantly and quietly in the background. I just happened to be there on a Thursday evening, after 9PM when they had live comedy in the lounge. Occasionally, they'll have live music on a weekend or special occasion, like a graduation or the Fourth of July.

The Trough's walls are the original barnwood from Crawford, Colorado, and from a ranch just down the road. Directly back from the host's stand is the bodega, a wine cellar with a wrought-iron gate, a fish tank and a rocking horse pig for the kids to play on while they down their PB&J and you select your bottle of wine. To the right of the entrance is a waiting area with a cushioned bench and just beyond is a Brobdingnagian fireplace with a 20-foot long hearth. Beyond this is the stage, lounge and bar. Throughout the restaurant, you'll see beautiful stained-glass in southwestern colors including a piece over the entrance to the bodega resembling three dead trees with an eerie-looking bluish-red background and a red, star-shaped piece in the corner of the lounge. This sizable restaurant is well designed in a circular pattern allowing a view of all areas from the host's stand and a cozy, romantic place to bring someone special.

SPECIAL ONE-TIME OFFER: Buy two entrées at the regular price and receive a complimentary appetizer (up to $10 value). This offer NOT valid in combination with any other offers. Please present to server at time of ordering. _____ Manager/Owner. _____ Date.

RECIPE

Pork Hawaiian

1 8-ounce pork tenderloin   Hawaiian Sauce:
Rice   Equal parts of teriyaki sauce,
Bell peppers   apple juice and pineapple juice
Onions   Pinch of cinnamon, ground clove
                                              and nutmeg. Cornstarch.

1. Marinate pork in just teriyaki sauce. Bring to a boil all ingredients for the Hawaiian sauce. Thicken with cornstarch.
2. Grill and slice pork over a bed of rice with grilled bell peppers and onions.
3. Pour Hawaiin sauce on top.

The Wine Cellar with Aquarium and Rocking Horse Pig at the Trough in Gunnison

Yesteryear at The Riverside Hotel and Restaurant in Hot Sulphur Springs

HEENEY

Heeney was named after Paul Heeney who owned much of the land bordering Green Mountain dam when it was built in 1938. Water from the Dillon Reservoir, 24 miles south of Heeney, flows north in the Blue River which dumps into the Green Mountain Reservoir. The town of Heeney, which developed around the building of the reservoir between 1938 and 1944, was supposed to be temporary for the dam builders but the Holderson family purchased the town from the U.S. Government and Heeney stayed in business. For all you hikers, lovers of "tiny livestock" and those who just appreciate the peculiar, bizarre and weird, Heeney has been hosting its own Annual Tick Festival in late spring (the end of tick season) since 1981. It began when a local resident, Faith Tjardes, recovered from tick fever. She left town, but the townsfolk decided to throw a celebration in her honor. Highlighting the day's events are the world's shortest parade (the town's only 1 block long), a spittoon toss, the crowing of the Tick King and Queen and for $1, festival-goers can tack a black paper tick on the wall of the Green Mountain Inn, reviewed below (remember, it's just a paper tick).
Zip Code: 80498. Area Code: 970. Population: 40. Elevation: Approx. 8,800'.

Green Mountain Inn
7101 County Road #30, 724-3812
Directions: Take Exit 205 from I-70. Go north on Highway 9 for 16.8 miles and turn left onto County Road 30 - Heeney Road (there is a green sign on the right for Heeney and Green Mountain Reservoir). Go 7.1 miles. The restaurant is on your right at the corner of Blue Ridge Street.

ESSENTIALS

Cuisine: Country
Hours: Memorial Day to Labor Day: Mon-Thu 11AM-10PM, Fri-Sun 8AM-10PM. Labor Day to Thanksgiving: Mon-Fri 3PM-10PM, Sat-Sun 8AM-10PM. Thanksgiving to Memorial Day: Mon-Fri 3PM-10PM, Sat/Sun 8AM-10PM. Breakfast served until 11AM, lunch starts at 11:30 or 3PM depending on opening time, dinner starts at 5PM.
Meals and Prices: Breakfast/ Lunch $-$$, Dinner $$-$$$$

Nonsmoking: No
Take-out: Yes
Alcohol: Full Bar
Credit Cards: MC, Visa
Personal Check: Local only
Reservations: Recommended on holiday weekends. Accepted otherwise.
Wheelchair Access: Yes
Dress: Casual, with country flair
Other: Catering, banquets and private parties available. Additional 15% service charge for parties of 5 or more.

HISTORY, PERSONALITY AND CHARACTER

The Green Mountain Inn (GMI) was built in the late 1940s as a meeting place for ranching families. The restaurant, located over the garage, was built in the mid-1960s. Current owners and managers Scott and Jeannette Astaldi, purchased the GMI in October 1993 and added a 1,600-foot deck on the Fourth of July 1994. Today, the GMI consists of an old-fashioned country store, rooms and cabins for rent, a tavern and a lake view dining room. Scott and Jeannette have been in the restaurant business since the early 1980s. Scott, who is the author of <u>High Country Crags, the Rock Climbing Guide to Summit County, Colorado</u>, worked at the Blue Spruce in Frisco from 1990 to 1993 and now runs the kitchen as well as playing handy man around the Inn. Jeannette was at Pug Ryan's in Dillon from 1988 to 1993 and oversees the front of the restaurant and the lodge.

FOOD, SERVICE AND AMBIANCE

They offer generous portions of good ol' agreeable country food. The curry chicken soup was stock full of vegetables and apples, but not overbearing on the spices, a good warm-up on a blustery spring day. My entrée, panfried trout with green chili aioli, was served butterfly-style with a lot of melted butter and savory flavor. It was served over a bed of pasta and vegetables. The aioli was made with mayonnaise, lime, green chilies, garlic, white pepper and salt.

If you arrive here for breakfast, you can order eggs with apple-smoked bacon, pan-fried rainbow trout, pancakes, charbroiled top sirloin, an omelet or French toast. The lunch/dinner appetizers include smoked trout with strawberry horseradish sauce, a southwestern shrimp cocktail, frazzled onions (tossed lightly with chili before frying), and stuffed jalapeños. The lunch menu features sandwiches, burgers (beef or soy-free vegetarian) and fried chicken. For dinner, you can choose from the house specialties (Colorado-raised choice beef and chicken pot pie), fried chicken, shrimp scampi, the catch of the day or Mexican. Chicken fried steak is offered at every meal. Friday is fish fry night and on Saturday, they have a prime rib special. For dessert, they were serving chocolate nemesis, Grannie's caramel apple and deep-dish apple pies the day I was here.

My server, the bar manager, had a great sense of humor (i.e. he laughed at all my little jokes). When you enter the building, the country store is on your left. The dining room is on your right past the tavern with hardwood floor and pool table. Country music emanates from the bar. The dining room itself has some interesting decor items, like a wood-burning stove (the only source of heat); mini organ; wagon wheel; brass-plated chandelier; 3½-foot diameter commercial saw blade with a painting of a mountain saloon, a couple of Harley-Davidsons, aspen trees and snow-capped mountains; a pair of skis hanging next to the saw blade; and a painting of the Colorado River near Kremmling in the autumn. The saw blade was painted by Tina Knapp and the painting was by Don Mertes, both local artists and both were in the tavern the day I was there (this is a really small town, folks!). The worn, green carpet in the dining room is easy to overlook and more than compensated for by the great view of the Green Mountain Reservoir and the Gore Mountain range. Still, it is only about one-third of what you will experience on the deck where you get a spectacular view in three directions up and down the Blue River. Try to visit when the weather is pleasant. They have live music inside on Saturday nights and outside on the deck on Sunday afternoons. During the summer and fall, you may even see deer or elk across the road. Country cuisine served with a down-home attitude in a place with a view is what you'll find at the Green Mountain Inn.

<u>Special One-time Offer:</u> Buy one entrée at the regular price and receive a second entrée of equal or lesser value FREE OR receive 50% off a single entrée. This offer NOT valid in combination with any other offers. _____ Manager/Owner. _____ Date.

<u>RECIPE</u>

Beef Teriyaki Kabobs
(Serves 4)

1 pound boneless beef sirloin steak
⅓ cup soy sauce
3 tablespoons apple juice
1 tablespoon molasses

2 teaspoons dry mustard
1 pinch ground ginger
1 clove minced garlic

1. Slice beef into ⅛-inch strips.
2. Mix all ingredients into marinade and marinate beef for 15 minutes at room temperature.
3. Drain meat and reserve for basting beef while meat cooks.
4. Place on uncovered grill over direct heat for 5 to 6 minutes; turn and brush with marinade often.

HOT SULPHUR SPRINGS

The town is named for the hot springs in the area and was once owned by William N. Byers, founder of the Denver Rocky Mountain News. Located in Middle Park and bounded by the Continental Divide to the east, Rabbit Ears pass to the northwest and the Gore mountain range to the southwest, the Hot Sulphur Springs area was previously inhabited by Ute and Arapaho Indians and French trappers. This is also the cradle of skiing in Colorado for it was here in 1911 that Norwegian champion Carl Howelson built the first ski jump west of the Mississippi River. Today, the primary industries are tourism and ranching.

Zip Code: 80451. Area Code: 970. Population: 347. Elevation: 7,680'.

The Riverside
509 Grand Avenue, 725-3589

Directions: From the east on Highway 40, turn right onto Grand Avenue as you enter town. Go 6 blocks (½ mile). The restaurant is on the right before the bridge over the Colorado River. From the west on Highway 40, turn left onto Grand Avenue and go one block. The restaurant is on the left.

ESSENTIALS

Cuisine: Country
Hours: Mid-MAY through SEP: Tue-Sun 5:30PM-9PM. Closed Mon. OCT to Mid-MAY: Thu-Sun 5:30PM-8PM. Closed Mon-Wed.
Meals and Prices: Dinner $$$
Nonsmoking: No
Take-out: Yes

Alcohol: Full Bar
Credit Cards: No
Personal Check: Yes, with I.D.
Reservations: Recommended in the summer
Wheelchair Access: Yes
Other: Available for banquets and special parties.

HISTORY, PERSONALITY AND CHARACTER

The Riverside Hotel and Restaurant was built in 1903 and has always had the same name. Expansions of the dining rooms and kitchen took place in 1919 and 1975. In October 1982, Abraham Renta Rodriguez purchased the red-framed building with its leaky roof and executed a major renovation. He restored the roof, painted the exterior walls white, added black shutters, laid wallpaper, installed wallboard, hired professional help to repair the wiring, plumbing and heating and reopened the hotel/restaurant in June 1983. Prior to coming to Hot Sulphur Springs, he lived in and renovated the Atwood-Jones House in Longmont. He shares kitchen duties with his former trainee, Jaime (Himeh) Hernandez, who has worked at The Riverside since 1984.

155

FOOD, SERVICE AND AMBIANCE

The food at The Riverside is down to earth, well prepared and a good value for your money. On my first visit, Abraham prepared a tasty cornish hen, stuffed with pimentos, topped with stewed tomatoes and served with fried rice mixed with onions, pickle relish, stewed tomatoes and stuffed green olives. On my last visit, I relished a whole panfried Rocky Mountain rainbow trout with lemon and capers cooked by Jaime. It was white, tender, moist, deboned meat with the skin still on that broke apart easily with a fork; served with an interesting array of fresh vegetables: white rice with corn, carrots with raisins, broccoli, tomatoes, onions, green peppers and green olives. Their clam chowder was a clear broth with a lot of vegetables and clams. Salad came with homemade Italian dressing (they also have homemade ranch and blue cheese). They serve bread, soups and apple and strawberry-rhubarb pies, all homemade. Sandwiches, burgers and salads are offered for lunch.

Owner, manager, chef, host and waiter, Abraham carts his blackboard and tri-pod from table to table as guests arrive for dinner and explains each of the evening's entrées like chicken fried steak, breaded pork chops, steaks, salmon steak, half roasted chicken and barbecued ribs. He is quite a character. On my last visit, he told the couple sitting next to me, "Everyone should have a blackboard menu . . . and a blackboard marriage. That way, if you don't like something, you could erase either one."

Classical violin and piano music are played in "Abe's Place". The first dining room has more antique charm with an old upright piano, a black and gold Fort Knox safe, a couple of oval portraits, a picture of the U. S. Capitol, an oil on canvas painting of Estes Park by Albert Bierstadt and a wood-burning rock fireplace. The second dining room has the picturesque view of the Colorado River as it flows toward the restaurant before veering off. Expect to enjoy a unique dining experience when you come to the Riverside.

SPECIAL ONE-TIME OFFER: 15% off the total food bill for 1 to 4 people. This offer NOT valid in combination with any other offers. Please present to server at time of ordering. _____ Manager/Owner. _____ Date.

RECIPE
Fail-Proof Basic Steps to Great Hardy Soups

Olive oil or vegetable oil	Cubed potatoes
Yellow onions, sliced	Diced carrots
Red peppers, diced (canned is OK)	Green beans
Granulated garlic	Diced celery
Pinch of oregano	Broccoli stems
Granulated black pepper	Tomatoes
Prime ingredient: Diced chicken, canned clams, hamburger meat or various kinds of fish	

1. In a stock pot, sauté in oil yellow onions and red peppers. Add granulated garlic, oregano and black pepper.
2. Just before onions are translucent, add the prime ingredient. Sauté the prime ingredient in stock pot until onions become translucent.
3. In a separate pot, boil potatoes, carrots and green beans. Do not over cook.
4. Just before serving, add the boiled potato mixture, celery, broccoli and tomatoes to the stock. The result is a hardy, tasty soup with crisp vegetables.

Why not pick up an extra copy of <u>Colorado Restaurants and Recipes</u> and keep one in your vehicle and the other in your kitchen?

HUDSON

Hudson was named after the Hudson City Land and Improvement Company of Denver, who purchased and developed the townsite.
Zip Code: 80642. Area Code: 303. Population: 918. Elevation: 5,000'.

Pepper Pod
530 Fir, PO Box 502, 536-4736
Directions: Located 31 miles northeast of Denver. From I-25 north of Denver, take I-76 northeast for 31 miles. Exit Hudson, turn right at the end of the exit ramp, then take another immediate right. The restaurant is a few hundred feet down the road on the left.

ESSENTIALS
Cuisine: American/Country
Hours: Wed-Mon 6AM-9PM. Closed Tue.
Meals and Prices: Breakfast/Lunch $, Dinner $$-$$$
Nonsmoking: Yes
Take-out: Yes
Alcohol: Full Bar
Credit Cards: MC, Visa, Amx, Disc
Personal Check: Yes

Reservations: Recommended for dinner
Wheelchair Access: Yes
Dress: Country casual
Other: Upstairs banquet room for receptions, business meetings, anniversaries and other social and business functions. Entrées prepared as a lo-fat, low cholesterol, healthy alternative indicated on the menu.

HISTORY, PERSONALITY AND CHARACTER
The Pepper Pod had two previous locations. The Peppers opened a modest cafe on Hudson's old Main Street back in the 1920s. Soon after opening, a larger building was needed to accommodate a flourishing business, so the restaurant was moved next to Highway 6. In 1956, the present building was constructed near Interstate 80 (now I-76). At that time, the Pepper Pod was known as the "Oasis on the Plains" (I like that name!) and was operated by Mr. Pepper's son-in-law, Bill Howard. In 1977, current owners David and Beth Martin bought the Pod from Mike Nanovich and began to build on the restaurant's reputation, serving buffalo year-around. This was a first-time restaurant venture for the Martins, one that has grown in popularity both with the locals and folks from the Denver area. It has been recommended to me several times since my first two restaurant guides were published. Dave is the head chef who gets help from Stella (over 20 years' experience), their baker, who prepares desserts, cinnamon and regular rolls, and corn bread.

FOOD, SERVICE AND AMBIANCE

Linda, my editor, and I tried their jumbo shrimp and chicken teriyaki combination and sirloin and lobster. The soup and salad bar was included with dinner. Their homemade chicken noodle came with lots of big wide noodles, but not much chicken. The 15-item salad bar included a thick cole slaw with carrot slices that I particularly liked and 5 homemade dressings made from recipes created by Irene Beard in the 1930s. The moist jumbo shrimps had a thick, but light breading. The sirloin had just enough fat for flavor. Dave selects well-marbled beef and does the aging and cutting himself. The ¼ to ½ pound lobster tail was just right, not rubbery but firm in texture. The chicken teriyaki was flavorful, but could have been more moist. Save room for one of their homemade pies. I would recommend the blueberry a la mode with 3 big scoops of vanilla ice cream. They also serve cherry, apple and others depending on the season. The breakfast menu offers omelets, pancakes, French toast, hot or cold cereal and fresh fruit in season. The lunch/dinner menu features appetizers like jalapeño cheese bites, hot wings and nachos; sandwiches made with steak, chicken, Polish or Italian sausage, and roast or corn beef; burgers; light entrées; salads; and entrées with beef, poultry, seafood, pasta, buffalo or pork. They also have a kid's menu, homemade cheesecake, sundaes and floats.

There is a staff of seasoned servers here, some dating back 10-20 years. Dave informed me that last year they only turned over 4 people from their staff of 36. Quite remarkable for this kind of business! The Pepper Pod does not offer music or entertainment. In the main dining room to the left of the entrance are three grand, imposing buffalo heads from a herd that grazed behind the Pod for many years. On the wall to the right of these heads is a photo that fascinated me. It was taken with a sweeping, wide-angle lens around the time of World War I in the middle of Hudson and everyone in town must have been in the picture! Check it out. They also have a gas fireplace in the dining room and a wood burning fireplace upstairs in the banquet room. The Pepper Pod is a long-lived, home grown place with a lot of local flavor.

SPECIAL ONE-TIME OFFER: Buy one entrée at the regular price and receive a second entrée of equal or lesser value FREE (Up to $25.00 value) OR 50% off a single entrée (maximum discount $12.50). This offer NOT valid in combination with any other offers.
_____ Manager/Owner. _____ Date.

RECIPE

Fiesta Chicken

1 stewing chicken
  3 to 4 pounds, cut as for frying
¼ pound butter
3 medium-size onions, chopped
1 large green bell pepper, chopped
1 tablespoon ground mild red chile
  (or more)
½ teaspoon freshly ground pepper
3 tomatoes, cut into thin wedges

1 cup chicken broth (or more
  as needed)
1 cup sour cream
3 tablespoons flour
2 tablespoons snipped fresh parsley
½ cup pitted black olives, cut into
  rings
2 tablespoons salt

1. Place cut-up chicken in a large casserole that has been generously buttered.
2. Melt butter in a frying pan and lightly sauté the onions and green pepper. Pour evenly over the chicken.
3. Season with the chile, salt and pepper. Cover with the tomatoes and chicken broth. Add more chicken broth if needed during baking. Bake in a 350-degree oven for 1½ hours or until tender.
4. When the chicken is tender when pierced with a fork, remove from casserole and remove chicken from the sauce.
5. Combine the sour cream with the flour and stir into the sauce in the casserole dish. Stir until well blended. Place over medium heat and simmer until thickened.
6. Serve the chicken drizzled with the sauce and sprinkled with freshly snipped parsley and black olive rings. A side dish of rice is a must for the gravy.

We use this as a special entrée and in catering. My Great-Grandma from New Mexico used red chile for tenderizing and flavoring meat — and this recipe came from that concept.

Beth Martin

IDAHO SPRINGS

Formerly known as Sacramento City, Idaho City, Idaho and Idahoe, the final name for the town may have been derived from an Indian word meaning "gem of the mountains", or it may have come from the word "Idahi", the Kiowa-Apache name for the Comanches. In either case, the town is the outgrowth of the camp of George A. Jackson who discovered gold in the area on January 7, 1859. Idaho Springs is another Colorado town with a rich history of mining. The Argo Gold Mine, which was used to retrieve gold, silver, copper, lead and other valuable metals between 1913 and 1943, has been restored and is now open for tours. A locomotive stands in the center of town on a section of the original narrow gauge track that connected Idaho Springs with two other mining towns, Golden and Georgetown.

Zip Code: 80452. Area Code: 303. Population: 1,834. Elevation: 7,524'.

Beau Jo's

1517 Miner Street, 567-4376, in Denver call 573-6924

Directions: Take Exit 240 from I-70. Proceed north one block to the stop sign. Turn right onto Miner Street. Proceed 2½ blocks. The restaurant is on your right just past 15th Street. Park in the street, or, turn right at 15th Street, go one block to Water Street, turn left, and enter the parking lot behind the restaurant.

ESSENTIALS

Type: Colorado-Style Pizza

Hours: Sun-Thu 11AM-9:30PM. Fri-Sat 11AM-10PM.

Meals and Prices: $$ per person for pizza.

Nonsmoking: Yes

Take-out: Yes

Alcohol: Full Bar

Credit Cards: MC, Visa, Amx, Disc

Personal Check: Yes, with guaranteed check card and driver's license.

Reservations: No

Wheelchair Access: Yes, from the front or back.

Dress: Casual - ski and outdoor wear.

HISTORY, PERSONALITY AND CHARACTER

Beau Jo's occupies 6 formerly separate buildings that date back to the 1870s. Originally an assay office for the local mining operations, this space went through several transformations, becoming a shoe store, department store and a 6-room hotel. The original Beau Jo's started on the corner of 15th and Idaho in 1971 by a local couple, who else, Beau and Joanne. "Chip" Bair, purchased the restaurant in April 1973 and moved it to its current location on Miner Street. Shawn Carter is the General Manager and has been with Beau Jo's since 1986. He has four assistant managers and 15 to 18 pizza makers who can turn out 60 to 70 pizzas in a half hour. Today, Beau Jo's has expanded with restaurants in Denver, Boulder, Arvada, Fort Collins and Colorado Springs with more Beau Jo's planned for the future.

FOOD, SERVICE, AND AMBIANCE

Beau Jo's offers a variety of specialty pizza pies and create-your-own mountain pies for the non-purist, unconventional, non-traditional pizza lover. I have tried 3 of their 4 breads, 3 of 4 thicknesses, 3 of 6 pizza sauces, 3 of 7 cheeses, and 11 of 29 ingredients. My preferences on their homemade dough are for the butter white bread, which makes for a lighter, more flavorful crust, and the sesame wheat bread, if you like sesame seeds. For thickness, I've graduated from a preference for thick, chewy crusts to the lighter thin and extra thin. I liked all three sauces that I tried: Beau Jo's pizza sauce, sweet and sour, and the white wine sauce. I plan to try the roasted garlic cream sauce next time. They also offer barbecue and taco sauces. I've tried their mozzarella, provolone, and Swiss cheeses. Cheddar, Monterey Jack, fontina-provolone, and no-cholesterol mozzarella are the other cheeses. Their ingredients are all prepped fresh daily. Their Mountain Man pizza with pepperoni, Canadian bacon, pineapple and spinach, and two specialty pizzas, the Thai pie and the shrimp Zapigh (named after Beau Jo's fabled French fur trapper founder, Pete Zapigh) were all scrumptious.

Some of the more interesting pizza ingredients on their menu are Cajun sausage, meatballs, Italian spiced chicken, zucchini, tofu, artichoke hearts, jalapeño peppers, broccoli and alfalfa sprouts. For those of you who yearn for some genuine Buffalo wings with Frank's hot sauce, order some at Beau Jo's. They're good and hot. The other appetizers on the menu are baked stuffed mushrooms and garlic bread with cheese. If you don't come here for pizza, your choices are limited to sandwiches, soup and the 20-item salad bar with six dressings. If you like a challenge, Beau Jo's has one for you. Two people have one hour to devour a 12 to 14-pound "Challenge", Grand Sicilian pizza on a super thick 16-inch crust. If you do, you get the $45 pie for free, $100, and 2 free Beau Jo's T-shirts. So far only one couple has been successful. Two cyclists, coming down from the mountains, came close, finishing off the pizza in 1 hour and 5 minutes. Beau Jo's "comped" the pizza and gave them the T-shirts, but not the cash. In 1994, Beau Jo's won Readers' Choice Awards for Best Pizza in the Rocky Mountain News and The Denver Post and Westword and was voted favorite place to stop after skiing by readers in the Rocky Mountain News.

Service here has always been very helpful and with a smile. One gets the impression that the folks here have a good time while they serve you. You will probably hear some moderate to mild rock songs playing in the background. The decor in Beau Jo's has two distinguishing themes: historical remembrances of the old mining town that was once here and a napkin art gallery. The napkins idea originated when Chip became annoyed with people writing on his pizza circle menus. He would hand them a napkin and tell them to "write on this". The idea just caught on and now you will see hundreds of personally artistic paper napkins nailed to the walls. Beau Jo's has expanded over time to 5-dining areas, bar, lounge and patio that can seat about 500 people. Throughout the restaurant, you will see old photos of Idaho Springs, including a 1909 photo of Bob

McClellan (the McClellan Tunnel was a major gold mining excavation between Idaho Springs and Black Hawk) holding a medicine ball; a series of four photos, end-to-end, in a single frame showing Idaho Springs in September 1925; and several old photos of the gold mines, the Hot Springs Hotel in 1926, 1890 gentlemen, an 1880 summer party, a big snow in 1913, celebration days in 1922, and Beau Jo's under construction. Along with the old photos are several old miner's maps, like the map of the Clear Creek gold belt between Idaho Springs and Black Hawk. The current restaurant has red brick walls to the far right and far left, a balcony to the far left, an original turn-of-the-century tin ceiling in the front, an old metal-siding ceiling in the bar room in the back, and uneven floor boards that creak in spots, especially near the bar. The restaurant's centerpiece, however, is their elevator shaft that has been disguised to look like a mine shaft. If you look down the shaft, you will see a big mining bucket that is slowly turning into a gold mine by itself. People have taken to throwing coins into the bucket like they would into a fountain. A rusty pair of ice tongs, an old cutting board, a model of a conestoga wagon, an old mining bucket rusted with holes, a pair of huge bellows, and a glass-enclosed case of old automobile headlights add even more character to Beau Jo's walls. Bathtubs with feet are used for the salad bars and in the bar/lounge in the back, you will see a huge safe with a big old cash register on top. In terms of pizza and decor, Beau Jo's is the most interesting restaurant you will find in Colorado. They have a gift shop upstairs if you want to take home a memorabilia of your experience here. Beau Jo's may be the chain pizzeria of the future, but there will only be one, unique, original Beau Jo's in Idaho Springs.

Special One-time Offer: Purchase any pizza and receive a complimentary pitcher of any soft drink. This offer NOT valid in combination with any other offers.
_____ Manager/Owner. _____ Date.

RECIPE
Cajun Pizza

1 13-inch pizza crust, thick
7 ounces pizza sauce
6 ounces Cajun sausage
4 ounces pepperoni

4 ounces onion
3 ounces jalapeño peppers, sliced
7 ounces provolone cheese, shredded
7 ounces cheddar cheese, shredded

1. Place pizza dough in a 13-inch round pan. Pour sauce over crust. Evenly distribute all ingredients, adding the cheeses last. For best results, toss cheeses together before putting on the pizza.
2. Bake at 450 for 20-25 minutes or until crust is golden brown.
3. Slice and serve hot.

163

KITTREDGE

It was established in 1920 when the Kittredge Town Company, owned by Charles M. Kittredge, purchased 300 acres of the Luther ranch. A year later, postal officials named the settlement after the Kittredge Family which had lived in the area since 1860. Zip Code: 80457. Area Code: 303. Population: 800. Elevation: 6,840'.

Tivoli Deer

26300 Hilltop Drive, PO Box 86, 670-0941

Directions: Take Exit 252, for El Rancho, from I-70 and follow Highway 74 south for 10 miles into Kittredge (2 miles past Evergreen). The restaurant is on the left just as you enter town and where the road bends to the right. An alternative route is to take C-470 to the Morrison Exit. Go west 10 miles to Kittredge. The restaurant will be on the right at the far end of town, right before the road bends to the left.

ESSENTIALS

Cuisine: Danish/Colorado
Hours: Mon/Wed-Sat: 11AM-3PM and 5:30PM-10PM. Sun 10AM-2PM and 5:30PM-10PM. Closed Tue.
Meals and Prices: Lunch $$, Brunch $$$, á la carte Dinner $$$, 4-course dinner $$$$$$$
Nonsmoking: All, smoking only permitted on patio
Take-out: Yes
Alcohol: Full Bar

Credit Cards: All 5
Personal Check: Yes, with I.D.
Reservations: Strongly recommended on weekends, recommended otherwise
Wheelchair Access: Yes
Dress: Casual to dressy on weekends, casual otherwise
Other: Special prices and portions available for seniors and youngsters under 12.

HISTORY, PERSONALITY AND CHARACTER

The Tivoli Deer is in a building originally constructed in 1974 for small shops: a television repair and Mountain Ranch Supply, now located next door. The Prospect, a cowboy restaurant with live rock music at the bar, took over in 1977. The Tivoli Deer Restaurant, which opened on June 17, 1982, is owned by Mogens Sorensen. The name is a combination of "Tivoli Gardens", a famous amusement park in Denmark, and a peaceful deer to add some Colorado mountain flair. In 1994, the patio was expanded and enclosed in glass.

Mogens was born in Herning, Denmark, and spent his youth working in his family's restaurant and bakery, "The Trianon". He graduated from the Aalborg and Copenhagen Schools of Hotel and Restaurant Management and went to work as a chef at Movenpick Restaurant in Geneva, Switzerland. The Fairmont Hotel System then brought Mogens to San Francisco as a management trainee in 1976. He managed several restaurants in the San Francisco Fairmont for 2 years, then was transferred to Denver as the Food and Beverage Director for The New Fairmont Denver. Mogens left the corporate world in 1982 to begin the Tivoli Deer.

FOOD, SERVICE AND AMBIANCE

Every summer, Mogens makes a trip back to Copenhagen, selects two graduating chefs from the Ringsted Culinary School and brings them back to Colorado. One is an assistant chef, the other a pastry baker. They spend a year at the Tivoli Deer practicing their trade. Mogens gives them the opportunity to create and improvise with the menu.

I've dined at the Tivoli Deer about a dozen times: once for lunch, once for dinner and the rest of the times for Sunday brunch. I have tried most of the brunch entrées at least once. They are all wonderful and I would highly recommend each one of them. The Pojarski was a homemade chicken sausage that had a fish texture. It was served on a buttered croissant with poached eggs, green and red peppers and hollandaise sauce. The fresh vegetable was a distinctive hollowed-out zucchini slice stuffed with mushroom pâté. The stroganoff crêpe (tenderloin tips sautéed medium rare in bordelaise, onion and mushroom sauce, then folded in a homemade crêpe) was tender and juicy. The garden brioche (filled with sautéed spinach, poached egg and hollandaise) was a savory vegetable dish. The French (two chicken and ham croquettes served with poached eggs on a croissant with hollandaise) was a gratifying mix of meats. The Nordic chicken (breast stuffed with deviled crabmeat in a light paprika shrimp sauce) was the tastiest of the Sunday fare. The smoke house (fresh smoked trout with scrambled eggs and chives) was a mouth-watering treat. The cheese blintzes (with three types of cheeses, blueberries and raisins, served with blueberry yogurt sauce) were sweet and delicious. The Aeggekage Danish (open-faced omelet with bacon, Jarlsberg cheese, tomato and onion) was a flavorful combination. Other spotlights on the brunch menu were filet mignon, Danish waffle, a combination seafood tart, and gravad lox and bagel.

Brunch includes a glass of champagne or soft drink, coffee or tea, Danish pastry, and fresh orange juice or fruit. Special cocktails, like mimosa, bloody Mary, fresh fruit daquiri, and a Danish Mary with Aquavit along with specialty coffee drinks are available. Most entrées come with fresh vegetables and pommes gratin dauphinoise (similar to scalloped potatoes with a crusty cheese and bread topping).

I ordered scrumptious Scotch eggs for lunch — a special that included soup or salad and cappuccino or dessert. For starters, I was served a fresh croissant made with cracked wheat that was fluffy on the inside and lightly browned and crisp on the outside — expertly prepared by Mogens' visiting pastry baker. The soup was a simple yet delectably thick cream of tomato topped with chives. The entrée had a whole hard boiled egg with ground lamb and beef encased in a puff pastry, served with wild rice (with slivered almonds and raisins) and green beans and mushrooms with garlic. This was my only opportunity (anywhere) for this unusual dish and if you're lucky enough to find it on the menu, go for it! The dessert was an ambrosial creation of homemade hazelnut ice cream with nougat-covered orange slices topped with a crunchy Italian crème meringue. Together with a cup of freshly ground coffee, they made a comme il faut ending to a fabulous meal.

The lunch specials change every two weeks. On my visit, the other specials were penne pasta with grilled chicken and vegetables, meatloaf with mushroom potato, English-style fish and chips and the Tivoli salad with marinated vegetables and tri-color rotini pasta. The regular lunch menu offered gravad lax (marinated salmon served with mustard dill dressing) as an appetizer; baked onion soup and a soup du jour; and seafood, herring or chicken curry salads. For sandwiches, they had Swedish meatballs, steak and hamburger. The specialties were breast of chicken Frangelico, 10-ounce sirloin, wiener schnitzel and sautéed gulf prawns provençale.

My sole dinner experience at the Tivoli was an enchanting one on the patio under a warm summer sky. Plan to spend two to three hours to fully relish this marvelous dining extravagance. Take your time, relax and feast! The four-course meal begins with your choice of appetizer or soup. My dinner companion and I ordered the herring trianon and the seafood cocktail. We enjoyed dipping the herring in each of the marinades (the tomato sherry, vinaigrette and horseradish and the curry and mayonnaise) and delighted in the Norwegian bay shrimp and scallops in Louis dressing made with mayonnaise, tabasco, sweet onion and pickle. The second course was the Tivoli salad. The ten dinner entrée selections featured everything from spaghetti to lamb. There's the Nordic chicken, tornedos marsala, squire coho salmon, breast of duck Danoise, emincé of veal Zurichoise, sweetbreads with crayfish tails en cocotte, roast saddle of lamb, beuf sauté stroganoff, seafood spaghetti and a daily special, usually fresh fish. We ordered the duck and the veal. The duck is basted a day in advance in its own juices and it was moist on the inside and crispy on the outside. Served along side potatoes with brown sugar glaze and red cabbage, it was positively outstanding! The veal and mushrooms in sour cream and chardonnay was no less spectacular. It was also prepared a day in advance and served on a rosty — similar to a potato pancake with onion, herbs and spices. Our final course was their mouth-watering, absolutely incredible desserts. We had the floderand — whipped cream layered between chocolate mousse between a top layer of strawberries and a bottom later of blueberries — and the coupe Denmark in meringue shell — hot ghirardelli chocolate on homemade vanilla ice cream with roasted almonds on top of a baked meringue shell. The combination of all ingredients made this a categorically irresistible dessert. I dare you — no matter how full you are — to take just one bite and stop! We complemented the ending of this extraordinary dining experience with Colorado coffee — made with kahlua, grand marnier, courvoisier and amaretto — with whipped cream and a sugar crystal stick.

It would be difficult to find better trained, more informed servers in small-town Colorado. Each server goes through a three-month training program and is well versed on the ingredients and preparation of every item on the menu. It is like having the chef at your table. They can answer every question you might have about food or drink and don't mind if you ask to repeat something. They will literally flood you with information. The service itself has always been cheerful, intelligent, professional and with a light-hearted attitude. At the Tivoli Deer, exceptional service is ordinary and the ordinary does not exist. They are simply the BEST!

The patio is a pleasing place to dine in the summertime. There always seems to be a cool breeze and the surrounding pines and firs provide a tranquil backdrop. There is a wall mural of two deer in a field with aspen trees in the background. Tiny white Christmas lights provide additional lighting to the table candles. The entire restaurant inside is decorated in blue and white, the colors of Denmark. There are white-laced table cloths and blue and white wallpaper. They have some rather unusual blue prints on how to make various dishes. These are in gold frames with dark blue matted backgrounds. They resemble the blue prints for a building project with specifications for materials and equipment, an isometric cut of the finished product and the ingredients; except they are for gourmet dishes and cocktails, like grand marnier souffle, boiled crab, a dry martini, a bloody Mary, a whiskey sour, a margarita and stuffed lobster. A framed poster of the Tivoli Gardens in Copenhagen also adorns the oak stained walls and there are some colorful plates on the top section of one wall. The bar and lounge area to the right has potted and hanging plants in the front window, a wine rack along the rear wall and tapestries from France showing wine drinkers in a garden. A diamond-shaped stained-glass fixture in a wood frame, with a picture of grapes in the middle, hangs in the back of the room also. Two deer heads are mounted on the wall.

I love the atmosphere at the Tivoli Deer — always comfortable and relaxed. They play classical music. The setting is perfect. It is a charming country/continental experience you soon won't forget and will yearn to repeat.

SPECIAL ONE-TIME OFFER: Buy one brunch, lunch or dinner entrée (à la carte or 4-course) at the regular price and receive a complimentary Tivoli cappuccino in our very own coffee mug that you can take home. Valid for every member of your party who purchases an entrée. This offer NOT valid in combination with any other offers. Please present to server at time of ordering. _____ Manager/Owner. _____ Date.

RECIPE
Frikadeller

8 ounces pork butt
8 ounces veal, bottom round
1½ cups all purpose flour
5 large eggs

1 quart 2% milk
¾ cup onion, minced
½ teaspoon salt
½ teaspoon pepper

1. Ground meat through fine holes. Combine in mixer: meat, onion, spices and flour. Run mixer at low speed for 2 minutes.
2. Add eggs, one at a time. Then add milk slowly. Mix well. Finally, add more salt and pepper if needed.
3. Shape into walnut-size balls and sauté in hot oil (about 1½ ounces each).
4. Mustard or any kind of honey-mustard sauce (dip) goes well with these meatballs.

The New Patio at the Tivoli Deer Restaurant in Kittredge

LA JUNTA

The town was formerly named Otero, after Miguel Otero, who established the town in 1875 when the Santa Fe railroad was built through the area. The name was changed to La Junta, the Spanish word for "junction", in 1878 when the town became a junction for the Santa Fe Railroad lines to Pueblo and Trinidad. Two items of local interest to La Junta are the Koshare Indian Museum and Bent's Old Fort. The museum is patterned after the Indian ceremonial kivas of the southwest and home of the famous Koshare Indian dancers. Several years ago the curator of the museum, a fellow named "Buck", who has since passed away, treated me to a tour of his private collection. Bent's Old Fort is a reconstruction of the original fort as it was in 1845. It was a major trading outpost on the Old Santa Fe Trail.

Zip Code: 81050. Area Code: 719. Population: 7,637. Elevation: 4,066'.

Chiaramonte's
208 Sante Fe Avenue, 384-8909

Directions: Take Highway 50 east from Pueblo 64 miles. As you pass through La Junta (Highway 50 is First Avenue), turn right on Sante Fe (one street past San Juan). Go 1½ blocks. The restaurant is on the right in the Town Square Mall (which actually is not a mall, but a two-door entrance to shops). The restaurant is down on the lower level.

ESSENTIALS

Cuisine: Steak and Seafood
Hours: 7 days: 11AM-2PM. Mon-Sat 5PM-9PM. Sun 5PM-8PM.
Meals and Prices: Lunch/Dinner $-$$$
Nonsmoking: No
Take-out: Yes
Alcohol: Full Bar
Credit Cards: MC, Visa, Disc
Personal Check: Yes

Reservations: Not required unless a party of 8 or more. Suggested if a holiday.
Wheelchair Access: No
Other: Private meeting rooms available: the Judge's Chamber seats 20 and the Jury can hold 40-45. The restaurant, by the way, is across from the courthouse.

HISTORY, PERSONALITY AND CHARACTER

Originally a furniture store, then office space, this lower level restaurant was formerly Georgio's, an Italian eatery from 1981 to 1984. In October 1984, Bill and Linda Chiaramonte took over and it has been Chiaramonte's ever since. Bill was former manager of the New Castle and Douglas Country Clubs and the Moose Club in Wyoming. He was also assistant manager of the Black Steer in Loveland and the Charcoal Broiler in Fort Collins. Bill's restaurant experience dates back to 1970, with 5 years off to farm, start a family and change lifestyles. Jodi Wheeler, their most capable chef, has been with the restaurant since its inception in 1984.

LA JUNTA

FOOD, SERVICE AND AMBIANCE

On my last visit here, I tried their steak 'n stuff, a ground sirloin sandwich served open-face with hot, melted mild cheddar and cold, diced green peppers, tomatoes and onions. The sirloin was very lean, a good cut. It comes with salad, but do not be afraid to ask to substitute a cup of soup. They will accommodate you. The homemade cream of potato was pretty much that - cream, potatoes and salt. No extras, fancy seasonings or exotic vegetables stirred in. Simple, but good. I liked their waffle-style crinkle-cut potatoes. The soup, sandwich and fries was just the right amount for lunch. I have dined here on several occasions, both alone and with associates. Their sandwiches, burgers, salads and steaks have all received favorable reviews from either myself or my compatriots. The combination lunch/dinner menu features chicken specialties, char-broiled steaks, seafood, a few Mexican selections and a kiddies menu.

Service was friendly and attentive. A tape of country music played pleasantly in the background. Chiaramonte's has a charm and elegance that is uncommon in this part of Colorado. At the same time, I found the atmosphere to be relaxing and easy going. The front dining room is darker, more romantic, with comfortable brown-cushioned chairs with armrests, red-brick and dark-wood walls, a low ceiling and hardwood walnut doors. The second dining room is more artistic with a large mirror on one wall and imaginative wood artworks on the other two walls resembling the Sun and Saturn with its rings and moons. This is a real jewel in the grasslands.

SPECIAL ONE-TIME OFFER: Buy one entrée at the regular price and receive a complimentary glass of house wine. Limit two glasses of house wine with the purchase of two entrées. This offer NOT valid in combination with any other offers.
_____ Manager/Owner. _____ Date.

RECIPE

Chef Jodi's Chicken Salad

1-1½ cup mayonnaise
Diced fine:
  1 medium onion
  ½ pound carrot
  1 pound celery stalk

1 whole chicken cooked, boned
  and diced
8 ounces crushed pineapple
½ pound chopped cashews
Salt and white pepper to taste

1. Add all ingredients together and blend in mayonnaise.
2. Add salt and ground white pepper to taste.
3. Use in stuffed tomato or filling in a croissant.

LA VETA

La Veta means "the vein" in Spanish referring to the many dikes emanating in all directions from West Spanish Peak. It was formerly named Francisco Plaza or Francisco Ranch by Colonel John M. Francisco who settled a home here while on a prospecting tour in 1834.

Zip Code: 81055. Area Code: 719. Population: 726. Elevation: 7,013'.

The Covered Wagon
205 South Main Street, 742-5280

Directions: Located 14 miles southwest of Walsenburg. From Highways 12 and 160, go 3 miles southwest into La Veta. The restaurant is just past Ryus Avenue on the left. The roof of the restaurant has a big white covered wagon with the initials CW on the side.

ESSENTIALS

Cuisine: Country
Hours: Tue-Sat 7AM-9PM (10PM from JUN to mid-OCT). Sun 7AM-3PM. Closed Mon. Closed NOV 15-30, 1995.
Meals and Prices: Breakfast/ Lunch $, Dinner $$-$$$
Nonsmoking: Yes
Take-out: Yes
Alcohol: Full Bar

Credit Cards: No
Personal Check: Yes, with I.D.
Reservations: Not required unless party of 6 or more.
Wheelchair Access: Yes
Dress: Country
Other: No separate checks. Additional 15% service charge for parties of 7 or more. No cigars.

HISTORY, PERSONALITY AND CHARACTER

The building occupied by the Covered Wagon dates back to the 1940s when it was used as a saloon for railroad workers. In the late 1950s, local pioneer Harry Willis opened Harry's Steakhouse. Harry, an octogenarian and the largest land holder in the area, was at the restaurant the evening that I visited. About 1970, the restaurant became The Covered Wagon. Over the last 10 years, the restaurant went through 3 or 4 owners, each time returning to Harry, and sat vacant for over a year before Alan Ireland took over. Alan is not your typical small-town restaurateur. Originally from Maine, he was an executive with "21" Club and worked for 30 years in the restaurant industry in places like New York, Chicago, Dallas and Houston. Alan is a talented man who has an understanding of what his guests want, believes in the integrity of his product and displays a genuine concern for the locals, his prime clientele. In fact, he even goes so far as staying open for breakfast year-around to meet the needs of a few locals when it is not particularly profitable. Tourists, flocking to cabins in the area during the summer, more than double La Veta's 700 population, causing the Covered Wagon's business to triple.

FOOD, SERVICE AND AMBIANCE

I had the beef barley soup with my dinner. It was <u>very</u> thick with barley, plenty of chunks of prime beef, carrots and celery and hardly any broth. No skimping on ingredients here. My entrée was pot roast, a favorite in these parts and for good reason. The beef was tender enough to break apart with your fork. The mashed potatoes were from real potatoes, lumpy, with their skins still on, and topped with a peppery cream gravy. Perfect! The pot roast, or what some might call beef stew, also had potatoes, carrots and a brown gravy. A side of corn and one of their delicious homemade garlic drop biscuits completed the plate. Folks, this is real home-cooked food and hearty portions! My half-order was plentiful. I had enough to take some home. All of their soups and desserts (fruit cobblers, bread pudding, cream pies) are also homemade and they buy their tortillas from a family in Sante Fe.

Breakfast is served 6 days a week until 11AM and includes omelets, burritos, chicken fried steak, pork chops, steak, home fries, French toast, pancakes and biscuits and gravy. Lunch offers Mexican specialties, sandwiches and daily specials like hot turkey or roast beef and lasagna. Dinner features fish, steaks, chops, chicken and baby back ribs. Sunday dinner, served from 11AM, includes ribs, chops, steaks, Mexican specialties, sandwiches and a western omelet. Every month, an ethnic specialty is offered, like Italian, Mexican, French, German or Chinese.

I spent most of my time talking with Alan, so I did not have much of an opportunity to experience the service. However, the dining area was sparsely filled when I arrived about 7PM, but by 8PM, there were people waiting for a table. The staff seemed to keep everyone happy and Alan even excused himself a couple of times to personally check with each table to make sure all was well.

The decor is "country cozy": paper napkins, walls made of board and batten Ponderosa pine from the San Luis Valley and a black-pipe stove furnace. Behind the front two dining rooms is a bar and lounge area that includes a huge red-brick fireplace and wall, a compact disk juke box, and various items hanging over the bar: a miniature chuck wagon, a cattle skin, an elk hide and saddles. Alan has plans to expand the restaurant into the building next door that occupies the corner to build a dance floor that would be separate from the dining area. Wholesome food served with as much care and love as your grandmother would give is what you'll experience when you dine at The Covered Wagon.

SPECIAL ONE-TIME OFFER: Buy one entrée at the regular price and receive a complimentary dessert (up to $3.00 value per dessert). Limit two desserts with the purchase of two entrées. This offer NOT valid in combination with any other offers. _____ Manager/Owner. _____ Date.

RECIPE

Grandma Ireland's Yankee Pot Roast
(Serves 8)

4 pounds Chuck roll, dust all
  sides with flour

1 pound cut fresh carrots, 1" to
  1½" long pieces
2 large onions, quartered
1 pound turnips, quartered
½ pound mushrooms, cut in half
1 pound red potatoes (baby), halved

Deglaze braising pan by adding:
  2 cups red wine (1 cup reserved for
    consumption while cooking)
  ¼ cup garlic in water, strained
  ¼ cup beef base
  2 bay leaves
  Salt and pepper to taste
  ½ gallon water

Roux:
  ¼ pound butter and ½ cup flour until
  thick roux is made.

1. Cover braising pan with enough olive oil to cover bottom of the pan.
2. Braise meat on all sides until brown. Place vegetables evenly into a 6-inch
   deep vegelene-coated pan.
3. Remove browned meat from braising pan and place evenly into full pans with
   vegetables.
4. To deglaze braising pan: Heat to boil all ingredients. Add Roux slowly until
   thickened.
5. Cover with foil and bake at 350 degrees for 2 hours.

*My grandmother from Ireland used to make this while I was a kid growing up on
a dairy farm in Maine.*

Alan Ireland

LAKE CITY

Lake City was named after nearby Lake San Christobal (Spanish for "Saint Christopher"), the second largest natural lake in Colorado. It is Colorado's largest historic district but the only town in Hinsdale, the least populated county in Colorado. The town is filled with Victorian homes having over 75 buildings from the late 1800s.
Zip Code: 81235. Area Code: 970. Population: 223. Elevation: 8,658'.

Crystal Restaurant
Corner of Highway 149 South and County Road 30, PO Box 246, 944-2201
Directions: Located on the south end of Lake City. From the south on Highway 149, the restaurant is on the left, .4 miles past the Alferd Packer massacre site, at the turn off for Lake San Crystobal (Country Road 30). Drive under the wood arches and go up the hill to the restaurant. From the north on Highway 149, the restaurant is on the right, .4 miles past Vickers Ranch. Drive under the wood arches, go up the hill and turn right to get to the restaurant.

ESSENTIALS
Cuisine: Country Gourmet
Hours: Memorial Day Weekend through SEP: Mon-Sat 8AM-10:30AM, 11:30AM-1:30PM and 5:30PM-8:30PM. Sun 8AM-1:30PM and 5:30PM-8:30PM. OCT to Memorial Day Weekend: Wed-Sat 8AM-10:30AM, 11:30AM-1:30PM and 5:30PM-8PM. Sun 8AM-1:30AM. Closed Mon/Tue.
Meals and Prices: Breakfast/Lunch $$, Dinner $$$
Nonsmoking: All
Take-out: Yes

Alcohol: Full Bar
Credit Cards: MC, Visa
Personal Check: Yes, with driver's license
Reservations: Recommended on holidays and during the summer, accepted otherwise.
Wheelchair Access: Yes
Other: Restaurant is part of lodge that features a heated pool and spa. Available for family reunions, retreats and small group conferences.

HISTORY, PERSONALITY AND CHARACTER
Roy Prye built the Crystal Restaurant in 1951 in what is now used as a conference room. The restaurant has gone through four owners but it has always been the Crystal. In 1968, Ralph Black built the bar which was converted to a restaurant in 1986 when the second dining room was built. Harley and Caryl Rodofsky owned the Crystal from 1977 until 1993 when Ann and Gale Udell, from California, took over on June 1st. They had been looking for a lodge and restaurant in Colorado for 3 years before settling here. Ann and Gale added the deck outside in the spring of 1994. Gale barbecues on the deck and Ann does most of the baking and desserts.

FOOD, SERVICE AND AMBIANCE

Their in-house chili was as good as Mom used to make, "thick as a brick" with big pieces of stewed tomatoes, kidney beans, ground beef, celery, green peppers and both temperature and spicy hot. The roast beef sandwich was nearly as good (Mom never used to make those), thinly sliced with sautéed mushrooms and onions and melted Swiss cheese on a croissant. Everything is prepared from scratch so you can expect fresh, high-quality food when you dine here. Their homemade delicacies include three daily soups, like matzo ball with chicken or beef barley; honey-mustard, herb-vinaigrette and cranberry-vinaigrette salad dressings; biscuits; salsa; jams; butter; and pies such as fresh rhubarb and Dutch apple. For their barbecue, they simmer ribs with herbs and spices then marinate for 24 hours in their own special barbecue sauce made with garlic, dry mustard, brown sugar, celery seed, salt, pepper and Worcestershire sauce. The chicken is mesquite smoked.

Sunday brunch highlights an assortment of delicious-sounding entrées: Rocky Mountain trout and eggs, salmon and shrimp with fettuccine, a seafood omelet, fresh blueberry pancakes, breakfast burrito, vegetarian skillet or sandwich, smoked chicken or turkey breast, meatballs with zesty meat sauce in a sesame seed roll and burgers. Lunch offers the same sandwiches plus vegetarian quiche. The dinner menu changes with an eclectic collection of prime rib, meats, wild game, seafood, pasta and Mexican dishes. This cumulation includes sirloin, pork, chicken and duck that are charbroiled, mesquite smoked, slow-roasted and seasoned or herb marinated. Expect to see some regional specialties like roast leg of Colorado lamb and Rocky Mountain trout as well as distant delights — Atlantic salmon, Louisiana lump crab cakes and jumbo shrimp jambalaya. A variety of pasta plates from penne, stuffed tortellini and jumbo shells to ravioli and fettuccine, in a number of rich and spicy sauces, are also available for your dining pleasure. Ann's whole chicken enchiladas showcase the Mexican choices along with grilled lime chicken breasts and shredded pork roast with smoky tomatoes, chorizo and roasted pablanos. No matter what you decide on, you're in for a treat!

Service was prompt and cheerful. Piano and other instrumental tunes played quietly in the background. The main dining room is decorated with a series of color photos of Lake City taken just south of town in the summer, winter and fall and a photo of Elk Creek Pass East of Montrose. In the small fireside room is a black-iron, wood-burning stove and a wall of photos and paraphernalia from the Sierra Madre Search and Rescue Team including picks, back packs and snow shoes. Gale was the member of the rescue team that found a 12-year-old lost boy scout in 1971 that made national news at the time. This display also includes a poster of a one-hour television special titled "The Search for Billy" by Alcoa and Life Magazine that aired in 1971, a letter of recognition to Gale from former President Richard Nixon and an October 1994 article in American Way Magazine, the magazine carried on American Airlines flights, titled "10 Great Drives" that features The Crystal Restaurant. Throughout the restaurant, you will see antique coffee grinders, scales and cast-iron utensils, the original Crystal Lodge neon sign and a couple of crystal-glass pieces of art. In warm weather, you can dine on the deck amongst the flowering planters and enjoy the view of Crystal Peak. If you haven't yet discovered the Crystal, it's time you paid them a visit.

SPECIAL ONE-TIME OFFER: Buy one entrée at the regular price and receive 50% off a second entrée of equal or lesser value (maximum discount $7.00). This offer NOT valid in combination with any other offers. Please present to server at time of ordering. _____ Manager/Owner. _____ Date.

RECIPE

Cajun Gratineed Shrimp
(Serves 6)

Shrimp:
- 36 jumbo green shrimp
- ¼ cup paprika
- ⅛ teaspoon cayenne pepper
- 1 bay leaf, crumbled
- ¼ teaspoon salt
- ¼ teaspoon dried oregano
- ¼ teaspoon dried basil
- ¼ cup olive oil

Fettucine:
- 1 pound fresh or dried fettucine
- Olive oil

Vegetables:
- 6 to 8 Roma tomatoes
- 1 small green bell pepper
- 1 small red bell pepper
- 1 cup sliced black olives

Sauce:
- 1 quart heavy cream
- 1 ¾-ounce package of fresh basil
- 1 teaspoon lemon juice
- 2 tablespoons melted butter
- 2 tablespoons all-purpose flour
- White pepper and salt to taste

Cheese:
- 1½ cups mozzarella cheese
- 1½ cups Parmesan cheese

---

1. Shrimp: Peel and butterfly, leaving the tails on. Combine dry ingredients in a large mixing bowl. Add the shrimp and olive oil to the mixing bowl. Using your hands, continue to gently blend shrimp with dry ingredients and olive oil.
2. Place shrimp on a hot grill or under the broiler. Cook until ¾ of the way done. DO NOT OVERCOOK. Place in covered bowl until ready to use.
3. Sauce: Place cream in a large sauce pan over very low heat. Add fresh basil and let heat for 30 minutes. Pour mixture through a strainer. Use the back of a wooden spoon to press juices from basil through the strainer. Discard the cooked basil. Return cream to sauce pan.
4. Place sauce pan on medium heat. Combine melted butter and all-purpose flour with a wire whip and add to cream. Continue mixing until thickened. Add lemon juice, salt and white pepper. Keep warm until ready to use.
5. Fettucine: Cook according to directions on package. Drain, sprinkle with olive oil, toss fettuccine to evenly coat and cover until ready to use.
6. Vegetables: blanche the Roma tomatoes in boiling water for 20 seconds or until skin splits. Remove from boiling water, peel and cut into 1" cubes. Dice the red and green bell peppers.
7. Cheese: Combine cheeses.
8. Assembly: On large oven-proof plates, divide the fettucine. Sprinkle the diced red and green bell peppers and slice black olives over the fettucine. Arrange 6 jumbo shrimps on top. Ladle approximately 4 ounces basil cream sauce evenly over fettucine, vegetables and shrimp.
9. Sprinkle cheese mixture over the top and arrange Roma tomatoes around the edge of the plate. Place the plates under the broiler until the cheese is bubbly. Serve immediately and enjoy!

I get bored cooking the same entrées so I am always dreaming of new or different combinations to serve our guests. The Cajun Gratineed Shrimp just came to me while I was prepping for dinner one night. It is an ideal entrée for either home or restaurant because all the work is done ahead of time. Just heat when ready to serve. It is an extremely popular dish and worth the effort.

Ann Udell

LAS ANIMAS

The town was named after the Las Animas River and was first established in 1869 about 6 miles to the east of its present location. In 1873, the Arkansas Valley Railway built a line from Kit Carson which connected to the Kansas Pacific Railroad 6 miles west of the original Las Animas. The town of West Las Animas was established at this junction and renamed Las Animas in 1886.

Zip Code: 81054. Area Code: 719. Population: 2,481. Elevation: 3,893'.

The Troll Haus Restaurant
604 Locust Avenue, 456-0062

Directions: Entering Las Animas from the west on Highway 50, the highway bends to the left before a bridge, then bends back to the right and turns into Ambassador Thompson Boulevard. Stay on this road to Locust Avenue and turn left. Go 1 block. The restaurant is on the right on the southeast corner of Locust Avenue and 6th Avenue. Entering Las Animas from the east on Highway 50, the highway bends to the left and becomes Bent Avenue. Stay on this road to 6th Avenue and turn right. Go 3 blocks. The restaurant is on the right on the southeast corner of Locust Avenue and 6th Avenue.

ESSENTIALS

Cuisine: Steak/Seafood/Fowl

Hours: Fri/Sat 5:30PM-9PM,
Sun 10:30AM-2PM.

Meals and Prices: Dinner $$-$$$, Sun buffet $$

Nonsmoking: Yes

Take-out: Yes

Alcohol: No

Credit Cards: MC, Visa

Personal Check: Yes

Reservations: Recommended. (They are occasionally closed for vacations, remodeling or private parties).

Wheelchair Access: Yes

Dress: Casual to Sunday dress

Other: In or outside catering available for banquets, special events and parties

HISTORY, PERSONALITY AND CHARACTER

The Troll Haus is in a former Episcopalian Church built in 1888. It remained a church until the late 1960s when John Flinn opened an art gallery in its place. In November 1984, Phyllis and Bill Lutz, who grew-up in Las Animas and graduated from the local high school, purchased the place from Flinn and opened The Troll Haus. Bill, a retired military man from the United States Air Force, has been in the food service business since 1961. He was a specialized cook — aide to the general — prior to retiring when he entered cooking schools at the Broadmoor and Antler's Plaza in Colorado Springs. Following this training, he and Phyllis opened The Troll Haus. Bill works the kitchen while Phyllis hosts and serves in the front.

FOOD, SERVICE AND AMBIANCE

The Lutzes have developed a worthy, American country cuisine in the serenity of a former church. I dined here for a special lunch on one of my restaurant tours, getting a sample of their 20-item salad bar that featured macaroni, fruit and cranberry salads and chocolate pudding — everything very fresh; breaded and fried jalapeños stuffed with cheddar cheese — a delectable appetizer that is now one of my favorites and that I highly recommend, and chocolate nemesis cake — a bitter sweet concoction in rich chocolate with the texture of fudge.

The cuts of steak on the dinner menu include top sirloin, rib eye, T-bone and filet mignon. The seafood selections are shrimp, crab legs, fried catfish or cod, lobster tail, grilled halibut and a seafood platter. Surf and turf combinations with top sirloin and either lobster or shrimp can be ordered. The chicken choices are Cordon Bleu, Kiev, strips or grilled breast. For a lighter appetite, they offer taco or seafood salads served with soup and dessert. For an appetizer, try breaded cheese or catfish nuggets, mini meatballs, chicken drumettes and breaded mushrooms. There is a children's menu. For dessert, you can delve into cheesecake, chocolate mousse, caramel or coconut custard, chocolate peanut butter or just plain peanut butter pie, or an ice cream parfait in your choice of crème de menthe, chocolate or strawberry flavors. The all-you-can-eat Sunday buffet consists of 3 changing entrées served with the salad bar, beverage and dessert. Highlighting the main-course dishes are roast beef, ham, beef stroganoff, chicken Tetrazzini, fried chicken, lasagna, sweet and sour turkey and stuffed peppers.

Service was handled well and Bill took me for a little tour of the church afterwards. A red carpet runs down the center aisle of the restaurant, just like it did when it was a church. The original pews are used for some of the seats and dining tables are set on what used to be the altar level. In case you're wondering how this restaurant got its name, Phyllis began collecting troll dolls when she and Bill were in the Air Force stationed in Norway. She brought them with her when they returned to the States and decided to "employ" them for the name of the restaurant and as a central decorative theme. You'll be delighted by several Norwegian and Swedish trolls with their short-hair heads and fuzzy tails, the North American trolls with shaggy-looking horse-hair tops, kid's trolls and even pictures of trolls. Colorful and attractive stained glass completes the former chapel's trim. Your charming hosts, the Lutzes and the trolls, will entertain and treat you to some distinctly healthy food in a tranquil environment.

SPECIAL ONE-TIME OFFER: Buy one entrée at the regular price and receive a second entrée of equal or lesser value FREE (up to $15.00 value). This offer NOT valid in combination with any other offers. Please present to server at time of ordering.
_____ Manager/Owner. _____ Date.

<u>RECIPE</u>

Chocolate Mousse
(Serves 3)

6 ounces semi-sweet chocolate	1 teaspoon vanilla
2 tablespoons Kahlua	¼ cup sugar
1 tablespoon orange juice	1 cup whipping cream

1. Melt first three ingredients over low heat then set aside to cool.
2. Whip last three ingredients till thick and smooth. Fold in melted chocolate gently.
3. Pour into parfait or small wine glasses. Demitasse cup may be used also.
4. Refrigerate. Just before serving, top with whipped cream.

The Troll Haus Restaurant in Las Animas with a friendly (if not befuddled looking) North American troll

LEADVILLE

When silver was first struck in Leadville in 1876, the town began with many names: Agassiz, Boughtown, Carbonate, Cloud City, Harrison and Slabtown. The name Leadville was chosen for the large amount of argentiferous lead ores in the area. In addition to being the "Silver Capital of the World" at one time ($15 million in silver was extracted from the area in 1880 when the town was the second largest in Colorado with a population of 30,000), gold, lead, zinc, copper and molybdenum deposits have also been mined over the past 120 years. Leadville is a historical treasure chest with the Healy House and Dexter Cabin, two original homes restored to 19th-century decor and turned into a museum; the Tabor Opera House; the Heritage Museum and Gallery which includes a diorama of the town's mining history and a styrofoam replica of the 1896 Ice Palace and the National Mining Hall of Fame and Museum which has exhibits dealing with the mining heritage here and throughout the nation. At 10,152' elevation, Leadville is the highest incorporated city in North America. It is a National Historic Landmark District with 70-square blocks of Victorian architecture and a 20-square mile mining district. Zip Code: 80461. Area Code: 719. Population: 2,629 (1990). Elevation: 10,152'.

Callaway's Restaurant

700 Harrison Avenue (in the Delaware Hotel), 486-1418, 1-800-748-2004, FAX 486-2214
Directions: Entering Leadville from the north, Highway 24 becomes Poplar Avenue. It turns to the west at 9th Street, then heads south again on Harrison Avenue. The restaurant is on the left at the southeast corner of Harrison Avenue and 7th Street. Entering Leadville from the south, Highway 24 becomes Harrison Avenue. The restaurant is on the right at the southeast corner of Harrison Avenue and 7th Street.

ESSENTIALS

Cuisine: American/Continental
Hours: 7 days 7AM-10:30AM, 11:30AM-2PM, and 5PM-9PM
Meals and Prices: Breakfast $, Lunch $$, Dinner $$-$$$
Nonsmoking: All
Take-out: No
Alcohol: Full Bar
Credit Cards: All 5
Personal Check: Yes, with I.D.
Reservations: Recommended for parties of 6 or more

Wheelchair Access: Yes
Dress: From casual to business to dressy
Other: Additional 15% service charge for groups of 6 or more. No separate checks for parties over 4. Separate plate charge $1. Available for wedding receptions, dinner meetings, parties and other special functions. They also do unique, entertaining evenings: theme costume parties, murder mysteries, medieval banquets.

LEADVILLE

HISTORY, PERSONALITY AND CHARACTER

In 1886, the Callaway Brothers (William, George and John) opened their Delaware Block Store, named after their home state, at an estimated cost of $80,000. After closing the business in 1890, the Callaways leased the first floor of the Delaware Block. In 1946, they sold the building for $40,000. In 1992, Scott and Susie Brackett purchased the hotel, made major renovations that included a redesigned interior, an elegant Victorian lobby and Callaway's Restaurant with unique period antiques, crystal chandeliers, brass fixtures and oak panelling, and reopened in April 1992. Suzi Benney has been their floor manager in Callaway's since 1993. Garth Duel and his wife, Jennifer, both graduates of the Culinary Institute of America, are the head chefs.

FOOD, SERVICE AND AMBIANCE

I stopped into Callaway's on a delightful late summer afternoon and enjoyed a cup of cream of mushroom soup with chopped celery and flavorful mushrooms that retained their texture. I also savored the tasty grilled chicken on focaccia bread with homemade basil pesto, fontina cheese, lettuce, tomato and red onion. It came with a half-dozen crisp, non-greasy, fluffy onion rings, made the way they should be so the onion doesn't slide out of the breading when you bite into them. Other tempting lunch items included a tortilla spiral roll (roast beef, lettuce, onion, cheddar and Russian dressing in a flour tortilla), sandwiches (Philadelphia cheese steak, Reuben, Monte Cristo, burger, club and veggie), Buffalo wings, pasta dishes, Southwestern green chili and salads (chicken Caesar with homemade dressing, chilled pasta and poached salmon).

The breakfast fare features traditional eggs and meats, eggs Benedict, huevos rancheros, egg and ham crêpes topped with hollandaise sauce or green chili, omelets, pancakes, French toast and a Continental breakfast. For dinner, you can select the soup du jour or French onion; an appetizer of pan-seared scallops, silver dollar mushrooms and artichokes, jalapeño poppers or Buffalo wings; a salad; a sandwich or one of their enticing entrées like filet mignon medallions, prime rib (on Fridays and Saturdays only), chicken marsala, chorizo sausage in mustard alfredo sauce over linguini, a fresh vegetable kabob, baked paprika salmon or the grilled pizza du jour. Enhance your dining with a bottle or glass of one of their California, French or Australian wines. There is a children's menu for lunch and dinner. For dessert, have a delicious piece of homemade bread pudding with either bourbon or Frangelico sauce, homemade strawberry or blueberry shortcake or tiramisu.

The Victorian charm of Callaway's is brought out with its high ceiling and windows, uneven wood slat table tops with wood chairs, an emerald green wallpaper with a flower-leaf pattern that complements the turquoise, pink and tan carpet, white-laced curtains and pictures of a fox hunt titled "Run to Earth" and 2 ladies of fashion chatting over a drink at a table. Further embellishing this ambiance are a picture of Sapphire Point in Summit County, old world maps and several pictures of famous sailing ships. Dwell in the "crown jewel" of Leadville, the same hotel that Butch Cassidy called home, while you relish in the Duels' fine cuisine.

SPECIAL ONE-TIME OFFER: Buy one entrée at the regular price and receive a complimentary dessert or glass of house wine. Limit 4 desserts or glasses of house wine with purchase of 4 entrées. This offer NOT valid in combination with any other offers. Please present to server at time of ordering. _____ Manager/Owner. _____ Date.

RECIPE

Penne Vodka
(Serves 4)

Vodka Sauce:
- ½ pound sliced mushrooms
- 1 onion, small dice
- 2 tablespoons garlic, minced
- 3 slices bacon, raw, diced
- 2 ounces vodka
- 2 8-ounce tomatoes, peeled, diced
- 1½ tablespoons basil, fresh, minced
- 1 tablespoon marjoram, fresh, minced

- 1 tablespoon thyme, fresh, minced
- ½ teaspoon rosemary, ground
- 1½ cups heavy whipping cream
- Salt and white pepper to taste
- As needed, Parmesan and Romano cheeses, grated
- As needed, green onions, cut on bias

8 ounces cooked penne pasta

1. Render bacon. Add and sauté onions and garlic until translucent. Add mushrooms.
2. Deglaze with vodka and add remaining ingredients except cream. Simmer for 45 minutes over low heat.
3. Turn off heat and add cream. Return to low heat. Do not boil.
4. Garnish with fresh Parmesan and Romano cheeses, green onions and garlic toast.

The Leadville Prospector Restaurant
2798 Highway 91, PO Box 554, 486-3955, 1-800-844-2828

Directions: From the intersection of Harrison Avenue (Highway 24) and 9th Street in Leadville, follow Highway 24 north for 3¾ miles. The restaurant is on the right. From the east on I-70, take Exit 195 and head south on Highway 91 for 20½ miles. The restaurant is on the left. From the west on I-70, take Exit 171 and head south on Highway 24 for 32 miles. At the intersection with Highway 91, turn left (north) on Highway 91. Go 1½ miles. The restaurant is on the right.

LEADVILLE

ESSENTIALS

Cuisine: Steaks/Seafood
Hours: Tue-Sun 5PM-9PM. Closed Mon. Closed Mid-OCT to Mid-NOV and 1st two weeks in APR.
Meals and Prices: Dinner $$$-$$$$
Nonsmoking: Yes
Take-out: No
Alcohol: Full Bar
Credit Cards: MC, Visa
Personal Check: In-state with I.D.

Reservations: Recommended, especially on Fri/Sat
Wheelchair Access: Yes, including restrooms
Other: No separate checks for parties of 6 or more. Additional 15% service charge on parties of 6 or more. Plate charge of $3.50 for adults splitting entrées and not ordering off the menu. Catering available.

HISTORY, PERSONALITY AND CHARACTER

The original "Prospector" building was brought down from the former mining town of Kokomo (near Climax) in 1958 by Phil Daughtery. It was used as a construction office until 1960, then opened as the Snow Valley Inn, a steak house. Emit Ossmond purchased the building in 1962, changed the name to The Prospector and built the mining portal entrance and the "moss" rock (red rock with streaks of lichen in different shades of green) bar with its wall and ceiling consisting of 2,000 local ore samples (gold pyrite or "fool's gold") set in seasoned mine timber. He also brought down a 20'-high mine hoist from the Climax mine, which you can see if you make an about turn right before entering the portal entrance. The hoist was used to lower 3 miners at a time into the mine shaft and bring ore back up.

Earl and Marcia Nordwall bought The Prospector in the early 1970s and gained a reputation for being one of the finest restaurants in the Rocky Mountains. In 1986, Bill and Sara Charvat purchased the restaurant and in 1992, it was sold to the current owners Bob and Pauline Alex and their son, Greg. This is the first restaurant that they have owned. Bob, the head chef, used to do catering out of his home and was a cook on a liner on the Great Lakes. Greg, who has a degree in Hotel and Restaurant Management, has been in the restaurant business since 1975 having managed in Alaska and the Virgin Islands. From 1986 to 1991, he worked as a catering supervisor for the Manor Vail and as a banquet captain at the Vail Marriott. He is the host and bartender and works the front of the restaurant. Pauline, a school teacher most of the year, works on the floor in the summers helping with the salad bar, busing tables and doing anything else that needs to be done. Before reopening the restaurant on July 13, 1992, the Alexes did some major remodeling and decorating of the dining areas and lounge.

FOOD, SERVICE AND AMBIANCE

I had two very pleasurable dining experiences at The Leadville Prospector. On my first visit, I delved into a delicate steak with sautéed mushrooms served with some super, big onion rings that broke apart easily without the onion separating from the batter. I also sampled their tasty and moist grilled chicken breast seasoned with fresh herbs. The second time, I was here on a Friday so I decided to order the prime rib (only offered on Fridays and Saturdays). It was aged, slow-roasted and succulent with garlic au jus on the side and baked potato (which I poured the au jus on rather than the customary butter and sour cream). The menu said it was 10 ounces, but it seemed closer to a pound. Completing the meal were appetizing julienne carrots l'orange, zucchini topped with grated Parmesan and fresh cantaloupe. Entrées come with soup, bean pot, salad bar and fresh mini-loaf of warm, soft white bread browned on top. The bean pot was elaborate and delicious. It featured black, garbanzo, red, kidney, pinto and northern beans; yellow and green split peas; lentils and tomatoes. The soup of the day was a hearty chicken-vegetable-rice with several ample chunks of chicken. Highlighting the salad bar were 3 pasta salads: bow-tie pasta with tomatoes, rigatoni with cauliflower and broccoli and spaghetti with pimentos and green peppers; potato salad; cheeses and fresh green and red peppers.

Leading the list of appetizers are Rocky Mountain oysters (when available), frog legs and Buffalo wings. Spotlighting the entrées are several cuts of steak, baby back ribs smoked in house and glazed with their own barbecue sauce, rack of lamb named after Mount Massive, seafood (steamed crab legs, salmon filet, shrimp scampi, Rocky Mountain trout and seafood Newburg), chicken (marsala, stir-fry and Cajun), pastas (fettuccine Alfredo and baked mostaccioli, a family recipe) and steak and seafood combinations. The dinner menu includes children's meals, selections for lighter appetites and veggie specialties. The daily dessert tray showcases delectable homemade delights like strawberry Prospector — a 20-ounce fish bowl filled with vanilla ice cream and fresh cut strawberries in Grand Marnier sauce with whipped cream, bread pudding with wild turkey liquor cream sauce and tiramisu. They also offer some luscious purchased treats: New York-style cheesecake, Snicker's pie and fresh fruits. Numerous Colorado micro brewery beers headline the choice of beverages.

Service was courteous and attentive and Greg is a hospitable host with the most. He greets and bids farewell to each of his quests and makes them all feel right at home. Slow-playing country music starring performers like Emily Lou Harris could be heard throughout the restaurant. Greg seized some old pieces of barnwood in Leadville for his walls and adorned them with enlarged photographs of mining scenes and logging taken from the Climax molybdenum mine; mining tools; several reversed paintings of fowl — ducks, quail, pheasants and geese — on glass (the artist painted the figures on the back sides of the pieces of glass); a sketch of the Little Jonny Mine; a $5,000 reward poster for the whereabouts of the body of Robert Leroy Parker (Butch Cassidy); a poster advertising Remington firearms; color etchings of Leadville; a wild west map of Utah with photos of Butch Cassidy, the Sundance Kid, Bill Hickman and Gunplay Maxwell next to a poster of Butch Cassidy's Wild Bunch; a photo of the famous 1896 Leadville ice castle; a map of Leadville's mining district and frosted glass pictures (Tabor House, Matchless Mine and Tabor Opera House; the Tabor Grand Hotel and City Hall). Shelves filled with rocks and bottles that Bob and Greg dug up, a fish tank, hanging ferns and philodendrons and a circular fireplace and hearth further embellish the restaurant's nostalgic atmosphere. Large picture windows look out onto hummingbird feeders and fir trees with a picturesque view of Mt. Elbert and Mt. Massive, the 2 tallest peaks in Colorado. The Leadville Prospector's latest owners advanced the standards of the cuisine while returning the ambiance to yesteryear.

SPECIAL ONE-TIME OFFER: Buy one entrée at the regular price and receive a complimentary dessert (up to $4.00 value). Limit 4 complimentary desserts with the purchase of 4 entrées. This offer NOT valid in combination with any other offers. Please present to server at time of ordering. _____ Manager/Owner. _____ Date.

RECIPE
Leadville Prospector's Cajun Angel
(Serves 1)

3 large shrimps
10 to 12 scallops
¼ teaspoon crushed red cayenne pepper
2 ounces white wine
2 tablespoons butter

¾ cup heavy cream
2 teaspoons salt
Capellini (angel hair pasta)
Pinch fresh garlic
1 tablespoon Cajun spice

1. Cook pasta (2 ounces per serving). Use 6 quarts of water per 1 pound of pasta. Add salt. When water is boiling, add pasta. Cook for 2 minutes and drain.
2. Dredge shrimp and scallops in flour. Pre-heat sauté pan with butter, Cajun spice and crushed red pepper. Add seafood and garlic.
3. Cook until golden brown. Add wine, reduce. Add heavy cream, reduce. Let simmer over low heat for approximately 5 minutes.
4. Add 1¼ cups of hot angel hair pasta to sauté pan and toss. Sprinkle with paprika. Top with shredded parmesan cheese. Garnish with a sprig of parsley.

Elegant Dining at Callaway's Restaurant in the Historic Delaware Hotel in Leadville

The Leadville Prospector Restaurant in Leadville

LOUISVILLE

Named after Louis Nawatny who led the first coal boring expedition after C. C. Welch discovered coal in 1877. Nawatny also owned the land on which the original settlement was located and filed the town plat in 1878.

Zip Code: 80027. Area Code: 303. Population: 12,361. Elevation: 5,337'.

Karen's Country Kitchen
700 Main Street, 666-8020

Directions: Take the Broomfield/Louisville Exit from the Denver-Boulder Turnpike (Highway 36) and go north 4.0 miles. Turn left on Highway 42. Go 2¼ miles. Turn left on Pine Street. Go ¼ mile. The restaurant is on the right at the corner of Pine Street and Main Street.

ESSENTIALS

Cuisine: Healthy Country
Hours: Mon-Fri 6:30AM-8PM
(Breakfast to 10:30AM, Lunch from 10:30AM, Dinner from 5PM). Sat 7:30AM-8PM (Breakfast to 1PM). Sun 8:00AM-1PM (Breakfast only).
Meals and Prices: Breakfast/Lunch $-$$, Dinner $$
Nonsmoking: All
Take-out: Yes
Alcohol: Full Bar
Credit Cards: MC, Visa, Amx, Disc

Personal Check: Yes, with I.D.
Reservations: Not Accepted
Wheelchair Access: Yes
Other: Available for outside catering. Homestyle bakery and gift shop on premises. Service charge of 15% added to parties of 6 or more. Children's meals available. "Happy Heart" meals indicated by a ♥ means margarine served instead of butter, skim milk instead of whole, etc.

HISTORY, PERSONALITY AND CHARACTER

Karen's Country Kitchen occupies 2 buildings dating back to the 1890s and is listed in the National Historic Register. The original shop on the corner was Louisville's first bank. In June 1974, Karen Mullholland started a gift shop and bakery and was soon serving sandwiches for lunch on their homemade bread. When waiting lines started to form for their 6 small tables, they found old doors on Dad's farm that could double as tables for the restaurant and as counters for jewelry displays. In 1979, Karen expanded into Selma's Bakery Shop next door, a building that started as the town's first post office. Now a century later, the 2 structures still stand much as they were when originally built.

In December 1995, Buddy and Amy Chick purchased the restaurant from Karen. They both handle the front of the restaurant and gift shop, managing and hosting. Buddy has been in the hospitality business, managing restaurants, resort properties and hotels, since 1974. Amy has been doing the same and catering since 1984. They worked in San Diego and at the renown La Quinta Hotel, Golf and Tennis Resort in California. Sandy

Aronson, who's been with Karen's since 1987 and started in the restaurant business in 1980, is the kitchen manager.

FOOD, SERVICE AND AMBIANCE

Linda, my editor, two friends and myself visited Karen's for one of their fabulous Sunday breakfasts. Karen, it seems, was born for what she's doing. A combination of natural talent, experience, qualified people, the freshest ingredients available, prize winning recipes and an on-site bakery where all baked goods are made from scratch are a few of the reasons why Karen's has become one of the most popular dining spots in the Denver-Boulder area, especially for breakfast.

I couldn't remember when, if ever, I had ordered steak and eggs for breakfast, so I chose the Country Special — a hearty, ½-inch thick, lean, tasty charbroiled sirloin with hashbrowns, eggs and Texas toast. Linda had the Jogger — fresh, homemade, crunchy granola topped with yogurt and served with thick, whole wheat, homemade bread. Sandi selected the heavenly cheese crêpes filled with real sour cream and cream cheese whipped together and topped with strawberry preserves. Ron elected to go with Jay's Special (named after Karen's produce man) — a delectable scramlette with fresh, crunchy broccoli, sautéed spinach, onions and mushrooms, cheddar cheese and sour cream. We all found our meals to be delicious and well-prepared with the freshest ingredients!

Highlighting Karen's other breakfasts are hashbrowns and eggs served with a variety of meats including grilled turkey breast, charbroiled beef patty and charbroiled turkey sausage; scramlettes — scrambled eggs with your choice of ingredients like ripe olive wedges, green chilies, pasta and herbed or jalapeño cheese; French toast made with their own bread; buttermilk pancakes with "just a perfect amount of whole wheat flour — enough for flavor but not so much as to make them heavy"; fresh Danish and fresh squeezed orange and grapefruit juices.

Homemade freshness doesn't stop with breakfast. Lunch offers salads (chicken Caesar, oriental, seafood or spinach) with homemade dressings; their own French Onion soup (you can request your favorite soup with a few days' notice); a host of vegetarian dishes (vegie club, vegie burgers and a Swiss cheese grinder); deli-style sandwiches, clubs and grinders on homemade breads with homemade side salads (potato, macaroni, pasta or cole slaw); award-winning burgers; burgers made with turkey, chicken or fried fish; and light meals of Buffalo wings, nachos and thin onion rings. Stop in for dinner and choose from New York strip, teriyaki or southwest chicken, shrimp, halibut or Italian chopped steak, all charbroiled; pasta primavera or baked ziti with their own Alfredo or marinara sauce; barbecued baby back ribs, marinated for hours; pot roast of beef, simmered for hours; liver and onions; fried chicken; eggplant Parmesan and chili rellenos. Real mashed potatoes and real gravy come with some meals and some entrées originally started when Karen's opened.

We waited 15 to 20 minutes to get a table and about a ½ hour to get our meals after ordering. This is a very popular place, so expect a bit of a wait — it's well worth it. This quaint, unique restaurant features several small rooms and little booths with picnic tables, trellis dividers and roofs, hanging baskets, minute pictures of columbines and roses, remnant cloth napkins, wreaths of dried leaves and dried chili peppers, a brass figure full of holes, stuffed animals and wood carvings. We dined in a cozy booth, one of many, next to a gazebo with a single table and a frosted-glass stencil of an antique car. Further embellishing this charming decor are Victorian-period paintings, a picture of a Parisian store front, tin walls with 3-dimensional flower patterns and a small bar (the original store had all tin walls and ceilings). When you dine at Karen's, you'll feel like you stepped back in time to a simpler era, but the food and service are one of the best that you'll find in any current-day country restaurant.

SPECIAL ONE-TIME OFFER: Buy one entrée at the regular price and receive a second entrée of equal or lesser value FREE. This offer NOT valid in combination with any other offers. Please present to server at time of ordering. _____ Manager/Owner. _____ Date.

Karen's Country Kitchen in Louisville

RECIPE

Lemon Meringue Pie

1 9-inch Pie Crust:
   3 tablespoons all purpose flour
   ¼ teaspoon salt
   1¼ cups granulated sugar
   3 tablespoons cornstarch
   1½ cups hot water

Meringue:
   3 egg whites
   ¼ teaspoon tartar sauce
   1 teaspoon vanilla
   6 tablespoons granulated sugar

3 egg yolks
2 teaspoons lemon rind
⅓ cup lemon juice
2 tablespoons butter

1. Pie crust: Mix together all ingredients with a wire whip. Place in a heavy pot and add hot water.
2. Boil until cornstarch is complete cooked. Taste to make sure the cornstarch flavor is gone. Pour some of this mixture into egg yolks and then back into pot. Boil 2 or 3 minutes longer. Turn off heat and add lemon zest, lemon juice and butter.
3. Meringue: Add the sugar slowly while beating. Beat until firm yet shinny. DO NOT OVER BEAT. It should be dissolved. Top pie and seal edges. Bake at 400 degrees until browned.

Have Benjamin James Bennis autograph your copy of Colorado Restaurants and Recipes at the Rocky Mountain Book Festival in October or the Holiday Food and Gift Festival in November, both at Currigan Hall in Denver.

LYONS

The town was named after Mrs. Carrie Lyons, pioneer editor of the weekly Lyons News which had a brief existence in 1890-91. The Lyons Family was also instrumental in quarrying superior sandstone, used in many buildings at the University of Colorado campus. Geographically, Lyons is the gateway to the Rocky Mountains with Highways 7 and 36 leading west to Estes Park and Rocky Mountain National Park. Zip Code: 80540. Area Code: 303. Population: 1,227. Elevation: 5,360'.

Andrea's Homestead Cafe

216 East Main Street, 823-5000

Directions: From Boulder, go north on Highway 36 for 14 miles. Turn left at the signal where the road comes to a "T" with Highway 66. Go 1.2 miles, the restaurant is on the north (right) side just before the street becomes one-way. From Longmont, go west on Highway 66 for 8½ miles. At the intersection with Highway 36, continue straight on Highway 36 for 1.2 miles. The restaurant is on the north (right) side just before the street becomes one-way. From Estes Park, go southeast on Highway 36 for 19 miles. At the intersection with Highway 7 in Lyons, turn left (east) onto Broadway. Just after the street becomes two-way, the restaurant is on your left.

ESSENTIALS

Cuisine: German (with Italian, American and Mexican)
Hours: Thu-Tue 8AM-9PM (later on weekends in the summer). Closed Wed.
Meals and Prices: Breakfast $, Lunch $$, Dinner $$$
Nonsmoking: Yes
Take-out: Yes
Alcohol: Full Bar

Credit Cards: MC, Visa, Amx, Disc
Personal Check: From local area only, with I.D.
Reservations: Recommended, especially in the evening, but no reservations for Sun Breakfast.
Wheelchair Access: Yes, including bathrooms.
Other: No cigar or pipe smoking.

HISTORY, PERSONALITY AND CHARACTER

Andrea Liermann has been the first, and only, restaurant owner on these premises, having purchased the property in 1977. It was formerly a filling station, or as Andrea jokingly states, "It still is a filling station". The back dining area, that includes the bar, was the original station area. Andrea had an outdoor deck added to the front when she bought the place. In 1985, she had the deck enclosed and in 1994, a banquet facility was added to the left of the entrance. Andrea, by the way, was the former manager at The Black Bear Inn next door with the original owners. Michael Ratzlaff is the restaurant's manager and head chef. He has been with the restaurant since 1990 and has 15 years' experience in cooking, having worked at several Estes Park restaurants including La Casa and the Gazebo.

FOOD, SERVICE AND AMBIANCE

Their cream of tomato soup was creamy rich in flavor with pieces of tomato, onion, a few carrot slices, parsley and pepper seasonings. The soup came with zwiebel rostbraten, a ribeye steak with grilled onions and mushrooms. The medium-rare steak, more rare than medium, was non-greasy, but had fat for flavor. German food being what it is, there wasn't any seasoning salt or spices added. The meal comes with a huge portion of German home fries and lightly-cooked carrots and zucchini. I have eaten here for breakfast, as well (or even better). The veal bratwurst is tender, juicy and lightly grilled; the French toast is thick, toasted golden brown, and served with warm maple syrup; and the eggs are done just right.

They serve one of the better breakfasts in Colorado with good things like eggs benedict, huevos rancheros, omelets, crêpes, blintzes, German apple-pecan pancakes, homemade blueberry glaze, and fresh warm apple streudel. Lunch is varied and good, as well, with salads (including charbroiled lemon peppered chicken breast); German, Italian and Mexican specialties; sandwiches; burgers; chicken dinners; turkey schnitzel; fish and chips; and Icelandic cod. The dinner menu features German potato pancakes or matjes — herring filet — as appetizers; sautéed turkey breast and gorgonzola and chicken salads; pork roast; sauerbraten; rahm schnitzel; yägerschnitzel; fettuccine with baby shrimp and crabmeat in a pesto cream sauce; pepper steak; German beef rouladen and Dijon or broasted chicken.

I found the service here to be top notch: very pleasant and professional, doing little things like seating me at a large table when I had writing materials with me and being very attentive to things like water, butter, coffee or just clearing away a finished plate. The decor is vintage Colorado with several stuffed animals, furs and skins: Scottish highlanders (with long horns), white-tail deer, black bear, buffalo, boar, big horn sheep, foxes, moose, beaver, elk, coyotes and caribou. On the far right wall is an octagonal-shaped stenciled window of ducks in a marsh. Stained-glass is used to divide the front and rear dining rooms. They usually play tapes of classical music, but on Friday and Saturday nights they provide live Bavarian and Austrian entertainment from a group of 5 guys who have played here since the mid-1980s. They include a harmonica player, bell ringer, slap dancer, guitar and vocal. Take in a piece of Old Germany, Colorado style, and dine at Andrea's.

SPECIAL ONE-TIME OFFER: Buy one entrée at the regular price and receive a complimentary dessert (up to $3.00 value). Limit two desserts with the purchase of two entrées. This offer NOT valid in combination with any other offers.
_____ Manager/Owner. _____ Date.

RECIPE

German Potato Pancakes

6 raw potatoes, peeled
2 cooked potatoes, peeled
  and cooled

8 to 10 whole eggs
Salt and pepper
Granulated garlic

1. Grate cooked and raw potatoes.
2. In mixing bowl, add eggs and grated potatoes.
3. Add 2 to 3 teaspoons granulated garlic, salt and pepper.
4. Heat skillet or griddle to 375 degrees.
5. Place 2 ounces of potato mixture in oiled skillet.
6. Spread mixture until very thin.
7. Cook until crisp on both sides.
8. Serve with homemade applesauce or lingonberry sauce.

Andrea's Homestead Cafe in Lyons

La Mariposa

112 East Main Street 823-5595

Directions: From Boulder, go north on Highway 36 for 14 miles. Turn left at the signal where the road comes to a "T" with Highway 66. Go 1.1 miles, the restaurant is on the north (right) side.

ESSENTIALS

Cuisine: Mexican
Hours: 7 days 11AM-9PM.
Meals and Prices: Lunch/Dinner $$
Nonsmoking: Yes
Take-out: Yes
Alcohol: Full Bar
Credit Cards: All 5

Personal Check: Yes
Reservations: Recommended for groups of 10 or more
Dress: A mix of blue jeans, slacks and blue collar
Wheelchair Access: Yes

HISTORY, PERSONALITY AND CHARACTER

The building used by La Mariposa was built in the late 1980s and was initially The Berlonva Restaurant (see page 198 in The Colorado Small Town Restaurant Guide). In 1992, Renee and Maria Cervantes opened La Mariposa. They started together in the restaurant business in 1986 with the original La Mariposa in Longmont and added a third Mexican Restaurant, Taqueria in Longmont, in 1994. Richie Webb, who started in the restaurant business at Andrea's up the street in 1985 and spent 8 years at the Fox Hill Country Club in Longmont, is the manager. Jesus Avila, who has been working since 1991 and trained as a sous chef at La Mariposa in Longmont, is the head chef.

FOOD, SERVICE AND AMBIANCE

Linda and I sat down to some light and crisp chips with a spicy, hot, homemade salsa that was like puréed tomatoes with jalapeño seeds. I reached for the ice water after my first chip and salsa. Linda ordered the camarones Acapulco, grilled shrimp wrapped in crisp bacon with mild jalapeños accompanied by a lettuce and tomato salad with Thousand Island dressing and Spanish rice. I selected the Parilladas beef and chicken combo. A tasty tray temptation of 10 corn tortillas served on a very warm cast iron skillet in a wood serving tray. The tortillas are topped with grilled meats and vegetables, including onions, tomatoes, green peppers and special seasonings. This hearty serving will fill one big appetite or two average ones.

Elsewhere on their Mexican menu, you'll find salads, like guacamole, taco or shrimp, burritos, enchilada dinners, taquitos, chile relleno dinners, fajitas, steak and pork meals, combination plates, shrimp, fish, menudo and egg dishes. You can down your Mexican choice with flavored or regular margaritas, wine beer or non-alcoholic drinks.

Finish the meal with vanilla, chocolate or fried ice cream, a sopapilla or a flan. There is a children's menu.

Service was friendly, with a smile and very attentive. Richie, who also waits tables, returned several times after our food was served to see how we were doing. Spanish vocal and instrumental songs, both romantic and lively, played throughout the evening. The pinewood panel walls in the front dining room look as fresh and new as when I visited Berlonva's in 1990. Mexican blankets and hats trim the windows. Mexican rugs, paintings of the Virgin Mary, pueblos, pottery, deserts and villages and a cute artwork of a chicken coop covered in chicken wire enhance the walls. The decor is not overdone, just a few fine touches.

The rear dining room has white stucco walls that resemble the building's exterior with two black iron enclosed wine shelves and matching black iron sconces. The covered patio behind this room displays a red brick floor, stucco ceiling and walls with a red trellis to the right. The theme has changed, but the ambiance is as warm and comfortable as Berlonva's, which I gave five stars to in my first book.

SPECIAL ONE-TIME OFFER: Buy one entrée at the regular price and receive a second entrée of equal or lesser value FREE (up to $8.00 value) OR receive 50% off one entrée (up to $4.00 value). This offer NOT valid in combination with any other offers. _____ Manager/Owner. _____ Date.

RECIPE

Flan

1 can of 12-ounce evaporated milk   4 eggs
1 can of 14-ounce Eagle brand condensed milk   ½ ounce vanilla
4 ounces of sugar

1. Blend all ingredients except sugar.
2. Heat sugar on stove until melted and brown.
3. Pour brown sugar into 9-inch cake pan. Add blended ingredients.
4. Place cake pan in larger pan containing water (or use double boiler).
5. Steam cook in oven at 375 degrees for 45 to 60 minutes until set and golden brown on top.
6. Chill one hour before serving.
7. Cut into 8 servings and serve cold.

196

MANCOS

The town was settled in the 1880s and named after the Mancos river which, in Spanish, means "one handed," "faulty" or "crippled". Two of the early settlers, Richard Wetherill, son of a successful Quaker rancher, and his uncle, Charles Mason, discovered three of the larger ruins of Mesa Verde in December 1888: the Cliff Palace, Spruce Tree House and Square Tower House. Richard Wetherill and his five brothers later provided guide services for visitors to the ruins and began a large collection of artifacts. Ten thousand of these items later found their way into The Colorado Heritage House in Denver. Ranching, tourism for hunters and fishermen, cattle and a match stick factory are Mancos' principal industries today.

Zip Code: 81328. Area Code: 970. Population: 842. Elevation: 7,030'.

Dusty Rose Cafe
200 West Grand Avenue, PO Box 419, 533-9042

Directions: Mancos is located 28 miles west of Durango and 18 miles east of Cortez. From the east or west on Highway 160, turn south onto Main Street at the Millwood Junction Restaurant (Highway 184 is to the north). Go two blocks, turn right on Grand Avenue. Go one block, the restaurant is on the right at the northwest corner of Mesa Street in the Old Mancos Inn. An alternative route is to exit Highway 160 at the Mancos business district, 1 mile east or west of town and drive into Mancos on Grand Avenue.

ESSENTIALS

Cuisine: Country Cafe/Northern Italian
Hours: 7 days 7AM-2:30PM, 5:30PM-10:30PM.
Meals and Prices: Breakfast/Lunch $, Brunch/Dinner $$
Nonsmoking: Yes
Take-out: Yes
Alcohol: Full Bar
Credit Cards: MC, Visa

Personal Check: Yes, with I.D.
Reservations: Not necessary for breakfast and lunch, unless its a party of more than 8. Recommended for dinner.
Wheelchair Access: Yes, including restroom.
Dress: Casual. Some dressy on Sunday after church.

HISTORY, PERSONALITY AND CHARACTER

The Dusty Rose is in a building originally constructed as a hotel in 1894, the year Mancos became incorporated. Over the years, different cafes operated here until the '90s. On May 16, 1994, Barry Sucherman, a former partner with Chris Chacos at the Village Smithy in Carbondale (see page 40) opened up the Dusty Rose. Barry's restaurant experience dates back to the '70s. He worked at the Original Pancake House in Chicago, the Atrium in Durango and the Millwood Junction (Mancos) before operating and cooking at the Dusty Rose. In May 1995, Barry brought in Chef R.J.(Dick) Pictor to prepare the Northern Italian and Continental cuisine in the evenings. Dick's wife, Becky, makes the desserts.

FOOD, SERVICE AND AMBIANCE

I had the chicken olé, charbroiled, smothered with Monterey Jack cheese, and overflowing with mild, diced green peppers on a toasted bun. The buns come frozen, par-baked and are completed at the restaurant (it actually tasted homemade). I doubled up on the chicken with chicken tortilla soup: big chunks of chicken with pieces of tortilla chips that they deep fry, all in a tomato soup with green and red chili and onion topped with Monterey Jack cheese. The taste of Mexico! For dessert, I had a big piece of homemade almond bread pudding made with poppyseeds and topped with lemon frosting. They have another homemade dessert, Mesa Verde mocha cake, that won 1st Place for most decadent dessert in the Chocolate Fantasy Contest at the 1994 Durango Winter Festival. They also make their own salad dressings: a low-fat yogurt dill, Italian vinaigrette, ranch with green chilies and a raspberry vinaigrette.

Breakfast features French toast, hotcakes, eggs, meats, huevos rancheros, McGurk's (hashbrowns smothered with cheddar, onions, tomatoes, mushrooms and bell peppers, the same one that you'll find at the Village Smithy in Carbondale), rancheros supreme (a combination of McGurk's and huevos rancheros), egg burritos, and omelets (served all day). Offerings for lunch include sandwiches (chicken Italian, veggie with avocado and Monterey Jack cheese, and grilled cheese deluxe); salads, including Italian hot chicken; burgers and a menu for smaller appetites. The weekend brunch specials are eggs benedict, vegetarian or neptune and crab omelet, all with homemade hollandaise sauce. Durango brewery beer on tap, California wines, mimosas, bloody Marys, tropical blend ice tea and freshly ground coffee are among the beverage choices. There is a lunch special every day like beef stew in a bread bowl or chicken quesadillas. Burgers, chicken sandwiches and super nachos with green chili are served on pub night on Fridays during the winter along with live jazz duets and acoustic blues.

Service was amiable and courteous. An old James Taylor tape played in the background. The restaurant was artfully decorated with a rose pattern on black tablecloths, veridian green walls decorated with wreaths of dried flowers, still-life paintings of flowers in vases, an Easter bonnet, curios of women and an outdoors vista painting in a classic gold frame. Stained-glass lamp shades, beveled-glass artworks and potted plants enhanced the country charisma. In the summertime, you can dine on their sidewalk cafe. This is an excellent morning or early afternoon stop on your way to Mesa Verde.

SPECIAL ONE-TIME OFFER: Buy one entrée at the regular price and receive a second entrée of equal or lesser value FREE (up to $8.50 value). This offer NOT valid in combination with any other offers. _____ Manager/Owner. _____ Date.

RECIPE

Chicken Artesun
(Serves 2)

2 6- to 8-ounce chicken breast boned and skinned	1½ tablespoon julienne, sun-dried tomatoes
2 ounces clarified butter	¼ cup white wine
5 artichoke hearts, halved	½ teaspoon chopped parsley
2 teaspoon julienne shallots	2 tablespoon cold, unsalted butter

1. Sauté chicken breast in clarified butter until browned lightly on one side.
2. Turn and add artichoke hearts and shallots. Cook for 2 minutes.
3. Add sun-dried tomatoes, parsley and white wine.
4. Cook 2 to 3 minutes to reduce liquid.
5. Remove from heat. Remove chicken to warm serving platters.
6. Add cold, unsalted butter to liquid and vegetables in pan and shake pan with back and forth motion until butter is creamed into sauce.
7. Serve over chicken at once.

The patio at the Dusty Rose Cafe in Mancos

Millwood Junction

101 Railroad Avenue, 533-7338

Directions: Mancos is located 28 miles west of Durango and 18 miles east of Cortez. From the east or west on Highway 160, turn south on Main Street (Highway 184 is to the north). The restaurant is on your right just past Railroad Avenue (the frontage road).

ESSENTIALS

Cuisine: Steak, Seafood
Hours: 7 days 5:30PM-10:30PM
Meals and Prices: Dinner $$$-$$$$
Nightly specials $$
Nonsmoking: Yes
Take-out: Yes
Alcohol: Full Bar

Credit Cards: MC, Visa
Personal Check: From local area only.
Reservations: Accepted. Highly recommended for concert nights.
Wheelchair Access: Yes

HISTORY, PERSONALITY AND CHARACTER

The Millwood Junction was built in 1978 with old barn wood from seven different buildings. The original and only owners of the restaurant have been Jake and Roma Riffel. Roma makes the desserts, like black bottom pie, raspberry torte, 3-berry cobbler and ice creams. Daughter JoAnn, along with another chef, now manages and cooks at the restaurant. She prepares all the homemade soups, salad dressings, sauces and dinner rolls, as well as the entrées.

FOOD, SERVICE AND AMBIANCE

I have had their steak, shrimp and barbecued baby-back pork ribs. Big steaks with a large order of fries are their specialty and they do a good job of it. The ribs are all meat and fall off the bone. Baby back pork ribs and barbecue sauce are the specialty of the house. The cole slaw is creamy and a little sweet. Their shrimp is quite good also. The rest of the dinner menu offers escargots and deep-fried vegetables for appetizers, a selection of light meals, pasta, steaks, seafood, house specialties (châteaubriand for two, steak Diane, steak au Poivre and beef stroganoff), sandwiches, a soup and salad bar and ice cream. There are specials every day including an all-you-can eat seafood buffet on Fridays that Joanne has been doing since 1983. It features oysters on the half shell, boiled shrimp, blackened catfish, 2-fish specials, a glass of wine and salad bar. Wine from California, France, Germany, Spain and Australia is available.

My server was soft spoken and quiet. Joanne is known for bringing entertainment to the Millwood Junction. Five or six times a year she'll book some top-quality live entertainers like Windham Hill artists Liz Story and Alex de Grassi, Jesse Colin Young, Boulder jazz player Peter Kater, Wind Machine, John Stewart, and Taj Majal. This rustic-style restaurant with unfinished wood has big wagon wheels and plants hanging in the divider openings, two stained-glass pieces, photos of wildflowers blooming and aspen, and blown-up photos of the old assay office at Red Arrow Mine and the Gold King Mine taken by a local photographer. This is still a lumber-producing community. When I drove through town, I passed by piles and piles of freshly cut timber. A lot of hard work has made the Millwood Junction a success going on two decades and is worthy of your attention.

SPECIAL ONE-TIME OFFER: Buy one entrée at the regular price and receive a complimentary glass of Millwood Junction house wine. Limit 2 glasses of Millwood Junction house wine with the purchase of 2 entrées. This offer NOT valid in combination with any other offers. _____ Manager/Owner. _____ Date.

RECIPE

Sautéed Lemon Chicken Breast with Mushrooms and Peas

Handful of mushrooms	1 tablespoon of fresh lemon juice
Chicken breast, skinless, butterflied	1 cup of heavy whipping cream
Butter	½ cup of frozen or fresh peas
1 teaspoon shallots, finely chopped	and mushrooms
¼ cup of white wine	Rice

1. Sauté a handful of sliced mushrooms.
2. Remove from pan.
3. Flour a boneless, skinless, butterflied chicken breast.
4. Sauté in butter until no longer pink inside.
5. Add shallots, white wine and lemon juice.
6. Remove chicken from pan.
7. Add heavy whipping cream.
8. Reduce heat. Cook until sauce is thick.
9. Add peas and mushrooms.
10. Pour over chicken. Serve over rice.

Have a favorite small town restaurant that you'd like to see in a future edition of this guide? Let Benjamin know about it. Call (303)978-0316.

MANITOU SPRINGS

Famous for its bubbling natural mineral springs, this small town was originally called Villa La Font or Fountain Village. It was renamed Manitou, the Algonquin Indian word for "Great Spirit", and became Manitou Springs in 1885. A few of the attractions which earned Manitou Springs a place on the National Historic District Register are Miramont Castle, a Victorian-style spa built of stone by Father Jean Baptiste Francolon in 1896; the Manitou Cliff Dwellings Museum, an outdoor architectural museum established in 1904 with the original stones from the Anasazi Indians in southwest Colorado; and the Manitou and Pike's Peak Railway, the highest cog railroad in the world ascending to the top of Pikes Peak at 14,110 feet.

Zip Code 80829. Area Code: 719. Population: 4,535. Elevation: 6,320'.

Craftwood Inn
404 El Paso Boulevard, 685-9000

Directions: Take Exit 141 from I-25 in southern Colorado Springs onto Highway 24 heading west. Drive 4 miles and exit at Manitou Springs. At the bottom of the exit ramp bear right onto Manitou Avenue. Go .7 miles and turn right onto Mayfair Avenue. Drive one block and take your first left onto El Paso Boulevard. The restaurant is down on the right.

ESSENTIALS

Cuisine: Hearty and Robust Colorado
Hours: 7 days 5PM-10PM
Meals and Prices: Dinner $$$-$$$$$
Nonsmoking: All
Take-out: Yes
Alcohol: Full Bar

Credit Cards: MC, Visa, Disc
Personal Check: Yes
Reservations: Suggested
Wheelchair Access: Yes
Other: 16% service charge added to parties of 7 or more.

HISTORY, PERSONALITY AND CHARACTER

The Craftwood Inn is an English Country Tudor-style building with beamed ceilings, stained-glass windows and a copper hood fireplace. It was built in 1912 by Rowland Bautwell as a coppersmith shop decorated with stained-glass personifying maidens from Italy and a Japanese shrine on the front column. In 1940, the Craftwood became a family-style restaurant and in the years that followed, the Craftwood's fine food and ambiance attracted dignitaries and celebrities like Cary Grant, Bing Crosby, Lawrence Welk, Liberace and Harry Truman's daughter. After three decades of popularity and success, the Craftwood deteriorated in the 1970s and closed its doors in the 1980s before the current owners, chefs and hosts, Cris Pulos and Rob Stephens, opened the Craftwood Inn in 1988. Chris was formerly at Finn's in Colorado Springs from 1980 until 1985 and at the Briarhurst Manor in Manitou Springs. Executive Chef Lawrence Johnson has been with the Craftwood since 1992 and formerly worked at Plaza of the Rockies in Colorado Springs and the Tyrolean Inn at Vail, always preparing wild game.

FOOD, SERVICE AND AMBIANCE

I've had two memorable dinners at the Craftwood Inn. On the first, I had roast duck with cranberry port sauce that sweetened and moistened this flavorful dish. On the second visit, Linda, my editor, and I spent a very pleasing winter evening in this charming, cozy restaurant. We both took pleasure in a light and fresh spinach salad with tomatoes and anchovies in a wild boar bacon vinaigrette. I thoroughly enjoyed the wild grill, a combination of tender, delicious paupiettes of venison; lean wild boar sausage with a crispy skin and delectable, thin slices of elk saddle steak — all in a very colorful plate setting showing green zucchini and asparagus, orange crinkly carrots, purple cabbage, brown potato skin and yellow acorn squash. Linda reveled in a superb king salmon filet that flaked away with a fork. It was in a blackberry beurre blanc, that enhanced the flavor without overpowering it, and served with mixed wild grains bread and quinoa.

There are several appealing à la carte soups, salads and appetizers to start your dining: elk consommé, crab and artichoke bisque, wild boar empanades, duck confit, rouladen of venison, Caesar salad and cold smoked salmon salad. The hearty and robust Colorado cuisine is revealed in the choices for wild game (roast pintelle pheasant, grilled Colorado boar, medallions of red deer and noisettes of caribou), the seafood selections (grilled pinon trout, shrimp sauté and lobster), various meat dishes (braised herbal chicken, veal scaloppine, Colorado striploin steak and tenderloin of beef au Poivre) and vegetarian platters. Seasonal specials like baked stuffed rabbit and sautéed Nilgai antelope are also offered. Wines, mostly from California and France, are available to enhance your meal and after-dinner cognacs, cordials, espresso and cappuccino drinks can accompany one of their scrumptious desserts like jalapeño white chocolate mousse.

Service was prompt and eager to take our order at first, then graduated into a more professional and laid-back tone. All in all, quite efficient from serving to cleaning the table. Classical music augmented the classic setting which was strengthened by artifacts discovered in a secret attic room during extensive renovations in the summer of 1988. Included in the find were a 1906 English lithograph from an original painting, 50 glass slides or negatives taken in Japan and Hong Kong by Bautwell and given to the local Historical Society, nonextant Manitou green stone (filled with copper) and paintings of George Washington's Inaugural taken from a home on Long Island and Martha Washington hosting a party that included Thomas Jefferson and Benjamin Franklin. The C.S. on the copper hooded fireplace signifies the original Craftwoods Shop. The terrace provides striking views of Pikes Peak. Colorado cuisine, historical ambiance and majestic vistas blend together in a powerful and unique dining experience at the Craftwood Inn.

<u>SPECIAL ONE-TIME OFFER:</u> Buy one entrée at the regular price and receive a complimentary glass of wine. Good for à la carte dining only. Good for every member in your party. This offer NOT valid in combination with any other offers. Please present to server at time of ordering. _____ Manager/Owner. _____ Date.

<u>RECIPE</u>

Game Chili

2½ pounds game meat (venison, caribou, elk), diced
½ pound cooked pinto beans
½ cup salad oil
1 large onion, diced
2 tablespoons cumin
1 tablespoon minced garlic
1 tablespoon oregano
3 tablespoons chili powder

3½ pounds crushed tomatoes
6 roasted green chilies, peeled and seeded or ½ cup of canned diced green chilies
2 teaspoons Tabasco
1 teaspoon salt
1 tablespoon basil
1 tablespoon ground black pepper
½ cup bread crumbs

1. Brown meat, garlic and onions in salad oil. Add remaining ingredients and simmer for 2 hours. Adjust spices.

Sleepy Cat Guest Ranch and Restaurant outside Meeker

MEEKER

Meeker was named after Nathan C. Meeker, one of the founders of Greeley, Colorado. In November 1879, Meeker and his fellow employees at the White River Ute Indian Agency were murdered by Indians and his wife and daughter were taken captive. After the massacre, a military post called "Camp on White River" was established four miles from the destroyed agency. The post was abandoned in 1883 and all the buildings were sold to the residents of the valley, leaving them a ready-made town.

Zip Code: 81641. Area Code: 970. Population: 2,098. Elevation: 6,239'.

The Sleepy Cat Restaurant
16064 County Road 8, 878-4413 or 878-5432

Directions: From Meeker, go north 2 miles (4.4 miles north of the intersection of Highways 13 and 64) to Country Road 8 and turn right. Go 16 miles, the ranch and restaurant are on your right.

ESSENTIALS

Cuisine: Steaks/Seafood/Ribs

Hours: Memorial Day Weekend to Mid-NOV: 7 days 8AM-11AM, 11AM-2PM, and 5:30PM-10PM. Mid-NOV to Memorial Day Weekend: Fri/Sat 5:30PM-10PM.

Meals and Prices: Breakfast $, Lunch $-$$, Dinner $$$-$$$$

Nonsmoking: No, but it usually is not a problem.

Take-out: Yes

Alcohol: Full Bar

Credit Cards: MC, Visa, Disc

Personal Check: Yes, with I. D.

Reservations: Recommended for dinner, accepted otherwise.

Wheelchair Access: Yes. There is a ramp in the back.

Other: Meeting room downstairs that leads to a patio facing the river. Available for banquets, family retreats, weddings and college study groups. Recent visitors have included Frankie Avalon, Hal Ketchum and Gary Morris.

HISTORY, PERSONALITY AND CHARACTER

The Sleepy Cat Guest Ranch, named after Sleepy Cat Peak several miles to the north, was built around 1946 by Otis McIntyre. Current owners Clark and Charlotte Wix bought the Sleepy Cat in 1964. Their philosophy is "high quality food and lodging at fair prices and a friendly, relaxed atmosphere will build the reputation that brings people back, with their friends". I'll vouch for the high-quality food, fair prices and friendly, relaxed atmosphere in the restaurant.

The original restaurant building burned down on January 5, 1991, but was rebuilt by October of the same year. Son Steve Wix, and his wife, Debbie, have managed the restaurant since 1984. Steve, who has been cooking since 1974, heads the kitchen staff with Paul Nold who joined the Sleepy Cat in 1989.

FOOD, SERVICE AND AMBIANCE

I ordered the Tom Cat-size prime rib, a massive, thick, meaty 16 ounces (actually, it seemed more like 24) that they cut in-house. This was one hearty prime rib without any special marinades or sauces. I did order a side dish of button mushrooms that, along with the horseradish, made for a perfect trio with the prime rib. Dinner comes with a 30-item soup and salad bar with homemade blue cheese dressing (the others are not homemade). The soup du jour was potato, a lightly seasoned broth with onions and big chunks of potato with skin left on. Their scones, a cross between French bread and a sopapilla, only better, were literally "too hot to handle". They were simply marvelous: chewy, doughy and slightly sweet. They're probably the best dinner bread I've tasted in Colorado and I'm pleased to present the recipe here. They use the left-over scone dough to make breakfast bread and French toast in the morning. Eggs, meats and Cinnamon rolls are also on the breakfast menu. For lunch, you can choose from burgers, sandwiches, fried shrimp or chicken or get a sack lunch to go. Other notable selections from their dinner menu are baby back pork and barbecue beef ribs; pork, lamb or elk chops; several steaks; shrimp scampi; baked scallops; catfish; trout; lobster tail and king crab legs. Sundae or sherbet is included with dinner or you can pay extra for cheesecake.

My server, Zippy, was just that plus cheerful, jolly, informative and helpful. You'll do well to have her wait your table. Mostly country music is played here, folks. As you enter through the solid pinewood and lead crystal doors, look straight ahead and you'll notice a grizzly bear posed upside down on the wall next to a picture of a mountain lion. Now turn around and take a look at the string of raccoon, possum, fox, muskrat and kit fox pelts. This is just the beginning of a trophy case of mounted animals and skins — a hunter's paradise. To the left is the bar, to the right is a fireplace with a full mount wolverine over the mantel and a full mount black bear cub to the side. Straight ahead is the dining room. At the host's stand is a wood carving of a sleepy mountain lion and a picture of a white owl. To the right of the host's stand is the salad bar with a wood carving of a mountain white fish, found in the White River, hanging over the soup pot. A stairway leads up to the loft with a first-rate view to the south of green hills, Elk Creek and the White River. Throughout the restaurant, you'll see knotty pine logs; heads of moose, bighorn sheep, deer, elk, buffalo, goat, coyote and American and African antelope; elk, deer, buffalo, raccoon and fox skins and hides; three full-length mounted Mexican marlin; an Alaskan king crab mounted on a framed black velvet mat; and full mount muskrat and mountain lion. Magnifying the rugged, western ambiance are wagon wheel chandeliers and a melange of changing photographs, paintings and prints by regional artists characterizing places like the Flat Tops Wilderness area, Marvine Lakes and Three Sisters Mountains. To entertain you, there are hummingbird feeders with a constant flutter of hummingbirds, especially in the evening. Now that you know about this place, don't you wish you were here?

SPECIAL ONE-TIME OFFER: Buy one entrée at the regular price and receive a second entrée of equal or lesser value FREE (up to $15.00 value) OR 50% off a single entrée (maximum discount $7.50). This offer NOT valid in combination with any other offers. Please present to server at time of ordering. _____ Manager/Owner. _____ Date.

RECIPE

Steve Wix's Sleepy Cat Scones

1 pound margarine	3 tablespoons yeast
4 tablespoons salt	8 cups water
8 cups milk	4 cups whole wheat flour
1 cup sugar	White all-purpose flour

1. Melt margarine and combine with salt and milk.
2. Combine sugar, water and yeast in mixing bowl and let set until yeast foams.
3. Combine all ingredients in mixing bowl except white flour.
4. Add enough white flour to make mixture firm enough to knead on a table.
5. Add flour as required to keep the dough from being sticky while it is kneaded.
6. Roll out about a half an inch thick and cut into two- or three-inch squares.
7. Let rise a few minutes then cook in deep fryer at 350.
8. Serve with butter and honey or ice cream.
9. Makes about 175 scones. Cut this recipe down a little unless you're expecting a crowd!

Sicily's Italian Restaurant in Montrose

MONTROSE

Montrose is located in the Uncompahgre Valley which was settled by Ute Indians. In 1874, O. D. Loutzenhizer, one of the founders of Montrose, visited the valley as a member of Alferd Packer's party. In 1881, a military post named Fort Crawford was established under General McKenzie and in 1881, under the demands of white settlers, the Ute Indians were "escorted" into eastern Utah. Pioneers, ranchers and farmers followed in their place and incorporated the town of Pomona on September 16, 1881. The name was later changed to Montrose by Joseph Selig in honor of the character, the Duchess of Montrose, from the novel Legend of Montrose by Sir Walter Scott. Zip Code: 81402. Area Code: 970. Population: 8,854. Elevation: 5,806'.

Sicily's

1135 East Main Street, 240-9199

Directions: From the intersection of Highways 50 and 550, go east on Highway 50 (Main Street) for .7 miles. The restaurant will be on your left at the northwest corner of Stough.

ESSENTIALS

Cuisine: Italian

Hours: 7 days, 11AM TO 9PM (10PM in summer)

Meals and Prices: Lunch/Dinner $$ Pizza $$-$$$

Nonsmoking: All

Take-out: Yes

Alcohol: Beer and wine

Credit Cards: All 5

Personal Check: In-state with I.D.

Reservations: Accepted

Wheelchair Access: Yes, through the main entrance on the North side

Other: 10% senior discount. Available for large parties or banquets.

HISTORY, PERSONALITY AND CHARACTER

Sicily's occupies a house built circa 1908. Some of the local old-timers claim the building was once used as a mortuary, although there does not appear to be any record of this, and that there is a ghost on the premises. It is known that a health food store was here for a few years before David Whigham purchased the building, added on a Garden Room, kitchen and deck and opened Sicily's on Mother's Day, 1994. David, from Colorado Springs, Colorado, managed a pizza shop in Fort Collins, Colorado, from 1985 to 1990, an Italian restaurant in Minneapolis, Minnesota, was sous chef at the Inn at Arrowhead in Cimarron, Colorado, and ran a small cafe at the Montrose Airport for a year before opening Sicily's. Head chef Michael Zimmerman started at Sicily's in the summer of 1995. He grew up in Brooklyn and is a graduate of the Culinary Institute of America in Hyde Park, New York. Apparently, the ghost I mentioned earlier is female with a sense of humor. She popped the lid off a can striking a cook in the head. She also bopped him in the head with an empty glass rack. (Maybe she's trying to tell him something!). She has been known to roll out toilet paper in the women's restroom. Ladies, beware!

FOOD, SERVICE AND AMBIANCE

Warm, homemade, rosemary herb bread with fresh, homemade marinara sauce loaded with Italian seasonings are served with the dinner pasta entrées. The house salad is better than most with shaved cheddar cheese, black olives, croutons, fresh mushrooms and a homemade Italian dressing made with wine. I ordered the manicotti with spinach and ricotta. The noodles were al dente, not overdone or burned on the edges like I see in some places. The marinara sauce was as good as I've had (I like to make my own the same way), and the cheeses and spinach were fresh. Everything is done from scratch here: the sauces, all the dough products and the desserts (mud pie, key lime pie and cheesecakes).

Antipasta, deep-fried mozzarella with marinara, zucchini and calamari are on the appetizer menu. For lunch, you can order a chef or seafood salad, minestrone soup, a dish of pasta, a meatball or Italian sausage sandwich, a pizza, or one of their calzones, stuffed with all kinds of good things like cheeses, meats, vegetables, spices and fresh herbs. The dinner pasta entrées include spaghetti, fettuccine Alfredo, lasagna, baked manicotti, pesto linguini, chicken parmigiana or marsala, shrimp scampi and linguini with fresh clams. Spumoni is offered for dessert. The wines are primarily from California and Italy and they boast the largest beer selection in western Colorado, offering over 60 beers including microbrewery beers from Boulder, Denver and Vail, Colorado; five other states; New Zealand and Italy. A children's menu is available.

My server was accommodating and eager to please. Very relaxing piano solos enhanced the laid-back atmosphere. The Garden Room features philodendrons growing on ceiling trellises and looks out onto the patio with stucco arches and a crab apple tree growing through the middle of the deck. Sitting on this patio on busy Main Street is as cosmopolitan as it gets in Montrose. David's wife, Julie, decorated the interior. At the restaurant's entrance and passageways, there are pictures of Italian villages, gardens and Venice. Artificial grape vines wrap their way around the archways between dining rooms and hallways. The rear dining room, in the old part of the building, is simple and plain, yet attractive with white and black sconces, wall to wall windows, a fireplace and decorative wallpaper that features bunches of grapes on a dark green background. Dave has put together a classy-looking corner of the world and the food (having grown up on Italian cooking) is the way I like it.

SPECIAL ONE-TIME OFFER: Buy one entrée at the regular price and receive a second entrée of equal or lesser value FREE (Up to $11.00 value). This offer NOT valid in combination with any other offers. Please present to server at time of ordering. _____ Manager/Owner. _____ Date.

RECIPE

Chicken Maria
(Family Style, Serves 5)

1½ pounds chicken breast, diced	½ teaspoon black pepper
1 large red bell pepper, in thin strips	½ teaspoon salt
1 large green bell pepper, in thin strips	4 ounces white wine
¼ cup green onions, chopped	2 cups marinara sauce
1 tablespoon garlic minced	¼ cup butter
2 tablespoons fresh parsley	¼ cup olive oil
1 teaspoon crushed red pepper	

1. Sauté chicken in butter and olive oil until slightly done.
2. Add garlic, herbs and peppers. Sauté for approximately 5 minutes; add wine and marinara sauce. Simmer for an additional 5 minutes.
3. Serve over choice of pasta. We recommend angel hair pasta.

The Whole Enchilada

44 South Grand Avenue, 249-1881

Directions: From the intersection of Highways 50 and 550, go west on Main Street for three blocks, over railroad tracks, to the first signal. The restaurant is on the left on the southwest corner of West Main Street and Grand Avenue.

ESSENTIALS

Cuisine: Mexican/Southwestern
Hours: Mon-Sat 11AM-9PM (10PM from Mid-MAY to Mid-SEP). Sun 12PM-8PM.
Meals and Prices: Lunch/Dinner $$
Nonsmoking: Yes
Take-out: Yes
Alcohol: Full Bar
Credit Cards: MC, Visa, Amx, Disc

Personal Check: Local area only.
Reservations: Recommended for Lunch or Dinner on Fri and Sat. Accepted otherwise.
Wheelchair Access: Yes (except patio).
Other: Additional 15% service charge for parties of 8 or more.

HISTORY, PERSONALITY AND CHARACTER

Built around the turn of the century, The Whole Enchilada is in a building that was originally an ore mill, then a grist mill for grinding grain, before being used for storage. Between 1975 and 1985, the Root Cellar Restaurant occupied the premises. Jerry Coffey opened The Whole Enchilada in November 1986 and sold it to current owner, Teri Lorimar, in June 1991. Teri worked in restaurants before, but this is the first one she has owned. Teri also manages, cooks and "does just about everything". Tony Manzanares has been the head cook since September 1994 and has been cooking in the Montrose area since 1983 at places like the Red Barn and the Elks.

FOOD, SERVICE AND AMBIANCE

I spent a very pleasant spring afternoon on their patio, eating both their mild and hot salsas with some salty corn chips. I ordered the estacado, a whole avocado filled with suremi (imitation crab), white fish, rice, parsley and spices, topped with cheddar and Monterey Jack cheeses and scallions. It came with a side dish I had not tried before: Chimayo corn — whole corn, onions, peppers, cheese, milk and eggs mixed together like a corn meal casserole; and pico de gallo. I found this southwestern meal considerably more to my liking than the Mexican fare I am used to and I would recommend it as a good alternative. Fillings and sauces are prepared fresh daily. Colorado ingredients are used whenever possible, and the beef and pork are from western Colorado. The estacado also comes with chicken instead of seafood. The other special on the menu is a beef or chicken stuffed sopapilla. The rest of the menu is fairly standard Mexican. They also offer hamburgers, a children's menu and an a la carte menu.

My server was friendly and helpful with a good sense of humor. The three-tiered patio has green and white umbrellas, river birch and aspen trees (that shed their "cotton" in the spring), a red brick wall and black iron gate at the entrance, a red brick wall in the rear, and a wood fence on the side. Inside, the bar and lounge to the right has a big screen television, ceiling fans, hanging philodendrums and dried red chilies, a sun roof, wood beams and posts. Rock music could be heard playing quietly in the lounge only. The dining room is straight back from the entrance in the mine part of the building. Sombreros, Indian art work and blankets, and an adobe latter decorate the red stone walls with pinewood dividers. For a good taste of the southwest and Mexico, visit The Whole Enchilada.

SPECIAL ONE-TIME OFFER: Buy one entrée at the regular price and receive a second entrée of equal or lesser value FREE (up to $11.50 value) OR 50% off a single entrée (maximum discount $5.25). This offer NOT valid in combination with any other offers.
_____ Manager/Owner. _____ Date.

RECIPE

Enchiladas Acapulco
(Makes 7 to 9)

White Sauce:
- 2 ounces butter
- 1 small onion
- 6 ounces of water
- 1 tablespoon of chicken base or stock
- ½ cup of green chilies
- ¼ cup of cornstarch
- ⅔ cup of cold water
- 8 ounces of sour cream

Enchiladas:
- 7 to 9 blanched corn tortillas
- Hot oil
- ½ pound shredded chicken
- Salt, garlic powder and onion salt to taste
- 2 ounces blanched, slivered toasted almonds
- 2 ounces black olives, sliced
- 1 ounce Monterey Jack cheese, shredded
- 1 ounce cheddar cheese, shredded
- Shredded lettuce, diced tomatoes and sour cream with toasted almonds

1. White Sauce: Dice onions and sauté in butter. Add water and chicken base or stock. Bring to boil. Add green chilies continuously to boil. Add cornstarch to cold water. Add to green chilies and boil to thicken. Remove from stove and cool. Add sour cream. Add more cold water to desired consistency.
2. Enchiladas: Dip tortillas in hot oil. Season chicken with salt, garlic powder and onion salt. Roll chicken, almonds, black olives and cheeses in tortillas. Top with white sauce and bake at 350 degrees in a greased pan for 5 to 10 minutes. Remove from oven. Top with lettuce, tomato and scoop of sour cream with toasted almonds.

MORRISON

The town was named after pioneer George Morrison who founded the town in 1859. Located at the base of the foothills just west of Denver, Morrison is best known for the adjacent Red Rocks Park Amphitheater.

Zip Code: 80465. Area Code: 303. Population: 465. Elevation: 5,800'.

The Fort

19192 Route 8, 697-4786, FAX 697-478

Directions: From C-470 and Highway 285 (Hampton Avenue) in Lakewood, go west on Highway 285 to the next exit for Highway 8. Take the exit and go north on Highway 8 for .1 mile. The restaurant is on the right.

<u>ESSENTIALS</u>

Cuisine: Early West

Hours: Mon-Fri 6PM-10PM, Sat 5PM-10PM and Sun 4PM-9PM.

Meals and Prices: Dinner $$$$-$$$$$

Nonsmoking: Yes. Smoking only in lounge areas. No pipes or cigars.

Take-out: Yes

Alcohol: Full Bar

Credit Cards: All 5

Personal Check: Yes, with I.D.

Reservations: Recommended

Wheelchair Access: Yes

Dress: Casual to formal

Other: 17% service charge for tables of 8 or more. No separate checks. Minimum service per person in dining room, $6.50. Menus available in Japanese, French, German, Spanish, Russian and Braille. Can accommodate large groups for special events.

<u>HISTORY, PERSONALITY AND CHARACTER</u>

The Fort Restaurant, built in 1962, is fashioned after the early Colorado fur-trading center, Bent's Fort, located near the town of La Junta, 160 miles southeast of Denver. It took 10 months for 22 New Mexican workmen from Taos to complete the project using 1,800 tons of earth to make 80,000 mud and straw adobe bricks, each weighing 45 pounds and measuring 14"x10"x4". The restaurant, with its 2-foot thick walls, was opened by Sam and Carrie Arnold on February 1, 1963. Sam and Carrie have owned and operated The Fort from 1963 to 1973 and from 1986 to the present. Sam is a restaurateur, food critic, author and historian. He has written 3 cookbooks and 2 historical books, travel articles for the Denver Post and food stories for the Rocky Mountain News. The Fort and Sam have been written about in numerous newspapers including the New York Times, Boston Globe and San Francisco Examiner and several periodicals such as Bon Appetit, Gourmet and Cuisine. Sam has also appeared on a number of television stations — BBC, CNN, the Food Network and the Discovery Channel — and been interviewed on quite a few television shows like the Today Show, Good Morning America, Regis and Kathy Lee and the MacNeil/Lehrer Report. Ron

Schickel, a graduate of La Varenne School of Cuisine in Paris and formerly Executive Chef at the Burnsley Hotel in Denver, has been the Executive Chef at The Fort since June 1995. Sam describes The Fort's operation like this: "I'm the composer, Ron is the conductor, our 30 cooks are the orchestra members and our 'music' is delivered to the customers by our servers".

The Fort is a place to bring out-of-town guests and for special occasions. It is probably the most sought after restaurant outside of Denver by conventioneers and tour groups coming to Colorado. I've dined at The Fort 10 times since 1991: twice for birthdays including my own on my first visit (see page 496 in <u>Restaurants from 101 Colorado Small Towns</u>), once with out-of-town family on my last visit, once for a graduation, once for a meeting, four times with tour groups (so I've experienced their catering capabilities) and once just for dinner (you don't <u>need</u> a special reason or to be part of a group to dine here). Several famous personalities have stopped by The Fort including James Michner, Dr. Arnold Toynbee, Ann Margaret, Louis Leakey, Sugar Ray Leonard, Michael Jackson and Bryant Gumbel.

FOOD, SERVICE AND AMBIANCE

Sam Arnold's Early West Cuisine highlights seafood, wild game, Colorado beef and fowl. A potpourri of "fur trade period potables" — authentic, and sometimes potent, concoctions with the unusual tastes of mid-19th century America — the Fort's own libational specialties and unique appetizers can be ordered before dinner. I've tried all but a few of their many menu items. I found the Trade Whiskey — made with tobacco juice, red pepper and gunpowder — to be a manageable shot. The gunpowder is made from sulfur, charcoal and saltpeter ("to preserve your bacon," Sam Arnold says). The first sip of the St. Vrain's Mule — a concoction of ginger brandy and ginger beer — tasted like ginger ale, but got better. The 1840 Hailstorm Premiere Julep, similar to a mint julep without peach brandy, was a sweet treat with French cognac (also available with Jack Daniels, Wild Turkey or Cutty). For a "lip-smacking good" departure from a familiar cocktail, try The Fort's frozen prickly pear margarita.

I enjoyed my first bites of Rocky Mountain oysters on my first visit to The Fort — small, tender and quite tasty small calf fries with tomato relish and onion cocktail sauce on the side. The Fort also introduced me to jalapeños stuffed with peanut butter and they became an instant favorite that I prepared myself for house parties and canoe trips. I liked the meat flavors on all of their appetizers: the soft textured roast buffalo marrow bones (also called "prairie butter") that you extract with a knife and spread onto toast, the thin and tender Texas rattlesnake braised, flaked and chilled with the texture of crab and the taste of chicken, the mild buffalo boudies sausage and the buffalo tongue served with Sam Arnold's famous capered horseradish. If you like guacamole with chips, they have that too — prepared with traditional Mexican guacamole made with avocadoes, tomatoes, onions, serrano chilies, cilantro, a little salt and a lot of lime.

Gonzales steak — top sirloin stuffed with real New Mexican pure green chili, then topped with a whole green chili pod, briefly broiled and prepared to perfection — was my savory entrée on my very first visit. It came with pan potatoes slightly undercooked the way I like them, peas and a sprinkling of toasted canola seeds. The meal was served with Indian blue corn and wild blueberry muffins and pumpkin and walnut muffins (The Fort has baked more than five million pumpkin and walnut muffins!). We finished out meals with glasses of port and sherry: a becoming conclusion to an exceptional meal.

On visits that followed, I ordered all of their game selections. The quail was moist, very flavorful, with a delectable seasoning and just slightly crispy. It was briefly marinated in teriyaki sauce, sherry and fresh ginger, then mesquite broiled. The pheasant was deliciously tangy and sweet, prepared with teriyaki and orange slices and glazed with honey. The deep pink New Zealand elk was very tender and the buffalo broke apart easily with a fork. Huckleberry sauce on the side is exquisite, but very sweet. It is something to try every few bites, but don't pour it over your entire meal. The quail was my favorite.

Their New York Strip steak was very low in fat and charbroiled. The prime rib, rubbed with herbs then slow roasted with a little onion peel smoke, was luscious. The mountain trout — broiled, basted in a mint sauce and topped with bacon bits — was mild and flaky. "The Bowl of the wife of Kit Carson", named after Kit Carson's granddaughter, who used to work at The Fort, was a spicy, pepper hot broth with chicken, rice, garbanzos, Monterey Jack cheese, smoky chipotle chilies and avocado. The Sante Fe chops — hefty, meaty and charbroiled — were served with New Mexico red chili sauce on the side. The pintade game hen, a charbroiled French delicacy served with Montana huckleberries, was moist and "taste like chicken wished it did". If you are a vegetarian, don't lose interest. They have a vegetarian plate, made to order, with in season vegetables like Arkansas Valley onions, white kernel shoe peg corn, Anasazi beans, cha-cha murphys (mashed potatoes mixed with a little green chili and cheese) and quinoa, "the super grain of the future". The salads, by the way, were excellent and I recommend the bayou dressing: a green garden dressing with a hint of anchovy. If you like vinegar, try the dill vinaigrette with ginger. The dessert selections vary, but you may see cheesecake (made with an amaretto crumb crust, rich dark Ghirardelli chocolate and Meyers Jamaica rum), wild Montana huckleberry sundaes, Kir Royale mousse, The Fort ice cream pie (made with Dutch chocolate ice cream, coffee, creme de menthe, slivered almonds and Hershey's syrup in a chocolate cookie crust), or an amaretto flan.

On my first visit to The Fort, the service was very pleasant and efficient. We wanted for nothing. Our waitress was quick and did not leave us waiting. My second visit was equally enjoyable only this time we had a jocular, self-professed "psychic" and flexible waiter who was prepared for anything. On the last 8 sojourns, the young men and young women servers have been professional, energetic and smiling.

The Fort has a very unique setting with an open air courtyard in the middle complete with bonfire in the summer and fantastic views of Denver and Pikes Peak. About 350 guests in nine dining areas can be served in this 12,000 square foot structure. Talk about authentic! A few of the more notable items of decor are a 350-pound church bell built in 1840 located in the cupola under the flagpole; a 27-star flag: the one used in 1845 just before Texas was annexed; two 18'x18' bastions or towers, one used for wine storage and tasting, the other as a special dining room with a fireplace; and cannons: a six-pound Napoleon, a 12-pounder on a naval carriage and a "thunder mug".

The St. Vrain bar, to the right of the front gate portal, has a herringbone planked ceiling with vigas and zapatas (footed supports). An adobe brick from the original Bent's Fort in 1834 can be found in a niche in the wall. As you pass through the dining areas of this restaurant, you will notice an American Indian selling jewelry, Indian sketches and sand paintings; Padre Martinez chairs (an early New Mexican style wooden chair made of ponderosa using peg construction), calico walls, decorated buffalo skulls, and oil paintings of the Bent brothers and San Miguel church in Sante Fe (the oldest church in the United States) as it looked in 1845. It would be difficult to find a more elaborate restaurant in small-town Colorado or one requiring more work.

Most places this large and this crowded would leave the average person feeling a little uncomfortable, or at least self-conscious, especially visiting the first time. Not so with The Fort. The air is filled with laughter, joviality and high spirits. If you are looking for a good time, come to The Fort. It is sure to delight your senses, enhance your mood, and by the time the evening is through, you may just find yourself reciting the Mountain Man's Toast. WAUGH!

SPECIAL ONE-TIME OFFER: Buy one entrée at the regular price and receive a complimentary Starbucks' espresso, cappuccino or latté with a chocolate dipped, La Tempesta biscotti. This offer NOT valid in combination with any other offers. Please present to server at time of ordering. _____ Manager/Owner. _____ Date.

RECIPE

Gonzales Steak
(Serves 1)

10-12 ounces, thick-cut top sirloin steak	1 clove garlic or dash of garlic salt
3 green Anaheim chile strips,	Pinch of Mexican leaf oregano
roasted and peeled (canned will do,	½ teaspoon salad oil
but fresh is best)	Salt and pepper to taste

1. Prick chilies and roast under the broiler till blistered and blackened. Turn them regularly as they blacken. Place in a Ziplock bag and pop into the freezer for 30 minutes. Then remove outer skin under running water. Cut off stems and remove the seeds.
2. With a very sharp knife, cut a horizontal pocket into the steak. Chop two of the chilies into a fine dice. Mix with garlic or garlic salt and oregano.
3. Stuff the chilies into the pocket. Oil the meat and remaining chile with salad oil.
4. Broil the steak both sides to desired doneness. Salt and pepper to taste.
5. Grill the remaining whole pod to get a nice patterning of grid burn onto the pepper. Lay it overtop the steak as a garnish when serving.
6. A teaspoon of brown butter on the steak is heaven!

Fresh chilies really are the best and simple to prepare. New Mexicans traditionally like to leave a few of the seeds in the dish. Seeds give it life, they say. In the old days, we'd heat butter until it turns a light brown color, then spill it overtop. But we're not allowed that anymore — down with those nasty food fascists!

Sam Arnold

The Fort Restaurant in Morrison on a clear day

MOSCA

Mosca was named after Mosca Pass to the east, which was named for Luis Di Moscasco, who succeeded De Soto in command of his exploration party after De Soto's death in 1542. The town had been known as Orean.

Zip Code: 81146. Area Code: 719. Population: 180. Elevation: 7,555'.

Great Sand Dunes Country Club

5303 Highway 150, 378-2356, Fax 378-2428

Directions: Located 4 miles south of The Great Sand Dunes National Monument. From Highway 17 just north of Mosca, take State Highway (or Lane) 6 east for 16 miles to Highway 150. Turn right (south) and go 1 mile. Look for the Rocky Mountain Bison, Great Sand Dunes Country Club & Inn signs. Turn right at the entrance and follow the gravel road to the inn and restaurant. From Highway 160, go north on Highway 150 for 12 miles and look for the same sign. Turn left at the entrance and follow the gravel road to the restaurant.

ESSENTIALS

Cuisine: Bison, Southwestern

Hours: APR-NOV: 7 days, 11:30AM-3PM and 6PM-9PM. DEC-MAR: Wed-Sun 11:30AM-3PM and 6PM-9PM. Closed Mon/Tue. Closed JAN.

Meals and Prices: Lunch $$, Dinner $$$-$$$$$

Nonsmoking: All

Take-out: Yes. Box lunches available.

Alcohol: Full Bar

Credit Cards: MC, Visa, Amx, Disc

Personal Check: Yes

Reservations: Required for dinner or parties of 6 or more.

Wheelchair Access: Yes

Dress: Casual, but you may want to dress up for dinner.

HISTORY, PERSONALITY AND CHARACTER

The inn and restaurant located on Zapata Ranch was built by the Linger family in 1928 and used as a ranch house until 1989. In 1948, two additions were added onto the house and in 1950, the stone wall encircling the building was constructed. No changes or restorations have been made since. In 1989, Rocky Mountain Bison, Inc., owned by Hisa Ota, purchased Zapata Ranch from the Stewart family and opened the Great Sand Dunes Country Club and Inn. The restaurant was the Stewarts' living room just a few short years ago. Head chef Philip Kenzoir, who started with the Sand Dunes in September 1995, learned his appreciation for cooking from his mother. He is certified by the American Culinary Federation and is a professional member of the Colorado Chef De Cuisine. Following his apprenticeship, Philip became chef at Cowboys Restaurant in Snowmass, Colorado. In his current position, he uses the best of the San Luis' Valley's offerings including quinoa, potatoes, fish, vegetables lamb and fresh produce grown in the garden on the ranch.

FOOD, SERVICE AND AMBIANCE

The 100,000-acre Zapata Ranch is home to the third largest bison herd in the country — 2,800 head in all. So naturally, I had to try their homegrown bison burger with real melted roquefort cheese for lunch. Actually, "homegrown" describes pretty much their whole menu. They grow their own herbs and vegetables in the summer. The fish is grown locally. Lamb is from the local area. They try to use as much organic produce as possible from the San Luis Valley (like potatoes) as well as Colorado products. The bison burger is a huge 10-ounce patty of lean bison. If you like blue cheese beef burgers, you will love this thick, hearty sandwich made with bison. Fries made with locally-grown potatoes are served on the side. I also tried the chef's daily soup selection, butternut squash and apple topped with spiced cream. I liked the fruit/vegetable mix and the tincturing of spiced cream was an added sweet savor — not too spicy, but definitely flavorful.

Dinner was a treat as I had my editor, Linda, my brother, Bill, and his wife, Ann, at the table. The chef's fabulous presentations appeared throughout the evening from appetizer to main course to dessert. For starters, I ordered the braised rabbit and blue corn quesadilla, cut into eighths and served in a circle like a pizza pie. It came with guacamole and red peppers with a corn husk sticking up in the middle of the plate and melted asadero cheese in 2 concentric circles around the edges — picturesque and tasty at the same time. Ann had the spicy lamb sausage in filo dough with carrot salad and red pepper jelly, dotted with specks of black pepper, drizzled cris-cross on the plate. Linda and Bill both liked the baby mixed greens with crunchy Tillamook cheddar puffs, artichoke hearts and apple smoked lardons, similar to bacon. We all went our separate ways on the entrées as we tried the veal, bison, duck and chicken. I delved into the roasted veal loin prepared confit style with shallots and garlic, served with a tangy yellow curry cream in a "lightning pattern" around the plate. My brother from Buffalo, New York, ordered the Zapata Ranch bison steak, lean and tender, spiced with tomatillo ancho chili sauce and served with Swiss chard and new potatoes. Linda opted for the moulard duck breast with creamy potato risotto, like minced potatoes, similar to potatoes au gratin, on a plate decorated with sprinkles of red peppers on the edge. Ann savored the almond crusted chicken breast with fava beans, morel mushrooms, wild asparagus and four types of snail-shaped pasta: spinach, saffron, tomato and plain. Four delectable desserts came our way to finish the evening: white chocolate and macadamia mousse in a filo dough pastry sandwich topped with blackberry sauce (my favorite); quinoa pudding with orange syrup, raspberry sauce and currants in a ring of strawberry slices; Valrhona chocolate and praline ice cream with hazelnut genoise and Godiva liquor; and a very tart lemon custard (created by greatly reducing the lemon) with bing cherries (they also use orange sorbet),

219

blood orange sauce criss-crossed on the plate and a fresh mint leaf — very elegant, high-quality dining where the edge of the San Luis Valley meets the Sangre de Cristo Mountains. The menu changes frequently as the chef will use the freshest available produce and meats found in the valley or state. Whatever the selection, you can be assured it will be inventive, different and expertly prepared.

For lunch, I was served by a charming waitress who put on a disk of Louis Armstrong singing "What a Wonderful World", a perfect accompaniment to the wonderful 60-degree February day we were having. For dinner, a chilly 50-degree July day, the white table cloths were brought out, the service was a little more sophisticated, but very pleasant at the same time and light jazz played in the background. Lunches are less formal. The 7-table dining room, which looks onto the golf course and grasslands, features a rock fireplace with pinewood walls, tables and chairs and a photo of the Great Sand Dunes by J. D. Marston. The Great Sand Dunes Country Club is isolated but not removed. You'll experience fine country dining prepared by a world-class chef and professional service in a unique setting.

SPECIAL ONE-TIME OFFER: Buy one entrée at the regular price and receive a complimentary appetizer or dessert (up to $10 value). Limit two appetizers or desserts with the purchase of two entrées. This offer NOT valid in combination with any other offers. _____ Manager/Owner. _____ Date.

RECIPE

Bison, Apple and Black Bean Chili
(Serves 6 to 8)

1½ cups black beans, dried	2 pounds bison stewing meat,
4 poblano chilies, medium	1-inch cubes
4 green bell peppers, medium	Salt and pepper, fresh ground
1 habanero chile, medium	1 onion, medium, finely chopped
10 tomatillos, medium, husked,	6 garlic cloves, minced
rinsed and quartered	1 tablespoon sugar
5 scallions, coarsely chopped	1 tablespoon cumin, ground
1 pound bacon, smoked	1 teaspoon salt
2 bay leaves	Cornbread
4 apples, peeled, seeded and diced	Sour cream
3 tablespoons vegetable oil	

---

1. Place the black beans in a medium saucepan and add 6 cups of water, bring to a boil over moderate high heat, and boil for 3 minutes. Remove from the heat and let stand for 1 hour.
2. Meanwhile, roast the poblanos, bells peppers and habanero under the broiler as close to the heat as possible or over a gas flame, turning frequently until blackened all over. Transfer to a paper bag and let steam for 10 minutes.
3. Peel the chilies and pepper under running water and remove the core, seeds and ribs. Drain and pat dry. Place them in a food processor with the tomatillos and scallions and purée until smooth.
4. Drain the black beans and return them to the saucepan. Add the bacon, bay leaves and 6 more cups of water. Bring to a boil over high heat. Cover, simmer over low heat, until beans are tender. Drain, reserving 1 cup of liquid. Discard the bay leaves and cut the bacon in ½-inch pieces and set aside.
5. Heat 2 tablespoons of oil in a large cast-iron casserole. Season the bison cubes with salt and pepper. Add some of the meat to the casserole in a single layer and cook over high heat, until well browned all over, about 5 minutes. Transfer to a plate and brown remaining in batches.
6. Heat 1 tablespoon of oil in the casserole. Add the onion and garlic and sauté until translucent. Return the browned bison meat to the casserole with the chile purée, sugar, cumin and 1 teaspoon of salt. Bring to boil, then lower heat, simmer until meat is very tender, about 2 hours. Stir in black beans, cubed bacon and apples with the reserve cooking liquid.
7. Season the chili with salt and pepper and spoon into bowls. Serve with cornbread and sour cream.

The Great Sand Dunes Country Club in Mosca

MT. CRESTED BUTTE

Mt. Crested Butte is named after the nearby mountain whose top resembles the crest of a rooster's head. It is 2½ miles from and 372' above Crested Butte and a popular resort for ski and snowboard enthusiasts.
Zip Code: 81225. Area Code: 970. Population: 264. Elevation: 9,280'.

Giovanni's Grand Cafe

500 Gothic Road (in the Grande Butte Hotel), PO Box A, 349-4999
Directions: From the intersection of Highways 50 and 135 in Gunnison, go 28 miles north on Highway 135 to Crested Butte. At the 4-way stop, continue straight for 2½ miles up to Mt. Crested Butte. Just past Snowmass Road, turn right into the underground parking garage at the Grande Butte Hotel. The restaurant is on the Plaza Level.

ESSENTIALS

Cuisine: Northern Italian
Hours: JUN through SEP: 7 days 7AM-10:30AM, 11:30AM-2PM and 5:30PM-9PM. Thanksgiving to Mid-APR: 7 nights 5:30PM-9PM. Closed Mid-APR through MAY and OCT to Thanksgiving.
Meals and Prices: Breakfast/Lunch $$, Dinner $$$$
Nonsmoking: All. Smoking only permitted in the lounge or on the patio.

Take-out: Yes
Alcohol: Full Bar
Credit Cards: MC, Visa, Amx, Disc
Personal Check: Yes. I.D. required if out of state.
Reservations: Recommended for dinner, accepted otherwise.
Wheelchair Access: Yes

HISTORY, PERSONALITY AND CHARACTER

The Grande Butte Hotel opened in 1986 with the Grande Cafe, a restaurant offering American cuisine. This was followed by the Spaghetti Slope. Giovanni's Grande Cafe opened in November 1991 under Crested Butte Mountain Resort (owners of 12 other restaurants opened during the winter): Ralph O. Walton Jr., Chairman of the Board; Bo Callaway, President and son Edward Callaway, in charge of operations. Sara Trees and Barry Hopkins are Co-Directors of Food and Beverage. They have been in the food service industry since 1982 and both joined the resort in 1986. Executive Chef for all resort restaurants is Mike Gumm. He has been working as a chef since 1985, obtained formal training and apprenticed in Switzerland and used to own his own restaurant in Gunnison, Colorado, the Coachline. Head Chef for Giovanni's since 1994 is Garrett Lazenby.

FOOD, SERVICE AND AMBIANCE

I relished over a savory bistecca for lunch: marinated New York strip, grilled and topped with fresh, sautéed red and gold peppers, onions and pancetta on crisp, crunchy and chewy focaccia spread with gorgonzola cheese. It came with a tasty pasta salad with red peppers, black olives and celery in a vinaigrette dressing. I found this to be a scrumptious and filling meal. Other lunch possibilities included spinach salad in a warm pancetta-leak vinaigrette, antipasto, frittata primavera, angle hair and fettuccine pasta dishes, a grilled eggplant sandwich and coppa salami with provolone cheese on Italian bread. Breakfast featured a fresh fruit plate, a southwestern skillet, omelets, Belgian pecan waffle, French baguette dipped in cinnamon-vanilla batter and crêpes filled with pastry cream and seasonal wildberry compote. Highlighting the dinner menu are appetizers like carpaccio, calamari and baked artichoke; minestrone soup and salads; first course pasta dishes: linguini with shrimp, eggplant lasagna, risotto with porcini mushroons, fettuccine with grilled chicken and spaghetti and meatballs; followed by second course entrées: veal dishes with prosciutto or asparagus; roasted gulf shrimp, maple leaf duckling and rack of lamb dishes; grilled chicken or beef plates and salmon baked in parchment paper. To complement your meal, you have a choice of about 100 wines, mostly form Italy and California, to choose from. Giovanni's has won the Wine Spectator Award of Excellence in 1993 and 1994.

Service was friendly and attentive. This second-story restaurant with wall-to-wall windows leads out to a patio and a grandiose view of the neighboring peaks. The interior, designed by Eric and Sammy Erickson from California, is embellished with Italian marble, black lacquer chairs, a silver-plated and glass chandelier, flower pots, aspen trees and modern artwork. In the lounge at the entrance, across from the host's stand, is a large wine rack behind tinted glass. Giovanni's offers you the best view with the finest dining in Mt. Crested Butte.

SPECIAL ONE-TIME OFFER: Buy one entrée at the regular price and receive a second entrée of equal or lesser value FREE (Up to $25.00 value) OR 50% off a single entrée (maximum discount $12.50). This offer NOT valid in combination with any other offers. Please present to server at time of ordering. _____ Manager/Owner. _____ Date.

RECIPE

Vittello con Asparagi
Veal with Asparagus
(Serves 4)

3 tablespoons unsalted butter
1 pound veal, thinly sliced and
pounded, 2 ounces each
1 tablespoon garlic, finely minced
½ cup dry white wine
1½ cups cream

¼ cup capers
20 asparagus tips, 4 inches long
3 teaspoons lemon juice
¼ cup tomatoes, ¼ inch diced
Salt to taste

1. Heat butter in a large heavy skillet over high heat.
2. When the butter foams, dredge the veal in flour and add, making sure not to crowd the skillet. If need be, cook the veal in 2 batches. Cook until the veal is lightly golden on both sides, about 2 minutes.
3. Transfer veal to a warm plate and set aside.
4. Add the garlic and cook until slightly browned.
5. Add the white wine and quickly stir to dissolve any meat deposits attached to the bottom. When the wine has reduced by half, add cream, capers and lemon juice.
6. Blanche the asparagus and add to sauce.
7. When the sauce has reduced by half, add the tomatoes.
8. Serve at once with a bit of sauce over each serving.

Benjamin James Bennis' three restaurant guides combined offer 667 restaurant reviews.

NORWOOD

Norwood was named by its founder, I. M. Coop, for a community in Missouri. The town is nestled atop Wrights Mesa with striking panoramas of the La Sal Mountains to the west, the Uncompaghre Plateau to the north and the San Juan and San Miguel Mountains in the east and south. Ute hunters, Spanish explorers and mountain men passed this way before Edwin Joseph homesteaded Norwood in 1879. In the late 1800s, Norwood became a timber and ranching support community for neighboring towns. Today, it is the destination of many outdoor enthusiasts. Norwood is one of the most popular hunting areas in Colorado with deer, elk, pheasant, grouse and duck found on the mesa and in surrounding national forests. Miramonte Reservoir, 17 miles to the south, offers windsurfing, swimming, water-skiing and year-around lake fishing. Nearby San Miguel and Dolores Rivers provide challenges for rafters, canoeists and kayakers. The San Miguel County race track and fair grounds host rodeo and horse racing.
Zip Code: 81423. Area Code: 970. Population: 429. Elevation: 7,006'.

The Back Narrows Inn Restaurant
1550 Grande Avenue, 327-4417, 327-4260
Directions: Located 33 miles west of Telluride and 17 miles west of the intersection of Highways 62 and 145 near Placerville. From the east on Highway 145, the restaurant is on the left (south) side just past Lucerne Street, 1.7 miles past the green National Forest Access sign for Miramonte Lake, Beaver Park and Lone Cone.

ESSENTIALS

Cuisine: Country
Hours: Year around: Mon-Sat 6PM-8:30PM. Mid-JUN to Labor Day: Mon-Fri 11:30AM-2PM. Closed two weeks in APR and 2 weeks in SEP.
Meals and Prices: Lunch $$, Dinner $$-$$$
Nonsmoking: No, but they will try to use the backroom for nonsmokers.

Take-out: No
Alcohol: Full Bar
Credit Cards: All 5
Personal Check: Yes, with I.D.
Reservations: Recommended for weekends or parties over 6. Accepted all other times.
Wheelchair Access: Yes

HISTORY, PERSONALITY AND CHARACTER

Built in 1885 as the Western Hotel, it was almost a century later in 1980 when the restaurant was added. The Back Narrows Inn and Restaurant was once two separate buildings: the Western Hotel and annex. The restaurant now occupies the area that used to be sleeping quarters and a storage room. In 1986, Richard and Nancy Parker purchased The Back Narrows. Their living quarters now occupy what used to be the Inn's old restaurant. Richard works the front of the restaurant while Nancy, who was trained at the

Cordon Bleu Culinary School in London and was a member of their staff for 5 years afterwards, prepares the delicious dishes.

FOOD, SERVICE AND AMBIANCE

Fresh-baked, homemade chips, light as a feather and puffy with air bubbles (they're marvelous), with the best salsa — tomatoes, onions and lots of cilantro — are served at your table. I had soup with my dinner: tomato and orange, a combination that works, at least the way Nancy makes it! For my entrée, I ordered breast of chicken with dumplings. The chicken was moist and broke apart easily with a fork. The dumplings were soft and fluffy, almost like fresh white cake. It came with plenty of white sauce from the chicken stock and broccoli, cauliflower and honeydew melon on the side. This was a big plate, very filling and must have added 2-3 inches to my belly (I have since forgiven Nancy).

The chalkboard dinner menu offers a few excellent choices: baked lasagna, filet mignon with Bernaise sauce, Colorado ribeye steak with sautéed mushrooms, poached halibut steak with shrimp in a cream sauce, fettucine Alfredo, and Mexican specialties: a tostada or salad with enchilada de carne or enchilada de pollo with green chili sauce. Nancy also prepares some delectable desserts: double fudge cake, butterscotch caramel cake, carrot cake with lemon cream cheese icing, banana hot fudge sundae and Viennese-style cheesecake with raspberry sauce. They also serve peach or black cherry frozen yogurt. Their summertime lunch menu offers light selections like salad plates (seafood with fresh fruit, chef, pasta, and cottage cheese with fruit), sandwiches (breast of chicken with cheese and Philly beef), and hot or cold soups, like chilled cucumber.

I found host and server Richard to be a very kindly and likeable fellow. The atmosphere is romantic and makes you feel like you just stepped back in time. Even the music of "Candlelight Magic" brought back memories of songs I remembered hearing at the movie theater as a child. This place is a true hidden treasure (that's what this book is all about!) and should not be passed up. I sat at the best table in the house — in front of the book shelf (with candles, beer steins, a tea kettle and wine bottle) looking out on the porch, street and town. It's not a "hurry up town", so a glance out the window every 10 or 15 minutes sufficed to catch everything that was going on. As you walk through the hallway from the hotel lobby to the restaurant, take note of the old Victorian-style paintings of pastoral settings. When you enter the restaurant, you will notice a small bar that used to be the hotel's front desk. Across from the bar is a small wicker couch and coffee table. Behind the couch are several original French posters glued to the wall. To the left of the posters are paintings of a woman sitting on a bench handling doves and a woman knitting at a table across from a man with a Napoleonic hat. This is stuff from a different era, preserved for your pleasure. The dining room to the right of this room (where I sat) has a cabinet, shelves and window sills with potted plants, and pictures of flowers, clipper ships and a boy herding sheep. The dining room to the left is decorated with old portraits, a picture of 3 Indian chiefs, and an Indian cloth art work. Old oak and cherrywood is used throughout the restaurant. The 20-seat patio is used for lunch and, weather permitting, dinner during the summer months.

SPECIAL ONE-TIME OFFER: Buy one entrée at the regular price and receive 50% off a second entrée (maximum discount $7.50). This offer NOT valid in combination with any other offers. _____ Manager/Owner. _____ Date.

RECIPE

Viennese Cheesecake
(Serves 10)

Crust:
  2 cups graham cracker crumbs
  ¼ cup powdered sugar
  6 tablespoons margarine

Filling:
  2 packages (1 pound) cream cheese
  ½ cup sugar
  Juice and grated rind of 1 lemon
  4 ounces white raisins
  1 cup lightly whipped heavy cream
  1 envelope of powdered gelatine

1. Put graham cracker crumbs in a bowl.
2. Mix and press into a 10-inch glass pie pan.
3. Cook 1 minute in microwave. Let cool.
4. In small sauce pan, sprinkle gelatine over ¼ cup cold water and let stand 1 minute.
5. In large bowl, with electric mixer, beat cream cheese, sugar, lemon juice and grated rind. Dissolve gelatine over low heat.
6. Into cheese mixture, fold in raisins, whipped cream and dissolved gelatine.
7. Pour into cold crust and refrigerate at least 1 hour.
8. Serve with fresh or frozen raspberries, sweetened with a little powdered sugar and 1 tablespoon of kirsch liqueur.

This is a family recipe which was developed in Scotland and passed on through three generations of family cooking.

Nancy Parker

Karen's

1610 Grand Avenue, 327-4840

Directions: Located 33 miles west of Telluride and 17 miles west of the intersection of Highways 62 and 145 near Placerville. From the east on Highway 145, the restaurant is on the left (south) side at the corner of Lucerne, 1.6 miles past the green National Forest Access sign for Miramonte Lake, Beaver Park and Lone Cone.

ESSENTIALS

Cuisine: Eclectic Country

Hours: Tue-Sat 7AM-2PM. Sun 7AM-12PM. Shut Mon.

Meals and Prices: Breakfast/Lunch $-$$

Nonsmoking: No, but no ash trays and Karen gives smokers a hard time.

Take-out: Yes

Alcohol: No

Credit Cards: No

Personal Check: Local area only

Reservations: Recommended for groups of 8 or more. Accepted otherwise.

Wheelchair Access: Yes

Dress: Casual/cowboy. People with suits get funny looks.

HISTORY, PERSONALITY AND CHARACTER

Karen's occupies a building that originally was a bank built in the early 1900s. The bank failed in 1929 and for almost a half century, the building went through a series of transformations. It was a movie theater, shoe store, jewelry store and apartments. Then in 1977, Karen LaQuey purchased the building, converted it to office space and rented to surveyors. Karen's love for cooking took her out of her job in the butcher shop and produce department of the local grocery. On October 22, 1984, she opened Karen's Restaurant. Karen is assisted by daughter, Kirsten, in the kitchen and a host of GMTs (gourmet maintenance technicians). Kirsten has been cooking since she was a little girl and has worked at the Hyatt Regency in Beaver Creek and various other establishments.

FOOD, SERVICE AND AMBIANCE

The menu is not extensive, but what there is promises high quality and great taste. For breakfast, I tried the green eggs and ham (No, Dr. Seuss was not dining with me that day). This was a scrumptious combination of eggs scrambled just right mixed with spinach and cream cheese. The meal comes with real grated potatoes, crisp on the outside without being burnt and tender inside without being undercooked, and honey wheat bread. For lunch, I ordered the soup du jour, fideo (fe-day-oh), a Mexican soup made with tomatoes and noodles that was delicious and the quiche du jour, seafood and asparagus that was fresh and flaky. Karen and Kirsten also prepare a "cream of everything" soup on some days (potatoes, vegetables and leftovers) and a ham and cheese quiche on other days. The pie dough, breads, rolls, sauces (including barbecue and Mexican Molé, chili sauce with chocolate), sweet and sour salad dressing (with a pink color from red onion), and hot mustard are all homemade. Other notable entries on the breakfast menu include new waveous (eggs, beans, cheese and salsa in a tortilla), breakfast in a bowl (potatoes, eggs and Hollandaise sauce), chorizo and eggs, eggs benedict, omelets, French toast, blueberry pancakes and pigs in a blanket. For lunch, you can choose from salad, create your own sandwich from selected meats and breads, or hamburgers, including an avocado green chili cheese burger and, on special days, a Cajun burger. A couple of their homemade cakes are poppyseed and Texas chocolate.

You probably noticed that I usually only devote a sentence or two to service (that's because in most restaurants, that's just about all you can say about the service). That won't be the case with Karen's. Karen is known throughout the San Miguel Basin for her hearty laughter, jovial nature and unsurpassed sense of humor. On my last visit, I asked to use the men's room, so Karen directed me to a narrow hallway at the back of the restaurant. At the end of the hallway was a door with the word "Ladies" on it. I looked at Karen and she said, "You have to go through the ladies' room to get to the men's room!" "You've got to be kidding" I said. As I walked into the hallway, I noticed a second short hallway to the left leading to the men's room that was not visible from the entrance to the first hallway. You have to be on guard with Karen. She won't pass up a chance to pull a joke on you. The pay-off, though, is that you get to hear and feel her infectious laugh. Service here is not just for laughs, though. Karen's motto is "We have no customers, only company". In fact, the first thing you may hear when you walk through the door is Karen's voice telling one of the servers "You have company," and that is just the way you will feel. Karen doesn't like to call her work in the kitchen "home cookin'". "Don't call it home cookin' 'cause people will think we're home cookin'" she says. You got to love these small town folks!

It would be a little difficult to describe the decor in Karen's in just a couple of sentences as well! She is a collector of odds and ends and antiques. Perhaps the best place to start would be with one of my favorite items in her restaurant — a citation, to Karen, from the American Restaurant Association, Gourmet Food Division. It states, "In recognition of superlative food, excellent service, garage sale furniture, leftover picnic dishes, and antique advertising," signed and dated December 28, 1987, in Washington, D.C. This was presented as a joke, of course, but it does accurately describe Karen's in a few words. Another notable item is a large picnic table in the rear dining room known as "the family table". It is a place for political discussions and town planning meetings and has acquired ("earned"?) the nickname "the liar's bench!" Other noteworthy articles include Ellen Brody's impression of Bridal Veil Falls in Telluride; a photo of Karen with grandson, Christopher, standing behind a sign saying "Under Old Management" (it was taken when Karen returned from a three-month hiatus from the restaurant); a zoom-lens photo taken of Norwood by Chuck Yeager at 31,000 feet on October 17, 1987; a photo of Telluride taken in the early 1890s, an original poster of a Rudolph Valentino film, "A

NORWOOD

Sainted Devil"; 3 shelves of boy scout cups from different troops around the country; civil war prints of Stonewall Jackson and the Battle of Franklin; a growing collection of photos (framed and under glass) of local customers; posters of Roosevelt and Truman (the election of 1944); and for children, which they encourage to visit, a toy box! Perhaps the sign in front of the restaurant sums up Karen's philosophy best. It's from Cicero. "Otium cum Dignatate", meaning leisure with dignity. Have a good time when you visit Karen's.

SPECIAL ONE-TIME OFFER: Buy one breakfast or lunch entrée at the regular price and receive 50% off a second entrée of equal or lesser value (maximum discount $4.00). This offer NOT valid in combination with any other offers. _____ Manager/Owner. _____ Date.

RECIPE

Karen's Famous House Dressing

1 medium red onion
½ cup sugar
¾ cup red wine vinegar
¾ teaspoon salt

¾ teaspoon celery seed
¾ teaspoon dry mustard

1½ cups salad oil

1. In a blender, blend first six ingredients to a pink liquid, then add the salad oil very slowly.

The Gold Creek Inn in Ohio City

OHIO CITY

Previously named "Ohio" after the Ohio residents who came to this area for the gold rush, Ohio is an Iroquois Indian word meaning "beautiful river". The town experienced 2 gold booms, one in the 1860s, the other in 1899.
Zip Code: 81237. Area Code: 970. Population: 60. Elevation: 8,583'.

Gold Creek Inn Restaurant

8506 Main Street (County Road 76), PO Box HH, 641-2086.
Directions: From the town of Parlin on Highway 50, 12 mile east of Gunnison, go north on County Road 76 for 8.6 miles to Ohio City. The restaurant is on the right just after Rowe's Ohio City Store and just before the bridge over Gold Creek.

ESSENTIALS

Cuisine: Continental
Hours: MAY-OCT: Tue-Sat 5:30PM to close. Closed Sun/Mon. Closed NOV-APR.
Meals and Prices: Dinner $$$-$$$$
Nonsmoking: All
Take-out: No
Alcohol: Full Bar/Wine Cellar
Credit Cards: MC, Visa
Personal Check: Local or pre-approved

Reservations: Highly Recommended
Wheelchair Access: Yes
Dress: Casual to comfortably formal
Other: No separate checks. Additional 15% service charge for parties of 6 or more. Available for special parties, luncheons, weddings, receptions and catering.

HISTORY, PERSONALITY AND CHARACTER

The Gold Creek Inn was originally built in the 1890s as a general store. After only 5 or 6 years, it was converted into a little cafe and boarding house and eventually into unrefined rental units with an outhouse in the back. The Inn had its share of ups and downs and periods of sitting vacant over the years. In the 1940s, Joe and Pearl Wright ran a cafe, boarding house and general store in this location and brought electricity to the building by means of an old paddle wheel and the force of Quartz Creek. It was the first building to have electricity in the Quartz Creek Valley. In 1971, they sold it to Ted Goodner who used the building for personal storage before selling to the current owner, Joe Benge, in 1977.

Joe and some of his friends spent 3 years renovating, adding pinewood logs and beams to the dining room so it would resemble the hand-hewn look of the original building. In the process of stripping away the old and adding on the new, Joe and Company discovered some old Chicago and east coast newspapers and letters (the building also served as Ohio City's first post office). Joe used the newspapers to add some country charm to the bathrooms. In May 1981, he opened the Gold Creek Inn and has been serving meals here every summer and fall since. Joe is owner, manager and executive chef. He has been in the restaurant business since 1976, is a graduate of Culinary Institute of America in Hyde Park, New York, a former Navy cook and has been a consultant to start-up restaurants in Crested Butte, Gunnison, Grand Junction (where he was born) and the Inn at Arrowhead in Cimarron (see page 46).

FOOD, SERVICE AND AMBIANCE

You have your choice of ordering an entrée a la carte with bread and vegetables or the full dinner which includes homemade soup, salad and potato. I chose the latter. The cream of carrot soup was rich in carrot flavor with onion and parsley in a light broth. I liked the flavor of the house Italian vinaigrette dressing on the mixed greens salad. Rice vinegar gave it a slightly sweet taste. The rib eye steak au poivre was a juicy piece of meat with plenty of au jus and pepper flavor. The steak is rubbed with pepper, panfried and flamed with brandy, and finally topped with a sauce consisting of brandy, cream, Dijon mustard and a deep, rich, reduced, brown sauce. The result was an exquisite sapor in both the meat and fat. Normally, I trim off the fat, but the fat on this cut was soft and tasty enough to devour. Real mashed potatoes with a few lumps and skins and sautéed zucchini accompanied the dish. For dessert, I delighted in a sweet ice cream parfait: sliced, toasted almonds on vanilla ice cream on amaretto sauce. They also served a parfait with strawberry, raspberry, chocolate or chocolate toffee almond crunch and New York-style cheesecake.

The regular menu items included roast prime rib au jus using choice, corn-fed beef, hand-rubbed with herbs and cut to order; a variety of cuts of choice steaks; broiled gulf shrimp in garlic; rainbow trout almondine; chicken breast pecan en crème; lemon pepper chicken and a nightly fresh fish special like yellow fin tuna, cod, halibut, sea bass or mahi mahi. The specials were broiled lamb loin teriyaki, rib eye with mushrooms and coho salmon with tropical salsa. Fresh ingredients and an experienced, trained chef guarantee you a marvelous dining experience.

My server was pleasant, helpful and informative. Joe personally visits every table when he's finished cooking to welcome and visit with old friends and new acquaintances. He's a very sociable guy. Some deep-down country music played very quietly in the bar. I had the cozy table in the corner nestled between the rock fireplace and window, great for viewing the roaring spring run-off on Gold Creek, but a disadvantage when it came to watching Joe at work in his open kitchen on the opposite side of the fireplace. The one-room dining room is decorated with an array of mining, lumbering, logging and farming tools collected by Joe's father, Harry "Buck" Benge. Adding to the rustic ambiance are a pair of old wooden skis, a piece of driftwood that I mistook for an antelope skull from where I was sitting, a rifle, a photo of Abe Lincoln that Joe inherited from his grandparents, copper pots and pans hanging over the fireplace, an antique sign for Friends Oats and sketches of buildings in Gunnison, Pitkin and Ohio

City. The bar at the entrance is embellished with an assortment of antique irons from Buck, more advertisements for Scotch Oats and Friends Oats and a 100-year-old frosted glass artwork detailing Indians, dogs and horses under a big oak tree. There is a small patio facing the creek with a covered wagon snuggled up against an old river willow tree, railroad tools, a few stellar jays helping themselves to a feeder and an old water wheel by the creek bed. It's a pleasurable drive over rolling hills and scenic landscape to get to the Gold Creek Inn Restaurant and a warm, comfortable place to dine once you arrive.

SPECIAL ONE-TIME OFFER: Buy one entrée at the regular price and receive 50% off a second entrée of equal or lesser value. Valid for up to two equal or lesser priced entrées at 50% off with the purchase of two entrées at regular price. This offer NOT valid in combination with any other offers. Please present to server at time of ordering. _____ Manager/Owner. _____ Date.

RECIPE

Steak Au Poivré
(Serves 2)

2 steaks (choice grade New York
  rib eye or tenderloin cut,
  approximately 8 ounces each)
2 teaspoons Dijon mustard
4 tablespoons cream or half and half

2 teaspoons Worcestershire sauce
  (Lea and Perrin)
2 teaspoons brandy
½ cup rich brown sauce, homemade
  or canned

1. Cook steaks to desired temperature in heavy pan. Flame the steak, dripping it with brandy until alcohol burns off. Add remaining ingredients.
2. Bring to simmer and top steaks.

Restaurant guides make unique gifts!

OURAY

Named after the famous Ute Indian chief, Ouray was first a silver camp called Uncompahgre or Uncompahgre City. In 1896, Thomas F. Walsh discovered gold here. Nestled in the San Juan Mountains, the youngest and steepest range of the Rocky Mountains, the entire town is listed on the National Register of Historic Districts. Ouray has been referred to as the "Gem of the Rockies" and the "Switzerland of America". Zip Code: 81427. Area Code: 970. Population: 644. Elevation: 7,811'.

Bon Ton Restaurant
426 Main Street, PO Box 667, 325-4951
Directions: Entering Ouray on Highway 550 (Main Street) from Ridgeway, continue on Main Street to the south end of town. The restaurant is on the right in the St. Elmo Hotel between 5th and 4th Avenues. Entering Ouray on Highway 550 from Silverton, the restaurant is on the left in the St. Elmo Hotel just past 4th Avenue.

ESSENTIALS

Cuisine: Italian/Seafood
Hours: MAY-OCT: 7 days 5PM-10PM, NOV-APR: 7 days 5:30PM-9PM. Year-around: Sun 9:30AM-1PM.
Meals and Prices: Brunch $$, Dinner $$$-$$$$
Nonsmoking: All
Take-out: Yes
Alcohol: Full Bar

Credit Cards: MC, Visa, Amx, Disc
Personal Check: In-state only with Driver's License
Reservations: Highly Recommended
Wheelchair Access: Yes (through the kitchen)
Other: Additional 15% service charge for parties of 8 or more. One check per table. Available for small banquets.

HISTORY, PERSONALITY AND CHARACTER

The Bon Ton is in the basement of the St. Elmo Hotel, built in 1898 by Mrs. Kittie Heit. The hotel is listed on the National Registry of Historical Buildings and is part of Ouray's National Historic District. The original Bon Ton Restaurant dates back even further, to the 1880s, and was on the site now occupied by the hotel's patio. When the hotel was completed, the restaurant moved into the hotel. The original Bon Ton building became a Chinese laundry and several other businesses before being replaced by the current hotel patio. The current owners, Sandy and Dan Lingenfelter, have operated the Bon Ton since 1983 and also own Buen Tiempo Restaurant in Ouray. Their son, Mike, is the general manager. Executive Chef Jon Kosh graduated from The American Culinary Institute in 1968 and has been with the Bon Ton since 1983. Chef Tim Eihausen studied under Jon 15 years ago and then expanded his cooking talents with 10 years of experience in some of the fine restaurants of New Orleans. He has been with the restaurant since 1992.

FOOD, SERVICE AND AMBIANCE

My editor and I tried two of their dinner specialties: veal piccata and eggplant Parmesan. We started our meal with Bear Creek (small button) mushrooms sautéed in butter, Madeira wine, parsley, red onions, peppers and garlic. They made for a tasty, light appetizer. The dinner salad was enlivened with red peppers, black olives and grated Parmesan cheese. The thin medallions of veal were prepared with lemon juice which gave the meal a delicately bitter taste that I found to my liking. The capers, mushrooms, white wine and onion all blended together deliciously. The eggplant was baked to a nice brown color on top and was tender, but not undercooked. The side dishes included a medley of vegetables and fettuccine with both madeira and pesto sauces.

The dinner appetizers include an assortment of cheeses, meats, vegetables, seafood, pastas and soups. The pasta entrées feature a variety of noodles and red, bechamel and marinara sauces with garlic, fresh basil, cream, pine nuts, Parmesan cheese, butter, white wine and vegetables. They serve three or four seafood selections, like seafood marinara, scampi and grilled salmon. Their other dinner specialties are beef Wellington, charbroiled filet, veal or chicken. There is a child's menu as well as a nightly dessert tray. To go with your champagne at Sunday brunch, you have your choice of eggs benedict with traditional hollandaise sauce or bernaise sauce prepared with chicken, spinach and salmon or spinach and artichoke hearts; quiche; fruit or vegetable crêpes; omelets; Mexican dishes; Belgian waffle and panettone French toast.

Our server was helpful, attentive and professional. New age music (Enya) played very softly in the background. As you descend down the stairs toward the restaurant, take notice of the two historic pictures on the wall displaying the hotel and original Bon Ton restaurant taken at the turn of the century. Once inside, you will see stone walls, frosted-glass and brass light fixtures, an antique dresser and mirror at the end of the dining room and stained-glass hanging lamps. The setting is exquisite and comfortably nostalgic, the staff will make you feel right at home and you'll delight in some exceptional dining at the Bon Ton.

Special One-time Offer: Buy one entrée at the regular price and receive 50% off a second entrée of equal or lesser value (up to $12.00). This offer NOT valid in combination with any other offers. _____ Manager/Owner. _____ Date.

RECIPE

Chicken Chipeta
(Serves 4)

1 pound egg fettuccine or pasta
of your choice
1 tablespoon butter
16 chicken tenders
Flour
⅛ teaspoon salt
⅛ teaspoon black pepper
2 tablespoons chopped fresh basil
3 cloves fresh garlic, chopped
1 medium red pepper, sliced
lengthwise into strips

1 medium green pepper, sliced
lengthwise into strips
1 small red onion, sliced
1 10-ounce can sliced black olives
1 10-ounce can green olives
½ cup white wine
2 tablespoons chopped parsley
3 tablespoons Parmesan cheese

1. Cook pasta according to package directions.
2. Melt butter in large sauté pan over medium heat until butter starts to smoke. Coat chicken tenders with flour. Sauté chicken on both sides until brown. Add salt, pepper, basil, garlic, red and green peppers, onion and both olives. Cook, stirring gently, until chicken is cooked through.
3. Add wine to deglaze pan, stirring gently as you add the wine. When wine is reduced by half, top with chopped parsley and Parmesan cheese.
4. Serve over hot pasta.

You can have both quantity and quality in choosing small town restaurants when you take along Restaurants from 101 Colorado Small Towns and Colorado Restaurants and Recipes

PAGOSA SPRINGS

Pagosa comes from the Ute Indian word, Pagosah, meaning "healing water". The hot springs located here were a favorite camping place of the Utes who found them medicinal and beneficial. In the early 1870s, the Pagosa Hot Springs were a welcome rest and relaxation stop for travelers and miners. In 1878, the U.S. Army built Fort Lewis across from the hot springs, but it only stayed three years before moving west to Durango. In the early part of the twentieth century, sheep herding, cattle ranches and lumber were the main industries in this area. Today, you can still find cattle ranches, cowboys and lumber mills, but tourism and sports, like skiing and biking, are the major industries.
Zip Code: 81147. Area Code: 970. Population: 1,207 Elevation: 7,105'.

Ole Miner's Steakhouse
3825 Highway 160, PO Box 1198, 264-5981
Directions: Located on Highway 160, 3 miles east of Pagosa Springs on the south side of the Highway.

ESSENTIALS

Cuisine: Steak, Seafood, Barbecue
Hours: Mid-DEC through OCT: 7 days 5:30PM-9PM. NOV to Mid-DEC: Mon-Sat 5:30PM-9PM. Open seasonally on Sun. Call in winter to confirm hours.
Meals and Prices: Dinner $$$-$$$$

Nonsmoking: No
Take-out: Yes
Alcohol: No
Credit Cards: MC, Visa
Personal Check: Local only
Reservations: Not accepted
Wheelchair Access: Yes

HISTORY, PERSONALITY AND CHARACTER

The building was built circa 1975. Although, one would swear it dates back much earlier. From the outside, Ole Miner's resembles an old boarded-up mine from Colorado's gold mining days, circa 1860. The original owner, Ray Watkins, opened a country general store. The Watkins family also owns the High Country Lodge next door. Later, the general store became a steakhouse and then a Mexican restaurant before current owners, Paul N. and Janet Aldridge, both former elementary school teachers, staked their claim on July 22, 1982. Manager/chef Paul Henry is also a former teacher and his wife, Cathy, (another ex-school teacher) is the head waitress. Janet just retired from teaching in 1994. This is their first venture in the restaurant business and if every restaurateur had the natural skill and creative ability that these folks have, there would be a lot fewer restaurant going out of business every year. Paul Aldridge prepares the homemade bread and barbecue sauce. His daughters, Laura Haynes and Linda Watkins, make the homemade desserts, like peach cobbler and fudge marble brownie.

FOOD, SERVICE AND AMBIANCE

Ole Miner's is known for their steaks, seafood and kabobs. I've tried their sirloin, shrimp, and barbecued sausage, beef and pork. They are all fabulous! The barbecue comes with Paul Aldridge's own homemade sauce. The sirloin is very lean, juicy, charbroiled and with just a speck of fat. The plump shrimp are served with melted butter, lemon and cocktail sauce. Dinner is served with a fresh, hot loaf of bread, straight from the oven, and brushed with butter. If it were any softer, it would float off the table! All of the meals included the salad bar with a choice between baked potato, grilled veggies or a trio of beans, coleslaw and corn. I chose the last. The sauce on the coleslaw is homemade as are the pinto beans, prepared with chopped hot links and salsa. I recommend the beans as a very tasty alternative to rice, baked potato or vegetables. I've also tried their lone appetizer, sautéed mushrooms. It is a plentiful serving of about 8 ounces of "piping hot" mushrooms with a couple of strips of red pepper in garlic butter. If you have a big appetite, order some of these.

Ole Miner's 49'er menu is actually up to 53 entrées that feature charbroiled steaks, seafood (like Alaskan king crab legs, lobster tail and shrimp), kabobs (made with assorted meats and seafood), fowl (chicken breast, rock cornish hen, and quail), fish (halibut, trout, catfish, and Alaskan salmon steak), charbroiled barbecue, and specials, when available. If there is a combination that you would like that is not on the menu, just order 'No. 53 - Go For Broke'. If you dine here, I am certain you will agree with their motto when you leave, "Truly a gold mine of good food!"

Service is pleasant and professional with a touch of real class. At the entrance, you will find rusty old gears, a shovel, saw and anvil. Inside, you will find one of the coziest and most romantic restaurants in Colorado! The front door is on a pulley with a steel-pipe weight at the end to close the door, much like a spring. The inner door to the restaurant is also on a pulley with an old gasoline can at the end. To the left of the entrance is the hostess' station. Just past there, to the left, is a small, very attractive and inviting Victorian-style waiting room. It is so enticing, in fact, that I think you should visit this restaurant some evening when you will have to wait 20 minutes for a table. The waiting room has two small speakers over the fireplace mantle playing the same soft guitar and instrumental music heard throughout the restaurant. Seating in this room is on very homey-looking reupholstered antique chairs and sofas in red velvet and a pretty flower pattern. The carpeting is a lush grey and the walls an appealing blue and tan. I want a room just like this one!

In the dining room, raw, natural barn-wood with knot holes separate each dining section which has only one or two tables. It would be difficult to find a restaurant that caters more to privacy, so bring your significant other here. Several small pictures and photos decorate each nook, cranny and alcove: scenes of trees, lakes, flowers, mountains, bays and ships, deer, and rolling hills with log cabins. Feel free to take a tour of the restaurant before or after dinner (they encourage that). You will see pairs of old snow shoes and skis, remains of a horse's harness, old books (the 1937 edition of The Encyclopedia and Gazetteer), a mirror and dresser, pick and shovel, even a salad bar upstairs made from a patented 1901 bath tub with oak trim. The restaurant literally goes right up to the attic, so make sure you take a trip upstairs. Then, visit their gift shop before you leave. Ole Miner's Steakhouse is unique, you won't find another one like it in Colorado; intimate, you practically have your own private dining room; and remarkably comfortable, you may be more at ease here than in your own living room.

Special One-time Offer: Buy one entrée at the regular price and receive a complimentary dessert. Good for every member of your party. This offer NOT valid in combination with any other offers. _____ Manager/Owner. _____ Date.

RECIPE

Easy Peach Cobbler

1 stick of butter
1 cup sugar
1 cup flour
2 teaspoon baking powder
⅛ teaspoon salt

1 cup milk
2 cups sliced peaches
(1 16-ounce can); if using fresh peaches, add 1 cup sugar

1. Melt butter in a 2-quart casserole.
2. Combine next 4 ingredients in a bowl.
3. Stir in milk. Mix well to make batter.
4. Pour batter all over melted butter in casserole. Do not stir.
5. Spoon peaches on top of batter. Do not stir.
6. Bake at 350 degrees for 45 minutes until crust rises and browns.

If Colorado were flattened it would be larger than the state of Texas!

The Rose

416 Main Street, 264-2955

Directions: The restaurant is the second building west of the intersection of Highway 160 and 4th Street (the signal in the middle of town) on the north side of the street.

ESSENTIALS

Cuisine: American Cafe/ Southwestern/Mexican
Hours: Year-around: Mon-Sat 7AM-2PM. Closed Sun. Memorial Day-Labor Day: Fri 5PM-8:30PM.
Meals and Prices: Breakfast/Lunch $
Nonsmoking: Yes
Take-out: Yes

Alcohol: No
Credit Cards: No
Personal Check: Yes
Reservations: No
Wheelchair Access: Yes
Other: Catering available and reservations taken for special occasions of 20 or more people.

HISTORY, PERSONALITY AND CHARACTER

The building that The Rose now occupies dates back to the 1920s. It was formerly the Mountain Greenery Flower Shop before The Wild Rose Bakery moved in from one street to the north. It became just The Rose in 1990. In January 1991, prior owners Roy and Shari Wedel took over operation of The Rose and in November 1994 they sold to Jerry and Cindi Owen, the current owners and managers. Jerry was in the clothing and service industry and Cindi came from the catering and flower business. This is the first restaurant for both and they have done a marvelous job of carrying forward an established tradition in Pagosa Springs, building on the menu before them and offering homestyle food at a reasonable price. They hail from Irving, Texas. Cindi cooks and prepares homemade soups and daily specials. Her mother, Betty Hodge, or Gran as she's called, does the baking: making pies, cakes like German chocolate, cobbler, cookies and biscuits.

FOOD, SERVICE AND AMBIANCE

I ordered the lunch special — pot roast. Four big chunks of beef with potatoes, carrots and corn, all cooked together in the beef's natural gravy and served with a couple of thick slices of toast. Perfect for a snowy March 1st! To top it off, I had warm apple cobbler, made by Gran, with a big scoop of cold vanilla ice cream in a small ceramic bowl. Good food for a wet day! The breakfast menu features huevos rancheros, omelets, breakfast quesadilla, a breakfast BLT (with egg), Belgian waffles, hotcakes, and pastries. Egg beaters can be substituted for eggs (plus 50¢). Regular lunch items include burgers, sandwiches (several chicken and turkey selections, vegetarian, fish and cheese), salads and entrées (chicken fry, Sante Fe chicken, fried shrimp and quesadillas — introduced to Pagosa Springs by Jerry and Cindi). Their most popular quesadilla, in season, is the fresh spinach, avocado and mushroom. Cindi's uncle owns a catfish restaurant in Oologah, Oklahoma, so she gets the coating mix for their catfish, a Friday special, straight from her uncle. Other specials you might run into include chicken and dumplings, meatloaf (sounds like home cookin' to me), chicken teriyaki or Mexican.

Service was friendly and accommodating. The decor is very appealing and colorful with rose-color wood, white plaster walls, mauve table covers, and paintings of cowboys in various settings: huddled around a campfire, stopping for water by a stream, having a cup of "Joe", and on a cattle drive. They are by local artists and for sale at about $200 each. The menu covers are prints of these original watercolors. The Rose offers home-spun meals provided by a warm, hospitable staff in a clean, attractive environment.

SPECIAL ONE-TIME OFFER: Buy one entrée at the regular price and receive a second entrée of equal or lesser value FREE (up to $6.95 value). This offer NOT valid in combination with any other offers. _____ Manager/Owner. _____ Date.

RECIPE

Chicken Enchiladas and Sour Cream
(Makes 16-20 enchiladas)

6 to 8 chicken breasts
2 teaspoon garlic
1 teaspoon pepper
1 teaspoon salt
1 10-ounce can condensed cream of mushroom soup
½ cup rotel tomatoes (or salsa)
½ cup chopped mild green chilies

Cooking oil
20-25 corn tortillas
1 cup grated Monterey Jack cheese
Jalapeño slices for garnish
Corn tortilla chips
Your favorite salsa

3 cups sour cream
¼ cup flour
3 tablespoons butter or margarine
Salt to taste
Milk

1. Cook chicken breast until tender or chicken begins to pull from bone. Remove bones and skin and shred using a fork.
2. Add remaining ingredients and mix well. This will hold until ready to serve.
3. In saucepan over moderate heat, melt butter. Stir in flour. Cook and stir until blended, about 2 minutes.
4. Slowly add sour cream and reduce heat. Heat only until well blended. Add milk to achieve a sauce consistency. Remove from heat. This will hold at room temperature until ready to serve.
5. Heat cooking oil in a pan (enough to immerse a tortilla). Using tongs, dip corn tortillas into hot oil for only 5 seconds or less. This will make the tortillas rollable.
6. Add chicken mixture to a single corn tortilla (approximately 4 tablespoons per enchilada), roll and place on a hot serving plate.
7. Each presentation will be much nicer on its own heat-resistant plate. Heat plates at 300 degrees.
8. Cover enchiladas with the sour cream sauce and top with grated cheese. Heat under broiler until cheese is melted.
9. Serve with rice and beans or salad and tortilla chips and salsa. Garnish with jalapeño slices.

The Rose in Pagosa Springs

PAONIA

Paonia was founded by Samuel Wade, a rancher who planted an orchard and established the first general store in the area. Peony flowers (genus peaonia) were common to the region, so Samuel suggested the name peony for the town. Postal authorities decided to change the name to Paonia.

Zip Code: 81428. Area Code: 970. Population: 1,403. Elevation: 5,645'.

Little's

PO Box 1167 (The post office gave out street numbers but the locals threw them all away!), 527-6141

Directions: Located on Highway 133, one mile west of Paonia next to the Redwoods Arms Motel. From the northeast (Glenwood Springs), go one mile past the turnoff for Paonia, the restaurant is on the left. From the southwest (Delta), go 8 miles past Hotchkiss, the restaurant is on your right.

ESSENTIALS

Cuisine: Steak/Seafood/Pasta
Hours: Mon-Fri 11:30AM-2PM.
7 days 5PM-10PM.
Meals and Prices: Lunch $$, Dinner $$$.
Nonsmoking: Yes, in the downstairs dining room.
Take-out: Yes
Alcohol: Full Bar
Credit Cards: MC, Visa, Amx
Personal Check: Local area only with I.D.

Reservations: They "love" reservations! Recommended for parties of 6 or more.
Wheelchair Access: Yes. They state, "We carry anyone in a wheel chair. We have strong women."
Other: Additional 15% service charge for parties of 6 or more and for separate checks. Available for receptions, special occasions and banquets. Live music and special menus for special events.

HISTORY, PERSONALITY AND CHARACTER

Owner, manager and cook Linda Little learned about the front part of the restaurant business at a Mexican Restaurant in Los Angeles before designing and building Little's in 1977. Her partner for the first five years, Kathy Goddard, came from Mexico, which happens to be where Linda was getting pregnant the day after Christmas in 1983 while her restaurant burned to the ground. It's like they say, you have to take the good with the bad in this life. (This is all true, folks). It took Linda less time to re-design and rebuild the restaurant than it took her to have her baby. Little's reopened in July 1984. In 1987, she leased out the downstairs to Colorado's first micro brewery which, unfortunately, only lasted about a year. If I had to pick one restaurant that was "The Best Kept Secret in Colorado" from each of my books, they would be Old Germany in Dolores from The Colorado Small Town Restaurant Guide, Ole Miner's Steakhouse in Pagosa

243

Springs from <u>Restaurants from 101 Colorado Small Towns</u>, and Little's in this book. I arrived for dinner on a March Monday. There were a half dozen cars parked out front, but when I entered, everyone got excited because I was the first customer of the evening. Garfield would have blamed the slow business on the fact it was Monday, the 13th! This was fortunate for me because I had the chance to be informed and humored by Linda, who is "a hoot". You should ask to meet her when you dine here.

FOOD, SERVICE AND AMBIANCE

I was in luck the day I arrived because their soup of the day was Hungarian Cream of Green, featured in the book <u>Favorite Restaurant Recipes</u> by Bon Appetit. It is prepared with chicken stock, zucchini or beans, potatoes, onion, fresh dill, garlic, ground pepper, sour cream and lemon. It was deliciously different from any other soup I've had, peppery and creamy. If they have it when you arrive, definitely order some! For my entrée, I selected the pepper steak. This is pepper steak made the way it should be! Linda trims the fat off the steak to make suet, grinds the pepper (but not too much, so it is still chunky and crunchy), "smashes" the pepper into the steak with the palm of her hand, cooks the steak in the suet and flames it in cognac for a nice finishing touch. I was in the kitchen when she poured in the cognac. She reared back as a flame shot up about three feet and roared with laughter exclaiming "grills and chills!" I loved this steak, one of the best pepper steaks I have ever eaten. The side dishes were great too: real mashed potatoes with a couple of dashes of paprika and fresh vegetables, which change with the season. Everything is cooked to order. The soups, salsas and sauces are homemade. They have a homemade house ranch dressing. If you prefer blue cheese, they crumble real blue cheese on top.

The lunch/dinner menu starts with appetizers like chili beer shrimp and Alaskan crab legs, followed by sandwiches (their most popular is the Budapest burger with sautéed onions, mushrooms and melted cheese), Mexicatessen (nachos, quesadillas and a chili burgerrito), salads, pasta (primavera and Cajun mushroom), steaks (one with garlic, one with mushrooms and onions and one naked), shrimp, chicken, crab, lobster and Mexican (chili verde enchiladas and a red and green burrito).

At the top of the steps leading to the restaurant, I was greeted by Sophie Schwartz — a short, black and shaggy haired dog with a high-pitch bark. That's Little's beloved mascot and chicken gourmet. She barks at dobermans, inspectors and bill collectors, but never bites. Inside the atmosphere was much better. They were playing Steely Dan and other 1970s rock songs. There is a round gas fireplace in the middle of the center dining room across from the bar. The high-back booths and tables are made of oak wood. The ceiling beams and vegas are made of lodgepole pine logs from west Yellowstone (before the fires). The white, rough plaster walls in the rear dining room are decorated with books, a big tapestry by Aspen artist, Hunter Hogan and mountain expressionist paintings by local, Carl Brown. The room downstairs has a cabinet and shelves from Hungary where Linda's parents are from, reeds covering one wall, a tropical waterfall in one corner that runs water in the summertime, a stained-glass artwork with Linda's logo, Linda's personal art collection from childhood including Salvatore Dali and batik, and pictures of the middle ages by Dutch painter, Hieronymous Bosch. I also liked the green cloth placemats and gold cloth napkins. In the summertime, they put tables with sun umbrellas on the deck.

SPECIAL ONE-TIME OFFER: Buy one entrée and receive one free dessert (up to $3.50 value). Limit two desserts with the purchase of two entrées. This offer NOT valid in combination with any other offers. _____ Manager/Owner. _____ Date.

RECIPE

Hungarian Cream of Green Soup
(Serves 3 to 4)

3 cups of good quality chicken stock	2 tablespoons snipped fresh dill
½ pound fresh green beans	2 small garlic cloves, crushed
2 small potatoes, peeled and quartered	Salt and freshly-ground pepper
½ large onion, quartered	¼ cup sour cream, room temperature
¼ cup (½ stick) butter	Juice of ½ lemon

1. Combine stock, beans, potatoes, onion, butter, dill and garlic in large sauce pan over high heat. Bring to a boil.
2. Reduce heat, cover and simmer until vegetables are tender (20 to 25 minutes).
3. Taste and add salt and pepper.
4. Transfer soup to blender in batches and puree until smooth.
5. Return to saucepan.
6. Stir in sour cream and lemon juice.
7. Cook on low till heated through.

PARKER

Formerly called Pine Grove, this town was a station on the old Happy Canon Road from Denver to Colorado Springs. The town was later named after James S. Parker, who served 33 years as postmaster. In the early 1860s, he was a stage driver on the Smokey Hill South stage route.

Zip Code: 80134. Area Code: 303. Population: 5,450. Elevation: 5,865'.

The Parker House Restaurant

10335 South Parker Road, 841-0539

Directions: Take Exit 193 from I-25 and go east on Lincoln Avenue for 5 miles to Parker Road (Highway 83). Turn right and go ½ mile. The restaurant is on the right. An alternate route from east Denver is to drive straight south on Parker Road (which is Leetsdale Avenue further north).

ESSENTIALS

Cuisine: Steak/Seafood/Mexican
Hours: Mon-Thu 11AM-9:30PM, Fri 11AM-10:30PM, Sat 10AM-10:30PM and Sun 10AM-8PM. Breakfast on Sat/Sun only 10AM-3PM, Lunch daily from opening to 4PM and Dinner daily from 3PM until close.
Meals and Prices: Breakfast $, Lunch $-$$, Dinner $$-$$$$
Nonsmoking: Yes
Take-out: Yes
Alcohol: Full Bar

Credit Cards: All 5
Personal Check: Yes
Reservations: Not necessary
Wheelchair Access: Yes
Dress: Casual, but more formal for dinner
Other: Available for wedding rehearsals and dinners and breakfast and lunch meetings; 15% service charge may be added to parties of 6 or more.

HISTORY, PERSONALITY AND CHARACTER

The Parker House Restaurant (The Parker House) was built in 2 stages. The front of the building was constructed in the early 1960s while the back section was added in 1984. The Ponderosa was the original restaurant on the premises. The Parker Steak House took over in the late 1960s and changed its name to just the Parker House in the late 1980s. A French restaurant operated here for a short period during the 1970s.

Dave and Sue Reed have owned The Parker House since May 22, 1995. Dave has been in the restaurant business off and on for 15 of the 25 years preceding his move to The Parker House. He used to manage Ichabod's in Denver and his sister owns the Double Tree Restaurant in Platteville (see page 396 in Restaurants from 101 Colorado Small Towns). Curt Jordon, who started with The Parker House as a busboy in 1982, has gone through extensive training, both in-house and formal, and worked his way up to head chef.

FOOD, SERVICE AND AMBIANCE

I've had lunch and dinner at The Parker House, relishing in their top-quality sirloin, the chicken chimichanga (a light, flour tortilla with big chunks of chicken, cheddar cheese, tomatoes and lettuce) and their lightly coated, crunchy honey-dipped chicken. The French onion soup with garlic croutons is without cheese but has a rich flavor without salt and a lot of onions. A 15-item salad bar was also available with cole slaw and pasta salad. I've taken delight in their luscious desserts made by former owner, Bea Kroehnke: the coconut cream pie with toasted coconut on top and the key lime pie with a slice of fresh lime. Both pies had whipped cream topping. Bea also prepares peanut butter, strawberry, mud, chocolate silk and pecan pies; meringue with strawberries; strawberry shortcake; angel food cake; German chocolate cake and pecan meringue torte. Other out-of-house desserts include orange sherbet, cheesecake, tiramisu, and from the Double Tree Restaurant where it's made, ice cream.

The Parker House is noted for steaks and prime rib and I would recommend these first, but their other fares are worthy of your attention as well. For dinner, you can select from veal piccata with capers, veal marsala, Alaskan king crab legs, Australian lobster tail, Rocky Mountain rainbow trout, pork schnitzel, chicken fingers, chicken-fried chicken, shrimp tempura or fettuccini, chili rellenos, fajitas, supreme enchiladas, quiche and burgers. There is a children's menu. Nachos, onion rings or Rocky Mountain oysters will get you started for lunch. In addition to burgers and steaks, you can have a mid-day sandwich like cold prime rib, a Parker Philly or a Monte Cristo; a croissant made with tiny bay shrimp, ham, turkey or cold prime rib; or a Mexican dish. Spotlighting weekend breakfasts are Belgian waffle supremes.

Service was cheerful and accommodating. Dave makes his presence known in the restaurant, chatting with diners both before and after their meals. There are 2 dining rooms with a lounge in the rear. The restaurant's interior is attractively decorated with white-laced curtains, antique cherry wood side boards, a combination of painted and frosted-glass ceiling lamps on chains and pictures of American Indians and ducks. All of this is accentuated by a red-brick wall and a large brown-rock fireplace. The lounge is decked with glass-covered, gold-framed beer posters, pictures of ducks, a 1910 Lanchester automobile, a television, stuffed ducks on the wall and a wall shelf filled with National Geographic Magazines, books, beer steins, trophies and other memorabilia. The Parker House presents a quiet and comfortable setting to enjoy a choice, juicy steak or other fine foods.

SPECIAL ONE-TIME OFFER: Buy one entrée at the regular price and receive a complimentary salad bar plus your choice of either a complimentary dessert or a complimentary drink. Limit to 8 people. This offer NOT valid in combination with any other offers. Please present to server at time of ordering. _____ Manager/Owner. _____ Date.

<u>RECIPE</u>

Veal Piccata

4 ounces veal round, pounded thin	2 tablespoons clarified butter
2 teaspoons capers	1 tablespoon fresh lemon juice
¼ cup white wine	1 teaspoon cold butter

1. Lightly flour veal. Sauté in butter for 1 minute until light brown. Turn over and add capers and lemon. Sauté for 30 seconds. Add wine and then cold butter.
2. Serve with fresh steamed asparagus and fettuccine Alfredo.

The dining room in the Redstone Inn in Redstone

REDSTONE

Named for the radiant red sandstone exposure nearby, Redstone was built as a model industrial village by the Colorado Fuel and Iron Company.
Zip Code: 81623. Area Code: 970. Population: 200. Elevation: Approx. 6,200'.

Redstone Inn

82 Redstone Boulevard, 963-2526

Directions: From the intersection of Highways 82 and 133, 12 miles south of Glenwood Springs, go south on Highway 82 for 18 miles to the town of Redstone. Turn left at the second entrance to town. Go .1 mile. The inn and restaurant are on the right.

ESSENTIALS

Cuisine: Colorado-style American
Hours: Year Around: 7 days 8AM-9PM (Breakfast 8AM-11AM, Lunch 11AM-9PM and Dinner 5PM-9PM).
OCT-MAY: SUN Brunch 9AM-1PM.
Meals and Prices: Breakfast $-$$, Lunch $$, Brunch/Dinner $$$-$$$$$
Nonsmoking: All. Redstone is in Pitkin County which, by law, requires all restaurants to be entirely smoke-free. The grill permits smoking after 5PM.

Take-out: Yes
Alcohol: Full Bar
Credit Cards: MC, Visa, Amx
Personal Check: In-state with I.D.
Reservations: Recommended
Wheelchair Access: Yes
Dress: Nicely casual to dressed up
Other: One check per table; 15% service charge added to tables of 6 or more. Breakfast and lunch are served in the Grill. Dinner and Sunday Brunch are offered in the dining room.

HISTORY, PERSONALITY AND CHARACTER

The Redstone Inn was completed in 1902 by John Cleveland Osgood to house bachelors who worked at another of Osgood's enterprises, the Colorado Fuel and Iron Company. A year later, Osgood, faced with insolvency, relinquished control of the company and left the Crystal Valley, returning only occasionally to visit. With the closing of the mines and coke ovens in 1909, the Inn deteriorated and was closed as well. In 1933, Osgood's third wife and widow, Lucille, reopened the Inn, tried unsuccessfully to run it as a resort, then sold it shortly thereafter. By 1941, the population of Redstone had dwindled to 12. Almost a half century later, John F. Gilmore and Deborah C. Strom, former owner and food and beverage manager, respectively, of the Hotel Jerome in Aspen, purchased the Inn in 1989. It is now listed on the National Register of Historic Places and a member of Historic Hotels of America. Master Chef David Zumwinkle, a chef since 1974, and formerly of the Ute City Banque in Aspen for 11 years, has been cooking at the Inn since 1993. He apprenticed under Sara Armstrong of Aspen's legendary Copper Kettle Restaurant and is assisted by Shawn Lawrence.

REDSTONE

FOOD, SERVICE AND AMBIANCE

Linda, my editor, and I enjoyed a very delightful evening dining in the Redstone Inn Dining Room. She ordered the wild mushroom pasta, a scrumptious dish combining hand-cut pasta with sautéed portobello and cremini mushrooms, spinach, sundried tomatoes, shaved Parmesan and garlic herb olive oil. I savored the delectable herb roasted chicken, honey glazed on sweet garlic cream sauce with chives and parsley, reduced with chicken stock and butter, and served with wild rice and mushroom pancakes. I still like potato pancakes, but this version, different in flavor and texture, was an inviting alternative. Preceding our entrées were Sonoma salads. Their generous portions met the quality standards of the food. We both had leftovers for lunch the next day.

Showcasing the dinner starters were elk in phyllo on roast shallot sauce and Carolina shrimp cake. Dinner classics featured Rocky Mountain rainbow trout and Colorado prime rib. Come earlier in the day and partake of some of these lunch items: vegetarian red chili, nachos grande, chicken Caesar, pizzas, burgers, Reuben, chuck wagon barbecue sandwiches, grilled vegetable quesadillas and tortilla lasagna. There is a children's menu, a good selection of imported and Colorado microbrew beers and premium wine by the glass. Come earlier yet and start your day with a fresh fruit bowl or cinnamon roll, special coffees, southwest scrambled with roasted chilies, lemon and ricotta pancakes (this is one I've got to try at home) and granola sundaes.

Our server, a local photographer by trade, was very friendly, talkative, helpful, willing to accommodate and, possessing a good sense of humor, quick with a joke. Slow jazz accompanied this very romantic dining room that has the historic architectural integrity of the original hotel. It comprises collector-item furniture like the dark oak side board, a Hazelton grand piano and several hand-pegged, Gustzav Stickley mission oak-style pieces. Historic wrought-iron sconces and chandeliers and a warm wood fireplace with a moosehead over the mantle embellish the setting. Except for beautifying the windows to accentuate the majestic vista, the place hasn't changed much over the century. You'll marvel at the comfort, high-quality service and the cuisine of an experienced master chef when you dine at The Redstone Inn.

SPECIAL ONE-TIME OFFER: Buy two dinner entrées at the regular price and receive a complimentary copy of Fabulous Valley — A Redstone History. This offer NOT valid in combination with any other offers. Please present to server at time of ordering. _____ Manager/Owner. _____ Date.

RECIPE

Sonoma Salad
(Serves 4)

Poppy Seed Vinaigrette Dressing:
  ¼ cup champagne vinegar
  ¼ cup honey
  2 tablespoons poppy seeds
  1 teaspoon minced shallot
  ¾ cup olive oil

Salad:
  2 heads Belgian endive, julienne
  4 cups spring mix or assorted
    baby greens
  1 cup strawberries, quartered
  4 ounces crumbled gorgonzola cheese

1. Dressing: Whisk ingredients in olive oil.
2. Dress to taste salad with poppy seed dressing.

El Capitan, circa 1940, in Rocky Ford

RIDGWAY

Named for R. M. Ridgway, superintendent of the Mountain Division of the Denver and Rio Grande Railroad, Ridgway was a station for wagon transportation to the mines. Zip Code: 81432. Area Code: 970. Population: 423. Elevation: 6,985'.

True Grit Cafe

123 North Lena Street, PO Box 401, 626-5739

Directions: From the intersection of Highways 550 and 62 in Ridgway, go west on Highway 62 (Sherman Street) for ½ mile. Turn right on Lena Street. The restaurant is in the first block on the left.

ESSENTIALS

Cuisine: Creative Cowboy

Hours: 7 days 11AM-10PM (9PM NOV-MAY).

Meals and Prices: Lunch/Dinner $$-$$$

Nonsmoking: Yes, smoking permitted upstairs and on the patio.

Take-out: Yes

Alcohol: Full Bar

Credit Cards: MC, Visa

Personal Check: Local only

Reservations: No

Wheelchair Access: No

Other: Available for special parties and meetings.

HISTORY, PERSONALITY AND CHARACTER

True Grit has a short but significant history. The restaurant was built in 1985, 15 years after John Wayne filmed the movie, "True Grit", in Ridgway. In the opening scene of the movie, the "Duke" walks by a red brick wall with the sign "Chambers Staple and Fancy Groceries". That wall is now the inside left wall of the True Grit Cafe. Current owner and manager, Terri Felde, took over True Grit on July 4, 1988 (one of John Wayne's favorite days). Terri has been in the restaurant business since 1976, working in restaurants in San Francisco and Orange County, California, before coming to Telluride, Colorado, in 1987. This is the first restaurant that she has owned and based on longevity and reputation, I'd say she is doing extremely well.

FOOD, SERVICE AND AMBIANCE

They serve a "mean", lean, green chili cheeseburger, an all-American burger, one that the "Duke" would have been proud of. He would have loved this juicy ½ pounder of meat hanging over the 4-inch diameter sesame seed bun. Get the picture? It was served with tart-tasting cole slaw sprinkled with parsley. This is a "no holds barred" cholesterol kind of place with chicken fried gravy made to order, a lot of butter and cream in almost everything and no "low fat anything". "Weenies" and "health food fanatics" should plan on bringing their own box lunch or dining elsewhere when they visit Ridgway, or just stay home. They use Colorado beef and make their own soups, salads, sauces, salad dressings (raspberry vinaigrette and sour cream) and True Grit Seasoning Dirt — great for cowboy cooking on ram, lamb, dogs, hogs and rattlesnakes (also available for purchase by the jar). The all-day menu is highlighted with chili, nachos, fresh green salads, half pound burgers, sandwiches, pasta dishes (beef and bell pepper or shrimp and chicken fries), supper dishes (jumbo burrito, steak and shrimp, chicken Dijon and grilled Idaho trout), pies and ice cream, 21 different beers and a children's menu. This is a hearty place. Bring an appetite to match.

Service was friendly and cheerful while they played old Cat Stevens songs and country rock. About twice a month, they have live music like fiddle and guitar either inside or out on the patio. If "yore" part of the rough and tumble crowd, you'll want to head upstairs to the loft where they have a Victorian couch, bookshelves, high tables, True Grit memorabilia, old cigarette signs like "Chesterfield, Best for You", an old weight machine that used to give a photo of a famous Hollywood star with each weight, world maps from school that roll-up, a series of train photos and prints of nature scenes by F. D. Ward. If you're closer to the family type, then grab a table downstairs by the towering two-story rock fireplace with antlers on the mantle; photos of a horse pull; miniature replicas of Ft. Smith, an out house and the Rusty Bucket Hotel and Saloon by Deadra Boland (who's also a server at True Grit) and photographs of old locals, property owners and ranchers by long-time Ridgway rancher herself, Marie Scott. From the front of the restaurant, you'll get a photogenic outlook of the San Juan Mountains, the Grande Mesa and the Cimarron Ridge. On the back patio, you can relax on picnic benches at tables with umbrellas. You'll get a kick out of dining at True Grit. For an even better time, rent the movie before you go.

SPECIAL ONE-TIME OFFER: Buy one entrée at the regular price and receive a complimentary 8-ounce jar of True Grit Seasoning Dirt. This offer NOT valid in combination with any other offers. Please present to server at time of ordering. _____ Manager/Owner. _____ Date.

RECIPE
Summer Sour Cream Dressing

1 cup sour cream
½ tablespoon "dirt" (True Grit Dirt, only available from the True Grit Cafe)

1 cup mayonnaise
½ teaspoon minced garlic
½ cup of milk

1. In a large bowl, mix together all ingredients with a wire whisk till smooth. Chill.
2. Dressing will thicken with time. Use only ¼ cup of milk for thick dip.

ROCKY FORD

Rocky Ford was originally located near a crossing of the Arkansas River about 3 miles northwest of the present site. When the Santa Fe Railroad was built through the area in 1875, Rocky Ford moved to be next to the railroad. The name is derived from the gravel-lined ford across the Arkansas River at the town's original site. If you are fortunate enough to be driving through Rocky Ford in late summer, August or September, be sure you stop at one of the roadside stands for some of their famous cantaloupes. Zip Code: 81067. Area Code: 719. Population: 4,162. Elevation: 4,178'.

El Capitan
501 North Main, 254-7471

Directions: Located 53 miles east of Pueblo on Highway 50. Take Exit 99 from I-25. Proceed east on Highway 50 for 53 miles to the town of Rocky Ford. At the only signal, in the middle of town, turn left onto Main Street. Go 2 blocks. The restaurant is on your left on the northeast corner.

ESSENTIALS

Cuisine: Steak and Seafood
Hours: Tue-Sat 5:30PM-8:30PM.
Closed Sun/Mon.
Meals and Prices: Dinner $$-$$$
Nonsmoking: Ash trays only passed out if requested. They try to place nonsmokers away from smokers.
Take-out: Yes
Alcohol: Full Bar

Credit Cards: MC, Visa
Personal Check: Yes
Reservations: Not required unless the party is 6 or more.
Wheelchair Access: Yes, and they have their own wheel chair which they let their customers use.
Other: Banquet facilities and catering available for receptions and meetings.

HISTORY, PERSONALITY AND CHARACTER

El Capitan, surprisingly, has <u>always</u> been El Capitan since 1900. It began as Hotel El Capitan with 40 stockholders, principal of whom was Mr. Capitan. In 1948, Irene and Lee Reed took over the establishment and held on for 40 years until selling to the current owner, Gloria M. Powers. This is Gloria's first restaurant venture. She has the help of her husband, Ed, who will show you to your table and take your money afterwards; her son, Lawrence, their chef; her son Doug, who waits tables, tends bar and backs up Lawrence; and her grandson, Christopher Berumen, who also waits tables. Just one big, happy family!

FOOD, SERVICE AND AMBIANCE

I have tried their prime rib, steaks and shrimp (their 3 main dinner entrées). Soup is not served. The meals themselves are plain — nothing added in the way of spices or special sauces. Their jumbo French fried shrimp are in a light, thin breading: plump and moist, yet firm. They are made with homemade bread and served with homemade cocktail or tartar sauce. The prime rib is only served on Fridays, Saturdays and special occasions. It is juicy and mouth-watering. The steaks are aged and charcoal broiled. They include porterhouse, T-bone, filet mignon, ribeye, sirloin and chopped sirloin. Ham, hamburger and chef salad are also on the menu. Marinated herring is offered as an appetizer and there is a children's menu. Dinner includes a small salad, a very big baked potato or French fries; a thick slice of homemade white bread; coffee, tea or ice tea; and a big scoop of vanilla ice cream with homemade wine, coffee, mint, chocolate or strawberry sauce. They also feature homemade, world famous, Rocky Ford cantaloupe preserves on request.

Service is casual and accommodating, but you will have to request melted butter or lemon with your shrimp. Gloria stays very busy serving to the Rotary, Lions and Shriners in addition to pleasing the public. Once a year, on Watermelon Day in August, she serves an annual Governor's luncheon to all the dignitaries of Colorado. Yet, she manages to be a sweet, charming lady, quick with a smile. There is no music or windows. The dining rooms are decorated with red velvet in gold frames and a gold chandelier hanging from a high ceiling. Come visit this family-run restaurant with a touch of historic elegance.

SPECIAL ONE-TIME OFFER: Buy one entrée at the regular price and receive a complimentary jar of homemade cantaloupe preserves. Limit one jar of preserves per book. This offer NOT valid in combination with any other offer. _____
Manager/Owner. _____ Date.

RECIPE
Tartar Sauce

1 quart salad dressing
½ cup chopped sweet pickles

½ cup finely diced onion
2 tablespoons prepared mustard

1. Mix all ingredients together.
2. Place in a tightly covered container for up to a month.

SALIDA

Salida, originally called South Arkansas, was founded by the Denver and Rio Grande Railroad when it reached here in 1880. The post office, after a recommendation by Governor A. C. Hunt, ordered the name changed in 1881. The governor had recently returned from a trip to Mexico where he had seen the word Salida on the exit of public buildings. Salida in Spanish means "departure" or "outlet".
Zip Code: 81201. Area Code: 719. Population: 4,737. Elevation: 4,870'.

Il Vicino

136 East 2nd Street, 539-5219

Directions: From Highway 50 in Salida, turn north on F Street. Go about a mile into the historic section of Salida and turn right onto 2nd Avenue. The restaurant is the third building on the left. Coming into Salida on Highway 291, which turns into 1st Street, turn right on E Street, go one block and turn right again onto 2nd Street. The restaurant is the second building on the right.

ESSENTIALS

Cuisine: Italian
Hours: Sun-Thu 11:30AM-9PM.
Fri/Sat 11:30AM-10PM. (JUN-AUG:
Closing time is 1 hour later)
Meals and Prices: Lunch/Dinner $-$$
Nonsmoking: Yes
Take-out: Yes

Alcohol: Beer and wine only
Credit Cards: MC, Visa
Personal Check: Local or with I.D.
Reservations: Not necessary
Wheelchair Access: Yes
Dress: Eclectic and casual

HISTORY, PERSONALITY AND CHARACTER

Tom Hennessy and his wife, Sandy, opened this restaurant/brewery in July 1994 in a building that was formerly a mortuary and that dates back to 1888. This is Salida's first brewery in 100 years! Tom has been in the restaurant business his entire life, owning 3 restaurants in Sante Fe and 2 in Albuquerque, one of which is also a brewery. Brewing beer has been a hobby of Tom's that he turned into a commercial venture in 1994. The manager/chef is Mike Mendicino who has been with the restaurant from the start and is familiar with the local area.

FOOD, SERVICE AND AMBIANCE

This is a great little place to stop for pizza, salad and brew while taking a look at their British holding vessels (barrels). I tried their pizza al pesto made with fresh basil pesto, pine nuts, mozzarella and roasted garlic — a deliciously different combination! All pizzas are 11" — just right for one hungry person or two small appetites — are prepared with homemade dough and sauces, and are cooked in a "wood oven". Actually, it is a lava rock oven that they use one side for burning oak wood and the other side to cook the

256

food. The temperature can get up to 1,100 degrees! Their pizzas take 3-4 minutes to cook and they come out on heavenly thin, crisp crust. There are 10 different pizzas to choose from and a host of extras to put on top, items like sundried tomatoes, calamata olives, roasted bell peppers, fresh spinach, green chili, oven roasted chicken, prosciutto, artichoke hearts and feta cheese. If you are not in the mood for pizza, you can choose a calzone, lasagna, salad or sandwich. My house salad had fresh romaine lettuce, tomato, slivered asiago cheese, Italian dressing and a piece of homemade bread with rosemary and red onion — a good two-some with the pizza. Their chocolate silk (flourless) cake is made from scratch.

Head brewmeister Tom makes a pale ale called Ute Trail, a winter (brown) ale named after Tenderfoot Mountain north of town and a porter for St. Patrick's Day. Wet Mountain, coined after the 1895 brewery in Westcliffe, is an Indian pale ale which won the bronze medal at the 1995 Great American Beer Festival. Loyal Duke is a Scotch ale named after a legendary dog who rescued some kids off railroad tracks in the 1800s. Their new amber ale is called Evan's Amber after a locally famous turn-of-the-century prostitute. They also serve homemade root beer, espresso, latte and cappuccino.

You place your order at the counter when you enter and then the food is brought to your table. They play mostly jazz and folk music, but I listened to some quiet rock music when I had lunch here. In the rear (smoking) dining room, you can see the barrels, each holding 14 kegs, that are piped directly into the taps in the front of the restaurant. This is a very popular place in the evening during ski season and during the summer. The tables are spread out, allowing a lot of room for standing. Il Vicino is a fun place to be for superb pizza and fresh microbrew beer.

SPECIAL ONE-TIME OFFER: Buy one entrée at the regular price and receive a pint of Il Vicino Ale FREE. This offer NOT valid in combination with any other offers. _____ Manager/Owner. _____ Date.

RECIPE

Pesto
(Makes 3 pounds)

4 ounces chopped garlic	1 tablespoon salt
4 ounces walnuts	1 tablespoon pepper
1 pound de-stemmed basil	Juice of 1 lemon
3 cups olive oil	1½ cups grated Parmesan

1. Purée garlic and nuts in food processor. Add basil and drizzle in oil.
2. Add salt, pepper and lemon juice. Add Parmesan.
3. When storing, cover with a thin layer of oil to prevent oxidation.

SILVERTON

The town was known by many other names — Bakers Park, Reeseville, Quito and Greenville — before Silverton was chosen in an 1875 election. Silverton averages 200 inches of snowfall a year and is perhaps best known today as the northern terminal of the Durango-Silverton narrow gauge railroad train.

Zip code: 81433. Area Code: 970. Population: 716. Elevation: 9,305'.

Natalia's 1912 Family Restaurant

1159 Blair Street, 387-5300

Directions: Entering Silverton on Highway 550 from Durango or Ouray (the highway does a loop and you enter Silverton from the West from both towns), go down Highway 550 (Greene Street) to 12th Street and turn right. Go one block and turn right on Blair Street. The restaurant on your right at the corner of 12th and Blair.

ESSENTIALS

Cuisine: American

Hours: MAY to Mid-OCT: 7 days 10:30AM-2:30PM. Closed Mid-OCT through APR.

Meals and Prices: Lunch $$

Nonsmoking: No, but they don't encourage smoking. You have to ask your waitperson for an ashtray. No cigars or pipes.

Take-out: Yes

Alcohol: Full Bar

Credit Cards: MC, Visa

Personal Check: Local only with I.D.

Reservations: Recommended for groups of 8 or more

Wheelchair Access: Yes, they will lift you up the few steps at the entrance

Other: Additional 15% service charge for six or more people

HISTORY, PERSONALITY AND CHARACTER

Natalia's was built in 1883 as a saloon and bordello called Mattie's. It had a trap door and hidden staircase leading down to the madam's quarters and 13 rooms (or "cribs" as they were called). Later, it was converted into a car showroom before becoming the Miner's Pick Restaurant, with picnic tables outside serving barbecue beef and beans. In 1983, Natalia and Robert Rezka purchased and renovated the restaurant adding the back bar which was moved from Green Gables Restaurant in Phoenix. Natalia has been in the restaurant business since the early 1970s and previously owned a restaurant in British Columbia. Natalia manages the front of the restaurant and waits tables while Robert is the Head Chef. He has managed and cooked in restaurants since 1970 at 3 Canadian restaurants and 4 in the U.S.: 2 in Washington State, 1 in Arizona and now Natalia's.

FOOD, SERVICE AND AMBIANCE

Natalia's is one of the many Silverton restaurants that caters to the passengers from the Durango-Silverton narrow-gauge train but one of the few with a family

258

atmosphere, as the name states. Most of the other restaurants in town have a saloon atmosphere. As you might expect, they serve good, wholesome, down-home cooking with a wide variety to choose from: everything from taco salad and seafood to burgers, sandwiches, pasta and "Natalia's fabulous luncheon buffet". Their pasta with fresh vegetables in oil and garlic was quite good — a light, delicious version of pasta primavera — and includes one trip to the salad bar. Several items are homemade — the chili, soup, Swedish meatballs and sauces — and Natalia bakes the fruit pies. The buffet includes several hot entrées like fried chicken, barbecue beef and oriental chicken, along with whipped potatoes, cooked vegetables and the salad bar. Their sandwich selections include hot or cold turkey or beef, Reuben, steak or meatball. If you like your chili hot, just ask. They'll spice it up with jalapeños. For those of you who prefer a bigger meal at lunch, they serve full meals of roast turkey, chicken fried or New York steak, and a 3-piece chicken dinner. Some menu items are designated for children under 12. Cheesecake with strawberry topping and carrot cake can complete your dining.

Service was very gracious, helpful and sincere. My waitperson took the writing materials I was carrying back to the table while I was visiting the salad bar and the other server was quick to refill the ice tea. Rock oldies from the 1950s played quietly in the background. This is an intriguing restaurant fashioned after early 20th century America (circa 1912). Its many attributes include a white tin ceiling and walls, several wall shelves with knickknacks (canisters, bottles, books, plates, pots and other cook wares) and white-laced curtains. Copper pans, mining and logging tools, decorator plates, elk antlers, pendulum clocks, old advertisements for Olympia Beer and Standard Seeds, Victorian-style paintings, a washboard, a 1940-ish waitress tray with a picture of a Coca Cola bottle, an old photo of the restaurant and paintings and photos of trains create a spellbinding collage of wall ornaments to look upon. Robert or a member of his staff is likely to great you at the frosted-glass front door. As you enter, take a look to your right at the old family photos showing Natalia's mother and father, her father's parents and Robert's parents. You'll feel like one of the family when you dine in Natalia's historic ambiance.

SPECIAL ONE-TIME OFFER: Buy one entrée at the regular price and receive 50% off a second entrée of equal or lesser value (up to $5.00 value). This offer NOT valid in combination with any other offers. Please present to server at time of ordering. _____ Manager/Owner. _____ Date.

RECIPE

Quick Stroganoff

8 ounces New York Steak
Butter
2 fresh cloves of garlic, diced
12 mushrooms, sliced

½ cup real whipping cream
2 tablespoons sour cream
Fresh cooked egg noodles

1. Cut steak into thin slices. Sauté in butter over high heat until brown.
2. Drain off most of the liquid from pan. Add garlic and mushrooms. Sauté for 3 minutes over high heat.
3. Add whipping cream and sour cream. Simmer until sauce has thickened. Pour over fresh cooked egg noodles.

Natalia's 1912 Family Restaurant in Silverton

SNOWMASS VILLAGE

Formerly known as West Village (the official mailing address), it was also known as Snowmass-at-Aspen for its closeness to Aspen and as Snowmass Resort because it is a ski resort. Snowmass is a young town established in 1967.
Zip Code: 81615. Area Code: 970. Population: 1,449. Elevation: (approx. 7,900').

Krabloonik

4250 Divide Road, PO Box 5517, 923-3953
Directions: On Highway 82, heading towards Aspen from the northwest, go 7 miles past the town of Snowmass. Turn right onto Brush Creek Drive. Go 5 miles (bearing to the right after 2½ miles where the road connects with Highline Road). Turn right onto Divide Road, go .9 miles and make a hair-pin right turn to enter the parking lot. From here, it's 70 steps down to the restaurant.

ESSENTIALS

Cuisine: Wild Game
Hours: Mid-JUN through SEP: 7 days 5:30PM-9PM. Thanksgiving to Mid-APR: 7 days 11AM-2PM and 5:30PM-9PM. Closed Mid-APR to Mid-JUN and OCT to Thanksgiving.
Meals and Prices: Lunch $$-$$$$, Dinner $20-$50
Nonsmoking: All
Take-out: No
Alcohol: Full Bar
Credit Cards: MC, Visa

Personal Check: Local only
Reservations: Highly Recommended
Wheelchair Access: Yes, by snowmobile
Other: One check per table. Additional 15% service charge for tables of 6 or more. Upstairs dining area for small parties, receptions and rehearsal dinners. Tours of the kennel available in the summer; dog sled rides given during the winter.

HISTORY, PERSONALITY AND CHARACTER

In the spring of 1974, Stuart Mace gave Dan MacEachen 55 of his world famous Toklat sled dogs. Dan named his kennel, Krabloonik, after the first lead dog that he raised while at Toklat, a kennel in Ashcroft, 11 miles south of Aspen. Krabloonik means "big eyebrows", the Eskimo term for "white man". The dogs are hybrids of Malamute, Eskimo and Siberian, commonly referred to as Husky. In 1983, Dan opened the Krabloonik Restaurant in what used to be the sled building to help with the kennel costs. Dan splits his time between Snowmass Village and Fairbanks, Alaska, where he has raced in the Iditarod, the 1,049-mile sled dog race from Anchorage to Nome. Gary Watts has been managing the restaurant since 1984 having worked previously at Staats and Charlemagne in Aspen. John Roberts, their executive chef since 1989, has been cooking since 1985, graduated from Johnson Wales Culinary School in Rhode Island and was a chef at the Nantucket Yacht Club in Nantucket, Connecticut, before coming to

SNOWMASS VILLAGE

Krabloonik. Jay Fletcher is their wine steward. Jane Steuben, pastry chef, has been with Krabloonik since 1986.

FOOD, SERVICE AND AMBIANCE

I hadn't tried wild boar before coming to Krabloonik. It was ground and sautéed, milder than beef without a beefy taste, closer to veal with more flavor and strength and served with a light, morel mushroom cream sauce containing tiny bits of mushroom. Preceding the entrée were sweet, homemade ginger and orange bread with a lightly-browned crust, homemade chokecherry jelly and a dinner salad with ginger-Dijon vinaigrette and roasted almonds. Accompanying the dish were a medley of vegetables, green beans, yellow squash, new potatoes and turnips, sprinkled with herbs.

Their house specialties include wild mushroom soup and homemade preserves which can be purchased to go or to be shipped. They have a smokehouse for smoking their own meats and they prepare desserts daily in their kitchen. Krabloonik offers one of the best wild game menus in the state. The sauces, presentations and preparations change every two weeks, but you can expect to see everything from smoked trout and wild game tartare for starters to Atlantic salmon, pheasant, quail, caribou, elk, fallow deer and Colorado lamb as entrées. The meats are prepared in a variety of ways — grilled, baked or roasted — with an assortment of sauces, like saffron cream and lemon-thyme beurre blanc, and glaces — red currant, apple-cranberry and juniper-madeira. (You can make a game out of guessing which sauce or glace goes with which wild game selection before you go to Krabloonik). The vegetarian dinner for the evening was penne pasta. The lunch menu featured many game choices in addition to buffalo mozzarella and smoked duck salads, smoked pheasant quesadilla, sandwiches (buffalo burger, grilled game sausage and roasted elk), minced crab linguini and free-range chicken. Over 300 wines from Europe and North America as well as nonalcoholic beer and wine and Colorado microbrews are available. Krabloonik has won the Wine Spectator Award of Excellence every year from 1990 to 1994. The list of delicious homemade desserts was highlighted by tortes: white chocolate raspberry, Reese's peanut butter cup with chocolate and coconut cream; traditional carrot cake; chocolate mousse with marshmallows and walnuts; and Swedish cream with kiwi and strawberries.

Service is very thorough and pleasant. Your server will go over the entire menu with you. The "call of the wild" greets you as you begin your 70-step decent to the restaurant with the howl of 250 Huskies to your right. Classical music played throughout the ponderosa pine log cabin restaurant with the continuous row of windows facing the west, offering splendid views of Mt. Daly and Capitol Peak. Framed pictures and posters of Huskies and a pair of snowshoes adorn the log walls. A black-iron, wood-burning stove further embellishes the "Northern Exposure" ambiance. Krabloonik is a most unusual, one-of-a-kind restaurant that you'll want to visit before leaving the Roaring Fork Valley.

SPECIAL ONE-TIME OFFER: Buy one entrée at the regular price and receive 50% off a second entrée of equal or lesser value (maximum discount $24.75). This offer NOT valid in combination with any other offers. Please present to server at time of ordering. _____ Manager/Owner. _____ Date.

RECIPE

**Roasted Rack of Colorado Lamb Vermont Style,
with Maple Syrup Glaze and Marsala Cider Sauce**
(Serves 6)

Marsala Cider Sauce:
 1¾ cups Marsala wine
 ½ cup white wine
 ¾ cup apple cider
 1 shallot, diced
 1 tablespoon honey
 1 teaspoon cider vinegar

Roasted Rack of Colorado Lamb:
 3 8-boned racks of lam, trimmed and frenched
 2 cups pure Vermont maple syrup
 1 teaspoon each salt and pepper

1. Sauce: Pour wines into large saucepan. Bring to a boil. Ignite by touching a match to the side of the pan (be very careful, for flames can be high). When flame burns out, add cider, shallots, honey and vinegar. Cook until liquid is reduced to 1½ cups.
2. Lamb: Preheat over to 400 degrees. Salt and pepper fat cap side of lamb. Place in roasting pan and bake for 15 minutes. Once a nice seared cap is attained, turn rack over and cover with maple syrup. Reduce heat to 325 degrees and bake until medium-rare, continuing to baste lamb with syrup in roasting pan.
3. Remove lamb from oven and brush with syrup in pan, allowing a candy coating to form. Return lamb to oven for 5 minutes prior to serving. Slice into chops.
4. Spoon sauce around plate and arrange lamb in center.

The Tower

45 Village Square, PO Box 5444, 923-4650

Directions: On Highway 82, heading towards Aspen from the northwest, go 7 miles past the town of Snowmass. Turn right onto Brush Creek Drive. Go 5¼ miles (bearing to the right after 2½ miles where the road connects with Highline Road). A ¼ of a mile past Divide Road, enter Upper Mall Parking. Park in Lot #6. Go across the street, walk past the Snow Village Bus Depot. Take the stairs to the Upper Level of the Mall. Turn Right and go about 100 feet. The restaurant, with its 60-foot tower, is on the right, just past Cottonwoods Restaurant.

ESSENTIALS

Cuisine: American

Hours: Thanksgiving to Mid-APR: 7 days 11:30AM-3PM and 5:30PM-10PM. Early JUN through SEP: 7 days 11:30AM-10PM (Lunch 11:30AM-3PM, Bar Menu 3PM-5PM and Dinner 6PM-10PM).

Meals and Prices: Lunch $$, Dinner $$$$

Nonsmoking: All

Take-out: Yes

Alcohol: Full Bar

Credit Cards: MC, Visa, Amx, DC

Personal Check: Local only with I.D.

Reservations: Highly recommended for dinner. Not accepted for lunch.

Wheelchair Access: Yes

Other: No separate checks. 15% service charge added for lunch parties of 8 or more and dinner parties of 6 or more.

HISTORY, PERSONALITY AND CHARACTER

The Tower originally opened as The Tower Fondue in 1968. In 1975, Michael Shore and John Denver purchased the restaurant and renamed it The Tower. Michael, who also manages The Tower, worked at The Refectory Restaurant in Snowmass from 1969 to 1975. This is John's first restaurant. Bill Jarrett has been with the restaurant since 1983 and is the head chef. He previously cooked at The Refectory and the Mountain Dragon in Snowmass. The Tower has 1 of only 3 Magic and Comedy Bars in the nation (the other two are in Chicago and Baltimore). It began in 1976. Bob Sheets, a former Chicago magician, and Kevin Dawson, a magician from Atlanta, were the first magic bartenders in The Tower. William H. "Doc" Eason, who learned bartending and magic from Bob, is the current performer along with rising star, Eric Mead, from Fort Collins, Colorado. The bartenders provide backup assistance with straight lines.

FOOD, SERVICE AND AMBIANCE

I spent a delightful spring lunch hour on The Tower patio luxuriating in the warm sunshine and cool breeze and relishing over a flavorous cup of cream of asparagus soup with a scrumptious Swiss chicken enchilada. The asparagus spear-filled soup was spiced with dill weed. The enchilada was filled with Swiss and Monterey Jack cheeses, chicken and green chili; topped with sour cream and chives, all in a creamy and peppery tomatillo sauce — a delectable combo. The rest of the lunch menu showcases burgers, sandwiches (prime rib, Reuben, grilled or battered and fried chicken, smoked turkey or German sausage and vegetarian), beef burgundy stew in a boule, award-winning chili, Caesar and pasta salads, homemade desserts (chocolate fondue with amaretto, sundae with chocolate fondue sauce, maple crème brûlée, three-layer chocolate cake, white chocolate lemon cheesecake and pies) and after lunch potions (special coffees, espresso and cappuccino).

Some tempting appetizers to start your dinner include fresh Maine mussels with sweet basil, fresh smoked Colorado rainbow trout, coconut shrimp and snow crab ravioli. Tower entrées are featured in four major food groups: meat, seafood, poultry and pasta. A few of the highlights are aged and slow-cooked Colorado prime rib; mountain elk; shrimp with John Denver's spicy, country, mustard barbecue sauce; roast duckling with orange blackberry sauce; chicken Sante Fe; pasta primavera and spinach manicotti. A children's menu is available.

Service was courteous, helpful and diligent. They were doing a good, late-spring ski-season business when I visited and the servers were kept busy. The two inside dining areas are embellished with John Denver's photography: beaches, close-ups of an insect, pine needles, a red ant, cotton weed, a mountain view, a regatta of sailing vessels and John on his boat. The bar exhibits a magic motif with posters of the Brookfarm Inn of Magic, David Copperfield makes the Statute of Liberty disappear — "The Illusion of the Century" and famed magician, Harry Blackstone Jr. Playing cards and mirrors adorn the area everywhere. The ambiance might create a phantasm, but the cuisine is for real and you'll take pleasure in both at The Tower.

SPECIAL ONE-TIME OFFER: Buy one entrée at the regular price and receive a second entrée of equal or lesser value FREE (up to $22.00 value). This offer NOT valid in combination with any other offers. Please present to server at time of ordering. _____ Manager/Owner. _____ Date.

RECIPE

Colorado Rocky Mountain Elk
(Serves 4)

1 tablespoon clarified butter

8 3-ounce elk medallions

1 tablespoon shallots, minced

4 shiitake mushrooms, cap julienned

4 ounces dry red wine,
 preferably Burgundy

4 ounces chicken stock

2 ounces demi-glace

Pinch of salt and pepper

Chopped fresh thyme and parsley

1. Heat butter in sauté pan until very hot but not smoking.
2. Salt and pepper medallions. Sear both sides in sauté pan and move to warm platter.
3. Sauté shallots and mushrooms briefly then add wine, stock, demi-glaze, salt, pepper, thyme and parsley.
4. Reduce heat until slightly thickened. Add medallions and any juices. Cook to desired temperature.
5. Place medallions on platter and top with sauce.

Don't leave home without this Guide!

SOUTH FORK

Initially a stage station to service lumbering and mining, South Fork was named for its location at the confluence of the south fork of the Rio Grande del Norte and the Rio Grande Rivers. Between the town and the headwaters of the Rio Grande, there are 47 tributaries with 500 miles of stream to fish. South Fork hosts the annual championship Rio Grande Raft Races in June and is the beginning of Colorado's historic Silver Thread Scenic Byway that follows the Rio Grande into the San Juan Mountains and the mining towns of Creede and Lake City.

Zip Code: 81154. Area Code: 970. Population: 280. Elevation: 8,200'.

Aspen Inn Restaurant

29257 Highway 160, PO Box 99, 873-5070

Directions: From the east on Highway 160, go .7 miles past mile mark 188. Turn right just past the building with the roof that says "Restaurant and Lounge" (that's the restaurant). There's also a sign by the road that says "The Inn Motel" before you turn right. The restaurant is on the frontage road. From the west on Highway 160, go 1.1 miles past the intersection of Highways 160 and 149. Turn left just before the Ute Bluff Lodge sign on the left. The restaurant is on the frontage road.

ESSENTIALS

Cuisine: American/Mexican/Italian
Hours: Tue-Thu 11AM-8PM, Fri-Sat 11AM-8:30PM, Sun 11AM-3PM (open an hour later each day from JUL to SEP). Closed Mon.
Meals and Prices: Lunch $-$$, Dinner $$-$$$
Nonsmoking: Yes

Take-out: Yes
Alcohol: Full Bar
Credit Cards: MC, Visa, Disc
Personal Check: Yes, with I.D.
Reservations: Recommended for groups over 6, accepted otherwise
Wheelchair Access: Yes, including bathrooms

HISTORY, PERSONALITY AND CHARACTER

The Aspen Inn Restaurant was originally built as a house with some adjacent cabins. In April 1995, Sara and Jon Middleton from Chicago and Texas purchased the property as their first restaurant venture. George Ruybal, who's been cooking since 1980 and used to own a restaurant in Antonito, Colorado, is their chef.

FOOD, SERVICE AND AMBIANCE

I dined alone (at my table and in the restaurant) for lunch and ordered the fried chile rellenos with thick, gooey cheese, a lot of hot (but not a "barn burner") red chili sauce, stuffed with Monterey Jack cheese and topped with cheddar cheese. It came with pinto beans and rice with a touch of tomato sauce that gave it a Spanish rice flavor. Their salsa is thick and tomatoey with green peppers, big, spicy hot chunks of red hot peppers

267

and onion, served with chips fried in-house. The Mexican food and some of their sauces are from scratch. They make their own beer batter for the salmon fillet.

Lunch offers a sizable selection of sandwiches, such as steak, Monte Cristo, chicken or steak Philly, chicken cordon bleu, Sante Fe chicken and club. For a dinner appetizer, try their pu pu platter, Rocky Mountain oysters, boiled crawfish, nachos or stuffed jalapeño. Dinner highlights include several cuts of steak, Italian dishes (shrimp and boursin fettuccine, manicotti, cannelloni and fettuccine Alfredo), seafood (lemon roughy, blackened tilapia and pan-fried catfish), Mexican specialties (fajitas, tacos, enchiladas and stuffed sopapilla), burgers and a lighter fare menu featuring salads and sandwiches. A children's menu is available. Several dinner menu items are also available for lunch. They also serve a large collection of Colorado microbrews and others from around the U.S.

Service was attentive and amicable. Light rock and new age music played lightly in the background. They also play some western. This is a two-dining room restaurant with one room used for casual, lunch-crowd dining and the other kept for dinner. The former is trimmed with knotty pine walls, a yellow and red brick fireplace set in a brick wall with a sketch of a moose on the wall. The room is adorned with artwork and potted philodendrons. The dinner dining room hosts a red brick wall and fireplace, a mural of aspen, knotty pine vegas and ceiling, white table cloths and metal gold aspen ornaments on either side of the fireplace. The Aspen Inn provides a diverse selection of entrées in a serendipitous setting making this restaurant your "best bet" before heading over Monarch Pass.

SPECIAL ONE-TIME OFFER: Buy one entrée at the regular price and receive a complimentary appetizer (up to $5.00 value). Limit 2 appetizers with the purchase of 2 entrées. This offer NOT valid in combination with any other offers. Please present to server at time of ordering. _____ Manager/Owner. _____ Date.

RECIPE

Chile Rellenos
(Serves 12)

24 large whole green chilies
Provolone cheese
Flour
Lard

Egg Mixture:
  6 eggs, separate whites from yolks
  ½ teaspoon salt

Green chile sauce, rice and beans

---

1. Wash the green chilies. You can leave the stems and seeds intact. Cut a 1- to 2-inch downward slit at the top (stem) of the chile and stuff with 1 to 1½-wide by 3- to 5-inch long strip of provolone cheese. The cheese strip size will be dictated by the size of each chile. Pat dry each chile and dunk in flour. Set aside while you melt lard in a skillet and make the egg mixture.

2. Melt lard in an iron skillet. The size of the skillet will determine how many rellenos you can fry at one time. Use enough lard to fill half the skillet when lard is melted and sizzling hot. While lard is melting, make the egg mixture.

3. Egg Mixture: Separate the eggs. Beat whites till stiff and add ½ teaspoon salt. Mix yolks with whisk and add to egg whites. Continue to beat while adding 1 to 2 tablespoons of flour. Add enough flour so the batter will coat the chile and not slip off.

4. Dunk a chile in the egg mixture and place in hot sizzling lard. Depending on the skillet size, you can fry two or three at time. When one side is golden brown, turn and brown the other size. Work fast as the egg mixture will liquefy in time.

5. Serve two rellenos covered with your favorite green chile sauce, rice and beans.

Feel free to introduce yourself to the owner, manager and/or chef at these restaurants. You have their names in the HISTORY, PERSONALITY AND CHARACTER section.

269

STEAMBOAT SPRINGS

Originally a summer playground for the Ute Indians, the town derived its name from a former mineral spring bubbling through a rock formation. To the trappers of the mid-1880s, it produced a sound similar to a "steamboat chugging". This spring, unfortunately, was destroyed during the construction of the Denver and Rio Grande Western Railroad in 1908. Steamboat is located in a big bend in the Yampa River with the springs on the south bank of the river. Today, Steamboat Springs is considered by many to be "Ski Town USA" because of the large number of Olympian and National Ski Team members produced here.

Zip Code: 80487. Area Code: 970. Population: 6,695. Elevation: 6,728'.

Antares

57½ - 8th Street, PO Box 775410 (80477), 879-9939

Directions: Located ½ block south of Lincoln Avenue (Highway 40) on the west side of 8th Street.

ESSENTIALS

Cuisine: Healthy "New" American
Hours: 7 days 5:30PM-10:30PM.
Meals and Prices: Dinner $$$-$$$$
Nonsmoking: All
Take-out: Yes
Alcohol: Full Bar
Credit Cards: MC, Visa, Amx
Personal Check: Yes, with I.D.

Reservations: Recommended
Wheelchair Access: No. There are several steps, but they will assist you if you so desire.
Other: Available for weddings, receptions and business meetings; full outside catering and wine maker dinners.

HISTORY, PERSONALITY AND CHARACTER

Antares is in a building dating back to 1903 that has been used for a livery barn, Ford Motor Company showroom and tractor repair shop. In the 1930s, it was purchased by Henry and Helen Rehder. The first restaurant to appear on this premise was the Brandywine, an upscale steak and seafood place, in 1972. In 1987, Gorky Park took over and on December 1, 1994, Antares was opened. The restaurant is named after the bright star in the neck of Scorpio that is visible in the southern sky in the summer and was used as a guide by the early pioneers in this area. The restaurant is owned jointly by Doug Enochs, Ian Donovan and Paul "Rocky" LeBrun. Doug moved to Colorado in 1980 and managed L'apogée. He is an accredited wine sommelier with the British Court, comparable to the designation given by the Wine Spectator, and holds wine seminars in Antares' bar. Ian grew up in restaurants, has worked as a headwaiter in the Sheraton Hotels in Australia and has been involved with restaurant contract openings in England and Australia. He also worked at L'apogée from 1989 to 1994. Rocky, a graduate of the Culinary Institute of America in Hyde Park, New York, started working in restaurants when he was 14 in Boston and studied cooking in France. He spent 5 summers at the Chanticleer Restaurant on Nantucket Island while working the winters at Mattie Silks in Steamboat Springs. Rocky also cooked at L'apogée for 5 years.

FOOD, SERVICE AND AMBIANCE

The chef's combo platter was heavenly and a great value. This assorted assembly of delectable delicacies featured brie cheese, ratatouille on French bread, mussels stuffed with avocado in a sake bisque, Mongolian beef skewer with peanut sauce and a piquant mushroom pâté with marsala wine and peppercorns, all with a colorful appealing presentation with shallots and parsley sprinkled on the plate's edge. My light supper entrée was even more exotic: tender, lightly barbecued prawn pagoong on crisp, chewy, homemade flat bread with avocado and ginger plum dressing. Tabouleh, served on the side, consisted of quinoa, red pepper, finely chopped celery and carrot, red wine, mint, and to add a taste of sour, vinegar and lemon juice. Meals like this one are why I love ethnic food so much.

The menu offers a combination of different ethnic backgrounds. Every dish offers something unique and exciting. This is not the place if you prefer bland food. You'll be able to choose from asparagus potato or asafetida lentil soups, green papaya and avocado salad, mung bean cabbage cakes, lemon crêpes filled with spinach and roasted red bell pepper, smokey eggplant, Ahi tuna in Pinot Grigio balsamic vinaigrette, kerala duck stew and Gujuarat spice crusted lamb chops. Chef Rocky uses fresh vegetable stocks and soy milk. Every Wednesday night is veggie night with a special selection of vegetarian appetizers, soups and dinners. To accompany your meal, they present 70 to 100 wines, mostly California with some French and Australian, for your pleasure. For dessert, try one of their homemade finishers like marquise au chocolate with pistachio Anglaise or mango mousse with strawberry chantilly. Antares will test every one of your taste buds. Their cuisine is truly "out of this world"!

My server was astute and attentive and the music selections were light jazz on a cool, comfortable spring evening. You'll find some intriguing original decor when you visit. The red gargoyle lamps on either side of the entrance to the lounge date back to the Rehders and are the same ones that Ian spotted on the street lights of Creel, Mexico. The stain glass, arched doorways and windows and rock walls are all original. They have a victrola with a 1904 patent that actually works. Additional embellishments include a white tin ceiling, a wine rack set into the rock wall, hand-carved wood chairs, a rock fireplace added in 1987, vaulted ceiling with lead-glass sky lights, etched glass works by a former local artist depicting hunting scenes, a cast-iron stove and charcoal in the corner of one dining room, left over from the old coal-burning stove. For a dissimilar dining experience that you'll treasure afterwards, visit Antares.

SPECIAL ONE-TIME OFFER: Buy one entrée at the regular price and receive a second entrée of equal or lesser value FREE (up to $15.00 value). This offer NOT valid in combination with any other offers. Please present to server at time of ordering. _____ Manager/Owner. _____ Date.

RECIPE

Tournedos of Beef in a Port Shallot Sauce
(Serves 4)

1 ¾-pound beef tenderloin
  cut into 8 3.5-ounce medallions
1 tablespoon vegetable oil
3 ounces balsamic vinegar
8 ounces ruby port, such as
  Fonseca Bin 27
8 ounces veal demi-glace
4 ounces whole unsalted butter
Salt and black pepper, freshly ground
3 large shallots, minced

½ pound cooked angel hair pasta
1 tablespoon virgin olive oil
½ tablespoon fresh oregano, chopped
1 tablespoon grated Grana
  parmesan cheese
40 spears fresh asparagus,
  steamed lightly
½ tablespoon virgin olive oil
Salt and pepper to taste

1. Tournedos: Sauté medallions of tenderloin to temperature in vegetable oil in large skillet over medium high heat. Remove from skillet and keep warm.
2. Port Shallot Sauce: Deglaze skillet with balsamic vinegar. Bring to a boil and simmer 1 minute. Add port, simmer 2 minutes. Add veal demi-glace, simmer 4 minutes to reduce. Season to taste with salt and pepper. Remove skillet from heat, whip in whole butter. Add shallots.
3. Toss cooked angel hair pasta with olive oil, parmesan cheese and oregano.
4. Arrange angel hair on 8 warm serving plates in twirls. Arrange 2 medallions over pasta on each plate.
5. Spoon port shallot sauce over medallions. Toss warm asparagus spears with olive oil, season with salt and pepper.
6. Garnish each plate with asparagus spears.

Hazie's

Top of Silver Bullet Gondola in Steamboat Resort Village, 879-6111x465, 1-800-922-2722
Directions: From South Lincoln Street (Highway 40), south of downtown Steamboat Springs, go east on Mt. Werner Road for .7 miles. Turn right on Mt. Werner Circle and go .6 miles to Gondola Square covered parking on the right. Exit the parking garage on foot from where you entered by vehicle, walk toward Gondola Square, past the

information kiosk. Go right under the maroon and white overhang for "Gondola Square". Go down the steps or ramp, turn left, go down more steps. At the bottom, make an immediate left into the activities center to get your gondola ticket, which is free with an advance reservation at Hazie's. Otherwise, its $12 during the day and $6 at night. (Hazie's will credit the cost of the Gondola ticket against your restaurant bill if you paid the $12). After you get your gondola ticket, walk across the square to the gondola entrance and take the gondola up to the restaurant. If you have reservations, you can go straight to the gondola.

ESSENTIALS

Cuisine: Continental
Hours: Mid-JUN to Labor Day: Fri/Sat 6:30PM-8:30PM. Sun 10AM-1:30PM. Sun Dinner served 4th of July and Labor Day Weekends. Thanksgiving to Mid-APR: 7 days 11:30AM-2:30PM. Mid-DEC through MAR: Tue.-Sat 6:30PM-9PM. Closed Mid-APR to Mid-JUN and Labor Day to Thanksgiving.
Meals and Prices: Lunch $$, Brunch $$$$, Summer Dinner $$$$, Winter 4-Course Dinner $47

Nonsmoking: All
Take-out: No
Alcohol: Full Bar
Credit Cards: All 5
Personal Check: No
Reservations: Required for dinner in the winter, suggested otherwise.
Wheelchair Access: Yes
Dress: "Resort casual" although some people do dress up
Other: Available for special parties, engagements, anniversaries, weddings and banquets.

HISTORY, PERSONALITY AND CHARACTER

Hazie's was built in 1986 and named after Hazel Ralston Werner, matriarch of one of the original homestead families in Steamboat Springs who died in February 1992. Her son, Buddy, a member of the 1964 Olympic Ski Team, died in an avalanche in Switzerland the same year. Her daughter, Skeeter, was a national champion skier in 1956 and placed 10th at the Olympics that year. She married Hall of Fame football player Doak Walker. Hazie's is owned by Steamboat Ski and Resort Corporation, one of a family of resort corporations owned by Kamori, Inc., the Japanese-based parent corporation. Jon Fyhrie is the Director of Food and Beverage. Dining Room Manager David Ferry has worked in restaurants his entire life, starting out bussing tables at the Grand Lake Lodge. From 1984 to 1990, he worked at the Club Car and Pepperoni's in Winter Park; then managed a Red Robin in Portland, Oregon, for 2 years before starting at Hazie's in 1993. The Executive Chef for the ski resort, Morten Hoj from Denmark, has been working in restaurants since 1968, is European trained as both a chef and waiter and attended the Culinary Institute of Copenhagen. He came to the U.S. in 1975 and went to work in the Danish Embassy in Washington, D.C. In 1980, Morton moved to

Steamboat where he became Executive Chef at Mattie Silks (1980-1985) and Ragnar's (1985-1986) before coming to Hazie's in 1987. Brian Krum, a California Culinary Academy graduate, has been the chef at Hazie's since 1994. He began his culinary career in 1975 at Pier 39 in San Francisco followed by stops at Fairmont Hotel Restaurants in Carmel, California, and Reno, Nevada. Brian helped to open the Home Ranch in Clark, 18 miles north of Steamboat Springs,

FOOD, SERVICE AND AMBIANCE

I highly recommend their exceptional Sunday Brunch Buffet. Their offerings are sensational: a heterogeneity of egg concoctions, meats, salads, specialty hot and cold soups and dishes, cheeses, breads, pastries, sweets and desserts. The choices are sure to please even the most finicky of diners. Some of my personal favorites were the thick, wholesome-tasting and flavorful Grand Marnier six-grain French toast, the sweet and delicious cottage and cream cheese blintzes with strawberry sauce, the crunchy and spicy Cajun catfish, the savory smoked salmon with onion and capers, the better-than-average basil pesto pasta salad, the delightful baked brie with lingonberries pastry, the smooth chocolate mousse and the scrumptious black raspberry and white chocolate cheesecake. For added good measure, I also reveled in the scrambled eggs with onions and bell peppers, the cucumber clam chowder, the German cambozoloa cheese and the fresh berries, including those dipped in chocolate. This was a luscious feast that would fill the heartiest of appetites.

Their soups, stocks, sauces, dressings (blue cheese, raspberry vinaigrette and virgin olive oil with balsamic vinegar) and most of the desserts are homemade; they use all natural, range-fed beef; the seafood is "jet fresh" and they proffer wild game specials, like buffalo and quail, regularly. Summer lunches spotlight chilled avocado cucumber soup, smoked salmon pompadour with asparagus, grilled marinated shrimp with a spicy peanut sauce, escargot bourguignonne au fromage and gourmet field greens with berries and roasted almonds. Dinner highlights include charbroiled salmon filet, Rocky Mountain trout, châteaubriand Bérnaise, lamb chops with roasted garlic rosemary sauce, veal Oscar, charbroiled duck breast with currant sauce and blackened chicken with rock shrimp. The 4-course dinners in winter feature 3 or 4 appetizers; soup or salad; 8 entrées including seafood, meat and specials like elk tenderloin with lingonberry sauce; and dessert. A 100+ wine bottle selection, mostly from California with some from France, is available for your pleasure.

Service was impeccable and pleasing. Classical music played in the background. In the winter, mid-December through March, Robyn Magnuson, who's been at Hazie's since 1993, plays the baby grand piano. This two-tiered restaurant provides majestic vistas to the south and west, super sunsets and a grand view of the gondola. The pink stucco walls are adorned by photos of the Steamboat area, circa 1919: Rabbit Ears Pass Road, Storm Mountain, the train, the bathhouse and outdoor pool and the high school band on skis (the only one in the country); and posters from California vineyards signed by the winemakers. The Werner family album is displayed everywhere: Hazie picking "spuds" in 1925, Buddy in Italy and being interviewed by Curt Gowdy, Skeeter in 1958, Ed "Pop" Werner in Winter Park in 1964, Loris — the second son — and Buddy flying through the air on skis in Sun Valley in 1957 and a framed portrait of Hazie. A spectacular panorama, elaborate dining and a piece of Colorado history — they're all here at Hazie's.

SPECIAL ONE-TIME OFFER: Buy one entrée at the regular price and receive a complimentary glass of Hazie's label chardonnay. Limit 4 glasses of chardonnay with the purchase of 4 entrées. This offer NOT valid in combination with any other offers. Please present to server at time of ordering. _____ Manager/Owner. _____ Date.

RECIPE
Charbroiled Duck Breast

2 duck breasts, halved, boned,
  skin removed

Marinade:
  ¼ cup walnut oil
  ¼ cup olive oil
  ¼ cup soy sauce
  3 tablespoons honey
  3 tablespoons finely chopped carrots
  3 tablespoons finely chopped celery
  2 tablespoons chopped parsley
  1 small garlic clove chopped
  ½ teaspoon fresh ginger root
  ¼ teaspoon crushed white peppercorn

Currant Sauce: (2 cups)
  2 tablespoons chopped shallots
  ⅓ cup red wine vinegar
  2 cups reduced duck stock or
  demi-glaze
  2 tablespoons currant jelly

1. Marinade: Combine all of the ingredients in a shallow dish and mix well. Add duck breast, turning to coat well. Cover with plastic wrap and refrigerate overnight.
2. Sauce: Place shallots and vinegar in sauce pan over high heat. Reduce to 2 or 3 tablespoons. Pour in duck stock on demi-glaze and currant jelly. If sauce is too thin for your taste, reduce further.
3. Grill duck breast 2 to 3 minutes on both sides to medium. Let the duck breast rest for a couple of minutes, then slice thinly. Serve with currant sauce.

TABERNASH

The town was named by E. A. Meredith, chief engineer for the Denver and Salt Lake Railroad — the company that provided the drive for the town's growth — for a Ute Indian by the same name who was murdered in 1879 by a white man named "Big Frank". The killing was a prelude to the Meeker and Thornburg massacres. Tabernash is located on the old Junction Ranch, homestead of Edward J. Vulgamott, an 1882 pioneer. The ranch was a popular place to stop for travelers on both Rollins Pass and Berthoud Pass Zip Code: 80478. Area Code: 970. Population: 350. Elevation: 8,326'.

The Ranch House

3530 County Road 83 (at Devil's Thumb Ranch Resort), PO Box 750, 726-5633

Directions: Take Exit 232 from I-70. Proceed north on Highway 40 for 32 miles. Two miles past Fraser, turn right onto County Road 83. Go ½ mile and bear right at the fork. Drive 3 more miles over gravel road. Proceed under the arched sign for "Devil's Thumb Resort". Drive toward the two log cabins and park. Walk uphill to the right 50 yards to the restaurant. Traveling from the north on Highway 40, the turnoff for County Road 83 is 10 miles south of Silvercreek.

ESSENTIALS

Cuisine: Gourmet Country

Hours: 7 days 8AM-10PM. Open at 7AM from Mid-NOV to Mid-APR. (Breakfast until 11AM, lunch 11AM-3PM, dinner from 5PM).

Meals and Prices: Breakfast/Lunch $-$$, Dinner $$$

Nonsmoking: All. Smoking only permitted in saloon in front of restaurant.

Take-out: Yes

Alcohol: Full Bar

Credit Cards: MC, Visa

Personal Check: Grand County only

Reservations: Recommended for dinner, especially weekends. Accepted otherwise.

Wheelchair Access: Yes, through a side entrance.

Other: Available for weddings (they have them almost every weekend in the summer in their chapel; actually its 6 or 7 pine logs set in a lean-to), family reunions, business conferences.

HISTORY, PERSONALITY AND CHARACTER

The Devil's Thumb Ranch Resort was originally built in 1937 as a homestead for the Yaeger family. They sold the property in 1966. The new owners developed it into a working dude ranch with a restaurant and saloon where the current saloon is now. The current dining area was added in the 1970s. In May 1994, Ranch Holding Ltd. purchased the resort, all 389 acres including the restaurant. The new owners are committed to preserving the area's pristine beauty and the resort's rustic charm. The resort offers dining and lodging accommodations on the site of a nordic skiing complex that was voted "Colorado's favorite" in a 1995 Rocky Mountain News readers poll.

Executive chef Alberto Sapien, winner of 8 gold medals at the Culinary Olympics in Germany and numerous other awards, started at The Ranch House in September 1995. Ken English is the sous chef.

FOOD, SERVICE AND AMBIANCE

I had the pleasure of stopping here for lunch and trying a bowl of carrot onion soup with the blackened chicken sandwich. Honey and sweet basil are added to onions that are caramelized "really well" to give the soup a sweet flavor. The chef says soups are a big seller in this area and at this high altitude, I tend to believe him. The chicken was a tender, moist piece smothered with cheddar on a flaky crust bun, served with big steak fries.

The menu changes seasonally with weekend specials offered Friday and Saturday nights. The breakfast menu includes traditional favorites as well as Ranch House specialties: trout and eggs with a pecan butter and nut-crusted French toast served with a Jack Daniels syrup. The lunch fare ranges from burgers and buffalo patty melts to paella. Dinner is where the restaurant really shines offering menu items that both tempt the eye as well as the palate, such as seed crusted pork medallions served with a berry gastrique and sweet potato shoestrings. On the weekend, you may see game specials like venison tenderloin or elk stew. Their philosophy is to bring a higher standard of food to the valley but still keep the old west charm the area is known for. It's what they call "Cordon bleu cooking at 8,700 feet".

I also sampled their delicious, homemade deep-dish apple cobbler, a biscuit dough layered with marmalade, custard, cinnamon apples and streusel. Heavenly sweet! They also make a flourless chocolate cake, souffles that pop up with the greatest of ease in this altitude, fruit tarts and tarte tartin, a classic apple tarte made with butter, cinnamon and sugar in a puff pastry. The full service saloon offers three beers on tap as well as a large selection of bottled domestics and imports. The wine list features wines from around the world and changes with the menu.

Service was prompt and friendly. Moderate to heavy rock music and golden oldies songs played quietly in this backwoods log cabin while I gazed through the windows at picturesque vistas of the unspoiled Ranch Creek Valley with the peaks of the Continental Divide as a backdrop. In the evenings, they play classical music and on the weekends they have live acoustic guitar, folk or country music in the saloon next door. Along the center of the back wall is a wood-burning, black-iron stove set into a fireplace. The Ranch House was a real hidden treasure for me and definitely worth the short drive off the main highway.

TABERNASH

RECIPE

Elk and Buffalo Stew

5 pounds game meat, cubed	Celery seed
22 ounces microbrew beer	Cayenne pepper
(e.g., Breckenridge Oatmeal Stout)	Black pepper
3 cups red wine	White pepper
5 cups large carrots, diced	Bay leaves
5 cups large onions, diced	Salt
5 cups large celery, diced	Flour
5 cups large potatoes, diced, optional	

1. Generously salt and pepper meat. Place into a heated, lightly oiled pot and sear on all sides.
2. Add vegetables and cook for 3-5 minutes. Add red wine, scraping the bottom of the pot to mix in caramelized meat at bottom.
3. Add beer and enough water to cover ingredients. Add spices to taste, bring to a boil, then reduce to a simmer.
4. Simmer until meat becomes tender, always making sure there is enough liquid.
5. Sift in flour to desired thickness, taking care to avoid lumps. Cook for an additional 15 minutes and serve.

The Ranch House Restaurant and Saloon in Tabernash

TELLURIDE

Founded as Columbia, the name was later changed to Telluride because of the tellurium ore — a rare element analogous to sulphur usually combined with gold or silver — found in the area. With the Denver and Rio Grande Southern Railroad reaching town in 1890 and the gold boom following the demonetization of silver in 1893, Telluride grew to new heights. The New Sheridan Hotel was built in 1895 and the Sheridan Opera House followed in 1914. However, as mining profits diminished and strikes crippled the industry, Telluride began to decline. After the closing of the Bank of Telluride in 1930, there were several failed attempts to create a ski area. In 1964, the town was designated a National Historic District for its important contribution to mining and its Victorian character. In 1968, entrepreneur Joe Zoline developed plans for a winter recreation area and in 1971, Governor Love dedicated the Telluride Ski Area. Combined with summer festivals, Telluride is a boom town once again.

Zip Code: 81435. Area Code: 970. Population: 1,309. Elevation: 8,800'.

The PowderHouse

226 West Colorado Avenue, PO Box 1709, 728-3622

Directions: Coming into Telluride on Highway 145 (Colorado Avenue), the restaurant is on the right, ½ block past Aspen Street.

ESSENTIALS

Cuisine: Colorado Rocky Mountain

Hours: 7 days 6PM-10PM. Closed Early APR to Memorial Day Weekend and Mid-OCT to Mid-NOV.

Meals and Prices: Dinner $$$-$$$$$

Nonsmoking: Yes

Take-out: Yes

Alcohol: Full Bar

Credit Cards: MC, Visa, Amx

Personal Check: From Telluride only

Reservations: Recommended

Wheelchair Access: Yes, through the kitchen

HISTORY, PERSONALITY AND CHARACTER

The PowderHouse was a turn-of-the-century arsenal for the mines, hence the name PowderHouse. The restaurant has had 3 owners since opening in 1972. The last, Tony Clinco, who took over in 1987, also operates Giuseppe's at the top of Lift 9. He's also the executive chef and has been in the restaurant business since 1970 with previous experience at the Sheridan and Radisson Hotels. Eric Ward has been the restaurant manager since 1990.

FOOD, SERVICE AND AMBIANCE

The PowderHouse version of Cioppino, the Portuguese fish stew, was a bona fide feast: tender, yet chewy mussels, lobster tail, calamari, crab, tuna, salmon, swordfish and shrimp in an ambrosial tomato broth of onions, tomatoes, basil, celery and oregano with white and wild rice pilaf. This mouth-watering dish was as good, or better, than any fish stew or paella I've had in Colorado. All of the seafood were left in their shells. A sweet-tasting mixed green salad with toasted wheat berries, sunflower seeds and Italian vinaigrette preceded the main course.

Several seafood appetizers, including escargots, smoked seafood platter and Cajun barbecued prawns, showcase the list of menu starters along with smoked game and Caesar salad. A half-dozen pasta selections feature fettuccine, angel hair pasta or ziti with seafood, salmon, chicken breast or artichoke hearts. House specialties and dinners include roast duckling or pheasant, Colorado rack of lamb, trout almondine, tournedos, stuffed quail, marinated elk, free-range chicken and veal scaloppine. Chef Tony uses a variety of innovative sauces with his meals, like rosemary, green peppercorn or a rich sherry demi-glace. Highlighting his exquisite homemade desserts are chocolate mousse, strawberry shortcake, white chocolate hazelnut cheesecake, jumble berry crumble with fresh berries, mud pie, tiramisu and affogado — honey and vanilla ice cream mixed with Frangelico and chilled cappuccino. They offer a wide range of delights both on and off the menu.

Service, with a smile, was helpful and cooperative. Dropping off a cold wet napkin for my fingers after I tackled the shellfish was a thoughtful gesture. New age music on the harp and guitar played overhead. The pink stucco walls were decorated with black and white photos of Anasazzi Ruins in Mesa Verde by Ilene Benjamin and old 1800s photos of Telluride. Use of color-stained, stenciled and frosted glasses as dividers and ornaments are made throughout the restaurant. You'll appreciate the setting and take pleasure in the food when you dine at The PowderHouse.

SPECIAL ONE-TIME OFFER: Buy one entrée at the regular price and receive a complimentary glass of wine. This offer NOT valid in combination with any other offers. Please present to server at time of ordering. _____ Manager/Owner. _____ Date.

With 365 restaurants to choose from, Restaurants from 101 Colorado Small Towns takes the guesswork out of where to dine in Colorado!

RECIPE

Organic Baby Greens with Sweet Basil Vinaigrette

Commercially mixed variety of greens
that comes with the following:
- Oakleaf lettuce
- Red tip lettuce
- Baby spinach
- Watercress
- Dandelion
- Chicory
- Rocket
- Sorrel
- Corn salad

Sweet Basil Vinaigrette:
- 2 cups canola salad oil
- 1 cup extra virgin olive oil
- 1½ cups red wine vinegar
- ½ cup water
- 1 cup yellow onion, diced
- 1 tablespoon fresh sweet basil, chopped
- 1 teaspoon Dijon mustard
- ⅛ cup sugar
- ½ teaspoon salt
- ½ teaspoon black pepper, coarse

1. Combine all ingredients for the vinaigrette in a blender, stick mixer or food processor and purée.
2. Store refrigerated in a sealed container.
3. Shake well before serving.
4. Lightly toss 6 ounces of mixed greens with 4 ounces Sweet Basil Vinaigrette. Serve on individual chilled salad plates.
5. Garnish each salad with fresh grated Parmesan cheese, toasted and lightly salted sunflower seeds and puffed cracked wheat berries.
6. Crumbled blue cheese may be used as an additional garnish, if desired.

There are several organic baby greens on the market today. Greens may be purchased individually or already mixed. There are many good pre-mixed greens sold by commercial farms that come in a variety of mixtures. At the PowderHouse, we use a commercially mixed variety of greens.

Tony Clinco

TRINIDAD

Named after the Holy Trinity, Trinidad was originally called Rio de Las Animas and first settled in 1859. The town began as a supply depot on the Mountain Branch of the Santa Fe Trail between Bent's Old Fort to the northeast and Raton Pass to the south. Later, Trinidad served as a railhead for cattle drives from Texas to New Mexico on the Goodnight Trail. Over the past century, Trinidad has prospered as the center of one of the world's richest coal mining district. Many famous western figures played a part in Trinidad's history: Bat Masterson, who was sheriff in the 1880s; Doc Holiday, who presumably gambled here with Bat Masterson; Wyatt Earp, who drove the stage; Billy the Kid and Kit Carson, whose statue graces the park that bears his name. While in Trinidad, I took an interesting side trip to Drop City, three miles northeast of I-25 and Exit 15, on Highway 239. Once a 1960s hippie settlement, there remains today a dome-shaped building made entirely of car parts, mostly fenders and doors. If you have an extra hour, take your camera and go see it.
Zip Code: 81082. Area Code: 719. Population: 8,580. Elevation: 6,025'.

Nana & Nano's Pasta House
415 University Street, 846-2696
Directions: Take Exit 14A from I-25. Go west one block, the restaurant is on the right.

ESSENTIALS

Cuisine: Italian
Hours: Labor Day-Memorial Day:
Tue-Fri 4:30PM-8PM, Sat 4:30PM-
8:30PM. Closed Sun/Mon. Memorial
Day-Labor Day: closing time is ½
hour later.
Meals and Prices: Dinner $$
Nonsmoking: All
Take-out: Yes

Alcohol: No
Credit Cards: MC, Visa, Amx, Disc
Personal Check: Local only
Reservations: Recommended on
Saturday and holidays. Not necessary
during the week.
Wheelchair Access: Yes
Other: Additional 15% service charge
for parties of 10 or more people.

HISTORY, CHARACTER AND PERSONALITY

Nana & Nano's (Italian for Grandma and Grandpa) Pasta House has been in business since 1988 under a corporation headed by Fran Monteleone and her Mom and Dad. Fran's father used to own a produce wholesale and deli store on West Cedar Street in Trinidad. When he retired in 1978, Fran took over and ran the business until she opened Nana & Nano's. Fran is owner, manager and head chef. She loves to cook and has been doing it her entire life. When she first opened her restaurant, she worked as both cook and waitress, often unbeknownst to her out-of-town customers. She says she likes to make sure her customers are happy. Judging from the business that she has been doing, I would say her customers are <u>very</u> happy!

The building occupied by Nana & Nano's dates to the early 1970s when it was the Burger Hub. The branding iron marks from that earlier establishment still remain on the upper portion of the dining room walls. Fran tells me the local ranchers love to come in and point out their mark. In the late '70s, Dairy Queen took over. From 1985 until 1988, the building was vacant.

FOOD, SERVICE AND AMBIANCE

This is the place for pasta! I have eaten their mostoccioli, a wide pasta noodle, and gnocchi, delectable chewy Italian potato dumplings with the texture of späetzle. Fran's diligence pays off in a consistently good product. You can order meatballs or their lean Italian sausage with your pasta. Most entrées, like spaghetti, ravioli, fettucine con sugo, polenta, rigatoni, and lasagna, are prepared with a homemade special Italian tomato sauce, not very rich or spicy, just plain good. Fran uses a 40-gallon tilt skillet to mix her tomato paste, garlic, olive oil and other fine ingredients. The sauce simmers from 9:30am through dinner. The meatballs and Italian sausage are also cooked in with the sauce giving them a soft texture. If you are not in the mood for pasta, you can choose from a few alternatives, like baked chicken or fish, rib eye steak, burgers or a meatball or Italian sausage sandwich.

The restaurant is not open for lunch, but you can visit their adjacent deli between 10AM and 5PM on Tuesday through Friday or 9AM TO 1PM on Saturday and order a homemade sandwich to go. While you are there, pick up some imported or domestic cheeses, fine meats, cold cuts or a copy of the cookbook that Fran and her two cousins, Genevieve Gurule and Shirley Compton, put together: Nana's Cucina (Grandma's Kitchen).

Dinner comes with a basic salad that seems to be popular in this part of the state. The sweet, homemade Italian salad dressing makes this salad a step above the rest. A creamy, spicy Italian dressing is also served, made with onion, salt, garlic, red bell peppers, paprika, parsley and vinegar. A warm loaf of homemade Italian bread is served at your table on a cutting board with a sharp bread knife and homemade garlic butter (Mmmm!). After your entrée, which comes in large or small portions, order one of their delectable homemade desserts, such as caramel Granny apple pie, torta tiramisu, bread pudding, baklava, key lime pie, spumoni or cheesecake.

They still play slow, romantic Italian melodies of Frank Sinatra, Andy Williams and others. Service is warm and friendly. My Mom would have liked this place. Maybe it is because I am half Italian, but I feel right at home here. The decor has changed in the last couple of years. Gone are the red and white checkered table cloths, replaced with green and white checked cloths. The red curtains are still there. As for the lack of alcohol, when Nana & Nano's first opened in 1988, there was an old town ordinance which forbade the sale of alcohol within 50 feet from a church or school. At the time, Nana & Nano's was next to a church. The church is no longer there and the ordinance

TRINIDAD

has since been removed, but Fran discovered that she really did not need to offer alcohol to keep people coming back for her pasta and other Italian delights.

SPECIAL ONE-TIME OFFER: Buy one entrée at the regular price and receive a second entrée of equal or lesser value FREE (up to $8.00 value) OR 50% off a single entrée (maximum discount $4.00). This offer NOT valid in combination with any other offers. _____ Manager/Owner. _____ Date.

RECIPE

Fran's alla Olio

1 pound spaghetti, cooked and drained   ¼ cup chopped garlic (in jar from the
½ cup butter   produce department)
½ cup olive oil   Parsley

1. Cook spaghetti and drain.
2. Melt butter, parsley, oil and garlic together over heat.
3. Pour mixture over spaghetti and serve hot.
4. Sprinkle with extra parsley on top of each dish.

The Nordic Inn in Twin Lakes (inset) and the view from the Inn

284

TWIN LAKES

Originally named Dayton after the city in Ohio, Twin Lakes was renamed in 1868 for the 2 neighboring natural lakes, each about 2 miles wide by 5 miles long. The discovery of silver west of the Sawatch Range in the Aspen area and the completion of the Denver and Rio Grande Railroad to Leadville and Granite resulted in the town's rapid growth. It seems Twin Lakes had its own version of the Lochness Monster back in the 1890s when sightings of a sea serpent sprang up. On January 21, 1962, a massive avalanche slid down Mt. Elbert fanning out to approximately 1 mile in width west of town and killing 7 people. Twin Lakes, situated in the heart of the Pike-San Isabel National Forest at the foot of Mt. Elbert, Colorado's highest peak, is a National Historic District.
Zip Code: 81231. Area Code: 719. Population: 75. Elevation: 9,220'

Nordic Inn
6435 Highway 82, PO Box 87, 486-1830, 1-800-626-7812, FAX 486-1830
Directions: From the intersection of Highways 24 and 82 south of Leadville, go west on Highway 82 for 6 miles. The restaurant is on the right as you enter town. Coming from Aspen on Highway 82 over Independence Pass, the restaurant is on the left as you enter town.

ESSENTIALS
Cuisine: German/American
Hours: Mid-MAY through OCT: 7 days 7AM-11AM, 11AM-3PM and 5PM-9PM. NOV to Mid-MAY (when Independence Pass closes): Fri-Sun 7AM-11AM, 11AM-3PM and 5PM-9PM. Closed Mon-Thu.
Meals and Prices: Breakfast $, Lunch $-$$, Dinner $$-$$$
Nonsmoking: Yes
Take-out: Yes
Alcohol: Full Bar

Credit Cards: MC, Visa
Personal Check: Yes ("We accept good checks from anywhere in the world.")
Reservations: Recommended for groups of 6 or more.
Wheelchair Access: Yes
Other: Banquet room available for wedding rehearsals and receptions, groups, clubs or meetings. Automatic 15% service charge added to parties of 6 or more. No menu substitutions.

HISTORY, PERSONALITY AND CHARACTER
The Nordic Inn, originally named the Twin Peaks Hotel after Mt. Twin Peaks south of the Inn, was constructed in 1879 by Maggie Webber of Wisconsin as a stagecoach stop between the silver mining camps of Aspen and Leadville. Maggie owned and operated the Inn until 1903. She then sold the place to the King family who operated the Inn for 50 years under the name "The Twin Lakes Hotel". The Inn accommodated the local miners by serving as a brothel until the 1920s. The large dining room with a bar wasn't constructed until the 1940s. The bar was moved in the early 1960s to its

285

present location in the Powder Guild Lounge, adjacent to the 2 dining rooms. The small dining room is believed to have been a porch at one time and was enclosed after the construction of the large dining room. In the 1950s, the "Hotel" was sold to the Stephans family and renamed "The Sportman's Lodge". During most of the 1960s, the Inn was closed and boarded up. In the early 1970s, Augie Freeville purchased the Inn and renamed it once again "The Twin Lakes Hotel". Frank Mueller bought the hotel in 1979, then sold it to Taylor Adams and Larry Overton in 1981. The current owners, Carol Slater and her sons John and Doug, purchased the Inn in 1986 and are in the process of completing an extensive 10- to 12-year remodeling and improvement plan that adds rustic charm and beauty to the Nordic Inn.

Carol and John operate the Inn, including the restaurant, while Doug, a colonel in the U.S. Army, is a silent partner. John, who has been cooking since 1968, is the head chef along with Tom Seidel who has been cooking since 1975. John worked in several New Jersey restaurants before moving to Colorado in 1981. He cooked at The Trough and Cattleman's Inn in Gunnison and The Prospector in Leadville before opening the Nordic Inn. Tom has been with the Inn since 1988 and previously worked at the Jackson Hotel in Poncha Springs, an establishment owned by John from 1989 to 1992.

FOOD, SERVICE AND AMBIANCE

I've delved into two of the Nordic Inn's delicious dinner entrées: the tarte and tangy sauerbraten made with spicy marinated Colorado beef and tender and savory Bavarian baked pork. The sauerbraten spiked my taste buds while the pork was very fresh with a light brown gravy — not a heavy dish. Both meals were served with fluffy and chewy knöeddle (potato dumplings), apple sauce sprinkled with cinnamon and either sweet German-style red cabbage or steamed vegetables. The soup du jour was chicken noodle with dumplings using bow-tie and kluski (egg) noodles and superbly flavored with tarragon and butter to give it a chicken kiev taste. German dark rye bread also comes with the meal: ideal, for those not too proud, for sopping up their delectable homemade gravy. To accompany your selection, you can choose from about 70 beers and wines from California, Germany and France.

Headlining the other German specialties are rinderrouladen, the Inn specialty — slow-roasted Colorado beef stuffed with onions and pickles; jaeggerschnitzel — breaded pork with mushroom sauce; bratwurst sausages boiled in beer then broiled and served with sauerkraut; marinated and broiled chicken with mushroom sauce and jumbo shrimp sautéed in garlic and butter. If you're wanting something more American, you can choose a charbroiled Colorado ribeye with mushrooms, rainbow trout, vegetable lasagna or a charbroiled hamburger. A soup, salad, baked potato and homemade bread combination and a grilled chicken salad are available for lighter appetites and there is a children's menu.

Breakfast at the Nordic Inn offers an authentic German-style meal consisting of Broetchen (a homemade roll), fresh fruit, cheddar cheese, 2 eggs and ham; an American classic of 2 eggs, home fries, whole wheat toast and choice of meat; a fruit and cheese plate; omelets; French toast and buttermilk pancakes. Lunch features kartoffel puffer (potato pancakes), broiled burgers, sandwiches (tuna fish, ham and Swiss, Reuben and turkey club) and a fruit plate.

Service on both my visits was courteous, prompt, cheerful and helpful. The staff was very accommodating. John and Carol were eager to converse with the patrons and answer any questions. They played a medley of instrumental show melodies, circa 1940s, interspersed with some folksy banjo tunes. John and Carol have done a marvelous job renovating and decorating the dining area to resemble a German Inn with Colorado flair. Carol, a frequent traveler to Germany, has returned with much memorabilia from the Homeland including a collection of nutcrackers which she proudly displays on the fireplace mantle; a solid copper plate over the mantle that describes 3 men sitting around a table drinking while a blacksmith looks on; rose wood inlays (made entirely from small pieces of stained wood) of Heidelberg and Rothenburg; colorful stained-glass ceiling lamps in bright reds, greens and yellows; a roll-top desk from her great-grandmother; beer mugs and steins that are on display in 2 cabinets; a potpourri of colored bottles in various shapes and sizes along with several figurines and knickknacks; and a plate collection depicting pictures of the German countryside and German life. She acquired them from the many volksmarches (walks) that she has been on in Germany (in the USA, you'd get a T-shirt). John has added a touch of Colorado by hanging several pairs of senior snowshoes and seasoned skis including a 9-foot-3-inch elongated pair dating back to 1875 that the post office used. In the lounge are photos of the 1962 avalanche on Mt. Elbert and vintage town photos taken in the early part of this century. Another unique highlight of the Nordic Inn is their books — they have thousands of them: on book shelves, on window sills, on wall ledges and in the rooms upstairs.

From your lodgepole pine chair and table, you have a view across Upper Twin Lake of the Twin Peaks, Mount Hope and Quail Mountain — all in the 13,000' range. During the winter, you can dine by the fireplace and, if you're lucky, catch a sight of the elk herd to the south. On warmer summer days, try reveling on their patio. No matter what time of year you dine at the Nordic Inn, John, Carol and company will serve you their exquisite cuisine with good cheer in a splendid setting.

SPECIAL ONE-TIME OFFER: Buy one entrée at the regular price and receive a second entrée of equal or lesser value FREE (up to $13.95 value). This offer NOT valid in combination with any other offers. Please present to server at time of ordering. _____ Manager/Owner. _____ Date.

RECILE

Rinderrouladen
(Serves 6 to 8)

3 pounds of flank steak | Dark spicy mustard
Bacon | Toothpick
Pickle wedge or slices | White flour
Onions, diced | Oil
Salt and pepper | Water
Paprika

1. Slice the steak in half. Pound all pieces thin with a rubber hammer, each piece should be 3 inches wide by 6 to 8 inches long by ⅛-inch thick.
2. Lay the pieces out flat. Each piece gets a piece of bacon, 1 pickle wedge or 4 pickle slices, ½ ounce diced onions, salt, pepper, paprika and 2 ounces of dark spicy mustard.
3. Roll each piece up as tight as possible. Use a toothpick or two to keep it rolled tightly.
4. Dip each rouladen in white flour, lightly cover the entire rouladen. Put each piece in a lightly oiled skillet. Lightly brown all the rouladens. Cover all the rouladens with water. Let simmer for 2 hours. Remove the rouladens and make your gravy out of the excess sauce.

This recipe has been with the Slater Family for about 100 years.
Carol and John Slater

VAIL

The valley of Gore Creek, where Vail resort now stands, was first settled in the 1880s by silver prospectors. Unsuccessful at silver mining, they developed homesteads instead and raised cattle and grew crops. Vail and nearby Vail Pass (10,603') were named after Charles D. Vail, Colorado State Department engineer and director in the 1930s and 1940s. The town of Vail is relatively new having been established in 1959 and incorporated in 1966. Vail ski area opened in 1962 and was chosen as the site of the 1989 World Alpine Ski Championships.
Zip Code: 81657. Area Code: 970. Population: 3,659. Elevation: 8,160'.

Uptown Grill

472 East Lionshead Circle, 476-2727
Directions: Take Exit 176 from I-70. Go south to the 4-way stop. Turn right onto South Frontage Road. Go .3 miles and turn left into the Lionshead Parking Garage. Park in the far west end and exit on foot down the steps to the southwest. Look for the green "Base Mountain Sports" awning and the rust-color "Cabbages and Kings" overhead sign. Walk between these two establishments. The restaurant is straight ahead about 100 feet.

ESSENTIALS

Cuisine: Modern American with a Southwest Flair
Hours: JUL to Mid-APR: 7 days 11:30AM-3PM and 5:30PM-10PM. Late-APR through JUN: 11:30AM-2:30PM and 6PM-9PM. Closed Mid-to-late APR.
Meals and Prices: Lunch $$, Dinner $$$$-$$$$$
Nonsmoking: Yes, smoking only permitted in the lounge

Take-out: Yes
Alcohol: Full Bar
Credit Cards: MC, Visa, Amx
Personal Check: Yes, with I.D.
Reservations: Accepted for dinner but not for lunch
Wheelchair Access: Yes
Dress: Nicely casual
Other: 15% service charge added for tables of 6 or more at lunch, 18% at dinner.

HISTORY, PERSONALITY AND CHARACTER

The building occupied by the Uptown Grill was originally The Place Restaurant built in the mid-1970s. In 1986, current owners and managers Joel and Susan Fritz opened the Uptown Grill. Joel is a long-time resident with over 32 years in Vail. Susan has been in the restaurant business since the mid-1960s. Their daughter, Amy, assists with the management of the restaurant. Peter Millette has been their Executive Chef since November 1994. He began his culinary career in 1983, graduated from the Western Culinary Institute in Portland, Oregon, and was sous chef at Sweet Basil from 1989 until 1994.

FOOD, SERVICE AND AMBIANCE

I savored a tasty portobello mushroom sandwich, a popular vegetarian lunch item, served with curly fries and mixed greens with Dijon sherry, oil and vinegar dressing. This was a prodigious, single mushroom the size of the large onion bun, topped with sundried tomato pesto and cilantro, two of my favorite garnishes — a scrumptious alternative to a burger. Chef Peter's southwest flair permeates the lunch and dinner menus. Items such as avocado, smoked onion salsa, sundried tomatoes, cilantro pesto cream, roasted eggplant, red pepper or smoked tomato chutneys, black beans, asadero cheese, pico de gallo, black bean or pumpkin seed sauces, Anaheim chilies, guacamole, pickled red onion, crème Fraiche, jicama, chili garlic or polenta croutons, black bean cake, cilantro blackbean ravioli, tomato maple mustard vinaigrette, mole sauce, tortilla hairs and warm gazpacho give prominence to the appetizers, salads, entrées and specialties. Headlining their spring menu were chili relleno, Southwest Caesar salad, calamari rings, mussels Vera Cruz and black bean soup appetizers; pizza and pasta dishes; southwest steak Caesar, soft shell crab sandwich and vegetable enchilada lunch specialties; rock shrimp salad; and rack of lamb, chicken pesto linguini, corn masa lasagna and grilled tenderloin of beef entrées. Each meal is prepared individually and to order. Special dietary requests are accommodated.

Joel was my amiable and helpful server. When you first enter the Uptown Grill, you are in the lounge decorated with pine wood poles and vegas, a wall constructed of wine boxes, red chili-pepper lights, copper table tops with matching lanterns, red brick floor, and sun roof covered with branches. See if you can tell which popular children's poem is described in pictures over the entrance to the dining room. The dining room is beautified in southwest colors — purple shutters and hanging red chilies — a wine rack and wall murals by popular local artist, Natalie DeStefano, whose works I came across in Fiesta's in Edwards and The Minturn Country Club. At the Uptown Grill, she has displayed a couple of diners under "The Uptown" sign and a scene from Monument Valley. Original oils created by David Parker for the Taste of Vail in 1994 characterize desert dining and a cowboy waiter. Porcelain sconces offset the colorful artwork. Dinner is presented with more formal service and white table cloths. The outside deck is adorned by hefty flower pots. For regional ambiance and a taste of the southwest, dine at the Uptown Grill.

SPECIAL ONE-TIME OFFER: Buy one entrée at the regular price and receive a complimentary glass of house wine. Limit two glasses of house wine with the purchase of two entrées. This offer NOT valid in combination with any other offers. Please present to server at time of ordering. _____ Manager/Owner. _____ Date.

<u>RECIPE</u>

Black Bean Soup
(Serves 8)

4 cups black turtle beans
2 medium poblano chilies,
  seeded and diced
1 small onion, diced
1 medium carrot, diced
1 stalk celery, diced
6 cloves garlic
6 to 8 cups homemade chicken stock
  or canned broth

2 tablespoons ground cumin
1 teaspoon ancho chili powder
½ cup sour cream
½ cup dry sherry
Salt and pepper to taste
Sprigs of cilantro, optional
4 6-inch flour tortillas, cut
  into eighths and fried to a
  golden brown

1. Rinse and sort beans, discarding discolored beans. Soak overnight in cold water.
2. Put the beans, onion, carrot, celery, garlic and water to cover in a large heavy pot. Bring to a boil and skim off any scum that rises to the surface.
3. Simmer slowly, loosely covered, until the beans are tender, approximately 2 hours. Add more water if the level falls below the surface of the beans and stir often to prevent sticking and to ensure that the beans cook evenly.
4. While soup is cooking, combine shallots and sherry. Simmer over medium heat until reduced by ¾ (about 5 minutes). Add to sour cream and refrigerate.
5. When the beans are cooked, purée in a food processor to rough consistency. Return beans to soup pot and add chicken stock, cumin and chili powder. Soup should be thick.
6. Heat stirring often so that beans do not stick to bottom of pot. Adjust seasonings when soup is hot.

VALLECITO LAKE

Vallecito Lake is a secluded resort community tucked away in the heart of 2-million-acre San Juan National Forest and borders 465,000-acre Weminuche Wilderness. Vallecito Lake has 22 miles of forested shoreline offering a variety of water sports in a mountain setting.

Zip Code: 81122. Area Code: 970. Population: 500. Elevation: Approx. 9,000'.

Old Lodge at the Lake Restaurant
(at The Wit's End Guest Ranch and Resort)

254 County Road 500, 884-4113, Fax 884-4114

Directions: From Bayfield: From the flashing signal at Highway 160 and County Road 501, go north on County Road 501 for 13.2 miles to the entrance to Vallecito Lake. On the right side of the road, there will be a large map of the lake and facilities. From this point, continue straight (do not turn right or you will wind up on the wrong side of the lake) for another 5.3 miles. Turn left onto County Road 500. Go .8 miles. Turn right and drive under the "Wit's End Ranch" sign. The restaurant is down the road and to the right. From Durango: From Main Avenue and 32nd Street go east on 32nd Street for 1.3 miles. Turn right on East Animas Road (County Road 250). Go .1 mile and turn left on Florida Road (County Road 240). Go 11.9 miles and turn right at Helen's Store (there's a Coors sign on the right). You'll be back on County Road 240. Go 2.8 miles and turn left onto County Road 501. Go 9.7 miles and turn left onto County Road 500. Go .8 miles. Turn right and drive under the "Wit's End Ranch" sign. The restaurant is down the road and to the right.

ESSENTIALS

Cuisine: American Country
Hours: Labor Day to Memorial Day: Open only on selective Fri/Sat 6PM-8:30PM. Memorial Day to Labor Day restaurant only open to ranch guests.
Meals and Prices: 6-course prie fix dinner $55
Nonsmoking: No
Take-out: No
Alcohol: Full Bar

Credit Cards: MC, Visa, Amx, Disc
Personal Check: Yes, with I.D.
Reservations: Required
Wheelchair Access: Yes
Dress: Western, casual or dressy
Other: 15% service charge automatically added to all checks. Available for weddings, wedding receptions, conferences, family reunions or corporate retreats.

HISTORY, PERSONALITY AND CHARACTER

The Old Lodge at the Lake Restaurant is a hand-hewn post and beam building built by John Patrick in 1870 as a barn. It remained a barn right up until 1988 when it was converted into a restaurant and tavern by Jim and Lynn Custer. They purchased the Wit's End Guest Ranch in 1986, refurbished before opening and later built a second wall around the outside of the building. The Custers were involved in realty, condos and rental properties and the aerospace industry in Kansas City and Phoenix before going into the ranch and restaurant business. Jim and Lynn run the ranch for the 5 high season months (May to October). Wit's End's chefs have won awards during their careers. The Wit's End Guest Ranch was featured in the August 1991 issue of "Country Inns", selected 1 of the 12 best country inns in America for 1991, and featured as a prize on the television show "Wheel of Fortune" since 1989. The Ranch has been described as a "world class" guest ranch by Durango magazine and headlined in Relax Magazine, Orange County Magazine, Bon Appetite and many other periodicals. Paul Harvey is one notable figure who has dined here.

FOOD, SERVICE AND AMBIANCE

Dining at the Old Lodge at the Lake Restaurant is as much a tour of the present and a walk back in time as it is an experience in eating. I began the dining part of my experience with creamy, well-seasoned cream of asparagus soup followed by lobster in a sherry cream sauce over linguini with Parmesan sprinkled on top. This delectable dish was served with plenty of garlic and butter along with parsley, lemon and the empty shell of the lobster's tail (a nice touch to the presentation, I thought). Also on the menu that evening were fried calamari with hot mustard or marinara sauce as an appetizer, mixed greens salad, roast prime rib au jus with glazed carrots and Italian roasted potatoes, scallops sautéed and flamed in sherry with bacon and chablis cheese sauce, and battered and grilled (sounds like a crime victim who then has to explain his side of the story to the police) Cajun chicken. The menu changes each weekend. Some items that you may see when you dine here are sautéed escargot in burgundy garlic sauce, baked mushrooms stuffed with shrimp in tarragon cream sauce or fried lobster buttons with sour dill sauce for appetizers; minestrone, wild mushroom or Mexican black bean soups; and homemade Italian, raspberry vinaigrette and Caesar dressings for your salad. Other entrées that Chef David prepares include fettuccine Alfredo, lobster diablo (seasoned in a spicy marinara sauce over pasta), grilled scallops with pesto cream sauce, châteaubriand and rack of lamb. He also makes all of his own sauces and stocks and the wheat bread is baked here as well. The wine list is mostly from California with some European and Australian imports.

They were short on staff the evening I visited, so service was a little sporadic. However, Dorothy did a fine job of helping out and "smoothing things over". Country music filled the air of this former three-story barn. On some evenings, there's live country music in the bar where you'll find the centerpiece of this multifaceted restaurant: the 1836 Crystal Tavern mirrors from the Crystal Palace in London. These mirrors, with the initials "CT" in 24-carat gold inscribed on each one, were displayed at the 1853 World Exposition in London. At another corner of the tavern, you'll find a sign that says "Not responsible for women left over night". A tour of the building at some point during your visit is in order. Downstairs you'll discover a rock, wood-burning fireplace with a stuffed pheasant, miniature log cabin and dried acorns, berries and straw over the mantel; an antler chandelier; stuffed big horn sheep and cougar; an artificial Christmas Tree by the front window with white lights; decorator plates with pictures of fish, turkeys, pheasants and ducks; log walls (with a steel wall added behind as part of the remodeling) and a pair of oil lanterns. At the foot of the old log stairway, you'll see a stuffed wild boar. As you head up the garland-wrapped stairway, you'll be able to view mountainous heads of moose, deer and elk. When you reach the second level, you're in a lounge with pool table, couches, coffee tables, chairs, rugs, cow hides and deer hides on an old wood floor. You are now in the middle of an old hay loft constructed of hand-hewn beams, timbers and logs dating back to 1872. Further up one more flight of stairs, you'll be in an antique library. When you return to your candle-lit dining table, you'll be seated at battenburg lace and flower-pattern tablecloths under glass. At The Old lodge at The Lake Restaurant, you'll feel as comfortable as John Patrick must have felt in his own homestead while you take pleasure in some fine dining.

SPECIAL ONE-TIME OFFER: Buy one prie-fix 6-course dinner at regular price and receive 50% off a second prie-fix 6-course dinner. This offer NOT valid in combination with any other offers. Please present to server at time of ordering.

_____ Manager/Owner. _____ Date.

RECIPE

**Grilled Sea Scallops with Roasted Bell Pepper
and Angel Hair Pasta**

1 pound sea scallops	12 ounces natural chicken broth
1 each yellow, red and green	1 tomato, peeled, seeded and chopped
bells peppers	1 tablespoon olive oil
8 leaves fresh basil, chopped fine	Salt and pepper to taste
1 pound angel hair pasta	Parmesan cheese and parsley flakes

1. In rapidly boiling water, add scallops for 30 seconds only. Immediately strain and add to ice water to stop cooking. Then drain and pat dry with clean towel.
2. On an open flame, char bell peppers black, then place in paper bag to sweat for 5 minutes. Then remove from bag and peel under cold running water making sure to remove all black skin and seeds from the inside. Cut into ¼-inch strips and set aside.

3. Prepare angel hair pasta according to package instructions, minus 1 minute cooking time.
4. Over medium heat, sauté olive oil, bell peppers, tomato, basil and chicken stock. Simmer for 8 minutes.
5. Toss scallops, salt, pepper and olive oil in bowl and place on medium hot grill for 2 minutes each side. Strain pasta and portion accordingly in desired serving dish. Add bell pepper, tomato and basil mixture on top of pasta.
6. Garnish with 2 or 3 grilled scallops. Sprinkle with Parmesan and parsley.

The entrance seating area for the Old Lake at the Lodge Restaurant in Vallecito Lake

Virginia's Steakhouse

18044 County Road 501

Directions: From Bayfield: From the flashing signal at Highway 160 and County Road 501, go north on County Road 501 for 13.2 miles to the entrance to Vallecito Lake. On the right side of the road, there will be a large map of the lake and facilities. From this point, continue straight (do not turn right or you will wind up on the wrong side of the lake) for another 4.4 miles. The restaurant is on the right just past the Circle S Lodge. From Durango: From Main Avenue and 32nd Street go east on 32nd Street for 1.3 miles. Turn right on East Animas Road (County Road 250). Go .1 mile and turn left on Florida Road (County Road 240). Go 11.9 miles and turn right at Helen's Store (there's a Coors sign on the right). You'll be back on County Road 240. Go 2.8 miles and turn left onto County Road 501. Go 9.2 miles. The restaurant is on the right just past the Circle S Lodge.

ESSENTIALS

Cuisine: Steak
Hours: MAY-OCT: 7 days 4PM-10PM.
NOV-APR: Thu-Mon 4PM-9PM.
Closed Tue/Wed.
Meals and Prices: Dinner $$$-$$$$
Nonsmoking: Yes
Take-out: Yes
Alcohol: Full Bar

Credit Cards: MC, Visa
Personal Check: Local only with I.D.
Reservations: Recommended for summer, accepted otherwise.
Wheelchair Access: Yes
Other: Live entertainment on selected Saturday nights during the winter

HISTORY, PERSONALITY AND CHARACTER

Virginia's Steakhouse was built circa 1930 and was formerly the Decker Ranch House. In the 1940s, it became the Semke Circle S Ranch owned and operated by Estelle Semke. In 1977, Virginia Jackson purchased the property from Semke and opened Virginia's Steakhouse. Her son, Steve Dudley, bought the restaurant in February 1993. He is also the head chef and has worked at different restaurants during the winter in Las Vegas, Boston and various locations in Arizona. His sister, Marilyn Zauberis, tends bar.

FOOD, SERVICE AND AMBIANCE

Virginia's has a gargantuan menu offering burgers, steaks, chops, ribs, veal, chicken, seafood, pasta and combinations. I started with a soup that I rarely see anywhere in Colorado, Manhattan-style clam chowder. It was a delicious and welcome change to the more popular New England version, temperature hot with several chewy and tender pieces of clam with vegetables in a tomato broth. For my entrée, I selected the steak cabellero, a savory petite New York strip topped with green chilies and cheddar with jalapeños and salsa on the side. I found this to be a very flavorful dish served with sautéed vegetables. At Virginia's, they bake their own bread, make their own soups, stocks, sauces and salad dressings, and serve trout that they catch daily from their own trout pond.

For an appetizer or light meal, you can choose from Rocky Mountain oysters, taquitos rancheros (crispy rolled tacos), Cajun rock shrimp, Buffalo wings, French onion soup, burgers and sandwiches (mesquite smoked beef brisket, prime rib or Cajun chicken). There are a number of different steak cuts prepared in a variety of ways: peppered, teriyaki or with mushrooms and garlic. Other meats include lamb or veal chops, rack of lamb, roast prime rib, pork or beef ribs, beef stroganoff, chicken fried steak, veal marsala or Oscar, and chicken boursin (cheese sauce) or piccata (with capers and shallots). For seafood lovers, Virginia's offers salmon, shrimp, scallops, swordfish, homegrown trout and Australian lobster tail in an assortment of preparations. Amongst the pasta picks are linguini and clams, tortellini carbonara and fettuccine alla burena with bacon, mushrooms and asiago cheese sauce. Nightly specials are offered during the winter, like pizza on Tuesdays, Mexican on Mondays and all-you-can-eat cod and catfish on Fridays. A children's menu is available and wines, mostly from California, specialty cocktails and hot drinks can be ordered for your dining pleasure.

Service was amiable and helpful. A CD jukebox is available for your listening enjoyment. Ponderosa pine logs are used in the construction of Virginia's poles, vegas and beams. A western theme is used throughout the restaurant. At the entrance, you'll see a stuffed bear, beaver and goat. Further back there is a stuffed deer head with antlers. There are blown-up replicas of 4 photos taken from western historical figures: Chief Ouray and Chipetta, Billy the Kid, Buffalo Bill and Sitting Bull. Indian figures and a painting of an Iowan chief adorn the fireplace mantel. A 750-gallon fish tank holds live trout. Indian artworks, paintings of Rocky Mountain wildlife, like a scene of a bobcat chasing down a deer, and a black-iron, wood-burning stove provide additional embellishments to the western motif. Whether you prefer meat or seafood, you'll have your choice of the best of both and a taste of the Old West just for seasoning.

SPECIAL ONE-TIME OFFER: Buy one entrée at the regular price and receive 50% off a second entrée of equal or lesser value. This offer NOT valid in combination with any other offers. Please present to server at time of ordering. _____ Manager/Owner. _____ Date.

RECIPE

Fettuccine a la Burena

Sliced mushrooms	Cooked fettuccine
Baby peas	Olive oil
Chopped shallots	Diced bacon, optional
Minced garlic	Heavy cream
White wine	Grated asiago cheese

1. In a sauté skillet, heat 2 tablespoons olive oil. Sauté mushrooms and bacon together. Drain excess oil.
2. Add garlic and shallots and sauté over high heat. Add peas. Sauté briefly and add a splash of wine. Bring to a simmer.
3. Add 1 cup heavy cream. Simmer on low heat for 3 minutes.
4. Thicken sauce with cheese. Season to taste with salt and pepper.
5. Drain cooked fettuccine and toss with sauce. Serve with garlic bread.

Chalet Lucerne in Winter Park

WALSENBURG

Walsenburg began as a little Mexican village called La Plaza de los Leones, for Don Miguel Antonio Leon, an early settler. Fred Walsen opened a general store here in 1870 and became a community leader. The village changed its name in his honor when it was incorporated in 1873. Postal authorities changed the name to Tourist City in 1887, but incensed citizens successfully had the old name returned.

Zip Code: 81089. Area Code: 719. Population: 3,300. Elevation: 6,182'.

Iron Horse
503 West 7th, 738-9966

Directions: From the north on I-25, take Exit 52 and follow Highways 85 and 87 for 2 miles into town where it turns into Walsen Avenue, then 1st Street and finally Main Street. Turn right at the second signal light onto 7th Street. Go 4 blocks. The restaurant is on the left just past the railroad tracks. From the south on I-25, take Exit 49 and head west on Guerrero Avenue which turns into Main Street. Turn left at the first signal onto 7th Street. Go 4 blocks. The restaurant is on the left just past the railroad tracks.

ESSENTIALS

Cuisine: Steak and Italian
Hours: JAN-APR: Mon-Fri 11AM-2PM. Tue-Sat 4:30PM-9PM. Closed Mon. MAY-DEC: Mon-Fri 11AM-2PM.
7 nights 4:30PM-9PM.
Meals and Prices: Lunch $, Dinner $$-$$$
Nonsmoking: No
Take-out: Yes

Alcohol: Full Bar
Credit Cards: MC, Visa, Amx, Disc
Personal Check: Local or with I.D.
Reservations: Recommended for holidays and parties of 12 or more. Accepted otherwise.
Wheelchair Access: Yes
Other: Banquet facilities available. Single tickets requested for parties of 6 or more.

HISTORY, PERSONALITY AND CHARACTER

The Iron Horse occupies a building that dates back to the 1920s. Originally a home owned by the Louie Dallafior family, it was converted into a restaurant in the 1960s. In the late 1970s, the restaurant was named Duffy's serving Italian and steaks. The previous owners from 1984 to 1988 were Frank, Martha and Karen Bak who changed the name to Iron Horse in commemoration of the train tracks that run behind the restaurant. They sold to the current owners, Jim and Pam Sperandio, first-time restaurateurs from Colorado Springs. Twenty-four trains a day pass by, but many of them are at night. I was here from about 12:30pm to 2:30pm and did not hear a single train. Susan Noga manages the restaurant with help from a very capable staff that has been with the restaurant for several years. Their chefs are Jim Valesquez, who has been cooking at the restaurant since 1989, is from Colorado Springs and has been cooking since 1980;

Gordon Lucero, who has been with Iron Horse since 1990 and has cooked in several restaurants in Cuchera and Trinidad; and Louis Martinez, who has been with the restaurant since 1993 and has been cooking since 1987. Pam also does gourmet cooking, catering weddings and preparing birthday cakes.

FOOD, SERVICE AND AMBIANCE

I had a bowl of their homemadē lentil soup, prepared with carrots and celery, along with the special — the barbecued roast beef marinated in their very own secret, tangy barbecue sauce. There was so much beef on the toasted roll that I had to turn it into an open-faced sandwich and eat it with a fork and knife. The soup was good, but the sandwich was excellent! The roast beef is cooked fresh every morning, smothered with garlicky sautéed mushrooms or cheddar cheese sauce and used on six different sandwiches. For lunch, if you are not an R.B. fan, you can also choose from marinated and grilled or breaded and deep-fried chicken breast, cod fish strips, 7 assorted burgers, a salad or club sandwich. The dinner menu features pasta (linguini, rigatoni, fettuccine chicken Alfredo or ravioli) char-broiled steaks, prime rib, broiled rainbow trout, batter-fried shrimp, broasted chicken and pork baby-back ribs. There are also senior citizen's and children's menus and sandwiches for the smaller appetite. Other homemade items include rolls, cinnamon rolls and desserts.

Service was prompt and accommodating. The front dining room has an attractive maroon and blue carpet to match the maroon tablecloths, while the rear dining room uses hardwood floors. All 3 dining rooms and the lounge are decorated with antique family pictures in original gold-leaf and walnut frames. The lounge exhibits a venerable photo of Jim's uncle, a wine maker. Each room is homey with artifacts like cherrywood sideboards, collectable buffets and a hoosier — a vintage kitchen cupboard with family photos of weddings and graduations (years gone by) and original cut-work linens and doilies made by Jim's grandmother and aunt. Complementing these curios are some very classy paintings by a local artist depicting valleys, forests, a sea shore and, one that I particularly like, two ladies in fine dresses and hats standing by a river. I liked the dichotomy between the carpeted and hardwood floors and between the old family photos and fresh paintings. The paintings, by the way, are for sale in the $200-$400 price range. You'll find something old and new, good old country-style service and healthy portions of your favorite foods at the Iron Horse.

SPECIAL ONE-TIME OFFER: Buy one entrée at the regular price and receive a complimentary glass of house wine. Limit 4 glasses of wine with the purchase of 4 entrées. This offer NOT valid in combination with any other offers. _____ Manager/Owner. _____ Date.

RECIPE

Berry Pie

2 cups whole fresh strawberries
2 cups fresh blueberries
2 cups fresh raspberries
1 cup fresh blackberries
½ to 1 cup sugar
4 tablespoons flour or tapioca
1½ teaspoons cinnamon
Dash nutmeg
Dash salt
2 teaspoons grated orange rind

4 tablespoons butter
Pastry for 2 crusts, 9-inch pies

Topping:
  1½ cups flour
  ½ teaspoon salt
  ½ cup sugar
  ½ cup brown sugar
  ⅔ cup soft butter
  1½ teaspoon cinnamon

1. Mix fruits together and toss well with sugar, flour or tapioca, cinnamon, nutmeg, salt and orange rind. Fill pastry shells, dividing fruit evenly between 2 pie crusts and dot with butter.
2. Make topping and crumble evenly on top of unbaked piece.
3. Bake at 350 degrees for approximately 50 minutes or until juices are bubbling and top is browned.
4. Let pies cool before serving so juices will thicken and set.
5. Topping: Mix all ingredients together until crumb forms. Make fist and press crumb mixture together to make chunks of the mixture and put on top of both pies, dividing evenly between both pies.

I have made this pie at the Iron Horse using many different types of berries, including elderberries, cranberries, and even diced rhubarb. This recipe was developed to use the wonderful berries and fruits that were in season at the time and many times were delivered to us here at the restaurant by a wonderful little grocery store in La Veta called Charlie's Cash and Carry. If the fruit is exceptional, Charlie will automatically think of us and deliver it down to us knowing it will be appreciated. Even though we now use fresh fruit, the first pie was made when a freezer at Charlie's went on the blink and he gave us cases of defrosted frozen strawberries, blueberries, raspberries and blackberries. Out of necessity, we were experimenting with all kinds of different fruit crisps and pies. Our berry pie seemed to be the best liked and we decided it was a keeper. Unfortunately, the fresh berries are not always available at the same time and that is why we have often experimented with different berries that are in season. So, enjoy with a little dollop of whipped cream and a hot cup of coffee. We think you will love it.

Pam Sperandio

WINTER PARK

Winter Park began as a construction camp for the Moffat Tunnel and was originally called West Portal, after the west portal of the tunnel. A ski area started up in 1927 with a 25 cents rope tow. Several years and two fires later, the world's first double chair lift was completed in 1947. Today, Winter Park is one of the finest winter sports centers in the country, home to a handicap ski clinic and host of the Special Olympics.
Zip Code: 80482. Area Code: 970. Population: 528. Elevation: 9,040'.

Chalet Lucerne
78521 Highway 40, PO Box 410, 726-5402
Directions: Take Exit 232 from I-70. Proceed north on Highway 40 for 29 miles to Winter Park. The restaurant is on the right just pass Park Plaza Center.

ESSENTIALS

Cuisine: Swiss

Hours: Mid-NOV to Mid-APR: 7 days 11:30AM-4PM and 5PM-9:30PM. Bar Menu 4PM-5PM. Memorial Day Weekend to Mid-NOV: 7 days 8:30AM-11:30AM, 11:30AM-2:30PM AND 5PM-9:30PM. Closed Mid-APR to Memorial Day Weekend.

Meals and Prices: Breakfast $, Lunch $$, Dinner $$$-$$$$

Nonsmoking: Yes

Take-out: Yes

Alcohol: Full Bar

Credit Cards: MC, Visa, Amx, Disc

Personal Check: No

Reservations: Highly suggested in winter, accepted otherwise.

Wheelchair Access: Yes, including the bathrooms.

Other: Some menu items available for children 12 and under at ½ price.

HISTORY, PERSONALITY AND CHARACTER

Chalet Lucerne was established in 1975 by Hilary and Barbara Henz. The original occupant of the building was Shelby's Restaurant in 1970. Since 1992, the Henzes have expanded the restaurant to include a second dining room, added a bar in the existing dining room, enlarged the kitchen area, added a 60-seat fountain patio and paved the parking lot. Barbara bakes the delicious desserts. Hilary is assisted in the kitchen by sons Mark and Greg. Mark has been cooking since 1980 and spent 2½ years in Switzerland in the mid-1980s and 2 years at the Hilton Fountain Blue in Miami before returning to Winter Park. Greg joined the cooking staff in 1994. Third son Ralph works out front and was my host on my last visit. He also worked for 3 years at the 5-star Hotel Schweizerhof in Luzern, Switzerland.

FOOD, SERVICE AND AMBIANCE

I've had the pleasure of dining here twice for dinner, taking delight in the Zurich-style veal, tender and delicious veal chunks with mushrooms in a creamy white wine sauce and the chicken sauté Swiss, a moist breast topped with chopped green peppers, mushrooms, tomatoes, garlic and Swiss cheese. I found the food here to be more exciting and zesty than most European restaurants. On both visits, I chose soup over salad, consuming a light, yet rich, deep-flavored, full-bodied beef consommé and a hot, thick, flavorful cream of broccoli prepared with chicken stock and plenty of broccoli. My side dishes varied on each visit. I've tried their chewy chopped spätzle; tangy red cabbage; white rice lightly seasoned with dill, parsley and onions and fresh steamed vegetables. Their dinner rolls come from a bakery in Granby just up the road. If you select a dinner salad, you'll have your choice of three homemade dressings: blue cheese, creamy garlic or raspberry vinaigrette. Their servings are plentiful, so come with a good appetite.

Breakfast offers juices, cereals, the usual eggs and meats, mussli with yogurt and fresh fruit, Belgian waffles, omelets and French toast. If you stop here for lunch, expect to see crêpe Florentine, seafood fettuccine, Swiss Raclette (boiled potatoes with melted Raclette cheese), sandwiches (corned beef, club, knockwurst, chicken breast cordon bleu and a burger) and salads (pasta primavera, chicken "Texan style", wurst and buendnerfleisch — air-dried beef). Escargot bourguignon, smoked or poached salmon and artichoke hearts are on the list of dinner appetizers. The light dinners include buffalo stew, tortellini and roast pork loin. Some of the highlights on the regular dinner menu are filet mignon, lamb chops, fresh catfish Nicoise, veal marsala, wienerschnitzel, sautéed lamb Bombay (in curry sauce), venison and pheasant. Fondues for two are served at your table. You can choose from beef tenderloin, a combination of Swiss Emmanthaler and Swiss Gruyere cheeses or veal. To whet your palate and accompany your dinner, you have 40 domestic and imported wines, champagnes and non-alcoholic wines to choose from. To finish your meal, try one of Barbara's homemade desserts: Swiss honey nut torte, apple streudel, black forest cake or créme caramel, with a cup of cappuccino, espresso or one of their special coffees.

My server was efficient, professional and friendly. Polkas on the accordion, choir music and even some yodeling were played throughout the restaurant. The decor demonstrates a consistent Swiss theme with long alp horns; dinner bells and cow bells (a centuries-old tradition in Switzerland); Swiss-made dinner plates; carved wood clocks and vases; decorator plates of the Brothers Grimm stories (Sleeping Beauty); the Swiss flag and cantons, or miniature flags, representing Switzerland's 26 states; and paintings and posters of Mount Eiger, Mount Monch, Mount Jung Frau, the Matterhorn, Lake of Lucerne, Rutli Meadow and the towns of Interlaken, Grindelwald, Zermatt and Bern, the capital. Complementing this setting are a gas fireplace with a copper flue; white crochet curtains from Germany; a vaulted wood ceiling; yellow-tinted brass light fixtures on chains; and Norman Rockwell decorator plates. The patio, with its running waterfalls, has majestic views of the Continental Divide and Berthod Pass ski area. Dining at Chalet Lucerne is a totally, authentic Swiss experience you should not miss.

WINTER PARK

RECIPE

Cheese Fondue
(Serves 4)

Garlic	Water
½ liter of dry white wine	2 ounces of kirsch
600 grams of grated cheese,	Pepper
half Emmenthaler, half Gruyere	Nutmeg
1 to 2 teaspoons cornstarch	Paprika

1. In a fondue pot which has been rubbed with garlic, warm the dry white wine while constantly stirring.
2. Add grated cheese.
3. Let it almost boil, then add one to two teaspoons of cornstarch mixed in water plus kirsh.
4. Let simmer and add pepper, nutmeg or paprika.
5. Carry proudly to the table!

Gasthaus Eichler in Winter Park

Gasthaus Eichler

78786 Highway 40, PO Box 3303, 726-5133

Directions: Take Exit 232 from I-70. Proceed north on Highway 40 for 29 miles to Winter Park. The restaurant is on the left just past Lions Gate Road and across from the road to Idlewild Ski Area.

ESSENTIALS

Cuisine: German

Hours: 7 days 7:30AM-11AM, 11AM-2PM, 5PM-9PM.

Meals and Prices: Breakfast $-$$, Lunch $$, Dinner $$$-$$$$

Nonsmoking: All, except the lounge and patio.

Take-out: Yes

Alcohol: Full Bar

Credit Cards: MC, Visa, Amx, Disc

Personal Check: Yes, with I.D.

Reservations: Recommended for dinner, accepted for breakfast/lunch.

Wheelchair Access: Yes. Many handicapped skiers come in.

Other: Some dinner entrées available in children's and senior's portions. Additional 15% service charge for parties of 6 or more. No separate checks. In-house catering available for wedding receptions, banquets, business lunches and parties.

HISTORY, PERSONALITY AND CHARACTER

Gasthaus Eichler, a European-style hotel and restaurant, was built in 1988 by then owners and long-time Winter Park citizens, Hans and Hannelore (Hanna) Eichler. The Eichlers had two previous locations in Winter Park for their restaurant dating back to 1965, where Deno's Swiss House and The Hideaway are now. In 1995, Jim Schlarbaum, wife Nancy Jackson, and partner and fellow chef Tim Luksa purchased the restaurant. Jim, a graduate of the Culinary Institute of America in Hyde Park, New York, has been in the restaurant business since 1975. He fulfilled his apprenticeship at the Fountain Blue Hotel in Miami before becoming sous chef at the Brazilian Court in Palm Beach, Florida. In Denver, he exercised his culinary skills at The Pantry Catering Company and was Director of Operations for Epicurean Catering when he met Tim, who was working as an executive chef. The two catered many high-class functions such as the International Golf Tournament at Castle Pines. Tim has been in the restaurant business since 1973 and has worked at several resorts in Wyoming and was executive sous chef at the Fairmont Hotel, now the Hyatt, in Denver. Nancy, who manages the hotel, has been catering since 1983. She was in catering sales at The Pantry, pantry chef at Boccolino's Restaurant and manager of The French Bakery in Castle Rock. Tony Howard has been the dining room manager since 1987. He has been in the restaurant business since 1979, tended bar in Maui, Hawaii and managed restaurants in Chicago.

WINTER PARK

FOOD, SERVICE AND AMBIANCE

New owners Jim, Nancy and Tim have kept the same distinguished dinner recipes that originated with Hanna's mother, who taught them to Hanna, who offered them to Hans, who passed them along to Jim and Tim. By doing so, they have preserved the best of a 30-year German dining establishment in Winter Park, while enhancing the menu with their own pasta creations and made-from-scratch items, like späetzle, lumpy mashed potatoes with the skins left on, chunky blue cheese dressing, freshly-baked breads (French, pumpernickel and banana nut) and homemade desserts (apple streudel, tortes, bread pudding with créme Anglaise and lemon cheesecake). They use home-grown herbs and tomatoes and procure fresh rabbits and chickens from Hans who raises them in nearby Fraser.

The two entrées that I enjoyed in the past, the rahmschnitzel (sautéed veal) with its exquisite and very rich creamy brandy sauce and the kassler rippchen (smoked pork loin) with the flavor of sauerkraut cooked into the meat are gladly still on the dinner menu which features 6 appetizers and over 30 entrées. Some of the more notable evening selections are rindsrolladen (rolled beef stuffed with onion, bacon and spices), paprika goulash, rehbraten in burgunder (venison braised in burgundy), châteaubriand for two, chicken Diane, filet mignon and Australian lobster tail combination, fresh rainbow trout and angel hair pasta with shrimp and bay scallops. A house menu, only served between 5PM and 6PM, features a dozen entrées priced between $10 and $12 that includes an appetizer, soup and salad.

While the dinner menu has remained intact, the breakfast and lunch menus have been revamped. For breakfast, you can cool off with a fresh fruit plate, yogurt, granola or a bagel with cream cheese. If you prefer something hot, order the kassler rippchen, a daily egg frittata (open-faced omelet) topped with a variety of ingredients, an omelet (with spinach, brie cheese and tomato or with green chili, cheddar and salsa), potato or buttermilk pancakes with pure maple syrup or a south of the border (potatoes with spinach, tomatoes and cheddar). Some lunch menu highlights are French onion soup, nicõise and sesame ginger chicken salads, grilled chicken pesto and Mediterranean (roasted vegetables marinated in Balsamic vinaigrette) sandwiches and rinderschmorbraten (beef braised in burgundy). I chose the shrimp späetzle sautéed in garlic herb butter with tomatoes topped with fresh, uncooked basil and white cheese and served with julienne zucchini. The shrimp were firm, but not overcooked. The späetzle was very tender without being too mushy. It was al dente or just right. This scrumptious lunch came with a tossed salad of fresh greens with the house Balsamic vinaigrette and French bread. Their fresh-squeezed lemonade is delicious: not too sweet, very refreshing and they offer free refills!

On my last visit for lunch, my smiling server, Erin, was hospitable, friendly and cheerful, similar to the service I received for dinner on an earlier occasion (see page 483 in Restaurants from 101 Colorado Small Towns). They played some light jazz inside while I reveled in a gorgeous spring day on the patio. In the evening, they shift to classical, instrumental and easy listening music for dinner. Almost all of the decor have remained from the "Eichler days". The lounge is still adorned with a stuffed pheasant and boar's head, plates popular in Bavaria, elk horns, antler-design wall light fixtures and a rock fireplace with beer steins on the mantle. For breakfast and lunch, the dining room has new English china with a fruit pattern set on pewter chargers, a typically German tradition. German-style china is brought out for the dinners. Jams, jellies and condiments are served in little glass ramekins. The carpet is new as are the French copper pots hanging on the wall. The predominantly German decor includes grapevine wreaths with dried flowers and ribbons, a favorite of Hana's; a poster of Rothenburg; a colorful, picturesque map of Deutschland (Germany); stained-glass pieces of hummingbirds and grapes; a German deer skin and picture puzzles of German cities and castles put together by Hana years ago. In the winter, they have a Christmas tree with German decorations. The dining area overlooks the Vasquez Creek and has all the appearance and atmosphere of a German lodge.

SPECIAL ONE-TIME OFFER: Buy one entrée at the regular price and receive a FREE appetizer. Limit 4 appetizers with the purchase of 4 entrées. Maximum Value $8 per appetizer. This offer NOT valid in combination with any other offers. Please present to server at time of ordering. _____ Manager/Owner. _____ Date.

RECIPE

Warm German Potato Salad

8 baking potatoes (Russet)	1 ½ cups water
¾ pound bacon, diced	Salt and pepper to taste
⅔ cup white vinegar	⅓ cup bacon fat
2 tablespoon cornstarch	¾ cup onions, diced
⅓ cup sugar	¼ cup chopped parsley

1. Bake potatoes until tender. Let cool and slice. Do not peel.
2. Sauté bacon until crispy and reserve ⅓ cup of the fat.
3. Remove bacon from pan. To the same pan, add vinegar and cornstarch. Mix until dissolved.
4. Add sugar, water and bacon fat. Cook on medium heat, stirring until sauce thickens.
5. Mix cooked bacon, chopped parsley and diced onions.
6. Add sliced potatoes and sauce. Mix gently.
7. Salt and pepper to taste.

> *This recipe has been in the Schlarbaum Family for many years and was given to Jim by his mother, Sally.*

Winston's

100 Winter Park Drive (in The Vintage Hotel), PO Box 1369, 726-8801
Directions: Take Exit 232 from I-70. Proceed north on Highway 40 for 25 miles to the entrance to Winter Park Resort and the rock sign for The Vintage Hotel. Turn left onto Winter Park Drive, take an immediate right and drive .2 miles up to Winston's at the Vintage Hotel. The restaurant is 3½ miles south of the town of Winter Park.

ESSENTIALS

Cuisine: Steaks/Seafood/Pasta
Hours: Memorial Day Weekend to end of SEP and Mid-NOV to Mid-APR: 7 days 7AM-10AM and 6PM-9:30PM. Mid-APR to Memorial Day weekend and end of SEP to Mid-NOV: 7 days 7:30AM-9:30AM (Continental Breakfast only). Wed-Sun 6PM-9:30PM.
Meals and Prices: Breakfast $-$$, Dinner $$$-$$$$
Nonsmoking: All, smoking only permitted at the bar.

Take-out: Yes
Alcohol: Full Bar
Credit Cards: All 5
Personal Check: In-state only with 2 forms of I.D.
Reservations: Recommended
Wheelchair Access: Yes
Dress: Varies: ski wear to formal to casual.
Other: Two banquet rooms (one that can be split) for receptions, meetings, parties or special events.

HISTORY, PERSONALITY AND CHARACTER

The Vintage Hotel and Winston's were built in 1987. In 1992, John Cahill, who owns hotels and restaurants in Flagstaff, Arizona; Jackson, Wyoming; Kauai, Hawaii; Park City and Alta, Utah and Billings, Montana, purchased and remodeled The Vintage. His business is buying troubled properties and redeveloping them. The renovation of Winston's included enclosing the deck and adding a bar moved from a little pub outside of London where Winston Churchill frequented to drink and smoke his cigars. See if you can find his cigar stain on the bar. Dace Voit, new to The Vintage Hotel, has taken over management of Winson's from Jennie Coulthurst, who managed Winston's from 1992 to 1995. Dace, who has been the manager of Winston's since June 1995, started his restaurant career in 1987 as a bus person for an upscale steak house in Louisville,

Kentucky. Since then, he has worked his way through each position in the restaurant business from Louisville to Winter Park, which has been his home since 1992. Joe Lovato, who started cooking at the age of 10 with Mom and professionally in 1980, has been their executive chef since 1994. Prior to coming to Winston's, he cooked at the Crooked Creek Saloon from 1993 to 1994, the Grand Lake Lodge, the Club Car, the Canterbury Inn in the Denver Technological Center and Bucci's Italian Restaurant in Denver. Ken English is the sous chef.

FOOD, SERVICE AND AMBIANCE

I ordered pork tenderloin with emphasis on tender — several mild medallions sweetened by a crust of crushed walnuts and brown sugar with a topping of sautéed brandy apples; a delightfully delicious dulcified display of lean meat. It was served with a colorful medley of vegetables: spinach, squash, red peppers, asparagus and carrots; baked potato; fresh-baked bread and a salad with homemade creamy garlic dressing that had a flavorful, spicy taste. They also make a blue cheese dressing, with real blue cheese, raspberry vinaigrette and Caesar. Soups, including lobster bisque, are homemade as well. A few of their appetizers to get you started are artichoke hearts with smoked provolone, mushrooms Boursin and sesame glazed shrimp.

Beef Wellington, carved at your table, is The Vintage specialty. Their dinner entrées offer pastas in a variety of sauces with appetizing ingredients like grilled salmon, smoked chicken and peppers, and black bean stuffed ravioli; chef specialties like steak au poivre, jumbo sea scallops and chicken breast stuffed with vegetables and cream cheese; several cuts of steak, chicken and seafood prepared on the grill and a selection of lighter items: beef and vegetarian burgers and flat bread — a butterless, bread dough with a varying selection of herbs, meats, vegetables and cheeses. You can make use of their suggested wines to complement your dining experience, then conclude your meal with a delectable apple caramel torte, a raspberry bash with white and dark chocolate, chocolate decadence, carrot cake or tiramisu. Occasionally, they will have homemade desserts like chocolate mousse or a poached pear. To crown your dessert or to finish your meal with the perfect touch, Winston's has a wide selection of port and dessert wines to choose from. The bar has a full selection including 7 microbrewed beers, one of which is root beer on tap, and a fine choice of bourbon whiskeys. For you Scotch drinkers, they serve 19 different single malt Scotches (probably the largest selection from any small town in the state).

During the off-seasons, spring and fall, they only serve a continental breakfast. The rest of the year, they provide a full, hot menu with create-your-own omelets, meat or vegetarian burritos, French toast, waffles and fresh corned beef. Egg beaters and egg white selections are available and during the winter, you can order a hot or cold skiers' buffet.

WINTER PARK

Service was pleasing and very accommodating as they permitted my order to go through when I arrived right after a group of 20 took their seats. The classic European—style dining room is divided by an entire row of hanging philodendrons facing a wall of windows with a scenic view of the Continental Divide and Berthod Pass. Named after Winston Churchill, the far end of the dining room spotlights several intriguing photographs of the great statesman and de Gaulle, Roosevelt, Giraud, Stalin, Eisenhower and Truman. Accompanying this compelling collection are a series of sporting paintings from the Chelsea Green Gallery in San Francisco demonstrating a fisherman, a fox hunt, a game of cricket, a golfer, and possibly the most popular sport of all, a group of "good ol' boys" smoking their long pipes by the fireplace. Good food, engaging decor and a gratifying view, it's all here at Winston's.

SPECIAL ONE-TIME OFFER: Buy one entrée at the regular price and receive a second entrée of equal or lesser value FREE (Up to $19.95 value) OR receive 50% off a single entrée (maximum discount $9.00). This offer NOT valid in combination with any other offers. Please present to server at time of ordering. _____ Manager/Owner. _____ Date.

RECIPE
Stuffed Chicken Breast with a Dijon Garlic Sauce

8-ounce chicken breast,
  boned, skinned and trimmed
Cream Cheese
Your favorite fresh herbs
Asparagus
Carrots
Red bell peppers
Summer squash
Cracker crumbs
Toothpicks

Sauce:
¼ cup white wine
1 tablespoon Dijon mustard
¼ teaspoon fresh garlic
¼ cup heavy cream

---

1. With a tenderizing hammer, pound the chicken flat.
2. Spread with softened cream cheese
3. Sprinkler with your favorite herbs.
4. Cut julienne all the vegetables.
5. Arrange on chicken breast.
6. Roll tightly and bread with cracker crumbs.
7. Secure with several toothpicks
8. Bake at 400 degrees for half an hour.
9. For the sauce, reduce white wine with mustard and garlic by ⅔ volume.
10. Add heavy cream and reduce.

Winston's in the Vintage Hotel in Winter Park

RECIPE INDEX

BEEF

Pan-Seared Thai Beef with Watercress Salad, Spicy Onions and Peanut Sauce. Piñons, Aspen, **11**

Sauerbraten. Black Forest Inn, Black Hawk, **22**

Grilled Steak Giambotta. Garlic Mike's, Gunnison, **148**

Beef Teriyaki Kabobs. Green Mountain Inn, Heeney, **154**

Grandma Ireland's Yankee Pot Roast. The Covered Wagon, La Veta, **173**

Gonzales Steak. The Fort, Morrison, **216**

Steak Au Poivré. Gold Creek Inn Restaurant, Ohio City, **233**

Quick Stroganoff. Natalia's 1912 Family Restaurant, Silverton, **260**

Tournedos of Beef in a Port Shallot Sauce. Antares, Steamboat Springs, **272**

Rinderrouladen. Nordic Inn, Twin Lakes, **288**

BREAD

San Carlos. Earth Song Haven, Cortez, **57**

Silverheels Chile, Cheese and Onion Rolls. Silverheels Southwest Grill, Golden, **134**

Cajun Pizza. Beau Jo's, Idaho Springs, **163**

Steve Wix's Sleepy Cat Scones. Sleepy Cat Lodge, Meeker, **207**

BREAKFAST

Breakfast Taco. Evergreen Cafe, Buena Vista, **38**

McGurk's Crispy Cheese and Potato Breakfast. The Village Smithy Restaurant, Inc., Carbondale, **42**

CHICKEN

Pollo ai tre Formaggi. St. Bernard Inn, Breckenridge, **33**

Chicken Mole Recipe. Casa del Sol, Buena Vista, **36**

Basil Chicken with Parmesan. Countryside Coffeehouse, Crawford, **59**

Tamari-Honey Chicken. Creede Hotel Restaurant, Creede, **65**

Petti di Pollo alla Diana. Ristorante Al Lago, Dillon, **81**

Fiesta Chicken. Pepper Pod, Hudson, **160**

Chicken Artesun. Dusty Rose Cafe, Mancos, **199**

Sautéed Lemon Chicken Breast with Mushrooms and Peas. Millwood Junction, Mancos, **201**

Chicken Maria. Sicily's, Montrose, **210**

Enchiladas Acapulco. The Whole Enchilada, Montrose, **212**

Chicken Chipeta. Bon Ton Restaurant, Ouray, **236**

RECIPE INDEX

Chicken Enchiladas and Sour Cream. The Rose, Pagosa Springs, **241**

Stuffed Chicken Breast with a Dijon Garlic Sauce. Winston's, Winter Park, **310**

DESSERT
Clafouti. Mirabella, Aspen, **9**

White Chocolate Bread Pudding. Cafe Alpine, Breckenridge, **29**

Tampico Torte. The Eatery, Delta, **76**

Cathy's Coconut Cream Pie. Rio Grande Southern, Dolores, **86**

White Chocolate Raspberry Cheesecake. The River Sage Restaurant, Evergreen, **106**

Bananas Flambé. Sopris, Glenwood Springs, **126**

Chocolate Mousse. The Troll Haus Restaurant, Las Animas, **180**

Lemon Meringue Pie. Karen's Country Kitchen, Louisville, **191**

Flan. La Mariposa, Lyons, **196**

Viennese Cheesecake. The Back Narrows Inn Restaurant, Norwood, **227**

Easy Peach Cobbler. Ole Miner's Steakhouse, Pagosa Springs, **239**

Berry Pie. Iron Horse, Walsenburg, **301**

DIPS AND DRESSINGS
Guacamole. Pegasus, Castle Rock, **45**

Sundried Cranberry Mandarin Orange Vinaigrette. Rackets, Copper Mountain, **54**

Tomato Chutney. The Slogar, Crested Butte, **73**

Charity's Hot Crab Dip. Charity's, Frisco, **115**

Karen's Famous House Dressing. Karen's, Norwood, **230**

Summer Sour Cream Dressing. True Grit Cafe, Ridgway, **253**

Cheese Fondue. Chalet Lucerne, Winter Park, **304**

LAMB
Lamb Chops Blue Spruce. Blue Spruce Inn, Frisco, **112**

Leg of Lamb Venison. The Gold Hill Inn Restaurant, Gold Hill, **129**

Roasted Rack of Colorado Lamb Vermont Style, with Maple Syrup Glaze and Marsala Cider Sauce. Krabloonik, Snowmass Village, **263**

PASTA AND RICE
Spanish Rice. Fiesta's, Edwards, **95**

Penne Vodka. Callaway's Restaurant, Leadville, **183**

Leadville Prospector's Cajun Angel. The Leadville Prospector Restaurant, Leadville, **186**

Fran's alla Olio. Nana & Nano's Pasta House, Trinidad, **284**

Fettuccine a la Burena. Virginia's Steakhouse, Vallecito Lake, **298**

RECIPE INDEX

PORK

Carne Adovada Burrito Casserole.
Mt. Blanca Supper Club, Fort Garland,
109

*Sautéed Pork Loin with Crab Meat
and Wild Mushrooms.* The Grand
Lake Lodge Restaurant, Grand Lake,
140

Pork Hawaiian. the Trough,
Gunnison, **150**

Frikadeller. Tivoli Deer, Kittredge,
168

SALAD, SAUCE AND SOUP

Eggplant Soup. The Dunraven Inn
Restaurant, Estes Park, **102**

Tuna and Mostaccioli Salad. The
Happy Cooker, Georgetown, **118**

Oriental Pasta Sauce. Grand Lobby
(Hotel Colorado), Glenwood Springs,
121

Red Curry Sauce. Rivers, Glenwood
Springs, **123**

*Fail-Proof Basic Steps to Great Hardy
Soups.* The Riverside, Hot Sulphur
Springs, **157**

Chef Jodi's Chicken Salad.
Chiaramonte's, La Junta, **170**

Hungarian Cream of Green Soup.
Little's, Paonia, **245**

Sonoma Salad. Redstone Inn,
Redstone, **251**

Tartar Sauce. El Capitan, Rocky
Ford, **255**

Pesto. Il Vicino, Salida, **257**

*Organic Baby Greens with Sweet Basil
Vinaigrette.* The PowderHouse,
Telluride, **281**

Black Bean Soup. Uptown Grill, Vail,
291

Warm German Potato Salad.
Gasthaus Eichler, Winter Park, **307**

SEAFOOD

Escoffier. Ricardino's, Avon, **15**

*Pan Seared, Oven Finished Filet of
Halibut with Fresh Beet Sauce,
Asparagus, Wild Rice with Three
Color Pepper.* The Savoy Restaurant
Français, Berthoud, **18**

BBQ Shrimp. Inn at Arrowhead,
Cimarron, **48**

Salmon Wellington. Bristol Inn
Restaurant, Creede, **62**

Seafood Risotto. Le Bosquet, Crested
Butte, **71**

Grilled Salmon with Squash Noodles.
Arapahoe Cafe, Dillon, **79**

Salmon Dijon. Red Snapper, Durango,
92

Shrimp Sarah. The Peck House,
Empire, **98**

*Shrimp and Feta Cheese Quesadilla
with Fresh Salsa.* Caroline's Cuisine,
Grand Lake, **137**

19 Shrimp Palermo. The Rapids
Restaurant, Grand Lake, **144**

RECIPE INDEX